# Expert Delphi

Robust and fast cross-platform application development

**Paweł Głowacki**

BIRMINGHAM - MUMBAI

# Expert Delphi

First published: June 2017

Production reference: 1300617

Published by Packt Publishing Ltd.
Livery Place
35 Livery Street
Birmingham
B3 2PB, UK.
ISBN 978-1-78646-016-5

www.packtpub.com

# Credits

**Author**
Paweł Głowacki

**Reviewer**
Dave Nottage

**Commissioning Editor**
Kunal Parikh

**Acquisition Editor**
Nitin Dasan

**Content Development Editor**
Anurag Ghogre

**Technical Editors**
Madhunikita Sunil Chindarkar
Rutuja Vaze

**Copy Editors**
Safis Editing
Muktikant Garimella

**Project Coordinator**
Vaidehi Sawant

**Proofreader**
Safis Editing

**Indexer**
Aishwarya Gangawane

**Graphics**
Abhinash Sahu

**Production Coordinator**
Shantanu Zagade

# Foreword

I have known and worked with Paweł Głowacki for more than 16 years. Paweł is one of the world-wide Delphi community leading experts. In this book, *Expert Delphi*, Paweł takes you on a learning journey that started in the early 1980s with Compas Pascal, Poly Pascal, and Turbo Pascal. For more than 20 years, Delphi has continued to evolve to meet the needs of developers around the world. During most of this time, Paweł has been a key team member and advocate for the continuous innovation of the compilers, frameworks, runtime library, integrated development environment, and tool chain, allowing developers to easily build applications across desktop, server, mobile, internet, and cloud platforms.

With FireMonkey (FMX), developers can build on top of a modern multiplatform framework based on a rich history of objects, components, and libraries and that has included Turbo Vision, Object Windows, and the VCL. Leveraging these frameworks, libraries, and tools allows developers to create applications for a wide range of architectures, databases, and distributed computing environments.

In his presentations and examples, Paweł shows you how easy it is to create a wide range of applications using SQL/NoSQL databases, XML, and JSON. Paweł also helps developers create multitier applications using the latest technologies, including REST.

As a member of and a leading advocate for the large, global Delphi community and ecosystem, Paweł is uniquely qualified to show you how to become a mobile developer superhero, become a hyper-productive software engineer, and build one source code application that can be compiled to all major mobile platforms and form factors. Paweł also shows you how to build stunning 2D and 3D multidevice graphical user interfaces with the FireMonkey library, providing an outstanding user experience for your application's users.

With *Expert Delphi*, you'll learn the best practices for writing high-quality, reliable, and maintainable code with Delphi's Object Pascal language and component architecture. After you complete Paweł's book, you'll understand how to take full advantage of mobile operating systems, frameworks, and hardware capabilities, including working with sensors and the Internet of Things.

Beyond developing apps for desktops and smartphones, you'll learn how to quickly and easily integrate with cloud services and data using REST APIs and JSON. You'll also learn how to architect and deploy powerful mobile backend services.

In *Expert Delphi*, Paweł encapsulates the knowledge gained through years as a world-class Delphi engineer, an entertaining presenter, a community leader, and a passionate advocate. With his words, step-by-step instructions, screenshots, source code snippets, examples, and links to additional sources of information, you will learn how to continuously enhance your skills and apps.

Become a developer superhero and build stunning cross-platform apps with Delphi.

**David Intersimone "David I"**

Vice President of Developer Communities, Evans Data Corp. and Embarcadero Community MVP.

Santa Cruz, California, USA

# About the Author

**Paweł Głowacki** is Embarcadero's European Technical Lead for Developer Tools. Previously, he spent over 7 years working as a senior consultant and trainer for Delphi within Borland Education Services and CodeGear. In addition to working with Embarcadero customers across the region, he represents Embarcadero internationally as a conference and seminar speaker.

# About the Reviewer

**Dave Nottage** is an independent software consultant who lives in Adelaide, South Australia.

Developing software with Delphi since 1995 when Delphi 1 was first released, he has been a valued member of Embarcadero's TeamB since 2001, and an Embarcadero MVP since 2014.

Dave is considered an expert in Delphi and has shared his expertise as a speaker at Delphi developer conferences, including BorCon, Delphi Live, and ADUG Symposia. He is an active member on Embarcadero forums and Stack Overflow, and his popular blog articles, which can be found at Delphi Worlds, provide solutions for common Delphi problems. His blog is followed by many developers across the globe and is considered a go-to source.

Having worked on projects for major global enterprises, corporations, and governments, he is now working on his own commercial product, a set of code libraries that aids developers in cross-platform development.

In his spare time, Dave enjoys playing bass guitar in a band, art exhibitions, puzzles that challenge the mind, and traveling the world.

Dave can be contacted at dave@delphiworlds.com.

# www.PacktPub.com

For support files and downloads related to your book, please visit www.PacktPub.com.

Did you know that Packt offers eBook versions of every book published, with PDF and ePub files available? You can upgrade to the eBook version at www.PacktPub.com and as a print book customer, you are entitled to a discount on the eBook copy. Get in touch with us at service@packtpub.com for more details.

At www.PacktPub.com, you can also read a collection of free technical articles, sign up for a range of free newsletters and receive exclusive discounts and offers on Packt books and eBooks.

https://www.packtpub.com/mapt

Get the most in-demand software skills with Mapt. Mapt gives you full access to all Packt books and video courses, as well as industry-leading tools to help you plan your personal development and advance your career.

# Why subscribe?

- Fully searchable across every book published by Packt
- Copy and paste, print, and bookmark content
- On demand and accessible via a web browser

# Customer Feedback

Thanks for purchasing this Packt book. At Packt, quality is at the heart of our editorial process. To help us improve, please leave us an honest review on this book's Amazon page at https://www.amazon.com/dp/1786460165.

If you'd like to join our team of regular reviewers, you can e-mail us at customerreviews@packtpub.com. We award our regular reviewers with free eBooks and videos in exchange for their valuable feedback. Help us be relentless in improving our products!

*For my beloved wife, Barbara, and son, Mateusz.*

*Thank you for all your love and support.*

*I love you!*

# Table of Contents

# Preface

The world of a mobile app developer is getting more and more complicated. The technology is not standing still. Every day, new versions of mobile operating systems are released to the market. Mobile devices are getting new capabilities. User expectations are constantly growing, and it is becoming increasingly harder to meet them.

The only way to meet and exceed all challenges in the contemporary world of mobile development is to become a developer superhero! Super heroes have super tools. In this book, we are going to embark on the journey of mastering Delphi development. We will learn how to gain amazing productivity powers and rapidly build stunning cross-platform mobile apps from one codebase.

We will start with getting comfortable with using the Delphi IDE. Then, we will review the key constructs of the Object Pascal language and everyday programmer tasks, so you can easily understand and write solid and maintainable source code. Over the course of this book, the fun levels are only going to increase. We will start our adventure with mobile development with Delphi from building small projects that will make you feel like a real Delphi developer. Having mastered simple things, you will be ready for doing more serious stuff. We will go deep into understanding the concept of FireMonkey styles, which is the cornerstone of building stunning cross-platform user interfaces that will make the difference in the end user experience of your apps. The rest of the journey is all about gaining practical knowledge of using more complex Delphi frameworks. We will get down to the metal and harness the full power of mobile hardware and operating systems. We will be working with sensors, extending to the Internet of Things, building data-driven user interfaces, embedding mobile databases, integrating with REST web services, architecting scalable, multiuser backends, and more.

This book is packed with practical code examples and best practices for you to become an excellent mobile developer!

## What this book is not about

If you have never written any line of code, this book is not for you. The chances are that you have been using Delphi already to build applications for Windows. You will not learn about Windows development in this book. We are going to focus on building mobile iOS and Android apps.

There are two main frameworks for visual development in Delphi: VCL and FireMonkey. The VCL, or the Visual Component Library, is designed for building Windows applications. VCL is arguably the best library for building Windows applications. This book is not about the VCL. There are many books and other resources that explain VCL development inside out. While the VCL is for Windows only, with FireMonkey, you can build apps not only for Windows but also for Mac, Linux, Android, and iOS. Mobile app development with the Delphi FireMonkey library is the main focus of this book.

# Why Delphi?

Mobile apps are everywhere. There are two main platforms for mobile apps that are dominating the mobile market: Android and iOS. It is a common requirement to develop an app for both the platforms. This typically means using different tools, frameworks, and programming languages. If you want to build a mobile app for iOS, you should probably use the Xcode development environment from Apple and use Swift or Objective-C as the programming language. Android development requires different tools. For Android, you would typically use a tool such as Android Studio from Google and the Java programming language. These are two different worlds that speak different languages. If you want to build your app for both, this means having two different sets of skills and, in practice, two different teams of developers. Mobile app development gets more and more fragmented. One can be an iOS developer, and somebody else can specialize in Android.

A mobile app is quite often more than just what you download from an app store and install in your phone or tablet. There must be a mobile backend deployed in the cloud that a mobile app is communicating with. This adds another dimension to mobile development landscape. One can be a frontend and one can be a backend mobile developer. There is a growing segmentation in the market and you might think that mobile app development is not for individuals anymore. Fear not! With Delphi, you can become a mobile developer superhero and gain unmatched productivity powers to build complete mobile apps using just one tool, one framework, and one programming language to create mobile apps for iOS, Android, and desktop applications for Windows, Mac, and Linux. With Delphi, you can also build scalable REST API backends that will power your mobile apps on all platforms.

This book is logically divided into two parts. In the beginning, we are going to build a complete, simple game that will be fun to play and will illustrate the basic concepts of architecting user interfaces for both 2D and 3D. In the second part, we will go deeper into understanding the inner workings of the FireMonkey visual library. We will see how to work with the different aspects of mobile operating system hardware and sensors, store data in an embedded database, and integrate with REST API backend using Delphi WebBroker and RAD Server frameworks. We will also cover all you need to know about putting your app on the Apple iOS App Store and Android Google Play.

Get ready! Boarding is complete, and we are just about to take off for the fascinating journey through the world of Delphi mobile app development!

# What this book covers

Chapter 1, *Fasten Your Seat Belts*, covers how to install Delphi and prepare it for mobile cross-platform development. We'll build a Hello World FireMonkey app and natively compile it from the same source code to Android and iOS.

Chapter 2, *Mind Your Language*, reviews the basic constructs of the Object Pascal programming language used in Delphi. After covering the fundamentals, we'll quickly move on to the discussion of more advanced language concepts used in FireMonkey programming, including class helpers, generics, anonymous code, and Runtime Type Information.

Chapter 3, *Packing Up Your Toolbox*, covers some of the most useful, everyday programmer skills, such as writing multithreaded code with parallel programming library and working with JSON and XML.

Chapter 4, *Playing with FireMonkey*, teaches the basics of building cross-platform mobile GUI with FireMonkey. you'll learn how to use shapes, effects, and animation components. We'll cover working with touch, multitouch, and gestures. At the end of this chapter, we'll write the complete mobile *Game of Memory* game.

Chapter 5, *FireMonkey in 3D*, explores how to build stunning interactive 3D graphical user interfaces, including working with wireframes, 3D controls, and importing 3D models into your Delphi apps.

Chapter 6, *Building User Interfaces with Style*, covers FireMonkey styling. We'll look into using built-in styles and custom styles with TStyleBook component, and customizing the styles with embedded Style Editor. We'll also cover working with frames and using inherited views for specific mobile form factors.

Chapter 7, *Working with Mobile Operating System*, covers how to access mobile hardware and operating systems with high-level components abstracting away underlying mobile APIs. We'll look into working with sensors, camera, address book, embedding web browsers, using maps, creating and consuming Android services, and working with language bridges for accessing APIs and frameworks not surfaced through the FireMonkey library.

Chapter 8, *Extending to the Internet of Things*, teaches how to build cross-platform mobile apps that communicate with IoT sensors and devices using Bluetooth LE communication protocol. We'll look into working with the TBluetoothLE components and also using specialized IoT components available via the GetIt Package Manager. We'll also cover building proximity-enabled apps that work with beacons using the TBeacon components and BeaconFence. The App Tethering framework is discussed as well for easy communication between mobile apps.

Chapter 9, *Embedding Databases*, covers building a *To-Do List* mobile app illustrating best practices for architecting data-driven solutions with a clear separation between user interface and data access layers. We use FireDAC database access framework for communicating with embedded SQLite mobile database and build user interface with the TListView component with dynamic appearance.

Chapter 10, *Integrating with Web Services*, looks at different Delphi frameworks and components for integrating with web services. We start from low-level native HTTP client library, consuming XML SOAP web services, and moving on to the REST and BaaS client components. In the last part, we will look into Cloud API for integrating with the Amazon and Azure clouds. We also replace the *To-Do List* app data access tier with logic to store JSON data in the Amazon Simple Storage Service (S3).

Chapter 11, *Building Mobile Backends*, explores building scalable multitier systems with Delphi. You'll learn how to build mobile backends with different Delphi frameworks, including WebBroker, DataSnap, and the RAD Server. During the course of this chapter, we will split the *To-Do List* app into separate client and server parts.

Chapter 12, *App Deployment*, covers practical steps of deploying Delphi mobile apps to the Google Play Store and the Apple iOS App Store. We'll also look at best agile practices for continuous enhancement of your apps with using version control, refactorings, and unit testing.

# What you need for this book

You are expected to have a basic knowledge of Delphi and an interest in building cross-platform mobile apps for Android and iOS.

The Delphi IDE is a Windows program, so you will need a physical or virtual Windows installation. In order to develop for iOS, you will need a Mac computer. You will also need an Enterprise or Architect license for Delphi itself. In the beginning of the first chapter of this book, we cover the installation process of Delphi in a great detail.

# Who this book is for

If you want to create stunning applications for mobile, desktop, the cloud, and the IoT, then this book is for you. This book is for developers who like to build native cross-platform apps from a single codebase for iOS and Android. A basic knowledge of Delphi is assumed, although we do cover a primer on the language.

# Conventions

In this book, you will find a number of text styles that distinguish between different kinds of information. Here are some examples of these styles and an explanation of their meaning. Code words in text, database table names, folder names, filenames, file extensions, pathnames, dummy URLs, user input, and Twitter handles are shown as follows: "The TForm class, which is an ancestor to TFormSettings, is, in turn, inherited from the TComponent class."

A block of code is set as follows:

```
Application.Initialize;
Application.CreateForm(TFormMain, FormMain);
Application.CreateForm(TFormSettings, FormSettings);
Application.Run;
```

When we wish to draw your attention to a particular part of a code block, the relevant lines or items are set in bold:

```
const EL = #13;

procedure TForm1.ButtonMultilineClick(Sender: TObject);
begin
  ShowMessage('Welcome!' + EL + 'Good morning!');
end;
```

**New terms** and **important words** are shown in bold. Words that you see on the screen, for example, in menus or dialog boxes, appear in the text like this: "In the **New Items** window, make sure that the **Delphi Projects** node is selected, and double-click on the **Console Application** icon."

# Reader feedback

Feedback from our readers is always welcome. Let us know what you think about this book-what you liked or disliked. Reader feedback is important for us as it helps us develop titles that you will really get the most out of. To send us general feedback, simply e-mail feedback@packtpub.com, and mention the book's title in the subject of your message. If there is a topic that you have expertise in and you are interested in either writing or contributing to a book, see our author guide at www.packtpub.com/authors.

# Customer support

Now that you are the proud owner of a Packt book, we have a number of things to help you to get the most from your purchase.

## Downloading the example code

You can download the example code files for this book from your account at http://www.packtpub.com. If you purchased this book elsewhere, you can visit http://www.packtpub.com/support and register to have the files e-mailed directly to you. You can download the code files by following these steps:

1. Log in or register to our website using your e-mail address and password.
2. Hover the mouse pointer on the **SUPPORT** tab at the top.
3. Click on **Code Downloads & Errata**.
4. Enter the name of the book in the **Search** box.
5. Select the book for which you're looking to download the code files.
6. Choose from the drop-down menu where you purchased this book from.
7. Click on **Code Download**.

Once the file is downloaded, please make sure that you unzip or extract the folder using the latest version of:

- WinRAR / 7-Zip for Windows
- Zipeg / iZip / UnRarX for Mac
- 7-Zip / PeaZip for Linux

The code bundle for the book is also hosted on GitHub at `https://github.com/PacktPubl ishing/Expert-Delphi`. We also have other code bundles from our rich catalog of books and videos available at `https://github.com/PacktPublishing/`. Check them out!

# Errata

Although we have taken every care to ensure the accuracy of our content, mistakes do happen. If you find a mistake in one of our books-maybe a mistake in the text or the code-we would be grateful if you could report this to us. By doing so, you can save other readers from frustration and help us improve subsequent versions of this book. If you find any errata, please report them by visiting `http://www.packtpub.com/submit-errata`, selecting your book, clicking on the **Errata Submission Form** link, and entering the details of your errata. Once your errata are verified, your submission will be accepted and the errata will be uploaded to our website or added to any list of existing errata under the Errata section of that title. To view the previously submitted errata, go to `https://www.packtpub.com/book s/content/support` and enter the name of the book in the search field. The required information will appear under the **Errata** section.

# Piracy

Piracy of copyrighted material on the Internet is an ongoing problem across all media. At Packt, we take the protection of our copyright and licenses very seriously. If you come across any illegal copies of our works in any form on the Internet, please provide us with the location address or website name immediately so that we can pursue a remedy. Please contact us at `copyright@packtpub.com` with a link to the suspected pirated material. We appreciate your help in protecting our authors and our ability to bring you valuable content.

# Questions

If you have a problem with any aspect of this book, you can contact us at `questions@packtpub.com`, and we will do our best to address the problem.

# 1
# Fasten Your Seat Belts

The key benefit of Delphi in mobile development is that you can design your app once and, from the same source code, you can natively compile it for both Android and iOS. This chapter is exactly about this capability. We are going to first install Delphi, create a simple one-button "Hello World" app, and then run the same app on Google Nexus 7 and on Apple iPhone 6S.

The **Integrated Development Environment** (**IDE**) is where the programmer spends the most of the time. Learning best practices of using the IDE will pay off in the future and will increase your developer productivity. Before going into building apps, you need to feel comfortable working in the IDE.

The objective of this chapter is to install the Delphi IDE, learn basic IDE functionality, and prepare it for mobile development.

## Delphi installation

Delphi is a Windows program, so you need to have a computer with a proper version of Windows installed and enough free space on your hard drive. You may want to install Delphi on a physical computer or onto a Windows virtual machine image using one of the available virtualization solutions such as VMware. Installing onto a virtual machine has some advantages in cross-platform development. In order to create iOS apps, you will need to have access to a Mac computer. This could be another computer available on a local network or the same physical machine. One of the most convenient configurations is to have just one physical machine that allows you to target all operating system platforms supported by Delphi.

In order to deploy to iOS devices, you need to use a physical Mac machine. At the same time, Delphi is a Windows program, so you will also need Windows. You can use both on one computer by running Windows in a virtual machine installed on Mac. Whether you choose to install Delphi onto a physical or virtual Windows machine, the installation process is the same.

Delphi is implemented as a native Windows 32-bit executable. As such, it can be installed to either 32-bit or 64-bit versions of Windows. Some parts of Delphi are written in .NET 3.5, so at the beginning of the installation, the installer may also install a .NET 3.5 redistributable package which is not installed by default in newer versions of Windows.

# Delphi versions

Delphi comes in different versions, so before downloading the installer, we need to decide which version to choose. There are four Delphi versions--Starter, Professional, Enterprise, and Architect:

- The **Starter** version is the simplest one and it does not contain features necessary for doing mobile development. This version is aimed at hobbyists, students, and in general for anyone that just wants to learn Delphi. *Starter* supports building application for Windows 32-bit only. That's not what we need.
- The next version is **Professional**. It also does not contain features for mobile development, but they can be installed separately in the form of *mobile add-on packs*. The *Professional* is a good choice if you plan to build applications for Windows and you do not need the possibility to connect to remote databases.
- The third version is **Enterprise**. This is the full version of Delphi and contains everything that is in the *Professional* plus more. It allows you to create apps for all supported mobile and desktop platforms including Android, iOS, Windows, Mac, and Linux. It also contains the **DataSnap** framework for building scalable, multitier systems that is not available in Professional edition. This is the version of Delphi that we are going to use in this book.
- The highest Delphi version is **Architect**. This is a product bundle that contains Delphi *Enterprise* and separately installed **ER/Studio Developer Edition** for modeling relational SQL databases and **DB Power Studio Developer Edition** that contains tools for working with SQL databases.

Delphi is available as a standalone product, but it can also be used as part of RAD Studio. RAD Studio contains Delphi and C++Builder. Delphi and C++Builder are two different *IDE personalities* of RAD Studio and both can be installed from the same RAD Studio installer into one deeply integrated environment. Both products, Delphi and C++Builder, provide the same capabilities of building mobile and desktop apps for different operating systems from the same source code using visual designers, and share the same component libraries, but differ in the programming language being used. Delphi uses Object Pascal and C++Builder uses standard C++.

I'm trying as much as possible to make sure that this book is not tied to any particular Delphi version. However, it is important to pay attention to which version of different pieces of software we are using.

In this book, we are going to use Delphi 10.2 **Tokyo Enterprise** edition. Delphi is produced by Embarcadero and you can find more information about different Delphi versions and features on the Embarcadero Delphi home page (http://www.embarcadero.com/products/delphi). You can get Delphi directly through the Embarcadero website or through one of many partner companies that represent Embarcadero in different countries. After purchasing Delphi, you will receive an automatically generated email with the download link to the Delphi installer and the serial number that you will need during the installation.

# Running the Delphi installer

Delphi installer is available in two different formats. You can either choose to install Delphi using the so-called **Electronic Software Delivery** (**ESD**) for short, or you can install from the ISO image of the full Delphi installation DVD. The first option is the default one and it makes for faster installation. The ESD installer is a relatively small application that downloads and installs only those parts of Delphi that you have chosen at the beginning of the installation process. After Delphi is installed you can always choose to install or uninstall different features. The second option is to install from the DVD ISO image. This is useful when the internet access is slow, unreliable, or for some security reasons the Windows machine that you install Delphi onto does not have internet access at all.

Here we are going to use the web installer. Download the installation file from the link provided in the email. You will need to have administration rights on Windows to be able to install Delphi. On one of the first installer screens you will be prompted to enter the serial number that you have received from Embarcadero and also you will need to enter your **Embarcadero Developer Network (EDN)** username and password. If you do not have an EDN account, you can quickly create one from within the installer. It is free and it makes the connection between the serial number that you have received and you as the user of the software.

During the installation, you can choose which platforms and additional features you want to install. You can always add or remove platforms and features from the IDE **Welcome Page** after the installation is complete, as shown in the following screenshot:

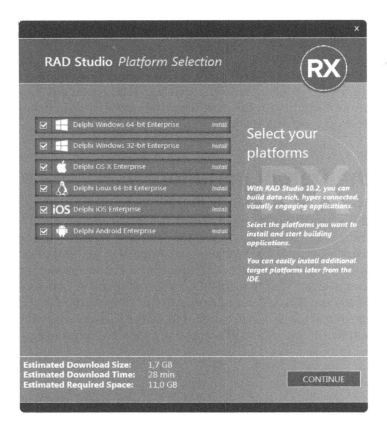

Platform Selection

After this, we need to select platforms and all additional features, as shown in the following screenshot:

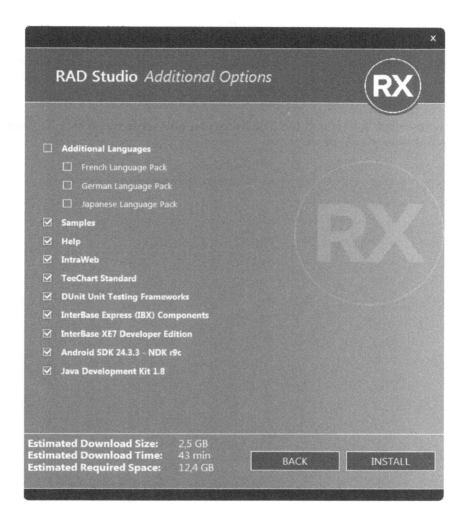

Additional Options

I'm going for the full install, so I have selected all platforms and all additional features to be installed, except for languages other than English. Depending on the speed of your internet connection, the installer should complete the installation in a couple of minutes. At the end of the installation, you will see the message that the installation is complete and you can start working.

If you run into problems during the installation, you can review the Delphi *Installation Notes* on the Embarcadero DocWiki
(`http://docwiki.embarcadero.com/RADStudio/en/Installation_Notes`).

Delphi is now installed. Run it and the first thing you will see is the **Welcome Page**, as shown in the following screenshot:

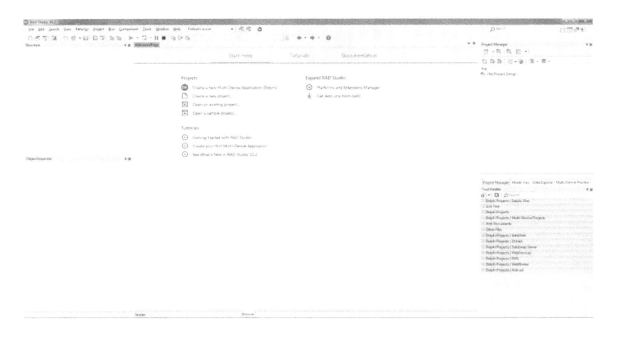

Delphi Welcome Page

Here you can display the **Platforms and Extensions Manager**, which will give you an opportunity to add or remove installed platforms and additional options. From the **Welcome Page** you can open sample projects, watch video tutorials, and access online documentation. You can also easily open recently closed projects. The projects that you frequently work with can be added to **Favorites** for quick access.

# Installing custom components

Delphi IDE has an open architecture and provides many ways to extend its functionality through additional packages. You can see the list of currently installed packages in the **Installed Packages** option available from the **Component** menu. The most typical Delphi building block is a **Component**. Technically, this is about taking the object-oriented programming principles and moving it one step further. With components, you have the ability to manipulate regular programming language object instances during the design time, before the project is built for a given platform. Packages may also contain custom property editors and the **Open Tools** API extension to the IDE itself that may add custom functionality to the IDE, such as additional menus and windows.

Out of the box, with the default Delphi installation, you will get a few hundred components already preinstalled. Depending on your Delphi version and selected features, this list may differ. Click on the **Installed Packages** option in the **Component** menu to verify which components are actually installed, as shown in the following screenshot:

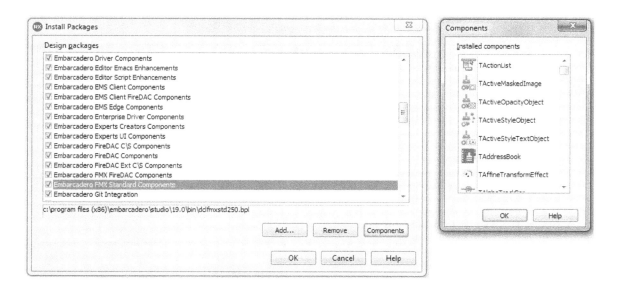

Installed Packages window with components shown for a selected package

There are many additional free and commercial component packages that are not installed by default. They can be installed with the integrated **GetIt Package Manager**. It is available either from the **Welcome Page** or from the **Tools** menu, as shown in the following screenshot:

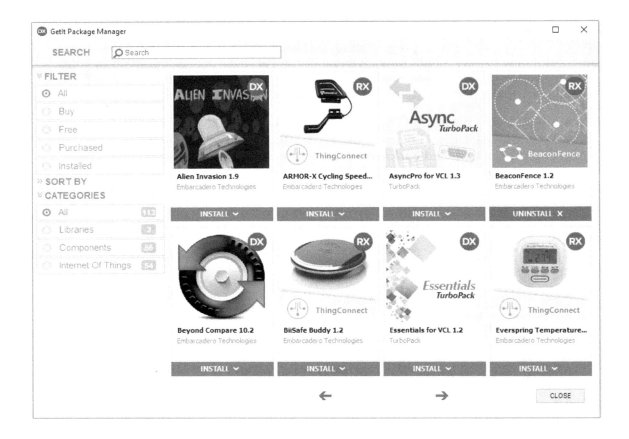

Delphi GetIt Package Manager

If you want to install any of the available component packages, just click on the **Install** button under the image of the package. The installation process is very straightforward. After accepting the license, the components are downloaded from the internet, compiled, and installed into the IDE.

# IDE options

You can manage all aspects of how the Delphi IDE works from the **Options** dialog available from the **Tools** menu. Here, you can control various aspects of how Delphi operates as a whole. Take a look at the following screenshot:

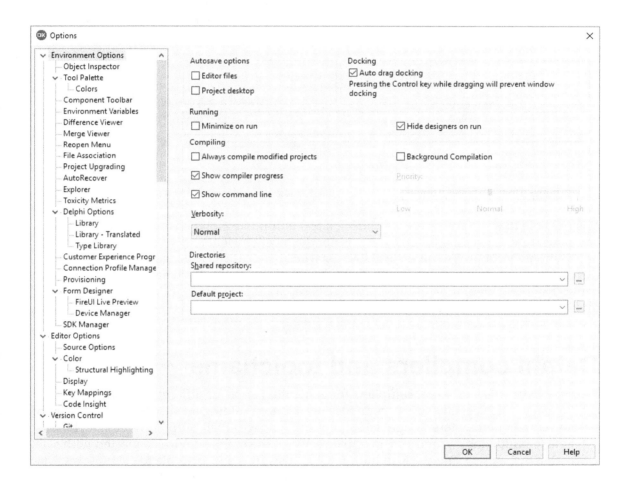

Delphi Options

# Riding the Integrated Development Environment

In a nutshell, Delphi is a program for making other programs. The actual program responsible for generating executable files from the source code is a compiler. It is typically implemented as a command-line application. When executing a command-line application, you can pass to it command-line parameters. Compilers take different command-line parameters, including the location of source code files necessary to generate the resulting binary file. Take a look at the following diagram:

Simplified compiler architecture

It is possible to write your programs using a text editor like Notepad and then execute the compiler from the command line, but it is not the most efficient way of creating applications. Most programmers use IDE for working on apps. The idea of an integrated development environment originates from the Delphi ancestor, **Borland Turbo Pascal,** and comes from the integration of three previously separate programs: Code Editor, compiler, and debugger.

# Delphi compilers and toolchains

Delphi IDE contains different compilers for generating apps for different platforms. The IDE manages all necessary source code files needed for building an app. It also takes care of passing correct parameters to right compilers and manages their output. In the IDE, it is possible to build, deploy, and run an app directly on the mobile device connected with a USB cable by just pressing the **Run** button. Obviously, it is also possible to generate an executable application without running it. Sometimes it is very handy to be able to step into an application as it is executed in the host operating system. This process is called debugging. In the Delphi IDE, you can run your program *with* or *without* debugging.

There are in total eight different Delphi compilers installed with the Delphi 10.2 version:

| Delphi compiler | Executable format |
|---|---|
| dcccaarm.exe | Android |
| dcciosarm.exe | 32-bit iOS |
| dcciosarm64.exe | 64-bit iOS |
| dcc32.exe | 32-bit Windows |
| dcc64.exe | 64-bit Windows |
| dccosx.exe | 32-bit Mac OS X |
| dccios32.exe | iOS Simulator |
| dcclinux64.exe | 64-bit Linux |

These compilers are typically installed into the C:\Program Files (x86)\Embarcadero\Studio\19.0\bin folder. The bin folder of Delphi has been added to the Windows path by the installer, so you can try and execute them directly.When executed with no parameters, Delphi compilers will just display their version numbers and possible command-line switches, as shown in the following screenshot:

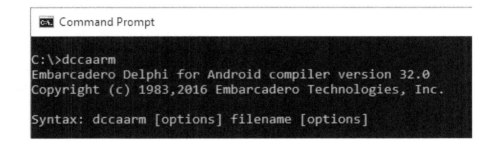

Delphi Android compiler invoked from Command Prompt

Take a look at the following screenshot:

```
C:\>dcciosarm64
Embarcadero Delphi Next Generation for iPhone ARM64 compiler version 32.0
Copyright (c) 1983,2016 Embarcadero Technologies, Inc.

Syntax: dcciosarm64 [options] filename [options]
```

Delphi iOS compiler invoked from Command Prompt

In the IDE, we do not need to invoke command-line compilers directly. The IDE is doing this for us when we choose to either run, build, or compile our project. It will also take care of outputting the resulting binary files into a separate folder per every supported platform and build configuration. When we build, deploy, and run our apps, we can see in the bottom part a log of all commands being executed, parameters passed to them, and their output.

# Hello World app

Starting with a new programming language or framework typically involves creating a program that displays the famous "Hello World" message, and we will follow this convention. Our app will have just one button. When you press the button, a `Delphi Hello World!` message will be displayed. Later in this chapter, we are going to put this app on an iPhone and on an Android device.

Click on the **Multi-Device Application - Delphi** option in the **File** | **New** menu, as shown in the following screenshot:

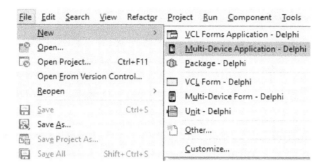

New "Multi-Device Application - Delphi" menu option

This will display the wizard with different multi-device project templates, as shown in the following screenshot:

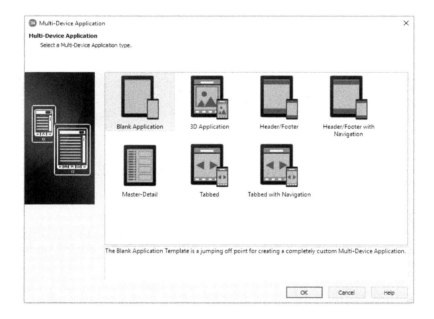

Multi-device application project templates dialog

Double-click on the **Blank Application** project template.

The first thing after creating a new project is to save it all. The Delphi project is made of multiple files that are managed by the IDE. The IDE will also create subfolders in the project directory for managing different artifacts such as compiled executable files, editor history, and recovery files, so it is always a good idea to save a new project into an empty directory.

Click on the **Save All** button in the Delphi toolbar just below the main menu to save all files in the project, as shown in the following screenshot:

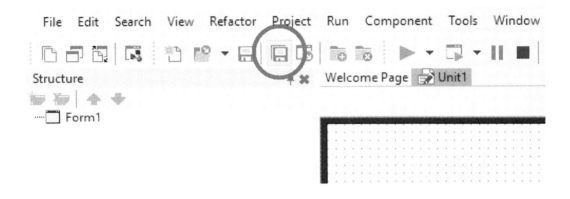

The Save All speed-button

Clicking from time to time on the **Save All** button is something that you do almost automatically.

First, we will be asked to save the main form of our application. Enter uFormHelloWorld in the file save dialog and click on **Save**. Then, the second file save dialog is displayed. Here we need to give our project a name. Enter DelphiHelloWorld and click on **Save**.

Delphi organizes all files necessary to build an app into a **Project**. The Delphi IDE contains a number of windows that help us work on our projects. There are different project types. It is possible to create a project group inside the IDE, but at any given moment of time there can be only one project active. You can see the name of the active Delphi project in the very top left corner of the Delphi window. Its name is also displayed in bold font in the **Project Manager**. Delphi IDE is context sensitive, so the contents of different windows and dialogs can vary. An example of a context sensitive dialog is **Project Options**. Select the **Options** item from the bottom of the **Project** menu. All options related to the current project opened in the IDE will be displayed, as shown in the following screenshot:

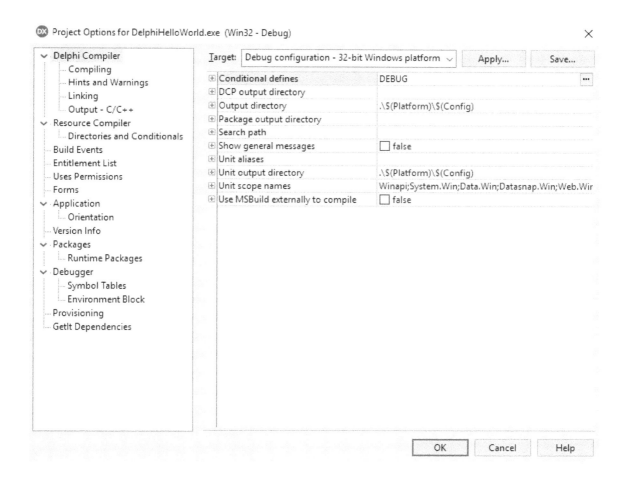

Project Options Dialog

Let's add a button to the form. The fastest way to work in the IDE is to use the **IDE Insight**. There are hundreds of different options, components, and windows in the IDE. If you know what you are looking for, you can just press *F6* or *Ctrl* and . keys at the same time. The IDE Insight combobox will receive focus. You can also just click on the IDE Insight combobox in the top corner of the IDE window. We want to add a button to the form. Just start typing what you are looking for and notice how, with every keystroke, the list of available items in the IDE Insight combobox is changing. Type b, u, and t and, after three keystrokes, the TButton component is the first on the list. Refer to the following screenshot:

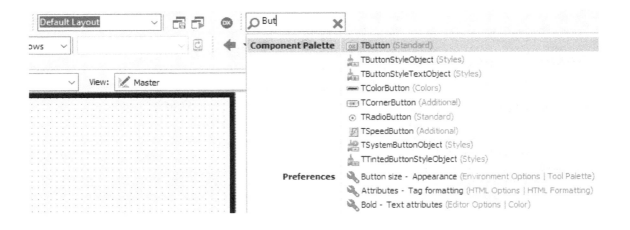

Incremental filtering in the IDE Insight combobox

Just press *Enter* and a button is added to the form. It is probably one of the single most useful productivity features of the IDE. Six keystrokes are needed to get the component added to the form. Alternatively, we could locate the TButton component in the **Tool Palette** window and double-click it to add it to the form. Over time, you will find that you press *Ctrl* + almost subconsciously, very much like clicking on **Save All**. In fact, you can click on **Save All** right now. :)

We have a button in the middle of an empty form. Let's start working on how our app will look--that's form design. What our app is going to do--that's coding. Click on the button and move it more toward the window's top left corner. In the left bottom part of the IDE there is the **Object Inspector** window. Here we can modify properties and events of components. We need to change the text that is displayed on the button. Make sure that TButton1 is selected in the **Object Inspector** and find its **Text** property. Replace the default Button1 with Hello World. Now, find the **Name** property of the button and change it to btnHelloWorld. Notice that the new name of the component has been immediately reflected in the **Structure** view above the **Object Inspector**. Now select the form. You can click somewhere on the form in the **Form Designer** to select it or just click on the form's node in the **Structure** view above **Object Inspector**. That's how the IDE works. Different windows are synchronized with each other, so selecting a component, changes the current component selection in other views as well. Find the **Name** property of the main form and change the default Form1 to FormHelloWorld. Now, find the **Caption** property of the form and change it to Delphi Hello World. Save all.

It is always good practice to give components and their properties meaningful names. There are different naming conventions. One of the most popular ones is to give components such name, that, just from the name itself, we could understand what the type of this particular component is. You also want to keep names short. If names are too long, you need to type more. Long names in the source code also tend to be less readable. It is up to you to decide what naming convention you use, but once you have decided, it is important to stick to it.

Now we need to define what will happen when the user of our app clicks on the button. For this, we need to attach an event handler to the OnClick event, of the btnHelloWorld button. We could switch to the **Events** tab in the **Object Inspector**, locate the OnClick event and double-click on the space next to it to generate an empty event handler. Let's do it faster. Just double-click on the button on the form. The IDE will switch from the **Form Designer** to **Code Editor,** and the cursor will be placed just at the beginning of an empty line between begin and end where we need to enter some code in the **Object Pascal** language. This code will be executed by our app in response to the click event. It could be misleading that this event is called OnClick, as you can use the mouse on desktop computers only. Fear not! If we compile our app to mobile targets, this event will be triggered in response to touching the button on the mobile device screen. In the code, we will invoke the built-in ShowMessage function and pass to it Delphi Hello World! as the string that we want to display in the message.

Click on **Save All** again. Now let's run the application. Refer to the following screenshot:

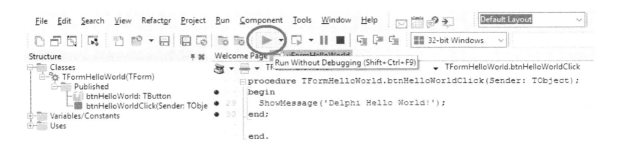

Run the current project without debugging

Click on the **Run** green arrow icon under the main menu to build and run the project. You will get the following output:

Delphi "Hello World" multi-device app running on Windows

We are on Windows and by default, we will compile our multi-device app as a Windows 32-bit executable. This is very useful during the developement of mobile apps with Delphi. During the development it is quicker to run our multi-device app on Windows to see that it does not contain any mistakes. If it compiles fine on Windows, then there is a big chance that it will also compile **OK** with mobile compilers. Building and deploying to a mobile device typically takes longer.

Every Delphi form is made of two source code files. You can switch between these files by clicking on the third button from the left in the toolbar with the Toggle Form/Unit (*F12*) hint or at the bottom of the screen using the **Code** and **Design** tabs. When we entered `uFormHelloWorld` as the name of the main form of our app, the IDE created two files: `uFormHelloWorld.pas` and `uFormHelloWorld.fmx`. The first file we can see in the **Code** tab is the source code, and the following is the screenshot of the toolbar with the toggle button to switch between the files:

Toggle Form/Unit speed button

The Code Editor is where we edit Delphi source files with the `pas` filename extension. We can see directly the contents of the file in the editor, as shown in the following screenshot:

Delphi Code Editor

The contents of the fmx file are managed by the **Form Designer** and we do not edit it directly. Every time we change something in the **Object Inspector** or in the **Form Designer**, these changes are stored in the fmx file. The **Form Designer** gives us a *what you see is what you get* user experience, so we can see how our app will look even before we run it. Refer to the following screenshot:

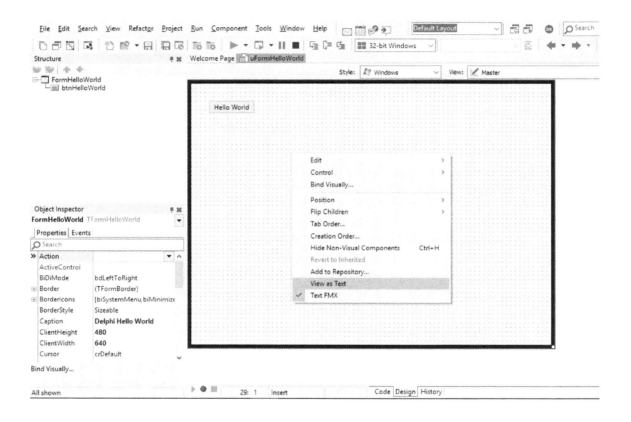

Delphi Form Designer - View as Form

You can preview the text of the form file by right-clicking somewhere on the form and selecting the **View As Text** option from the context menu.

To return to the form view, just right-click on the editor again and select **View As Form** from the context menu, as shown in the following screenshot:

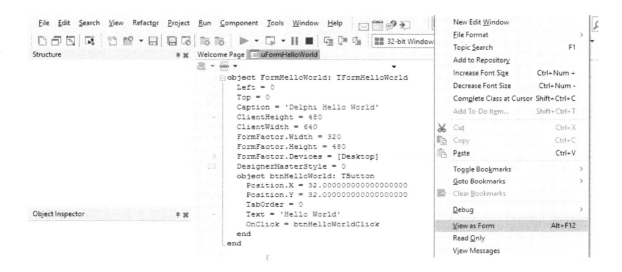

Delphi Form Designer - View as Text

The most important window in the IDE is the **Project Manager**. It provides a graphical interface to work with all files that make up our projects and lets us switch between different compilers and build configurations. You can build your applications in either *debug* or *release* mode. The debug mode is used during the development of an app. The resulting binary file will have additional binary information embedded that is used by a debugger. When our app is ready to be built for distributing to an app store, then we can switch to release mode.

This will generate an app in the form that is suitable for distribution. Take a look at the following screenshot:

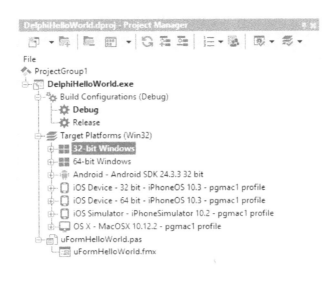

Delphi Project Manager

Let's have a look at different files that make up a Delphi project. If you want to quickly find the folder where the current project is located, you can do it easily. Click on the name of the project in the **Project Manager**. In the **Object Inspector,** you should now see, **Full Name** and **Full Path** properties. Copy the content of the **Full Path** property to the clipboard, paste it into Windows Explorer, and then hit *Enter*, as shown in the following screenshot:

Current project path and file name in Object Inspector

You should now see all the files and folders that make up our DelphiHelloWorld project:

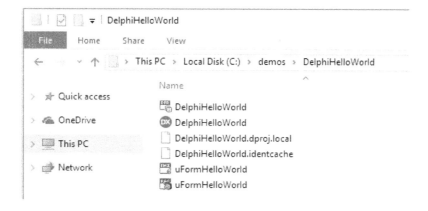

Files that make up a Delphi project in Windows 10 File Explorer

Alternatively, you could also right-click on the project name in the **Project Manager** and select the **Show in Explorer** option.

Among others, you will see here two files named `uFormHelloWorld` and two project files with the same name as our project `DelphiHelloWorld`, but with different extensions. The first one has the extension `dpr`, which stands for **Delphi Project** and contains the main program file of our application. We can preview this file inside the IDE by going to the **Project** | **View Source** menu, as shown in the following screenshot:

```
program DelphiHelloWorld;

uses
  System.StartUpCopy,
  FMX.Forms,
  uFormHelloWorld in 'uFormHelloWorld.pas' {FormHelloWorld};

{$R *.res}

begin
  Application.Initialize;
  Application.CreateForm(TFormHelloWorld, FormHelloWorld);
  Application.Run;
end.
```

Delphi project source code

It is the application main program file which is managed by the IDE and most of the time, we need to change anything there. The second project file has a `dproj` extension. If we open it in Notepad, we will see that it contains XML code with build instruction, for the MSBuild engine that is used by Delphi to manage all files and resources that are needed to build our project for different targets and configurations, as shown in the following screenshot:

```
DelphiHelloWorld - Notepad
File   Edit   Format   View   Help
<Project xmlns="http://schemas.microsoft.com/developer/msbuild/2003">
    <PropertyGroup>
        <ProjectGuid>{B2049BF3-149A-448A-BF5C-4EBBC2936EA2}</ProjectGuid>
        <ProjectVersion>18.1</ProjectVersion>
        <FrameworkType>FMX</FrameworkType>
        <MainSource>DelphiHelloWorld.dpr</MainSource>
        <Base>True</Base>
        <Config Condition="'$(Config)'==''">Debug</Config>
        <Platform Condition="'$(Platform)'==''">Win32</Platform>
        <TargetedPlatforms>1119</TargetedPlatforms>
        <AppType>Application</AppType>
    </PropertyGroup>
    <PropertyGroup Condition="'$(Config)'=='Base' or '$(Base)'!=''">
        <Base>true</Base>
    </PropertyGroup>
    <PropertyGroup Condition="('$(Platform)'=='Android' and '$(Base)'=='true') or '$(Base_Android)'!=''">
        <Base_Android>true</Base_Android>
        <CfgParent>Base</CfgParent>
        <Base>true</Base>
    </PropertyGroup>
    <PropertyGroup Condition="('$(Platform)'=='iOSDevice32' and '$(Base)'=='true') or '$(Base_iOSDevice32)'!=''">
        <Base_iOSDevice32>true</Base_iOSDevice32>
        <CfgParent>Base</CfgParent>
        <Base>true</Base>
```

Contents of the dproj project file

There is also a `win32` subfolder here. It contains a subfolder called `debug` and two files: `DelphiHelloWorld.exe` and `uFormHelloWorld.dcu`. The first file is a regular Windows 32-bit executable program that we have just built. It does very little. It only has a button and displays a message. The second file is the product of compiling a form file and is only useful for the IDE during the build process. You can safely delete the `win32` folder and its contents. The next time you run the application, all folders and files will be recreated. That's where the difference between *building* and *compiling* the project comes. The very first time, both commands do exactly the same--they generate all binary files in the output folder. In fact, `dcu` files are generated first and the `exe` file is generated next. If we select **Build** every time, all binary files are recreated. If we select **Compile**, only those `dcu` files are recreated that have changes. This really speeds up running a project inside of the IDE.

# Deploying to mobile devices

Our `DelphiHelloWorld` project is now ready for deployment to mobile devices. We have already built and run it on Windows. Now, we are going to first deploy it to an Android device and then to iOS.

This is a one-time preparation for mobile development that you need to go through after Delphi is installed. We want to get to the point that you can see your devices as targets inside the **Project Manager**.

For Android, all steps to configure your system to detect your device are described at `http://docwiki.embarcadero.com/RADStudio/en/Configuring_Your_System_to_Detect_Y our_Android_Device`.

# Deploying to Android

Deploying apps from Delphi to Android devices is simpler then deploying to iOS. You only need to have an Android device and a USB cable to connect your device to a Windows machine where you have Delphi installed.

Before deploying to an Android device, you need to find out if your device is supported by the version of Delphi you are using. For details, consult `http://docwiki.embarcadero.com/RADStudio/en/Android_Devices_Supported_for_Appli cation_Development` for the list of currently supported Android versions.

The first step is to enable USB debugging on the device. This option can be set in **Developer options** on your device. This option is not easy to find. It is, in fact, hidden. On your Android device, go to the **Settings | About** menu. Tap the **Build number** seven times to make **Settings | Developer options** available. Then, check the **USB Debugging** option. Connect your Android device with a USB cable to a computer where your PC is running. If you are using VMware make sure that your Android device is connected to the virtual machine where you have Delphi and not to your Mac. The first time you connect your Android device, you may see a message displayed on the device to **Allow USB debugging** from the computer, identified by a string of hexadecimal numbers that represents the computer's RSA key fingerprint. Check the **Always allow from this computer** option and click on **OK**.

More info on enabling USB debugging on Android devices is available at `http://docwiki.embarcadero.com/RADStudio/en/Enabling_USB_Debugging_on_an_Androi d_Device`.

The next step is to install the USB driver for your Android device on the machine where Delphi is installed. The test device that I'm using is Google Nexus 7.

Probably the easiest option to download all the necessary bits for Android development is to download and install Android Studio for free from Google. It will download all necessary Java SDKs and tools that are needed in order to build an Android `apk` executable file. For reference, I'm using Android Studio version 2.2.2. On the splash, select the **Android SDK** option. In the dialog, select the **SDK Tools** tab and check the **Google USB Driver** option. Click **OK** and the driver will be downloaded and installed, as shown in the following screenshot:

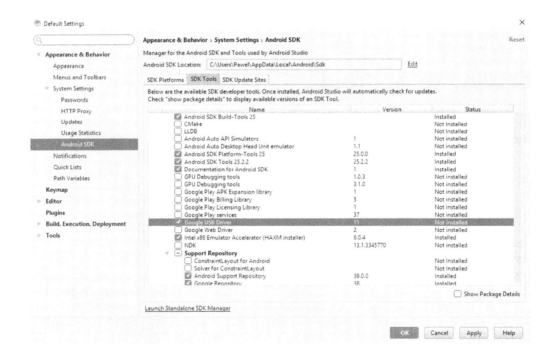

Android SDK Tools with the "Google USB Driver" option checked

In order to make sure that the device driver has been installed successfully, go to the **Device Manager** window in **Control Panel** and you should find your device listed. If you right-click on the device, there is an option to **Update Device Driver**. I could find my Nexus 7 listed there and the device driver was up to date. Refer to the following screenshot:

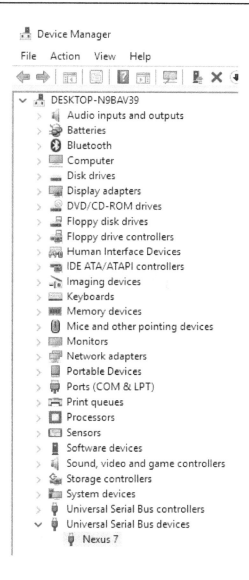

Nexus 7 in Device Manager

Depending on your device, the steps may be different. You can find detailed information on how to install the USB driver for your Android device at
`http://docwiki.embarcadero.com/RADStudio/en/Installing_the_USB_Driver_for_Your_Android_Device.`

Now, back to Delphi IDE. Make sure that our `DelphiHelloWorld` project is still open in the IDE. In the **Project Manager,** expand **Target Platforms** and click on **Android**. The first time you click on the **Target** node, you will see the message **Android SDK tools are required. Do you want to download and install Android SDK tools automatically?**. Click on **Yes**. The process to download and install SDK tools will start and you will see in the Command Prompt window the progress of the operation. After a moment, you should see your device listed under **Tools** in the **Project Manager**.

Double-click on the **Android** node to select the Android target. It should display in bold font. Now this is the current target, so when you click on the Run green arrow, the IDE will build our Delphi Hello World app using the Delphi Android compiler and the executable `apk` Android file will be created, deployed to the device, and run in just one operation.

Click on **Run**. The project will be compiled, deployed to your Android device, and run:

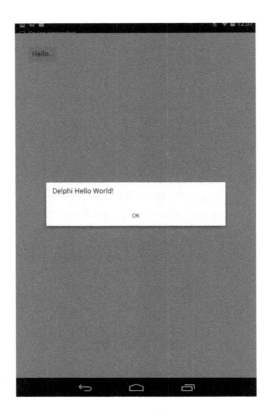

Delphi "Hello World" app running on Android

You can find more information about preparing your IDE for running apps on Android devices on DocWiki at
`http://docwiki.embarcadero.com/RADStudio/en/Android_Mobile_Application_Developm ent`.

# Deploying to iOS

Deploying apps from Delphi to an iOS device requires a Mac computer. As compared to Android, deploying to iOS requires more steps because you also need to enroll for the Apple iOS Developer Program and to provision the device you want to deploy to.

First, you need to make sure that the iOS device that you want to deploy your application to is compatible. In case of iPhone, the oldest supported model is 4GS, but you want to have a device that can have iOS 10 installed. In my case, it is iPhone 6S.

The first steps to prepare your Mac and an iOS device for deployment are exactly the same that any iOS developer needs to do. This is something that you do once. During the process of deploying to an iOS device, an app needs to be digitally signed with the special command-line tool that comes with Apple Xcode installation. You could install just the Xcode command-line tools, but in practice it is easier to install the whole Xcode development environment from Apple.

In order to be able to deploy apps to an iOS device, it needs to be provisioned first. The process of provisioning iOS devices, joining the Apple iOS Developer Program, and installing various certificates is the same as in the case of any app developed with Xcode. In order to be sure that you will be able to deploy an app from Delphi into iOS, it is recommended to create an empty app from a template in Xcode and try to run it on the device. If this is successful, the next step is to install a special **PAServer** Mac program on the machine where you have Xcode installed. The `PAServer19.0.pkg` installable package is installed in the `PAServer` subdirectory of Delphi. Just copy it over to your Mac and execute. This will install the PAServer. The PAServer is implemented as a command-line app, and after it is launched on Mac, it will display a command-line interface where you will be prompted to enter your Mac password. Your Mac will also display a dialog asking if it is OK to give PAServer debugging permissions. Accept it.

You can think about the PAServer as an agent that performs operations on behalf of the Delphi IDE that runs on a remote Windows machine. In order for Delphi to be able to connect, you need to know the IP address of the machine where the PAServer is running. You can find out the IP address by issuing the i command from the PAServer's Command Prompt. The list of all available command-line parameters to PAServer is displayed when you enter ? in the Command Prompt, as shown in the following screenshot:

```
                          pg — paserver — paserver — 80×24
Last login: Wed May 31 17:48:00 on console
/Applications/PAServer-19.0.app/Contents/MacOS/paserver ; exit;
Pawes-MacBook-Pro:~ pg$ /Applications/PAServer-19.0.app/Contents/MacOS/paserver
; exit;
Platform Assistant Server  Version 10.0.1.23
Copyright (c) 2009-2017 Embarcadero Technologies, Inc.

Connection Profile password <press Enter for no password>:

Acquiring permission to support debugging...succeeded

Starting Platform Assistant Server on port 64211

Type ? for available commands
>?
q - stop the server
c - print all clients
p - print port number
i - print available IP addresses
s - print scratch directory
g - generate login passfile
v - toggle verbose mode
r - reset, terminate all child processes
>
```

PAServer running on Mac

Now we need to configure Delphi, so it can find the iOS device you want to deploy to. The goal is to find your device listed in the **Project Manager**. In general, you could have multiple different Macs visible to your Delphi installation. For every Mac you want to deploy to, you need to define a connection profile.

Make sure that our DelphiHelloWorld project is open in the IDE.

Double-click on the **iOS Device - 64 bit** node under **Target** to make it active. It will be displayed in bold. Now, right-click on the node and select **Properties**. You will see a small **Platform Properties** dialog where you will be able to select the proper iOS SDK. Click on the SDK combo box and select **Add New...** from the dropdown.

Then, select **Add New** from the connection profile combo. The **Create a Connection Profile** wizard will be displayed. I have entered `DelphiDev` as the profile name. Click on **Next**. On the next tab of the wizard dialog, we need to enter the address and port of the remote machine. Keep the default port `64211` and enter your Mac password in the last field. Now click on the **Test Connection** button to verify that the IDE can communicate with the remote PAServer. If everything went well you should see the message that the connection to your Mac succeeded. Click on **Finish**, as shown in the following screenshot:

"Create a Connection Profile" dialog

Now, back in the **Add a New SDK** dialog, select the SDK version to add and click on **OK**:

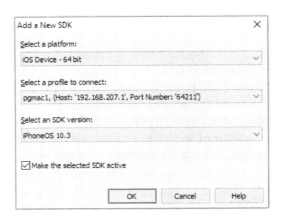

Add a New SDK dialog

This will initiate the process of updating the local file cache, with files being downloaded from Mac that are needed by the Delphi iOS compiler to generate an iOS executable file. Refer to the following screenshot:

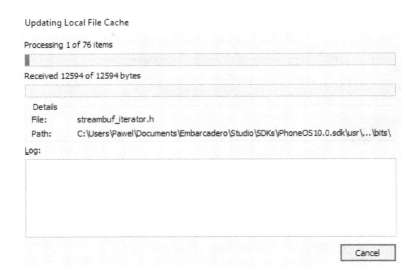

Updating Local Cache

After the cache is refreshed, the IDE should automatically update the iOS 64-bit `Target` node and you should see your device listed there:

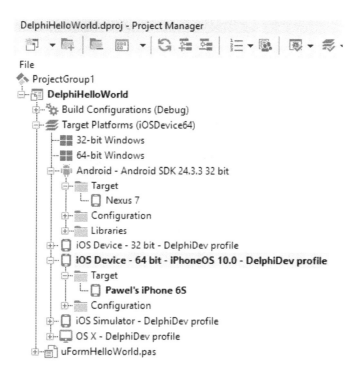

Project Manager with an iPhone device listed as a target

Now click on the **Run** button. This will locally build the iOS `ipa` executable file and send it to the Mac machine where PAServer is running. The PAServer will invoke the command-line tool from the Xcode installation to digitally sign the executable, and then it will be deployed and run on the physical iOS device--all in one operation.

And here is how our Delphi Hello World app looks on my iPhone 6 running iOS 10:

Delphi "Hello World" app running on iOS

More information about deploying apps to iOS devices from Delphi can be found online at
http://docwiki.embarcadero.com/RADStudio/en/IOS_Mobile_Application_Development.

# Summary

In this chapter, we have installed Delphi and configured it for mobile development. We have also learned the basic functionality of the Integrated Development Environment.

Now we are going to change gears and focus on Object Pascal, the programming language of Delphi.

# 2
# Mind Your Language

The Object Pascal language used in Delphi is constantly evolving. With every new version of Delphi, new features are added to the language. For every mobile and desktop operating system, there is a different Delphi compiler with slightly different functionality, such as automatic reference counting for mobile. Fluency in using the Object Pascal language is a key skill for every Delphi developer.

This chapter will cover the following points:

- The basic Object Pascal language features
- Advanced constructs, such as generics, anonymous methods, class helpers, custom attributes, and Runtime Type Information (RTTI)

The objective of this chapter is gaining fluency in using the Object Pascal language with a focus on mobile Delphi compilers. This chapter is not a definitive reference to every single feature of the programming language of Delphi. The goal is to cover most of the everyday constructs, to be able to understand the FireMonkey library source code, and to write solid and maintainable code.

# Do you speak Object Pascal?

The Object Pascal language has been designed for teaching good programming practices. It is a high-level, modern, and strongly typed compiled language that supports structured and object-oriented programming.

In order to solve a problem using a computer, you need to define a finite set of actions that operate on certain data or, in other words, to define an algorithm. An algorithm expressed in a programming language is a computer program, and its actions are described as programming language instructions.

One or more actions performed on certain data can be encapsulated in the Object Pascal language as a routine or a class. In Object Pascal, routines are called **functions**. If a function does not return a value, it is called a **procedure**. Classes are the corner stones of object-oriented programming, which is the most important approach to building apps in Object Pascal. Objects group the data and the operations performed on this data together, providing encapsulation and reusability.

In the previous chapter, you learned about compilers. The job of a compiler is to process one or more files that contain the text of the programs that we write in a programming language and generate a binary file that can be loaded by an operating system and executed. Compilers may also generate other types of binaries, such as packages or services. In this chapter, we will focus on the contents of the files that contain the source code of our programs. Source code files are regular text files that can be opened in an arbitrary text editor. The default extension of a file that contains the Object Pascal source code is `.pas`. When you install Delphi, it will register itself with Windows as the default program for opening different file types related to Delphi programming, including `.pas`, `.dpr`, `.dpk`, `.dproj`, and a few more.

The source code file needs to contain proper content according to the rules of the programming language. If you try to compile a file that is not properly structured or that contains programming language errors, the compiler will stop the compilation and report an error message describing the location and nature of the error. Sometimes the error message might not be obvious, but we would typically get the name of the source file and the text line number where the error is located.

# Program structure

Each program begins with a heading, which specifies the name of the program, followed by an optional `uses` clause and a block of declarations and statements. Object Pascal programs are typically divided into modules of source code called **units**. The optional `uses` clause contains the list of units that are used by the program. These units, in turn, may use other units specified in their own `uses` clauses.

Every Object Pascal program uses the built-in `System` unit. This unit contains predefined constants, types, functions, and procedures, such as basic functions to write and read from the command line or work with files. If you explicitly place the `System` in the `uses` clause, you will get an error message that this unit is already used and that it is not legal to use a unit multiple times in one unit. Apart from the `System` unit, Delphi comes with many units that are not used automatically. They must be included in the `uses` clause. For example, the `System.SysUtils` unit is typically used in every Delphi project because it provides some basic functionality, such as the declaration of an exception class needed for structured exception handling. Unit names may contain dots, such as in the case of `System.SysUtils`. Only the last part is the actual unit name, and all the preceding identifiers constitute a *namespace* that is used to logically group units. In some cases, it is possible to skip the namespace part, and the compiler will still be able to compile a unit. The order of the units listed in the `uses` clause is important and determines the order in which they will be initialized.

The first time you compile an app or a package (a special type of project custom components and editors used by the IDE), the compiler produces a compiled unit file (`.dcu` on Windows) for each unit used in the project. These files are then linked to create an executable file. In the **Project** menu, or in the **Project Manager** context menu, there are options to either **Compile** or **Build** the current project. When you compile your project, individual units are not recompiled, unless they have been changed since the previous compilation or their compiled units cannot be found. If you choose **Build**, all the compiled units are regenerated. In fact, the compiler just needs the compiled unit to generate the executable, so it might not have access to the source code of a unit at all. With pre-compiled units, you can build even very big projects very quickly.

# Console application

The simplest possible type of program that can be written in Delphi is a console application. It does not contain any graphical user interface. Console programs can be executed from the command prompt and can optionally take command-line parameters. A console application may output some text back to the command line, perform some calculations, process files, or communicate with remote services running somewhere on the internet.

Let's create a simple Delphi console app. It will be an interactive program that will take our name from the command line and will display a greeting. In the **File** menu, select **New** and **Other**. In the **New Items** window, make sure that the **Delphi Projects** node is selected, and double-click on the **Console Application** icon:

Console
Application

The IDE has generated a console application for us that currently does nothing. The first thing we always do after creating a new project is to save it. Click on **Save All** in the **File** menu, click on the **Save All** icon in the toolbar, or just press *Ctrl + Shift + S* on the keyboard:

Always save a new project into an empty folder. Enter Greeter as the name of the new project and click on **OK**. Notice that the IDE has changed the identifier in the first line of the code and, also, the name of the file where the program is stored. Every Delphi executable program source code needs to start from the Object Pascal keyword, program, followed by the name of the program. The name of the program should match the name of the file it is stored in. The identifier in code should match the physical file name. Otherwise, the compiler will fail to process the file.

If you now browse the folder where the project is saved, you will find two files named Greeter but with different extensions. One is the Greeter.dpr file that contains the source code of the program that we see in the Code Editor. The second one is Greeter.dproj and contains the MSBuild XML code that the IDE uses for storing different settings belonging to the project that are used for compilation. By convention, the main file of the Delphi app, the one that starts with the program keyword, does not have the .pas extension but .dpr, which stands for **Delphi project**.

Let's replace the content of our program with the following code:

```
Greeter
 1  program Greeter;

    var
       s: string;

    begin
       Write('Enter your name: ');
       Readln(s);
       Writeln('Welcome ' + s + '!');
10     Readln;
    end.
```

Save and run the application. It should display an Enter your name: message and then display the welcome message. On my machine it looks as follows:

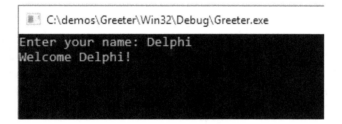

```
C:\demos\Greeter\Win32\Debug\Greeter.exe
Enter your name: Delphi
Welcome Delphi!
```

Procedures for reading and writing to console come from the built-in `System` unit, so in our simple demo program, there is no need for a `uses` clause at all. The last empty `Readln` statement is there in the program, so we could actually see the output from the previous `Writeln` statement before the program closes. `Write` is used to output text to the console and `Read` is used to read the input from the console into a string variable. The `Writeln` and `Readln` variations of these methods additionally advance to the next line in the console.

Before the `begin` keyword, there is a variable declaration. Object Pascal is a strongly typed language. You need to declare a variable and its type before you can use it. In our example, `s` is declared as `string`, so it can hold an arbitrary string of Unicode characters. Traditionally, in the Pascal language, the individual characters of a string can be accessed with a 1-based index. Delphi mobile compilers follow conventions used in other languages and use a 0-based indexing. There is a special compiler directive, `ZEROBASEDSTRINGS`, that can change this behavior.

The Code Editor helps us in a visual way to work with our code. In the screenshot from the Code Editor, on the left-hand side, in the gutter, there is a green line. It is completely green because I just saved the code. If I start typing, the color of the gutter next to the modified row will change to yellow to indicate that there are some unsaved changes. Every time you save a file, its local copy is stored in a hidden `__history` folder. At the bottom of the Code Editor, there is the **History** tab. In the **History** view, you can browse through changes, compare file versions, and restore a file to a previous revision.

Blue dots in the gutter indicate all *executable* lines of source code. This is where you can place a breakpoint if you want to debug this program. The instructions that make up the Object Pascal program start with the `begin` keyword and end with the `end` keyword, followed by `.`. Everything that goes between them contains statements. Each statement is separated with a semicolon (`;`) character. It will still be a valid program if we remove the semicolon after the last `Readln` instruction because the semicolon's role is to be a *separator* and not a *terminator*. The indentation of the source code and text formatting does not have any meaning for the compiler, but it is a good practice to use indentation and empty spaces for better readability. That is why the `begin` and `end` keywords start from the beginning of the line and all the other statements are indented. To increase the indentation of a block of code in the Code Editor, select the lines, keeping the *Shift* key pressed, and use the *Ctrl + Shift + I* key combination. To decrease the indentation, use *Ctrl + Shift + U*.

You can put arbitrary text in your source code in the form of comments, which are ignored by the compiler. Comments are multiline or single-line. Multiline comments are enclosed within curly braces ({ }) or a bracket and star character combination ((* *)). The two types of multiline comments can be nested within each other.

Some multiline comments start with a dollar sign. They are displayed in a different color in the Code Editor because they are compiler directives. In the default source code generated for a console application, there are two optional compiler directives. The first one tells the compiler that this program is a console app and the second one, with the R switch, instructs the compiler to embed in the resulting executable any binary resources that may be found in the resource file with the same name as our project, but with the .res extension.

Single-line comments start with two slashes (//). A compiler ignores all the characters that follow until it encounters the end of line control characters. If you want to quickly comment *out* or *in* a block of code, use the *Ctrl + /* key combination. If a comment starts with three slashes, it is treated as a special *documentation* comment, which can be used for displaying documentation hints in the Code Editor and documentation generation. It is a good practice to properly document your code with comments, so it is easier to read and maintain it.

# Forms applications

It is time to start building our first fully functional mobile app *The Game of Memory*. In this chapter, we will only create the main architecture. Our app is going to be very simple. There will be two forms--one main form will contain a grid of squares, which will serve as the game board, and the second form will contain the game settings. This simple architecture will help us understand the structure of a typical Delphi *forms* applications.

Projects

 Create a new Multi-Device Application (Delphi)

Close the `Greeter` program if it is still open. Create a new `Multi-Device Application - Delphi` program. Select the **Blank Application** template and click on **Save All**. Save the file that contains the main form of the application as `uFormMain` and the project as `GameOfMemory`. Change the **Name** property of the application form to `FormMain`. Add another form to the project:

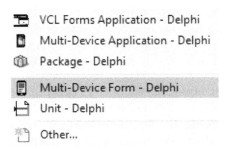

In the **File | New** menu, select **Multi-Device Form - Delphi**. In the dialog to select the form type, keep the default **HD** selection. The other option is **3D**. We will get to building 3D user interfaces later in the book. **HD** stands for **high definition** and is just a more fancy way of specifying that we just want a regular 2D form. Save the file as `uFormSettings` and change the **Name** property of the new form to `FormSettings`.

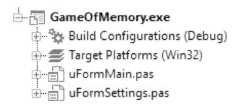

Our project contains two forms now. Where is the program file of our app? Click on the **View Source** option in the **Project** menu, or in the context menu in **Project Manager**. You should now see the following code. This is the main program of our **GameOfMemory** app:

```
program GameOfMemory;
uses
  System.StartUpCopy,
  FMX.Forms,
  uFormMain in 'uFormMain.pas' {FormMain},
  uFormSettings in 'uFormSettings.pas' {FormSettings};

{$R *.res}
```

```
begin
  Application.Initialize;
  Application.CreateForm(TFormMain, FormMain);
  Application.CreateForm(TFormSettings, FormSettings);
  Application.Run;
end.
```

The main program file in our project is managed automatically by the IDE, and in most cases, there is no need to edit it manually. This is a very typical project file.

The first line contains the program heading. The lines following it contain the uses clause. Next, there is a compiler directive that links the resource file of the project into the program. What follows is the block of statements executed when the program runs. The project file ends, like all the source code files, with a period.

The uses clause lists all the units incorporated into the program. These units may, in turn, have their own uses clauses. The logic of a program is defined between reserved words, begin and end. In this program, executable statements are simply method calls to the global Application object of the project. The block can also contain declarations of constants, types, variables, procedures, and functions. These declarations must precede the statement part of the block.

The Delphi Code Editor has a built-in hyper-navigation functionality to quickly jump to other units. For example, we may want to see where the Application global object variable reference is declared. If we move the mouse cursor over Application somewhere in the code, we will see a hint that tells us in which unit a given symbol is defined, as shown in the following screenshot:

If you press the *Ctrl* key at the same time, the symbol turns into an underlined hyperlink that you can click to quickly jump to the unit where a given symbol is declared. Alternatively, you can right-click on the symbol in the editor and select the **Find Declaration** option. Take a look at the following screenshot:

The blue arrows in the IDE toolbar let you move back and forth through the history of your navigation in the Code Editor.

Currently, at the startup of our program, both the application forms are created. In fact, we do not need to create the **Settings** form when the application starts. It may so happen that the end user will just play the game and close the application, without going into **Settings**. Another important consideration in mobile apps is the application startup time. You want to keep it to the minimum. The call to create the **Settings** form, depending on the processor speed of your mobile device, may delay the moment when the end user sees the screen of the app by a couple of milliseconds. We can just manually delete the line of code in the Code Editor that contains `Application.CreateForm(TFormSettings, FormSettings)`, but there is a more elegant way of doing so. In the **Project** menu, click on **Options** at the bottom of the menu. In the **Project Options** dialog, select the **Forms** node and move **FormSettings** from the list of "**Auto-create forms**" to the list of **Available** forms. Take a look at the following screenshot:

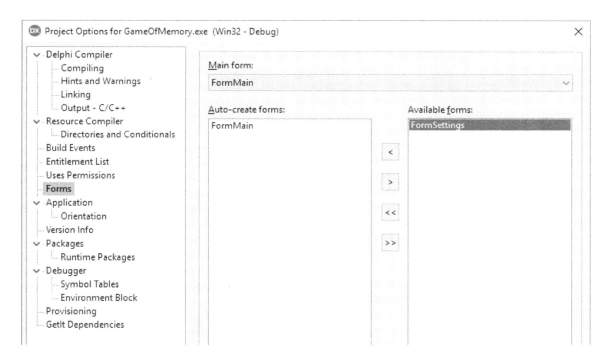

Note that the line of code responsible for creating the **Settings** form disappeared from the main program block.

Now, we are going to implement basic navigation between the forms and, at the same time, have a closer look at the structure of the Object Pascal unit.

The main form of the application is displayed at application startup, and its lifetime is the same as the application. Let's add a toolbar to the main form of the app and a speed button in the top-right corner, which will display the **Settings** form. In the **Settings** form we will also add a speed button on the left-hand side of the toolbar with the left arrow image for going back to the main application form.

Make sure that the `FormMain` unit is open in **Form Designer**. If you are in the Code Editor, you can switch to **Form Designer** by clicking on the **Design** tab at the bottom of the screen. Press the *Ctrl* and *.* keys at the same time to focus the IDE insight and just start typing the `TToolbar` that we want to add to the form. After the first three letters, the `TToolbar` should be at the top of the list. Just press *Enter* to add it to the main form, as shown in the following screenshot:

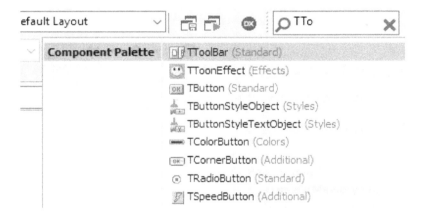

It will automatically align to the top of the form. In the same way, using the IDE Insight, add the **TSpeedButton** component on the toolbar. Change its **Align** property to **Right**, so it always stays in the top-right corner of the screen regardless of its size or orientation. Change the **Name** property of the speed button to **spdbtnSettings**. Now, we need to give it a nice icon. We can do it by changing its **StyleLookup** property.

By default, when we create a new multi-device form, it uses the default Windows style. What we really want is to see how the form will look on a mobile target, be it iOS or Android. Change the selection from Windows to iOS in the combobox above **Form Designer**. Refer to the following screenshot:

Now, if we open the **StyleLookup** property of the speed button in **Object Inspector**, we should be able to select from one of the built-in iOS styles for a given control. Select the **drawertoolbutton** style from the list. If we switch to Android, the look and feel of the form will change, including the styling of the toolbar and also the icons available for styling the speedbutton. Refer to the following screenshot:

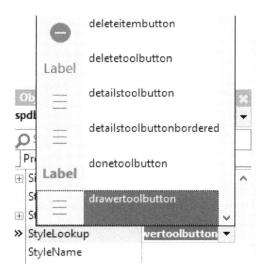

Save the form. Now go to the **Settings** form. Change **Style** in the preceding combobox the form to iOS. Following the same steps, add a toolbar and a speed button. Change the Name property of the speed button to **spdbtnBack**, its **StyleLookup** property to **arrowlefttoolbutton**, and **Align** property to **Left**.

Now we will implement the functionality to navigate between these forms. In the main form, when we click on the **Settings** button, we want to call the Show method of the **Settings** form. However, **FormMain** does not know about **FormSettings**. We need to add **FormSettings** to the uses clause of **FormMain**. We could do it manually, but the IDE again can help us with it. Make sure that the **uFormMain** file is open in the Code Editor and click on the **Use Unit...** option in the **File** menu, as shown in the following screenshot:

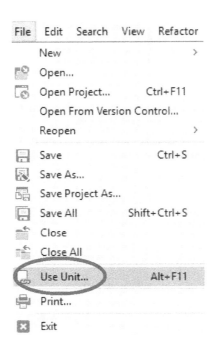

In the **Use Unit...** dialog, select **FormSettings** and keep the default selection to add this unit to the uses clause of the implementation section of the FormMain unit. This dialog will list all the other units in the current project that are not yet used by the currently selected unit. Take a look at the following screenshot:

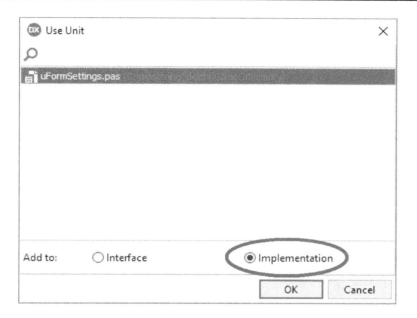

The next step is to do the same thing in the **FormSettings**. Add **FormMain** to the implementation section of the uses clause of **FormSettings**. Double-click on the Back speed button and enter one line of code to show the main form of our application:

```
unit uFormSettings;

interface

uses
  System.SysUtils, System.Types, System.UITypes, System.Classes,
System.Variants,
  FMX.Types, FMX.Controls, FMX.Forms, FMX.Graphics, FMX.Dialogs,
FMX.StdCtrls,
  FMX.Controls.Presentation;

type
  TFormSettings = class(TForm)
    ToolBar1: TToolBar;
    spdbtnBack: TSpeedButton;
    procedure spdbtnBackClick(Sender: TObject);
  private
    { Private declarations }
  public
    { Public declarations }
  end;
```

```
var
   FormSettings: TFormSettings;

implementation

{$R *.fmx}

uses uFormMain;

procedure TFormSettings.spdbtnBackClick(Sender: TObject);
begin
   FormMain.Show;
end;

end.
```

This is a fairly simple Object Pascal unit. Every unit file begins with a unit heading, which is followed by the `interface` and `implementation` sections. After the `implementation` section, there could be optional `initialization` and `finalization` sections with instructions to be executed before and after the main application logic.

The interface section of the unit starts with the reserved word, `interface`, and continues until the beginning of the implementation section. The `interface` section declares constants, types, variables, procedures, and functions, which are visible to other units in the project. The `interface` section does not contain any executable code. The declaration of a procedure or function includes only its heading. The block of the procedure or function follows in the implementation section. The interface declaration for a class includes declarations of all its members, including the ones that are private to the class and not accessible to the code outside the declaring unit. The `interface` section may include its own `uses` section, which must appear immediately after the `interface` keyword.

The implementation section of a unit starts with the `implementation` keyword and continues until the beginning of the initialization section or, if there is no initialization section, until the end of the unit marked with the `end` keyword followed by a period. The implementation section contains declarations of constants, types, variables, procedures, and functions, which are visible only to the declaring unit. This introduces better organization to the program structure through encapsulation and the *separation of concerns*. The implementation section of the unit contains the executable code defined in either standalone functions and procedures or belonging to classes and in this case called **methods**. Only those functions and procedures that additionally have their headings declared in the interface section of the unit are visible to the code residing in other units. The implementation section of the unit may have its own `uses` clause section, which follows immediately after the `implementation` reserved word.

A given Object Pascal unit may contain a reference to other units only once, either in its implementation section or its interface section. If you are unsure where to put a unit reference, always use it in the implementation part of the unit. Sometimes, you have to put a unit reference in the interface section of the unit. For example, our uFormSettings unit declares the TFormSettings class type, which inherits from the TForm class, which is defined in the FMX.Forms unit, so this unit has to be listed in the interface section of the unit.

If unit A depends on unit B, and unit B depends on unit A, then they are mutually dependent. This is the case between the two units in our GameOfMemory project. If the two units are mutually dependent, at least one of them should list another in its implementation's, and not interface's, uses clause.

The initialization section is optional. It starts from the initialization keyword and continues until the beginning of the finalization section, or if there is no finalization section, until the end of the unit. The initialization section contains statements that are executed at the program startup. The order in which the units are listed in uses clauses is important because it is what determines the order in which initialization statements are executed.

The finalization section is also optional and can only appear in units that have an initialization section. It starts from the reserved word, finalization, and continues until the end of the unit. The finalization section contains statements that are executed when the program terminates. The finalization sections are executed in the opposite order of initializations.

The uFormSettings unit contains the declaration of the TFormSettings type. Type declarations follow the reserved word, type. After the declaration of the form's type, there is a variable declaration, FormSettings, of the TFormSettings type. Variable declarations start with the var keyword. When you define a variable, you must also state its type. The Object Pascal language is strongly typed. The more complex your programs begin, the more you will appreciate the fact that it is not the job of a compiler to guess the type, but it is you, the programmer, who decides about types. The Delphi compiler works in a top-down fashion and, typically, just makes one go through all the dependent units in your project. This also means that the TFormSettings type needs to be declared before it can be used to declare the type of the variable. Because the FormSettings variable is defined in the interface section of the unit, it can be used outside the unit, for example, in the main program file.

Inheritance is a very important concept in object-oriented programming. Our **Settings** form has everything that a standard multi-device form has. You can inspect the declaration of the TForm class in the FMX.Forms unit. A class declaration defines the name of the class and the class it inherits from in the brackets after the class keyword. The class declaration is divided according to visibility. Different class members can be private, then they are visible to the defining class only. It is also possible to have members defined as protected. This means that a given member--variable field, constant, or a method--is also visible to the descendant classes. The two other important visibility specifiers are public and published. The first one means that the class members are visible to all the other units in the project. Published has public visibility, but, additionally, published class members are also accessible at the design-time in the IDE.

The three lines right after the class declaration of the form contain two field declarations for the toolbar and for the speedbutton. There is also a method, or more specifically an event handler, for the OnClick event of the button. These declarations do not have an explicit visibility specifier, and they are treated as published. This part of the form class is managed by the IDE. Every time you add a component to the form or create an event handler, the corresponding declaration is added automatically. Also, the interface uses clause is updated by the IDE every time a different component is added to the form in **Form Designer**. The form's class declaration also has placeholders for optional private and public declarations that the programmer may want to add.

The implementation section of the unit starts with the $R compiler directive that instructs the compiler to link into the unit the form file that is managed by the IDE and contains component properties set by **Form Designer** and **Object Inspector**. What follows is the implementation of the TFormSettings.spdbtnBackClick(Sender: TObject) event handler. Its name is made of two parts separated by a period. The first part is the name of the class and the second part is the name of the method. In brackets, there is one Sender parameter that is passed to the method and, in this case, is a reference to the spdbtnBack control of the form. The Show method in the body of the event handler has been inherited from the TForm class and, as such, is available in the descendant TFormMain class reference defined in the other form.

One last thing is to implement the functionality to show the **Settings** form in the OnClick event of the main form. Remember that we have removed the TFormSettings from the list of autocreated forms. This means that we are now responsible for creating an instance of this class before we can manipulate it in code.

Enter the following code in the OnClick event handler of the spdbtnSettings
speedbutton:

```
implementation

{$R *.fmx}

uses uFormSettings;

procedure TFormMain.spdbtnSettingsClick(Sender: TObject);
begin
  if FormSettings = nil then
    FormSettings := TFormSettings.Create(Application);

  FormSettings.Show;
end;

end.
```

The global FormSettings variable stores the reference to an instance of the
TFormSettings class. We only need to create the **Settings** form once in code. This is a
common *lazy creation* pattern, where an object is created just before it is used for the first
time in code. If the end user never clicks on the **Settings** button, this object is never created.
Here, we are entering a whole new world of different expressions and instructions of the
Object Pascal language. In short, what happens here is that if the FormSettings variable is
nil, then we assign to it the reference to the newly constructed instance of the
TFormSettings type. Create is a special constructor method that may perform the
initialization of an object, but most importantly, it allocates memory for the object. There are
also *destructors* that are responsible for freeing the object's memory. The TForm class, which
is an ancestor to TFormSettings, is, in turn, inherited from the TComponent class. This is
where the Create(AOwner: TComponent) constructor is defined. Here, we specify that
the global Application object is the owner of the newly created form and it will be
responsible for calling the form's destructor when the application is terminated.

This is another feature of Object Pascal. Not only do you need to define the types of
variables, but you are also responsible for managing memory. Once you get some memory
through a call to a constructor, you should also think about when it is released. In fact, in
the case of Delphi mobile compilers, there is an *automatic reference counting* mechanism in
place that will automatically call a class destructor when the object reference is no longer
accessible in code. However, it is always a good practice to call destructors and think about
memory management as if there were no automatic reference counting.

# Object Pascal Phrase Book

This book is aimed at Delphi programmers with some previous Delphi experience. The Object Pascal language of Delphi keeps evolving, and knowing it well is of the utmost importance to every programmer, even the experienced ones. Not all the concepts that you can find in many Object Pascal tutorials are discussed here, but the idea is to have a solid walkthrough of even the fundamental language concepts, with the focus on newer constructs and those that are important to mobile development with Delphi.

# Tokens

Tokens are the smallest meaningful pieces of text that a compiler understands. Tokenization is the very first thing that the compiler does when starting to process a source code file. There are different types of tokens, including identifiers, numbers, strings, constants, and special symbols. An Object Pascal program is made up of tokens and separators. A separator is either a blank space or a comment. There must be at least one separator between tokens.

In Object Pascal source code, you can use any Unicode characters for identifiers, but it makes a lot of sense to stick to just ASCII characters and consistently use just the English language in your code. Different Object Pascal language elements are in English, and it is easier to work with other programmers who might use other languages as their mother tongue.

The Delphi Code Editor displays different fragments of Delphi source code using different colors. Some words are displayed in bold and some others in italics. The color scheme of the Code Editor can be customized in the IDE Options, but here we will stick to the defaults.

The Object Pascal language defines a set of *reserved words* that the compiler knows about, and they cannot be used as identifiers in our code. Keywords are displayed in bold, so they are easy to spot. Keywords have a special meaning to the compiler. For example, if you try to save your program as `program`, you would get an error message that `program` is a reserved word and cannot be used as an identifier. If, for some reason, you really want to use a keyword as an identifier in your code, you can escape it by prepending the identifier with the & character.

Identifiers are used for constants, types, variables, procedures, functions, units, programs, and fields in records. An identifier must begin with a letter or an underscore character and cannot contain spaces. Letters, digits, and underscore characters are allowed after the first character. Identifiers and reserved words are not case sensitive. Sometimes, you may want to qualify an identifier with its unit name to avoid ambiguity.

# Constants

A constant is an identifier that marks a value that cannot change. The normal decimal notation is used for numbers that are integer or real constants. A hexadecimal integer constant uses a dollar sign as a prefix. It is also possible to use the engineering notation, where an exponent follows the E or e character.

A character string is a sequence of zero or more characters written in one line in the program and enclosed within apostrophes. A character string with nothing between the apostrophes is called a `null` string. Two sequential apostrophes in a character string denote a single apostrophe character.

For example, a string constant would print out as just `Paweł's computer`, as shown in the following program:

```
const
    s = 'Paweł''s computer';
```

Object Pascal allows the use of *constant expressions*. The compiler evaluates them at compile time without actually executing the program.

Object Pascal makes it possible to embed control characters in character strings. The # character followed by an unsigned integer in the range of 0 to 255 means a character of the corresponding ASCII value. A useful example of this capability is embedding a newline character in a string constant, so it is displayed in multiple lines. For example, check out the following code snippet:

```
const EL = #13;

procedure TForm1.ButtonMultilineClick(Sender: TObject);
begin
    ShowMessage('Welcome!' + EL + 'Good morning!');
end;
```

Embedding the new ASCII 13 *newline* control character displays the message in two lines. For readability, the actual newline character is defined as a constant.

# Types

Writing applications in Object Pascal starts from defining custom types. Only the simplest programs can get away with just using built-in types. Once you have defined your types, you start writing code and implement algorithms that operate on your types or data structures. The more carefully your types are designed, the more clean and readable your code will be.

Object Pascal comes with many different built-in types that you can use to define your own custom types. With experience, it will become more obvious how to model your problem domain. If you write an app to manage grades in a school, you would probably want to model the abstraction of a school grade. Should it be a constant, an enumerated type, a record, or a class?

Every country and education level has different grading schemes. As an example, let's consider the grading system that was used in my primary school in Poland. There were only four grades: very good (5), good (4), sufficient (3), and insufficient (2). At first, we could be tempted to use numbers as grades in our code. Refer to the following code snippet:

```
var
  grade: integer;
```

That is not an optimal design. What if our application assigns a value by mistake to a `grade` variable that is negative or too big?

In this particular case, it would be better to define a school grade as an enumerated type. This will make our code less error-prone and much more readable. There are two different ways of defining an enumerated type. Traditionally, we would define the `TSchoolGrade` enumeration as follows:

```
type
  TSchoolGrade = (sgVeryGood, sgGood, sgSufficient, sgInsufficient);
```

Somewhere in our code, we have a variable of the `TSchoolGrade` type, which can only hold one of the four possible grades defined by this type. Now our code is better. The `sg` prefix helps us remember that the `sgGood` identifier, for example, is, in fact, one of the possible school grade values. The other possibility is to use the enumerated values in the fully qualified form. With the `SCOPEDENUMS ON/OFF` compiler directive, we can enforce using a fully qualified form of an enumeration, as shown in the following code snippet:

```
{$SCOPEDENUMS ON}
type
  TSchoolGrade = (VeryGood, Good, Sufficient, Insufficient);
```

```
procedure DoWork;
var sg: TSchoolGrade;
begin
  sg := VeryGood; // error, needs scope
  sg := TSchoolGrade.VeryGood; // correct syntax
  // ...
```

Now, we do not really need the sg prefix anymore. It is up to your personal taste as to which form of defining enumerated types to use. The first one is more compact. The second one may be more readable.

# Sets and arrays

After defining a type, we will use it in our code, either as a standalone variable or as a collection. The most basic collection type is a set. It is very powerful and not available in other programming languages. We could, for example, define a set of *qualifying* school grades. The elements of a set are enclosed in square brackets. Refer to the following code:

```
type
  TSchoolGrade = (sgVeryGood, sgGood, sgSufficient, sgInsufficient);
  TSchoolGrades = set of TSchoolGrade;

const
  QUALIFYING_GRADES: TSchoolGrades = [sgVeryGood, sgGood, sgSufficient];

function IsQualifyingGrade(sg: TSchoolGrade): boolean;
begin
  Result := sg in QUALIFYING_GRADES;
end;
```

Using the in operator, we can check if a given value belongs to a set. It is also possible to use other operators to combine sets, calculate their intersections, and, in general, implement other set theory operations.

Another built-in type for dealing with collections of values is an array. Arrays can have either a fixed or a varying size. If it is fixed, then we need to define upfront how many elements an array can hold. It is also possible to use *dynamic arrays*. In this case, we can change the size of an array in code using the SetLength procedure and check its current size with the Length function. Once we are done with using a dynamic array, it is a good idea to pass it to the Finalize procedure, so the memory it occupies can be properly freed.

One interesting usage scenario for fixed arrays is defining a record constant array. Such an array needs to have a fixed size because it is embedded in the program during the compile time. This way, you can avoid writing code for initializing an array and adding elements to it.

Let's consider chess. Chess pieces do not change, and sometimes, it makes sense to assign a relative value to them, so a simple chess program can make decisions if it makes sense to exchange pieces. Why not to hardcode this information?

```
type
  TChessPiece = record
    Name: string;
    Value: Double;
  end;

const
  CHESS_PIECES_COUNT = 6;

  CHESS_PIECES: array[0..CHESS_PIECES_COUNT-1] of TChessPiece =
    (
      (Name : 'Pawn'; Value : 1),
      (Name : 'Knight'; Value : 3),
      (Name : 'Bishop'; Value : 3),
      (Name : 'Rook'; Value : 5),
      (Name : 'Queen'; Value : 9),
      (Name : 'King'; Value : 0)
    ) ;
```

Obviously, this is only an example, and chess piece valuations can be different depending on the phase in the game and expert opinions.

Instead of using an array of a fixed size, it is more common to use dynamic arrays. We can initialize them as if they were of a fixed size and perform set operations on them, as shown in the following code snippet:

```
var fruits: array of string;
begin
  fruits := ['Apple', 'Pear'];
  fruits := fruits + ['Banana', 'Orange'];
// ...
```

Dynamic arrays also allow using the `Insert` and `Delete` procedures for adding and removing a specified number of elements from a given position in an array.

# Helpers

Manipulating types in code can be even more readable when we define type `helpers`. Helpers extend a type `vertically`. You can define them on simple types, enumerations, records, or even on dynamic arrays. Delphi already comes with helpers defined for many built-in types, so they are easier to use in code. One good example is the very common task of converting an integer to a string, so it could be displayed as shown in the following code:

```
var s: string; i: integer;
begin
  i := 10;
  s := IntToStr(i); // "old" style
  s := i.ToString;  // more readable
  s := 10.ToString; // that would work too
```

Just right-click on the `ToString` method in this code and jump to the declaration. In the `System.SysUtils` unit, you will see helpers defined for many built-in types providing some additional useful methods, such as the minimum and maximum values for given built-in numerical types.

It is easy to define your own helper classes. Until Delphi 10, using helpers it was possible to access some private functionality of types that come out of the box with Delphi libraries, but since then this hack no longer works.

We already have the `TSchoolGrade` custom enumerated type. It would be useful to provide methods to convert a school grade value to a string or to a number. With helpers, it can be done in a really elegant way, as shown in the following code:

```
type
  TSchoolGrade = (sgVeryGood, sgGood, sgSufficient, sgInsufficient);
  TSchoolGrades = set of TSchoolGrade;

const
  QUALIFYING_GRADES: TSchoolGrades = [sgVeryGood, sgGood, sgSufficient];

type
  TSchoolGradeHelper = record helper for TSchoolGrade
  public
    function ToString: string;
    function ToInteger: integer;
    function IsQualifying: boolean;
  end;

{ TSchoolGradeHelper }

function TSchoolGradeHelper.IsQualifying: boolean;
```

```
begin
  Result := self in QUALIFYING_GRADES;
end;

function TSchoolGradeHelper.ToInteger: integer;
begin
  case self of
    sgVeryGood: Result := 5;
    sgGood: Result := 4;
    sgSufficient: Result := 3;
    sgInsufficient: Result := 2;
  end;
end;

function TSchoolGradeHelper.ToString: string;
begin
  case self of
    sgVeryGood: Result := 'Very Good';
    sgGood: Result := 'Good';
    sgSufficient: Result := 'Sufficient';
    sgInsufficient: Result := 'Insufficient';
  end;
end;
```

We use the `self` pseudo-variable in the implementation of a helper method to refer to the current value of the type we operate on.

Also, the function to check whether a given grade qualifies has been refactored as a helper method. It is more readable and improves the code structure.

# Generics

One of the most powerful concepts in the Object Pascal language is a *generic type*. This way, we can write our code in a more generic way, so the same algorithm can operate not on just one data type, but many. Generics are *things* that can be parameterized by type. The code is not fully specified, providing the implementation details to the code that uses generics. There could be generic types where the whole type definition is parameterized by an unknown type, or we can just define generic methods that operate on a type that is not fully specified.

As an example, let's consider a `fillable` class. Many languages have the concept of `nullable` values, but we will be different and use "fillable". It seems more natural. One useful example of using nullables or fillables is mapping between the data stored in a relational database and the entities in our code. A field in a database record may contain a value, such as a string or an integer, or it might be `null`. In order to properly represent the data coming from a database in our code, we need an extra logical flag that will say whether a value of the given type contains a valid value or `null`. If we represented this data using an object, we would have the possibility to have a `nil` reference, but it is more efficient to work with plain, simple built-in types the lifetime of which does not need to be directly managed. Without generics, we would need to implement a `fillable` class for every field type duplicating the same logic for clearing the flag, returning information if the value is *filled* or adding two *fillables* together:

```
type
  TFillable<T> = record
    Value: T;
    IsFilled: boolean;
  end;

  TFillableString = TFillable<string>;
  TFillableInteger = TFillable<integer>;
  // ...
```

If our implementation cannot deal with arbitrary types, we can specify a constraint on a type parameter using a colon. We can, for example, say that a generic type TFmxProcessor can be parameterized by any type, but it needs to be a class derived from TFMXObject, and it needs to have a public constructor:

```
type
  TFmxProcessor<T: TFMXObject, constructor> = class
    // ...
  end;

  TRecordReporter = class
    procedure DoReport<T: record>(x: T);
  end;
```

Another example where generics are useful is a custom sorting algorithm. There are many possible implementations, such as *bubble sort* or *quick sort*. It does not matter if we are sorting characters, integers, or real numbers. The algorithm's logic is the same. With generics, you do not need to implement the sorting algorithm for all the possible types it can operate on. You just need to have a way to compare two values, so they can be ordered properly.

Delphi comes with the System.Generics.Collections unit, which defines many useful generic collection types, such as enumerations, lists, and dictionaries that we can use in our code.

Consider the following TPerson class:

```
unit uPerson;

interface

type
  TPerson = class
    FirstName, LastName: string;
    constructor Create(AFirstName, ALastName: string);
    function Fullname: string;
  end;

implementation

{ TPerson }

constructor TPerson.Create(AFirstName, ALastName: string);
begin
  FirstName := AFirstName;
  LastName := ALastName;
end;

function TPerson.Fullname: string;
begin
  Result := FirstName + ' ' + LastName;
end;

end.
```

Before the introduction of generics, you could manage a list of objects with the TList class. Let's check out the differences between managing lists with and without generics.

Here is some code that iterates through an object list of the `TPerson` instance and logs their full names using `TList`, as shown in the following code snippet:

```
procedure DoPersonsTList;
var
  persons: TList; p: TPerson; i: integer;
begin
  persons := TList.Create;
  try
    // not safe, can add any pointer
    persons.Add(TPerson.Create('Kirk', 'Hammett'));
    persons.Add(TPerson.Create('James', 'Hetfield'));
    persons.Add(TPerson.Create('Lars', 'Ulrich'));
    persons.Add(TPerson.Create('Robert', 'Trujillo'));

    for i := 0 to persons.Count-1 do
    begin
      p := persons.Items[i];
      Log(p.Fullname);
    end;
  finally
    persons.Free;
  end;
end;
```

`TList` defined in the `System.Classes` unit can be used to manage a list of pointers of an arbitrary type. In order to access the `Fullname` method of the `TPerson` class, we need to perform a typecast by assigning a pointer reference to a variable of a proper type. If the object is not `TPerson` or its descendant, we will get an error at runtime, as shown in the following code snippet:

```
procedure DoPersonsGenerics;
var
  persons: TObjectList<TPerson>; p: TPerson;
begin
  persons := TObjectList<TPerson>.Create;
  try
    // safe, can only add TPerson or descendant
    persons.Add(TPerson.Create('Kirk', 'Hammett'));
    persons.Add(TPerson.Create('James', 'Hetfield'));
    persons.Add(TPerson.Create('Lars', 'Ulrich'));
    persons.Add(TPerson.Create('Robert', 'Trujillo'));

    for p in persons  do
      Log(p.Fullname); // no typecast needed

  finally
```

```
      persons.Free;
    end;
  end;
```

Using a generic list is much cleaner. The compiler, at compile time, knows that it deals with a list of `TPerson` objects and will not compile code that tries to add incompatible references. We can use the more readable `for..in..do` loop, and there is no need for a typecast. Using generics, in general, improves the quality of your code.

# Anonymous code

Anonymous code is all about treating code as data. You can assign an implementation of a function or procedure to a variable; you pass functions as parameters to other functions and receive them as results. This is a very powerful feature of the Object Pascal language. With anonymous code, the source code of your app can be more compact and maintainable.

A declaration of an anonymous method type has the following syntax:

```
type
  TStringProc = reference to procedure (s: string);
```

We are saying that `TStringProc` is a procedure that takes a string parameter. Now, we can define variables of this string type, assign implementation to them, pass them to functions, or, simply, just call them. Refer to the following code snippet:

```
procedure CallMe(const proc: TStringProc; msg: string);
begin
  proc(msg);
end;

procedure DoStringProc;
var
  proc: TStringProc;
begin

  proc := procedure(x: string)
  begin
    Log('Declared proc got: ' + x);
  end;

  CallMe(proc, 'Hello');

  CallMe(
      procedure(v: string)
      begin
```

```
          Log('Inline code got: ' + v);
        end,
        'World');
  end;
```

Here, we have a `CallMe` procedure that takes as a parameter a chunk of code compatible with `TStringProc` and a string variable. There is also a `proc` local variable of the `TStringProc` type. In the first lines of the `DoStringProc` routine, we assign implementation to the `proc` variable. Note that there is no identifier after the `procedure` keyword. The parameter declaration follows immediately. This is why it is called *anonymous* code. It does not need a name because it is never referenced by name. In the first call to `CallMe`, we pass the `proc` variable as a parameter. The second call to `CallMe` is even more compact; we define the implementation of an anonymous procedure, *in-place*.

A more useful example of using anonymous code could be the sorting of a generic list. We can define the `TPersonList` class and implement the `SortByFullName` method:

```
unit uPersonList;

interface

uses
  System.Generics.Collections, // TObjectList<T>
  uPerson;   // TPerson

type
  TPersonList = class(TObjectList<TPerson>)
    procedure SortByFullName;
  end;

implementation

uses
  System.Generics.Defaults, // IComparer, TComparison
  System.SysUtils; // CompareStr


{ TPersonList }

procedure TPersonList.SortByFullName;
var
  Comparer : IComparer<TPerson>;
  Comparison : TComparison<TPerson>;
begin
  Comparison := function(const p1, p2: TPerson): integer
  begin
    Result := CompareStr(p1.FullName, p2.FullName);
```

```
    end;
    Comparer := TComparer<TPerson>.Construct(Comparison);
    inherited Sort(Comparer);
  end;

  end.
```

The generic object list class defines the Sort method, which can be overridden in the descendent classes. As its parameter, it expects a generic comparer class, which is only responsible for comparing any two elements of the underlying class; it returns an integer value that needs to be negative if the first element is less than the second, "zero" if they are the same, or a positive value if the first element is greater than the second one. Here, we construct the TComparer class, which is responsible for comparting to TPerson objects. Luckily in the System.SysUtils unit, there is a very handy CompareStr function that we can use directly. Our comparer is referenced by its implementing interface, and that's why we do not need to free it afterwards. It will be freed automatically by the interface reference counting mechanism.

# Operator overloading

Your code can be more readable with operator overloading. You cannot overload the meaning of arbitrary operators in Object Pascal, only the built-in operators. You can also implement implicit conversion operators that make it possible to assign different types to a given type and define what would happen during the assignment. You can also define comparison operators to define the results of the built-in operators, =, <, and >.

Operator overloading leads to more compact, more readable code. For example, Delphi comes with a System.Math.Vectors unit with different useful types such as TVector3D with useful overloaded operations, as shown in the following code snippet:

```
uses
  System.Math.Vectors;

procedure DoSomeVectorMath;
var
  A, B, C: TVector3D;
begin
  A := TVector3D.Create(1,2,4);
  B := TVector3D.Create(2,3,1);
  C := A + B;
  // ...
```

Another good example is the `TAlphaColorF` record type defined in `System.UITypes`, which defines different operations on colors using real numbers.

Operator overloading cannot be used with class types, only with records.

# Custom attributes

Custom attributes let you add custom information to a class itself or to its individual members. Many libraries that come with Delphi use custom attributes. They are useful when we want to mark certain types or type members that need to be treated in a special way. For example, in the `DUnitX` unit testing framework that comes with Delphi, we use the `Test` custom attributes to mark a method as `testable` and optionally provide parameters to be used by the unit test runner. Another example is the REST API resources, which are published from EMS modules. With custom attributes, we can tell the framework what should be the name of the REST resource to access a certain method.

A custom attribute is just a regular class that inherits from the `TCustomAttribute` type defined in a built-in system unit.

Let's consider the definition of a custom `documentation` attribute. A programmer could use such an attribute to associate a given class member in code with a custom URL, with more information about it. Take a look at the following code snippet:

```
unit uDocAttribute;

interface

type
  DocAttribute = class(TCustomAttribute)
  private
    FURL: string;
  public
    constructor Create(URL: string);
    property URL: string read FURL write FURL;
  end;

implementation

{ DocAttribute }

constructor DocAttribute.Create(URL: string);
begin
  FURL := URL;
end;
```

To apply an attribute, it needs to be placed just before the element it applies in square brackets. Optionally, it can take parameters that just come as a list in brackets. This will implicitly call the custom attribute constructor:

```
uses uDocAttribute;

type
  [Doc('http://mydocs/MySuperClass')] // skipping "...Attribute"
  TMySuperClass = class
  public
    [DocAttribute('http://mydocs/MySuperClass/DoSomething')]
    procedure DoSomething;
  end;
```

By convention, custom attribute class names end with `Attribute`. Delphi compiler allows us to skip the optional `Attribute` part of the attribute class name.

That's nice, but how do I know in my code that there are attributes applied to classes that my code operates on? This and many other capabilities are provided by the Runtime Type Information (RTTI) system.

# Runtime Type Information

RTTI provides reflection capabilities to the Object Pascal language. With reflection, different types of *meta-programming* scenarios are possible. You can, for example, write code that will be able to operate on objects that it does not know about. RTTI provides abstractions for all the different types available in the Object Pascal language in the `System.Rtti` unit that comes with Delphi. All classes and built-in simple types can be treated in a unified way using the `TValue` record. If you want to programmatically inspect a type and to know whether it is a class and what members it contains, you can use `TRttiContext`, which has a `GetType` method that returns an instance of the `TRttiType` reference, which has methods that let you *inspect* a given type and iterate through all its members if it is a class.

In our `documentation` attribute example, we can use RTTI to retrieve documentation URLs for the type itself and for its methods. Refer to the following code snippet:

```
uses RTTI, uDocAttribute, uMySuperClass;

procedure TFormDemo.Button1Click(Sender: TObject);
var
  ctx: TRttiContext;
  t: TRttiType;
  m: TRttiMethod;
  a: TCustomAttribute;
```

```
begin
  ClearLog;

  ctx := TRttiContext.Create;
  try
    t := ctx.GetType(TMySuperClass);

    for a in t.GetAttributes do
      if a is DocAttribute then
        Log(Format('Type = %s; Attribute = %s, URL = %s',
          [TMySuperClass.ClassName, a.ClassName,
DocAttribute(a).URL]));

    for m in t.GetMethods do
      for a in m.GetAttributes do
        if a is DocAttribute then
          Log(Format('Type = %s; Method = %s; Attribute = %s, URL = %s',
            [TMySuperClass.ClassName, m.Name, a.ClassName,
DocAttribute(a).URL]));

  finally
    ctx.Free;
  end;
end;
```

The RTTI context object owns all the intermediate objects that represent different class members such as TRttiMethod or TRttiAttribute.

# Summary

In this chapter, we reviewed different basic and more advanced elements of the Object Pascal language used in Delphi. There are many tutorials and language primers that cover each and every element of the language in detail.

In the first part, we reviewed the structure of a typical Delphi application from the perspective of the Memory Game app that we are going to build in the next chapters. The second part of the chapter covered selected elements of the Object Pascal language, such as type helpers, generics, anonymous code, and more, which are needed to better understand the code that comes with the Delphi installation and which you need to use very frequently, such as generic lists of objects.

In the next chapter, we are going to build on our language knowledge and review the functionality of some key classes for doing some common things that every programmer must know how to do, such as working with files, streams, and much more.

# 3
# Packing Up Your Toolbox

There are many simple every day programming skills that every Delphi developer needs to have. Pack your every day programmer toolbox with everything you will need from simple things such as file I/O to more complex things such as working with JSON and the Parallel Programming Library.

This chapter will cover the following points:

- Parallel Programming Library
- File I/O
- JSON
- XML

The objective of this chapter is to become fluent in using a Delphi programmer with every day useful techniques, such as working with files, streams, JSON, and XML. We will also look into making your apps faster and more responsive with the Parallel Programming Library (PPL).

## Parallel Programming Library

Writing multithreaded code is considered to be one of the most difficult things in programming. Debugging multithreaded apps is even more difficult. When an operating system starts an app, it creates an operating process for it. In each process, there could be one or more threads running. Processors that power mobile devices typically have multiple cores. This means that there could be multiple threads executing in parallel on each core. A typical app executes in one thread, which runs on just one processor core. All other cores do nothing.

Since the very early versions of Delphi, there is a `TThread` class that represents the concept of the operating system thread. PPL provides the concept of `TTask`, which is more abstract than a thread and makes it easier to write multithreaded code. The very first thing to do in order to use PPL is to add a `System.Threading` unit to the `uses` clause of your program. Instead of creating threads directly, the library maintains on behalf of the app a self-tuning pool of threads that are used to execute tasks. Tasks can be easily synchronized. There are methods to wait for any or all tasks to complete.

# Parallel loops

The most easy concept to grasp in the PPL is a *parallel for loop*. This is useful when calculations for different values of a control variable are independent and it is not important in which order they are executed. A good example of this use case comes from the ray tracing algorithm used in computer graphics. To generate an image, we need to calculate the color of each pixel that makes up the resulting image. This is done by calculating the path of each ray of light in space. Calculating the color of a given pixel is completely independent from other pixels and can be performed simultaneously to generate the resulting bitmap faster.

Instead of implementing a ray tracer here, let's create a really simple demo that would allow us to observe how much faster a parallel loop would execute as compared to a traditional loop. Instead of calculating pixel colors in each iteration of the loop, we will just call, `Sleep` procedure that will make the current thread sleep for a given amount of milliseconds and then it will continue to run. Create a new multi-device project in Delphi. Drop two buttons on the form and write the following code that will display in the caption of each button, how much time it took to execute the loop.

For calculating the elapsed time, we are using the `TStopwatch` record type from `System.Diagnostics` unit; refer to the following code snippet:

```
uses
  System.Threading, // parallel programming library
  System.Diagnostics; // TStopwatch

procedure TForm1.DoTimeConsumingOperation(milis: integer);
begin
  Sleep(milis);
end;

procedure TForm1.btnForLoopRegularClick(Sender: TObject);
var sw: TStopwatch; i: Integer;
begin
  sw := TStopwatch.StartNew;
```

```
  for i := 0 to 99 do
    DoTimeConsumingOperation(10);
  sw.Stop;
  (Sender as TButton).Text := sw.ElapsedMilliseconds.ToString + 'ms';
end;

procedure TForm1.btnForLoopParallelClick(Sender: TObject);
var sw: TStopwatch; i: Integer;
begin
  sw := TStopwatch.StartNew;
  TParallel.For(0, 99, procedure(i: integer)
  begin
    DoTimeConsumingOperation(10);
  end);
  sw.Stop;
  (Sender as TButton).Text := sw.ElapsedMilliseconds.ToString + 'ms';
end;
```

The TParallel.For method has a lot of overloaded versions. In this example, it takes the starting index, ending index, and an anonymous procedure that takes an integer parameter as an index.

Depending on the number of cores in your device, you will see that the regular loop executes in more then a second and the parallel loop executes roughly as much faster as the number of cores available to your app.

# Tasks

One of the key use cases for multithreading code is to keep the user interface responsive while performing some long running operation, such as downloading data from the internet or performing calculations. The main thread of the application, the one when the user interface runs, should not be busy with those time consuming operations. They should be executed in the background thread to keep the user interface responsive.

Add two more buttons to the form and enter the following code in their OnClick events:

```
procedure TForm1.btnNonResponsiveClick(Sender: TObject);
begin
  DoTimeConsumingOperation(3000);
  (Sender as TButton).Text := 'Done';
end;

procedure TForm1.btnResponsive1Click(Sender: TObject);
var aTask: ITask;
begin
```

```
   aTask := TTask.Create(procedure
   begin
     DoTimeConsumingOperation(3000);
   end);
   aTask.Start;
   (Sender as TButton).Text := 'Done';
 end;
```

When you click the first button, the form freezes for 3 seconds. When you click on the second button, the form stay responsive because a *time consuming operation* is executed in a different thread and the main app thread can process user events normally. In fact, the *Done* message is displayed almost immediately because the main thread continues to execute just after it started the task. If you would like to display the *Done* text on the button after the task is complete, you would need to do it from inside of the background thread. You can only manipulate the user interface from the main app thread; that is why the call to the change button's Text property needs to be synchronized as shown in the following code snippet:

```
procedure TForm1.btnResponsive2Click(Sender: TObject);
var aTask: ITask;
begin
  aTask := TTask.Create(procedure
  begin
    DoTimeConsumingOperation(3000);
    TThread.Synchronize(nil,
      procedure
      begin
        (Sender as TButton).Text := 'Done';
      end);
  end);
  aTask.Start;
end;
```

Now the label changes not immediately, but after 3 seconds.

A task is a bit like an anonymous procedure. You can declare it, but it only starts to execute when it is told to. You need to call Start and only then the task starts.

# Futures

PPL also provides the notion of a future. It is a specialization of a task. It is a task that returns a value. In the case of a task, you call its `Start` method to execute. In the case of a future, you can just declare it and assign it to a variable. When you try to retrieve the value of this variable, then the future is executed in a background thread and the value is returned.

There are some interesting use cases when futures are useful. For example, you may want to calculate something based on the values of two or more parameters that need to be calculated first. Instead of calculating these parameters sequentially, we could perform these calculations simultaneously.

For example, a management board of some large organization would like to know what is the ratio of actual versus planned expenses for the last year. Calculating both values could be a lengthy process. At the end you get just two currency values that you want to divide.

Let's first have a look at how we could implement this functionality without futures, just by using standard code:

```
function GetPlannedExpenses: currency;
begin
  Sleep(1000);
  Result := 100;
end;

function GetActualExpenses: currency;
begin
  Sleep(2000);
  Result := 110;
end;

procedure TForm1.btnFuture1Click(Sender: TObject);
var
  planned, actual: currency;
  ratio: double;
  sw: TStopwatch;
begin
  sw := TStopwatch.StartNew;

  planned := GetPlannedExpenses;
  actual := GetActualExpenses;
  ratio := actual / planned;

  sw.Stop;
  (Sender as TButton).Text := ratio.ToString
```

```
              + ' (' +  sw.ElapsedMilliseconds.ToString + 'ms)';
    end;
```

The ratio has to be calculated and we can see that it took about 3 seconds. That is what has been expected. The first calculation took 1 second and the second took 2 seconds.

The same functionality, but this time implemented with futures, looks like this:

```
procedure TForm1.btnFuture2Click(Sender: TObject);
var
  planned: IFuture<currency>;
  actual: IFuture<currency>;
  ratio: double;
  sw: TStopwatch;
begin
  sw := TStopwatch.StartNew;

  planned := TTask.Future<currency>(function: currency
  begin
    Result := GetPlannedExpenses;
  end);

  actual := TTask.Future<currency>(function: currency
  begin
    Result := GetActualExpenses;
  end);

  ratio := actual.Value / planned.Value;

  sw.Stop;
  (Sender as TButton).Text := ratio.ToString
    + ' (' +  sw.ElapsedMilliseconds.ToString + 'ms)';
end;
```

This code executes in about 2 seconds. This is how much the longer of the two calculations takes.

Future is a generic class method that belong to TTask type. When you access the Value of a future, then the actual calculation takes place and it is happening in the background thread. The calculation of actual and planned values is done in parallel and not consecutively.

# Working with files

Almost every app needs to persist data. You have just downloaded an app, worked with it for a while, and the next time you open it, you would like to see that it remembers what you have done so far. An app can store its data in the cloud, in an embedded database or in a file. This last option is the most easy to use. A local file can store information in different formats. It could be a binary file, which is just an array of bytes, that is left to an app to make sense of, or it could be a text file. Your app can store information in plain text or it can use some of the file formats, such as JSON or XML, to make it easier to process text information.

Imagine that you would like to write a small mobile app to keep track of your favorite locations on the internet. To keep it simple, it could be just a list of favorite items made of two strings: an URL and a caption. Let's go for it! Create a new multi-device application in Delphi. Select a blank application template. Save the main form as uFormFavMain and the whole project as FavoritesDemo. Add a new unit to the project and save it as uFavorite. Let's define there a simple TFavorite class for individual favorite items. It will contain only two public string fields, URL and Caption. For convenience, let's add there a constructor that will take initial values for both fields. If we define a custom constructor that takes parameters, we will not be able to call a normal parameterless constructor, so we also need to explicitly define one. We could have defined both string fields as properties, but in fact there is no need for properties here.

There is also the TFavorites class definition, which is a generic object list of TFavorite objects. It is going to be easier to use it in code instead of the full generic notation with < and > characters, as shown in the following code snippet:

```
unit uFavorite;

interface

uses
  System.Generics.Collections;

type
  TFavorite = class
    URL: string;
    Caption: string;
    constructor Create; overload;
    constructor Create(AURL, ACaption: string); overload;
  end;

  TFavorites = class(TObjectList<TFavorite>);
```

```
implementation

{ TFavorite }

constructor TFavorite.Create;
begin
end;

constructor TFavorite.Create(AURL, ACaption: string);
begin
  URL := AURL;
  Caption := ACaption;
end;

end.
```

We will be first storing favorites in a text file using a convention that each two consecutive strings in the file represent one favorite entry: the first for the URL and the second for the Caption. Later in the chapter, we will use specialized file formats such as JSON and XML.

The main form of our demo app will contain a private field, accessible through a public property, with a list of sample favorite items, which we are going to access from other forms in the application, so we do not duplicate code. That's a proper way of encapsulation. External code will not be able to destroy this instance, because the reference is read-only.

Create an OnCreate event for the main form where we are going to construct a Favorites list and add some sample favorite entries. In the OnDestroy event, we destroy the list. One could argue that Delphi mobile compilers have **Automatic Reference Counting (ARC)**, but it is a good practice to write code, as if there were no ARC in place.

Another good practice is to avoid long identifiers, because your code gets less readable. That is why instead of Favorite in many places of the demo app, we just use Fav as a handy abbreviation, as shown in the following code snippet:

```
uses
  // ...
  uFavorite;

type
  TFormFavMain = class(TForm)
    // ...
    procedure FormCreate(Sender: TObject);
    procedure FormDestroy(Sender: TObject);
  private
    FFavs: TFavorites;
    procedure AddSampleItems;
```

```delphi
public
  property Favs: TFavorites read FFavs;
end;

var
  FormFavMain: TFormFavMain;

implementation

{$R *.fmx}

procedure TFormFavMain.AddSampleItems;
begin
  FFavs.Add(TFavorite.Create(
    'www.embarcadero.com/products/delphi',
    'Delphi Home Page')
  );
  FFavs.Add(TFavorite.Create(
    'docwiki.embarcadero.com/RADStudio/en',
    'RAD Studio online documentation')
  );
end;

procedure TFormFavMain.FormCreate(Sender: TObject);
begin
  FFavs := TFavorites.Create;
  AddSampleItems;
end;

procedure TFormFavMain.FormDestroy(Sender: TObject);
begin
  FFavs.Free;
end;
```

There are many different ways of creating files in code. For example, one could use Delphi classic built-in functions such as AssignFile, Rewrite, Reset, and CloseFile. Another option is to use functionality from specialized classes such as TMemo or TIniFile that provide methods such as SaveToFile and LoadFromFile that could be used directly. There is also the TFile class in System.IOUtils that can be used to write and read different types of data such as strings or just raw arrays of bytes.

Probably the most easy way to work with files is to use the TStreamWriter and TStreamReader classes from the System.Classes unit. They provide an elegant programming model for doing file operations.

The main form of our demo app will also work as a menu to display other forms where we will be trying different approaches of working with text files. Let's add a new multi-device form to our project. Save it in the uFormFavTextFiles unit and rename the form to FormFavTextFiles. That is another useful convention to follow. The name of the unit that stores a form starts with u followed by the name of the form.

First we are going to add some navigation code for moving from the main form to the additional form and back. First add the new form to the uses clause in the *implementation* part of the main form. Then add a button to the form with a call to show the form, as shown in the following code snippet:

```
uses
  uFormFavTextFiles;

procedure TFormFavMain.btnTextFilesClick(Sender: TObject);
begin
  FormFavTextFiles.Show;
end;
```

In the other form, we add exactly the same logic to display back the main form.

Now we can focus on implementing the functionality to write favorites from the list in our main form into the text file and to read it back. Add two buttons to the form and align them to the top. In this way, they will always look good at different screen factors on mobile devices. Also add a TMemo component, rename it MemoLog, and align it to Client. Optionally, change all four Margins of the memo from 0 to for example 4, so that there is a little margin around the memo that looks better on a mobile screen. The first button will be used to write favorites to a text file and the second to read this information back and display in the memo, so we know that things work OK.

First we are going to define a separate function, GetFilename, that will centralize accessing the name of the file, so both functions for writing and reading are accessing the same file.

On mobile operating systems, unlike traditional desktop ones, an app can only create and read files from its Documents folder. In the System.IOUtils unit that ships with Delphi, there is the TPath class that offers a number of class methods to work with paths. The location of the Documents folder can be obtained with the TPath.GetDocumentsPath call. In order to construct the full path to our file, we also need to use a delimiter before the actual name of the file. A delimiter can be different on different targets; that is why it is a good practice not to hardcode it. If our text file is called favs.txt then the actual code to get the full filename of the favorites text file could look like this:

```
uses
    System.IOUtils;

function TFormFavTextFiles.GetFilename: string;
begin
    Result := TPath.Combine(TPath.GetDocumentsPath, 'favs.txt');
end;
```

Double-click on the first button on the form and enter there the following code to put the favorites information into the plain text file:

```
procedure TFormFavTextFiles.btnWriteClick(Sender: TObject);
var sw: TStreamWriter; fav: TFavorite; favs: TFavorites;
begin
    favs := FormFavMain.Favs;
    sw := TStreamWriter.Create(GetFilename, False, TEncoding.UTF8);
    try
        for fav in favs do
        begin
            sw.WriteLine(fav.URL);
            sw.WriteLine(fav.Caption);
        end;
    finally
        sw.Free;
    end;
end;
```

We are using the Favorites list from the main form. To simplify the code, in the first line we put this property reference into a local variable favs, which is easier to use in code. The rest of the implementation is quite trivial. We are constructing an instance of the TStreamWriter class and in the for loop writing URL and Caption properties of each TFavorite item in the list.

Now let's read this information back. In the `OnClick` event of the second button, insert the following code:

```
procedure TFormFavTextFiles.btnReadClick(Sender: TObject);
var sr: TStreamReader;
begin
  sr := TStreamReader.Create(GetFilename, TEncoding.UTF8);
  try
    while not sr.EndOfStream do
      MemoLog.Lines.Add(sr.ReadLine);
  finally
    sr.Free;
  end;
end;
```

Now run the app. Navigate to the **Text Files** screen and click on the "write" button first and then on the "read" button. You should see the list of favorites in the memo, as shown in the following screenshot:

The problem with this approach is that there is no structure in the data. By convention, we know that every two lines of text contains one favorite entry. The first is the URL and the second is the description.

# JSON

A better format for storing favorite entries is JSON. This is currently the most popular data interchange format. Its strength is its simplicity. The JSON specification makes for an interesting read at `http://json.org`. With a very simple type system, JSON is able to represent complex data structures. One of the key design objectives of a JSON is to keep it simple. Most programming languages can process JSON and Object Pascal is not an exception.

There are two main ways to work with JSON in Delphi. One approach is to build an in-memory representation of JSON tree using objects from the `System.JSON` unit. The second approach is based on streaming and provides sequential access to JSON data. In reality, both ways have their advantages and disadvantages. Let's look at both.

JSON is a very popular format for sharing information. You have just locally downloaded a piece of JSON and now what?

Here is our favorites information expressed as JSON:

```json
{
  "Favorites": [
    {
      "URL": "www.embarcadero.com/products/delphi",
      "Caption": "Delphi Home Page"
    },
    {
      "URL": "docwiki.embarcadero.com/RADStudio/en",
      "Caption": "RAD Studio online documentation"
    }
  ]
}
```

Notice that unlike plain text the favorites data is more structured. Here we have an object with just one property called `Favorites` and its value is an array made up of two objects. Each object contained in the array has two string properties: `URL` and `Caption`. In a programmer's life, a typical objective might be to convert JSON data into programming language constructs that can be manipulated in code or to output JSON text from a program.

Add another form to the demo app and call it `FormFavJSON`. Add all the functionality to navigate to this form and back to the main form exactly like we did for the `FormFavTextFile` form.

# Writing JSON

First let's look at different ways of generating JSON. We will save this information to a file and later we will read this information back into a local favorites list.

Again we are going to start with implementing a `GetFilename` function, but this time to write and read from the `favs.json` file:

```
function TFormFavJSON.GetFilename: string;
begin
  Result := TPath.Combine(TPath.GetDocumentsPath, 'favs.json');
end;
```

We will also need a simple function to write a string with JSON text to a file. It is so simple with the `TStreamWriter` class that we saw earlier. Refer to the following code snippet:

```
procedure TFormFavJSON.WriteJsonTextToFile(txt: string);
var sw: TStreamWriter;
begin
  sw := TStreamWriter.Create(GetFilename, False, TEncoding.UTF8);
  try
    sw.WriteLine(txt);
  finally
    sw.Free;
  end;
end;
```

The first approach for generating JSON is based on building an in-memory graph of JSON data and then converting it to a string in one operation. For this we will define the `FavListToJsonTextWithDOM` method that will return JSON text generated from our global `TFavorites` list in the main form of the demo app:

```
uses System.JSON;

function TFormFavJSON.FavListToJsonTextWithDOM: string;
var
  fav: TFavorite; favs: TFavorites;
  objFavs, objF: TJSONObject; arrFavs: TJSONArray;

begin
  favs := FormFavMain.Favs;

  objFavs := TJSONObject.Create;
  try
    arrFavs := TJSONArray.Create;

    for fav in favs do
```

```
begin
  objF := TJSONObject.Create;
  objF.AddPair('URL', TJSONString.Create(fav.URL));
  objF.AddPair('Caption', TJSONString.Create(fav.Caption));
  arrFavs.Add(objF);
  end;
  objFavs.AddPair('Favorites', arrFavs);

  Result := objFavs.ToString;
finally
  objFavs.Free;
end;
end;
```

In this approach, we need to define local variables for all JSON objects to build a graph in memory and then output it with the `ToString` method of the root `objFavs` instance. Note that we only need to free the root object. All other objects are owned by the root object and if we try to free them in code, we would get an error.

Note that with this approach it is not very easy to visualize the exact JSON that this function will generate.

Add a button to the form, align it to the top, change its **Caption** property to `Write with JSON DOM`. Double-click on the button and enter the following code in its `OnClick` event and implement the actual functionality of writing JSON to the file:

```
procedure TFormFavJSON.btnWriteDOMClick(Sender: TObject);
var s: string;
begin
  s := FavListToJsonTextWithDOM;
  WriteJsonTextToFile(s);
end;
```

The second approach for generating JSON involves using the `TJsonTextWriter` class. Let's define the `FavListToJsonTextWithWriter` method in the form class that is returning a string like this:

```
uses System.JSON.Writers, System.JSON.Types;

function TFormFavJSON.FavListToJsonTextWithWriter: string;
var
  fav: TFavorite; favs: TFavorites;
  StringWriter: TStringWriter;
  Writer: TJsonTextWriter;
begin
  favs := FormFavMain.Favs;
```

```
    StringWriter := TStringWriter.Create();
    Writer := TJsonTextWriter.Create(StringWriter);
try
    Writer.Formatting := TJsonFormatting.Indented;

    Writer.WriteStartObject;
    Writer.WritePropertyName('Favorites');
    Writer.WriteStartArray;

    for fav in favs do
    begin
        Writer.WriteStartObject;
        Writer.WritePropertyName('URL');
        Writer.WriteValue(fav.URL);
        Writer.WritePropertyName('Caption');
        Writer.WriteValue(fav.Caption);
        Writer.WriteEndObject;
    end;

    Writer.WriteEndArray;
    Writer.WriteEndObject;

    Result := StringWriter.ToString;

finally
    Writer.Free;
    StringWriter.Free;
    end;
end;
```

The constructor of the `TJsonTextWriter` class expects as its argument an instance of `TTextWriter` that will be responsible for the actual process of outputting the resulting JSON text. Notice that the `TTextWriter` class is a class with virtual abstract methods that just define the interface to the text writing functionality so we need to use one of the text writer descendants such as `TStringWriter`. This is a very elegant approach and makes it easy to use other types of writers without changing the logic for JSON writing.

Before calling different `write*` methods, we set the `Formatting` property of the writer to `TJsonFormatting.Indented`, so the resulting JSON will be nicely formatted. Note that in the DOM approach, we just got JSON in one, not formatted string. The code to write JSON with a text writer is much more verbose and does not allocate any temporary objects. Now the code is much more readable. Just by glancing at it, we can figure out how the resulting JSON is going to look like.

The third approach for generating JSON is based on using *fluent builders*. The idea is to make the code even more verbose and more resembling the resulting JSON. Take a look at the following code snippet:

```
uses System.JSON.Builders;

function TFormFavJSON.FavListToJsonTextWithBuilder: string;
var
  StringWriter: TStringWriter;
  Writer: TJsonTextWriter;
  Builder: TJSONObjectBuilder;
begin
  StringWriter := TStringWriter.Create();
  Writer := TJsonTextWriter.Create(StringWriter);
  Builder := TJSONObjectBuilder.Create(Writer);
  try
    Writer.Formatting := TJsonFormatting.Indented;

    Builder
    .BeginObject
      .BeginArray('Favorites')
        .BeginObject
          .Add('URL', 'www.embarcadero.com/products/delphi')
          .Add('Caption', 'Delphi Home Page')
        .EndObject
        .BeginObject
          .Add('URL', 'docwiki.embarcadero.com/RADStudio/en')
          .Add('Caption', 'RAD Studio online documentation')
        .EndObject
      .EndArray
    .EndObject;

    Result := StringWriter.ToString;

  finally
    Builder.Free;
    Writer.Free;
    StringWriter.Free;
  end;
end;
```

As in the previous example, we still need `TStringWriter` and `TJsonTextWriter` instances, but on top of them we need to instantiate `TJsonObjectBuilder` that accepts `TJsonTextWriter` as an argument to its constructor.

Just from the structure of this source code, we can visualize what kind of JSON we are going to generate. The problem is that we cannot really use *fluent builders* for outputting data coming from an external data structure, such as our `TFavorites` list, because it is just one long chain of method calls on the builder class instance.

# Reading JSON

The JSON specification does not provide any way for expressing the schema or a metadata describing the structure of JSON information. Consequently, when we write code that processes JSON, we are assuming to find there certain data structures. There are two ways of reading JSON. One that is based on its in-memory representation and the second based on streaming.

The key to parsing JSON using DOM is the `ParseJSONValue` class method belonging to the `TJSONObject` type. This an overloaded method defined in `System.JSON` and it takes JSON text in form of a string, stream, or array of bytes, parses it and returns a `TJSONValue` reference which points to the root of a graph of JSON objects in memory. If JSON passed to this method is malformed then this method does not raise an exception, but just returns a `nil` reference. Take a look at the following code snippet:

```
uses
  System.JSON.Readers, System.JSON.Types;

procedure TFormFavJSON.btnReadDOMClick(Sender: TObject);
var
  favs: TFavorites; valRoot: TJSONValue; objRoot: TJSONObject;
  valFavs: TJSONValue; arrFavs: TJSONArray; i: integer;
begin
  favs := TFavorites.Create;
  try
    valRoot := TJSONObject.ParseJSONValue(ReadJsonTextFromFile);
    if valRoot <> nil then
    begin
      if valRoot is TJSONObject then
      begin
        objRoot := TJSONObject(valRoot);
        if objRoot.Count > 0 then
        begin
          valfavs := objRoot.Values['Favorites'];
          if valFavs <> nil then
          begin
            if valFavs is TJSONArray then
            begin
              arrFavs := TJSONArray(valFavs);
```

```
          for i := 0 to arrfavs.Count-1 do
          begin
            if arrFavs.Items[i] is TJSONObject then
              ProcessFavObj(favs, TJSONObject(arrFavs.Items[i]));
          end;
        end;
      end;
    end;
  end;
end;

  DisplayFavsCount(favs);
finally
  favs.Free;
end;
end;


procedure TFormFavJSON.ProcessFavObj(favs: TFavorites; favObj:
TJSONObject);
var fav: TFavorite; val: TJSONValue;
begin
  fav := TFavorite.Create;

  val := favObj.Values['URL'];
  if val <> nil then
    if val is TJSONString then
      fav.URL := TJSONString(val).Value;

  val := favObj.Values['Caption'];
  if val <> nil then
    if val is TJSONString then
      fav.Caption := TJSONString(val).Value;

  favs.Add(fav);
end;


procedure TFormFavJSON.DisplayFavsCount(favs: TFavorites);
begin
  if favs <> nil then
    ShowMessage('Favorites count: ' + favs.Count.ToString)
  else
    ShowMessage('Favorites reference is nil');
end;
```

Note that we have here a separate `ProcessFavObj` that is responsible for processing a single `TJSONObject` representing just one *favorite* item. There is also the `DisplayFavsCount` method which is called at the end of the processing to verify that we actually successfully parsed JSON. There should be two `TFavorite` items in the resulting list.

Processing JSON in this way is very tedious. Even for a simple JSON, like in our demo sample, the resulting code is quite complex and involves a lot of checking for `nil` and typecasting to expected types of JSON values. There is also an overhead of having to create a lot of in-memory objects that represent JSON.

A much better way is to use a streaming model and process JSON text sequentially with the `TJsonTextReader` class, as shown in the following code snippet:

```
procedure TFormFavJSON.btnReadReaderClick(Sender: TObject);
var jtr: TJsonTextReader; sr: TStringReader; favs: TFavorites;
begin
  favs := TFavorites.Create;
  try
    sr := TStringReader.Create(ReadJsonTextFromFile);
    try
      jtr := TJsonTextReader.Create(sr);
      try
        while jtr.Read do
        begin
          if jtr.TokenType = TJsonToken.StartObject then
            ProcessFavRead(favs, jtr);
        end;
      finally
        jtr.Free;
      end;
    finally
      sr.Free;
    end;

    DisplayFavsCount(favs);
  finally
    favs.Free;
  end;
end;

procedure TFormFavJSON.ProcessFavRead(favs: TFavorites; jtr:
TJsonTextReader);
var fav: TFavorite;
begin
  fav := TFavorite.Create;
```

```
while jtr.Read do
begin
  if jtr.TokenType = TJsonToken.PropertyName then
  begin
    if jtr.Value.ToString = 'URL' then
    begin
      jtr.Read;
      fav.URL := jtr.Value.AsString;
    end

    else if jtr.Value.ToString = 'Caption' then
    begin
      jtr.Read;
      fav.Caption := jtr.Value.AsString;
    end
  end

  else if jtr.TokenType = TJsonToken.EndObject
  begin
    favs.add(fav);
    exit;
  end;
 end;
end;
```

We no longer need to create temporary objects. We just move through the stream of JSON tokens. Notice that we do not need to encapsulate the structure of the whole JSON in this code. It could be part of a bigger structure. We just iterate through tokens and if we encounter the `BeginObject` token, we can start a separate processing in the specialized procedure that only cares about objects that represent one favorite.

Using JSON readers instead of DOM is faster and requires less memory and processing power.

# XML

Before JSON dominated the world, XML was the most popular format for data interchange. With the addition of many new specifications, XML became very complex, but it is a practical thing to understand how to process XML in case you need to.

XML processing in Delphi is based on building an in-memory representation of the XML file using XML parsers from different vendors. The key component for working with XML is TXMLDocument. XML parsing is considerably more difficult then JSON. TXMLDocument has a pluggable XML parser architecture and Delphi comes with a number of XML parser implementations from different vendors. There are different vendor implementations available depending on the target platform. Take a look at the following screenshot:

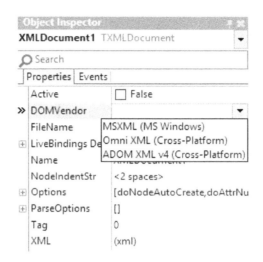

Let's have a look at how to implement writing and reading XML information from a file. In the **New Items** dialog, there is the **Web Documents** category, where you can find a wizard to create a new XML file. We can add an XML file directly to our FavoritesDemo project. Click on the XML File icon and save the file as favs.xml.

Our favorites sample data expressed in XML could look like this:

```xml
<?xml version="1.0" encoding="UTF-8"?>
<Favorites>
  <Favorite>
    <URL>www.embarcadero.com/products/delphi</URL>
    <Caption>Delphi Home Page</Caption>
  </Favorite>
  <Favorite>
    <URL>docwiki.embarcadero.com/RADStudio/en</URL>
    <Caption>RAD Studio online documentation</Caption>
  </Favorite>
</Favorites>
```

The XML standard has two different formats for describing metadata. The first one is **Document Type Definition (DTD)**. It is very old and hardly used. The second one is called **XML Schema** and is widely used. This is the metadata mechanism that JSON is currently lacking. With XML Schema, we can *validate* the structure of an XML file and it can also be used to automatically generate code for processing XML files. Delphi provides the **XML Data Binding** Wizard that can be found in the **New Items** dialog in the **XML** category of new **Delphi Projects**.

XML Data
Binding

With this wizard, we can generate, Object Pascal unit for processing XML files of a known structure. Double-click on the wizard icon as shown in the following screenshot:

In the first screen of the wizard, we need to specify either an XML or schema file as source:

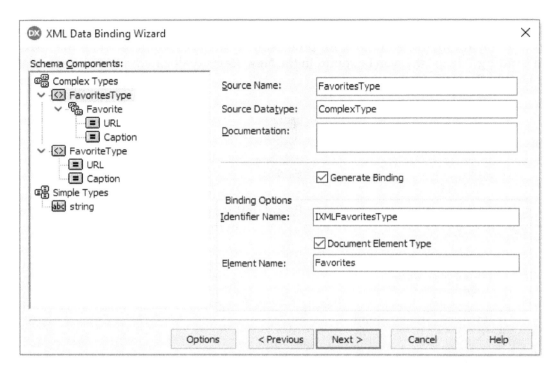

In the second screen, we can preview simple and complex types detected in the source file as shown in the following screenshot:

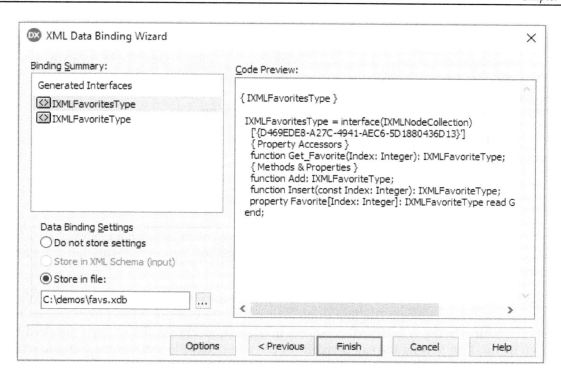

In the last screen, we can preview the source code that is about to be generated by the wizard. The actual XML Schema with all the modifications done in the wizard, which will be used by the wizard to drive the code generation, can be optionally saved into an `.xdb` file.

After clicking on the **Finish** button, the wizard will generate a `Favs.pas` file that is automatically added to the current project. This *binding* file contains interface and type definitions that corresponds to all complex types detected in the source data. In our case, there are `IXMLFavoritesType` and `IXMLFavoriteType` interfaces and their corresponding type declarations. The first interface is derived from the `IXMLNodeCollection` class because it could contain multiple favorite items and the second interface inherits from just `IXMLNode` because it represents just an object.

Working with XML in code is all about traversing a graph of objects in memory that represents individual pieces of data. It is similar to JSON DOM support. We could just use `TXMLNodeCollections` and `TXMLNode` classes to write similar code like in the case of JSON where we deal with objects from the `System.JSON` unit. The XML data binding adds type information to XML nodes so there are properties that map to elements from the XML or XML Schema files. This helps to simplify the code we need to write.

At the end of the interface section of the unit generated by the wizard, there are three global functions that can be used to work with XML. Refer to the following code snippet:

```
function GetFavorites(Doc: IXMLDocument): IXMLFavoritesType;
function LoadFavorites(const FileName: string): IXMLFavoritesType;
function NewFavorites: IXMLFavoritesType;
```

The first can be used to obtain the `IXMLFavoritesType` interface from an existing data loaded into `TXMLDocument`. The second one can be used for reading information from a file and the last one can be used to create a new XML file.

Let's add another form to our `FavoritesDemo` project for writing and reading XML. We are going to call it `FormFavXML`. The first thing is to add the navigation to and from the main application form in the way described earlier in the chapter. We will also need the already known method for getting the full filename of the `favs.xml` file that we are going to write and read.

The next step is not obvious. We want to make sure that our app will use the correct XML parser implementation that would work on mobile platforms. For this we need to make sure that somewhere in the `uses` clause of our project there are correct units added, so the XML parser implementation gets compiled into our app. The easiest way to do so is to drop on the form a `TXMLDocument` component, select the desired value in the `DOMVendor` property, and save the form. Correct units will be added automatically to the form interface `uses` clause. If we select **Omni XML** as the **DOM Vendor**, the following units will get added:

```
uses
  // ...
  Xml.xmldom, Xml.XMLIntf, Xml.XMLDoc, Xml.omnixmldom;
```

The first three are related to `TXMLDocument` components and the last one is the actual DOM vendor implementation.

Now let's add a button to the form, align to `Top`, and change its `Text` property to `Write XML`. Double-click on it and in the `OnClick` event handler enter the following code:

```
procedure TFormFavXML.btnWriteClick(Sender: TObject);
var
  favs: TFavorites; fav: TFavorite;
  favsXML: IXMLFavoritesType; favXML: IXMLFavoriteType;
begin
  favs := FormFavMain.Favs;

  favsXML := NewFavorites;
  for fav in favs do
  begin
    favXML := favsXML.Add;
    favXML.URL := fav.URL;
    favXML.Caption := fav.Caption;
  end;

  XMLDocument1.LoadFromXML(favsXML.XML);
  XMLDocument1.SaveToFile(GetFilename);
end;
```

Reading the XML is even more straightforward.

```
procedure TFormFavXML.btnReadClick(Sender: TObject);
var
  favs: TFavorites; fav: TFavorite;
  favsXML: IXMLFavoritesType;
  i: integer;
begin
  favs := TFavorites.Create;
  try
    favsXML := LoadFavorites(GetFilename);
    for i := 0 to favsXML.Count-1 do
    begin
      fav := TFavorite.Create;
      fav.URL := favsXML[i].URL;
      fav.Caption := favsXML[i].Caption;
      favs.Add(fav);
    end;

    DisplayFavsCount(favs);

  finally
    favs.Free;
  end;
end;
```

The call to `LoadFavorites` takes the filename and returns the reference to the `IXMLFavoritesType` interface, which we can use to iterate through favorites data and to populate a local favorites list. Similarly to the JSON example, at the end we are calling the `DisplayFavsCount` method to verify that we have the correct number of favorite items in the list before destroying it.

# Summary

In this chapter, we have learned some useful everyday skills that a Delphi developer can benefit from.

In the first part, we have looked into PPL. With constructs such as parallel `for` loops, tasks, and futures, we can really make our Delphi apps faster and more responsive.

The second part of the chapter was related to working with text files. One can work with just plain text, or take advantage of popular structured file formats such as JSON and XML. We have looked into working with both file formats through building their in-memory representation. In the case of JSON, we have also looked into reading and writing data using dedicated readers and writers. For completeness, it should be noted that we have not covered the `TJson` class from the `REST.Json` unit that can be used for serializing Delphi objects to their JSON representation and back.

In the next chapter, we will be playing with FireMonkey through small, but funny demo apps.

# 4

# Playing with FireMonkey

Delphi development is, first of all, great fun. The best way to learn how to build mobile apps is to start by creating a few small apps. In this chapter, we are going to build a simple *Game of Memory* application using primitive components such as layouts, shapes, effects, and animations. We are also going to learn how to deliver a great mobile user experience with touch, multitouch, and gestures.

This chapter will cover the following points:

- Using shapes, effects, and animations
- Using images and image lists
- Controlling the user interface with layouts, alignments, anchors, and margins
- Learning about touch, multitouch, and gestures
- Using timers

The objective of this chapter is to learn the basics of FireMonkey programming.

# Drawing in code

The key to FireMonkey cross-platform support is its rendering architecture. When you create a new multidevice project with Delphi, on the first page of the wizard you can choose an application type. This effectively just selects the type of the first form to add to a new app. You can choose **Blank Application**. This will add to the project a form inherited from TForm, which is a basic two-dimensional form. The second choice is **3D Application**. This will add a form inherited from TForm3D. All other choices give you a TForm descendant with some additional controls already added. Check the following screenshot:

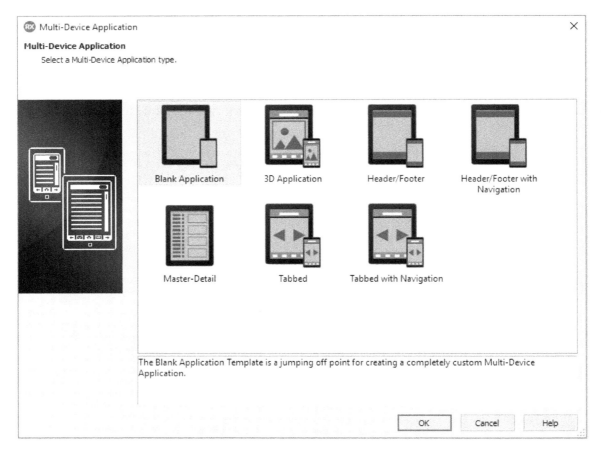

If you decide to add more forms to the project, then you can see the real choice. It is either an **HD Form** or a **3D Form**. **HD** stands for **High Definition** and is just a different name for **2D**. Depending on the chosen platform, FireMonkey forms are rendered using different graphics APIs such as OpenGL or DirectX. These are the same APIs that many developers use to implement graphically intensive games.

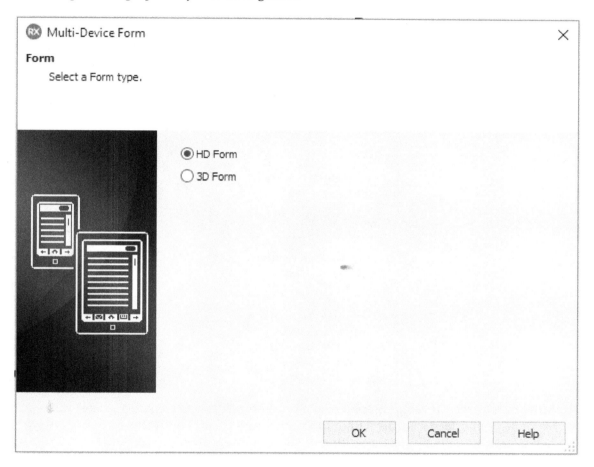

The TForm class inherits from TCustomForm, which, in turn, derives from TCommonCustomForm and implements the IScene interface. The key method of this interface is GetCanvas, which returns the TCanvas instance. TCanvas is the main abstraction for 2D drawing in FireMonkey. It is an abstract class that defines a common denominator for writing cross-platform drawing code. It has different implementations for different targets. If you look into the Delphi source directory, you will find units with different TCanvas implementations, depending on the platform. If we compile our app for Windows, we will be using the TCanvas implementation based on Windows Direct2D graphics defined in FMX.Canvas.D2D. The same app compiled for other targets will use OpenGL graphics and the TCanvas implementation from FMX.Canvas.GPU. This is a typical pattern in the FireMonkey cross-platform library. A base abstract class provides an interface for a programmer's code, and its implementation is platform-specific. See the following diagram:

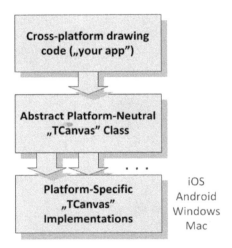

FireMonkey is based on vector graphics, so a programmer can easily scale, rotate, and transform user interface controls without loosing graphics fidelity! At the lowest level, we can just use TCanvas methods for writing cross-platform drawing code.

If we want to draw on the FireMonkey form using its `Canvas` directly, we can use a convenient `TPaintBox` control. It has an `OnPaint` event that provides access to `Canvas` as its parameter. Typically, code that is responsible for drawing on canvas is enclosed within the `BeginScene` and `EndScene` calls:

```
procedure TForm1.PaintBox1Paint(Sender: TObject; Canvas: TCanvas);
begin
  Canvas.BeginScene;
  try
    // access "Canvas" methods and properties here
  finally
    Canvas.EndScene;
  end;
end;
```

The `TCanvas` class has many methods for drawing lines, ellipses, rectangles, and other geometries. An actual drawing call is done with a current brush and other properties of a canvas, so these must be set before a call to draw something.

Let's draw a simple scene with a blue sky and a beautiful yellow sun. Create a new Delphi multidevice project and select **Blank Application** as the project type. Save the form's unit as `uFormSunCodeStatic` and the project as `SunAppCodeStatic`. Drop the `TPaintBox` component on the form and align it to `Client`. Double-click on the `OnPaint` event and enter the following code there:

```
procedure TFormSunCodeStatic.PaintBox1Paint(Sender: TObject; Canvas:
TCanvas);
const
  DEFAULT_OPACITY = 1; POS_X = 150; POS_Y = 150;
  SUN_RADIUS = 50; RAY_COUNT = 12; RAY_LENGTH = 100;
var
  aRect: TRectF; x, y, r, angle: double; i: integer; a, b: TPointF;
begin
  Canvas.BeginScene;
  try
    // draw blue sky
    Canvas.Fill.Color := TAlphaColorRec.Skyblue;
    Canvas.FillRect(PaintBox1.BoundsRect, 0, 0, [], DEFAULT_OPACITY);

    // draw yellow sun solid circle
    Canvas.Fill.Color := TAlphaColorRec.Yellow;
    Canvas.Fill.Kind := TBrushKind.Solid;
    x := POS_X;
    y := POS_Y;
    r := SUN_RADIUS;
```

```
  aRect := RectF(x-r, y-r, x+r, y+r);
  Canvas.FillEllipse(aRect, DEFAULT_OPACITY);

  // prepare stroke for drawing sun rays
  Canvas.Stroke.Color := TAlphaColorRec.Yellow;
  Canvas.Stroke.Kind := TBrushKind.bkSolid;
  Canvas.Stroke.Thickness := 5;

  // draw sun rays
  for i := 0 to RAY_COUNT-1 do
  begin
    angle := i * pi * 2 / RAY_COUNT;
    a := PointF(x, y);
    b := PointF(
      x + RAY_LENGTH * cos(angle),
      y + RAY_LENGTH * sin(angle));
    Canvas.DrawLine(a, b, DEFAULT_OPACITY);
  end;

  finally
    Canvas.EndScene;
  end;
end;
```

If we run the app, we should see a beautiful sun shining on a blue sky, as shown in the following screenshot:

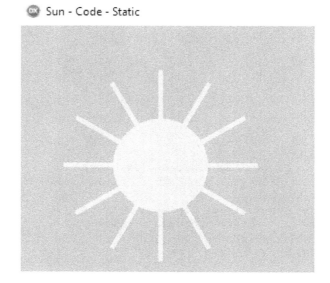

Code for drawing lines and filling rectangles can be simplified by defining a class helper for the TCanvas class; thus, instead of three to four lines of code, we can write just one. Additionally, we can define some default values for parameters, so the code could become even simpler:

```
unit uFmxCanvasHelper;

interface

uses
  System.Types,
  System.UITypes,
  FMX.Graphics;

type
  TFmxCanvasHelper = class helper for TCanvas
    procedure Line(A, B: TPointF; aColor: TColor; aThickness: Single = 1);
    procedure SolidRect(aRect: TRectF; aColor: TColor =
TAlphaColorRec.White);
    procedure SolidCircle(A: TPointF; R: Double; aColor: TColor);
  end;

implementation

const
  DEFAULT_OPACITY: Double = 1;

{ TFmxCanvasHelper }

procedure TFmxCanvasHelper.SolidRect(aRect: TRectF; aColor: TColor);
begin
  self.Fill.Color := aColor;
  self.FillRect(aRect, 0, 0, [], DEFAULT_OPACITY);
end;

procedure TFmxCanvasHelper.Line(A, B: TPointF; aColor: TColor;
  aThickness: Single);
begin
  self.Stroke.Color := aColor;
  self.Stroke.Kind := TBrushKind.bkSolid;
  self.Stroke.Thickness := aThickness;
  self.DrawLine(A, B, DEFAULT_OPACITY);
end;

procedure TFmxCanvasHelper.SolidCircle(A: TPointF; R: Double;
  aColor: TColor);
var aRect: TRectF;
```

```
begin
  aRect := RectF(A.X-R, A.Y-R, A.X+R, A.Y+R);
  self.Fill.Color := aColor;
  self.Fill.Kind := TBrushKind.Solid;
  self.FillEllipse(aRect, DEFAULT_OPACITY);
end;

end.
```

Now, we can just add this unit to the `uses` clause of the form that we want to draw on a FireMonkey canvas.

Now the painting code is simpler, because it uses the new helper class for `TCanvas`.

```
uses uFmxCanvasHelper;
procedure TFormSunCodeStaticHelper.PaintBox1Paint(Sender: TObject; Canvas:
TCanvas);
const
  DEFAULT_OPACITY = 1;
  POS_X = 150; POS_Y = 150;
  SUN_RADIUS = 50; RAY_COUNT = 12; RAY_LENGTH = 100;
var
  angle: double; i: integer; a, b: TPointF;
begin
  Canvas.BeginScene;
  try
    // draw blue sky
    Canvas.SolidRect(PaintBox1.BoundsRect, TAlphaColorRec.Skyblue);
    // draw yellow sun solid circle
    Canvas.SolidCircle(PointF(POS_X, POS_Y),
      SUN_RADIUS, TAlphaColorRec.Yellow);
    // draw sun rays
    for i := 0 to RAY_COUNT-1 do
    begin
      angle := i * pi * 2 / RAY_COUNT;
      a := PointF(POS_X, POS_Y);
      b := PointF(
        POS_X + RAY_LENGTH * cos(angle),
        POS_Y + RAY_LENGTH * sin(angle));
      Canvas.Line(a, b, TAlphaColorRec.Yellow, 5);
    end;
  finally
    Canvas.EndScene;
  end;
end;
```

When defining helpers for some fundamental library classes, always make sure that there is no helper already defined because any given type can have only one helper applied to it.

# Get moving with timers

Let's take one further step, and, instead of having a static scene, let's add an animation. It is a normal thing for the sun to ascend in the morning. In order to achieve the effect of sunrise every time the form is repainted, we will change the *y* coordinate that is used for painting the sun's circle and rays. Let's add to our TFormSun class a private member FSunPosY: double, which will store the current vertical sun position.

The simplest way to change our scene over time is with the TTimer component. Drop TTimer on the form. It has only one event, OnTimer. The frequency of these events is controlled by the Interval property, which specifies the number of milliseconds between firing the OnTimer event. The default value of the Interval property is 1,000, which means that the timer fires its event every second. For a smooth animation, this is too much. Change the Interval property to 20 and double-click on the OnTimer event. Here, we want to constantly increment the FSunPosY member that we will be using in the OnPaint event. We also want to force the form to repaint itself. This can be done through *invalidating* the form's canvas. Here is the updated drawing code that uses a timer to achieve the animation effect, and we also use the canvas helper to simplify the drawing code:

```
type
  TFormSunCodeAnim = class(TForm)
    PaintBox1: TPaintBox;
    Timer1: TTimer;
    procedure PaintBox1Paint(Sender: TObject; Canvas: TCanvas);
    procedure Timer1Timer(Sender: TObject);
    procedure FormCreate(Sender: TObject);
  private
    FSunPosY: double;
  public
    { Public declarations }
  end;

var
  FormSunCodeAnim: TFormSunCodeAnim;

implementation

{$R *.fmx}

uses uFmxCanvasHelper;
```

```
const
  END_SUN_POS_Y = 150;

procedure TFormSunCodeAnim.FormCreate(Sender: TObject);
begin
  FSunPosY := self.Height + 150;
end;

procedure TFormSunCodeAnim.Timer1Timer(Sender: TObject);
begin
  if FSunPosY > END_SUN_POS_Y then
    FSunPosY := FSunPosY - 10;

  Invalidate;
end;

procedure TFormSunCodeAnim.PaintBox1Paint(Sender: TObject; Canvas:
TCanvas);
const
  DEFAULT_OPACITY = 1; POS_X = 150; // POS_Y = 150;
  SUN_RADIUS = 50; RAY_COUNT = 12; RAY_LENGTH = 100;
var
  x, y, angle: double; i: integer; a, b: TPointF;
begin
  Canvas.BeginScene;
  try
    // draw blue sky
    Canvas.SolidRect(PaintBox1.BoundsRect, TAlphaColorRec.Skyblue);

    x := POS_X;
    y := FSunPosY;

    // draw yellow sun solid circle
    Canvas.SolidCircle(PointF(x, y),
      SUN_RADIUS, TAlphaColorRec.Yellow);

    // draw sun rays
    for i := 0 to RAY_COUNT-1 do
    begin
      angle := i * pi * 2 / RAY_COUNT;
      a := PointF(x, y);
      b := PointF(
        x + RAY_LENGTH * cos(angle),
        y + RAY_LENGTH * sin(angle));
      Canvas.Line(a, b, TAlphaColorRec.Yellow, 5);
    end;

  finally
```

```
      Canvas.EndScene;
    end;
end;
```

This technique of drawing on canvas gives you a lot of flexibility in graphics effects; however, the code gets really complicated and difficult to maintain.

# Precise timing

Note that the `TTimer` component cannot be used for very precise timings. If your animation code is time-sensitive, for example, when you are using a physics engine, it needs the exact amount of time that elapsed from the last `OnTimer` event. In this case, you could use the `TStopwatch` record type from the `System.Diagnostics` unit, which makes it easy to read the precise timer information from the underlying operating system clock in a cross-platform way. `TStopwatch` needs to be initialized, so somewhere, for example, in the `OnCreate` event of the form, you need to call its `StartNew` method. The `GetTimeStamp` method returns the current number of underlying operating system `ticks`, which is the most precise available timing information. Luckily, there is also a `Frequency` property, which gives us the number of ticks per second. By dividing these two values, we can get the raw reference time in seconds.

Let's create a simple test app. Declare the `FLastTime:  double` private field in the form's class. Drop a timer component and implement the `OnTimer` event. The default value for the `Interval` property is one second but, as we will see, it is never exactly one second between every two `OnTimer` events:

```
uses
  System.Diagnostics;

// ...

procedure TFormTiming.FormCreate(Sender: TObject);
begin
  TStopwatch.StartNew;
  Log('Stopwatch Frequency = ' + TStopwatch.Frequency.ToString);
end;

function TFormTiming.GetRawReferenceTime: double;
begin
  Result := TStopwatch.GetTimeStamp / TStopwatch.Frequency;
end;

procedure TFormTiming.Timer1Timer(Sender: TObject);
```

```
var t, elapsed: double;
begin
  t := GetRawReferenceTime;
  elapsed := t - FLastTime;
  FLastTime := t;
  Log('t=' + t.ToString + '   elapsed=' + elapsed.ToString);
end;
```

If we run this app, we will see the precise difference in seconds between timer events. See the following screenshot:

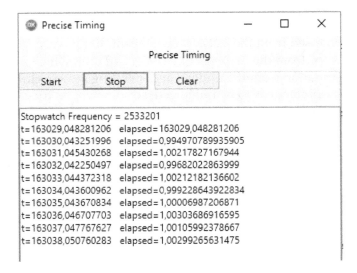

This technique could be useful if you need very precise timing in your next high-end game written in Delphi. Even in an almost empty app, the timer is accurate up to a few milliseconds. In a more complex app, this difference could be bigger.

# The power of parenting

One of the nicest things about the FireMonkey architecture is *parenting*. Essentially, any FireMonkey component can contain, or *be a parent* to, other components. What is cool about it is the fact that all the children inherit different properties of their parents, such as position, scale, and rotation. This also gives a lot of possibilities in building user interfaces because we can create *composite* controls without having to declare completely new classes.

# Shapes

A lot of low-level drawing code can be avoided by using different controls from the **Shape** category on the **Tool Palette**. There are lines, circles, ellipses, rectangles, pies, paths, and more. They just encapsulate drawing on the canvas, so you need not write so much code.

Let's try to recreate our sun visualisation with shapes to better compare these two possible approaches to drawing. Add a new **Form HD** to the project. Drop the TRectangle component on the form and align it to **Client**. Change its **Name** property to rectSky. Expand its **Fill** property and change **Color** to Skyblue. Drop the TCircle component on the form and name it circleSun. Change its **Width** and **Height** properties to 100 to make it bigger, and its Position.X and Position.Y properties to 100 to move it towards the top-left corner of the screen. Change its Fill.Color and Stroke.Color properties to Yellow. So far, we have been changing the color, position, and dimension of FireMonkey shapes, but we can also scale them horizontally and vertically, rotate them using RotationAngle and RotationCenter properties, as well as change their Opacity. This gives a lot of possibilities to show off your artistic skills while designing user interfaces with FireMonkey.

It is time to add some sun rays now! Make sure that the sun circle is selected on the form; drop the TLine component on it, and rename it to LineRay01. Change LineType to Top, so it is horizontal and not diagonal. Change its **Width** and **Height** properties to 100, its Stroke.Color to Yellow, and **Thickness** to 5.

Now for the important part, make sure that the line component *belongs* to the circle. In the **Structure** tree view, it should be a **leaf** of the circle. We will be adding more lines to the circle, and they all need to be children of the sun. See the following screenshot:

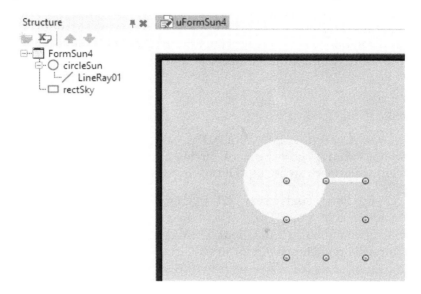

Children properties are set relative to their parents. This is very powerful because changes made to parent properties automatically propagate to children. Make sure that **Position.X** and **Position.Y** of the line component are both set to 50, so the ray starts exactly in the center of the sun. If we now change the position of the circle, the line will go with it. This is *parenting*, and it is one of the most important and powerful aspects of the FireMonkey architecture.

Now, we will add the remaining rays by coping the first ray and changing their rotations. Right-click on the line and select **Copy** from the **Edit** context menu. Click on the circle to select it. Right-click again and select **Paste**. A copy of the line has been added to the form. Now, in the **Structure** view, drag the new line onto the circle, so it becomes its child. Change its `Position.X` and `Position.Y` properties to 50 to make sure it starts exactly at the center. Now we want to rotate the second ray. Change the `RotationAngle` property to 30 degrees. Note that this is not the exact rotation that we wanted to achieve. By default, shapes are rotating around their center, but we want the line to rotate around its top left corner. How to do that? There is also a `RotationCenter` property with default values of *X=0.5* and *Y=0.5*. These properties control the rotation center relative to the dimensions of the control. Just half and half means center. If we change both the values to 0, we will achieve the desired rotation.

Now, paste ten more lines onto the form, setting the same position and rotation center for each of them but incrementing the rotation angle by 30 degrees. We should now have a beautiful sun with twelve rays. See the following screenshot:

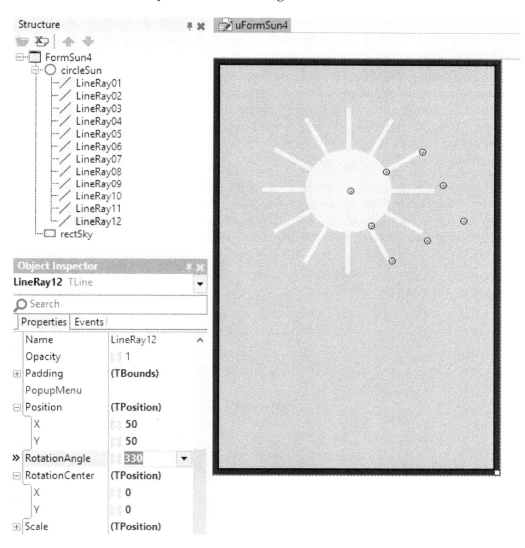

Note that we have achieved the very same graphical result as previously, but this time we have not written a single line of code. Everything has been done visually, at design time. That is another benefit. You do not even need to run the app to see how it is going to look.

# Animations

No coding, just shapes. The next step is to recreate the animation of the rising sun in the new app, which is made of components only. The easiest way to add an animation is to use special *animation* components. On the **Tool Palette**, there is a separate category for **Animations**. There are different animation components for animating the values of different types over time. There is TFloatAnimation for changing float values, TColorAnimation for changing colors, and so on.

Instead of dropping an animation component on the form, we can create it directly from inside the Object Inspector. In our demo, we would like to change the Position.Y property of the circle component. Just expand this property in the Object Inspector and select the option to **Create New TFloatAnimation**. See the following screenshot:

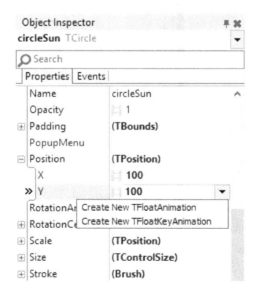

Animation components make it very easy to change the values of different properties over time in background threads, without having to use timer components. When we create an animation from the Object Inspector, then it is already properly parented under the component; the property it is going to manipulate and its `PropertyName` are also already set. See the following screenshot:

An animation is just a component, so we can adjust its properties at design time with Object Inspector. Set the **Duration** to two seconds, **Enabled** to **True**, **StopValue** to **100**, and **StartValue** to **600**. In fact, we might want to set the `StartValue` property in code to accommodate different display heights. We want the sun to start ascending from outside the border of the screen. Enter just one line of code in the `OnCreate` event of the form:

```
procedure TFormSunCompAnim.FormCreate(Sender: TObject);
begin
  FloatAnimation1.StartValue := rectSky.Height + 150;
end;
```

The last property that we can optionally adjust is `Interpolation`. By default, it is set to **Linear**, which means that the value changes linearly from `StartValue` to `StopValue` through the `Duration` of animation. Change the **Interopolation** to **Sinusoidal** for a slightly more interesting visual effect.

Our animation is **Enabled** at design time, which means that it will start right after our app is run. Animations execute in separate threads, so our app stays responsive.

It is also possible to do animations in code. Instead of using animation components, we can also animate the properties of different objects with the `TAnimator` class.

# Programmable effects

We can make our graphical user interfaces really stunning by using programmable effects. These are also components, such as shapes and animation, with properties and events that can be used to add this extra artistic touch to the FireMonkey user interfaces. They are implemented using shader programs that are executed in the **Graphical Processor Unit** (**GPU**), so they are very fast. See the following Effects:

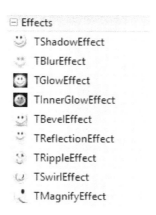

Out-of-the-box, Delphi comes with more then sixty effect components.

Right now, our sun animation is a bit static. The sun rises and stays in the same place. We can add a glow effect to make it more realistic. Drop `TGlowEffect` on the form and drag it in the structure view onto the sun's circle component, so it is one of its children-like lines, and the vertical position animation component. By default, the **Color** property of the glow effect is set to **Gold**, which we can leave as-is. The **Softness** property controls how far the glow effect extends. Setting it to 1 will make the sun look better. See the following screenshot:

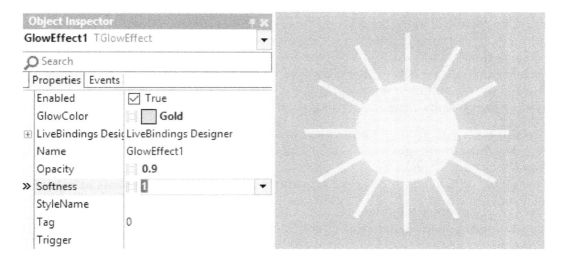

We do not need to wait until our app runs. At design time, we can already see the glow effect in action. This can go further. We could have now added an animation to the **Softness** property to make the visualization even more interesting.

That's the power of building user interfaces with components. We can use shapes, animations, and effects, and build complex visualizations without writing a single line of code. Later on, we will see that this technique is used internally by FireMonkey to render complex user interface controls.

# Touch me

Up to this point, we were focusing on generating great graphics but with no user interaction. Great apps are all about great user experiences. In order to get some feedback from apps, users are busy touching the screen in all possible ways.

FireMonkey forms provide support for handling simple touch, multitouch, and gesture events. You can use standard and interactive gestures, such as zoom and rotation, to make your apps more dynamic and interactive.

# Touch

FireMonkey forms are used for building both mobile and desktop applications. It is just a matter of changing the selected **Target Platform** and recompiling the project. Certain concepts exist on the desktop and do not exist on mobile platforms and vice versa. For example, on mobile devices, there is no concept of a mouse, which does exist on desktops. FireMonkey forms provide different mouse events, which, on mobile platforms, are fired in response to simple touch events. When the end user touches the screen, the `OnMouseDown` event is fired. There are also other events such as `OnMouseUp` and `OnMouseMove` that are fired when the the end user stops touching the screen, or when the touch point changes. For individual controls, the `OnMouseEnter` and `OnMouseLeave` events are additionally defined.

If a scene is built in code, then we can just implement mouse events on the form itself. It is more common in FireMonkey to create visualisations with shapes and complex controls. Higher-level components, such as `TButton`, offer events such as `OnClick` that centralize touch support. When building a scene just with shapes, we need to understand how touch events work.

Every shape component derives from the `TControl` class. In this class, all user interactions, including touch, are handled. If a control does not need to respond to touch events, we can set its **HitTest** property to **False**. This can be important when we are combining different primitive shapes into something more complex. Typically, we just want the parent shape to receive touch events.

Let's modify our *sun* app, so the end user will be able to change the position of the sun. This involves handling the `OnMouseDown` and `OnMouseUp` events. In the `OnMouseDown` event, we just set the Boolean flag that we are in the process of *moving* and store the initial *x* and *y* coordinates of the touch event. In the `OnMouseUp` event, we do the actual `move` operation and reset the `Moving` flag.

There is also our initial *sun rising* animation played when the app starts. We do not want the end user to move the sun before it is in its target position on the form. That's why we also add the `FReady: boolean` private field to the form that is set to `False` in the `OnCreate` event of the form and set to `True` in the animation's `OnFinish` event.

Double-click on the `OnMouseDown` and `OnMouseUp` events of the form and, the following code to events, and declare new fields in the form class itself:

```
type
   TFormSunMove = class(TForm)

// ...
   private
     FReady: boolean;
     FDown: TPointF;
     FMoving: boolean;
   end;

var
   FormSunMove: TFormSunMove;

implementation

{$R *.fmx}

procedure TFormSunMove.FormCreate(Sender: TObject);
begin
   FMoving := False;
   FReady := False;
   FloatAnimation1.StartValue := rectSky.Height + 150;
end;

procedure TFormSunMove.FloatAnimation1Finish(Sender: TObject);
begin
   FReady := True;
end;

procedure TFormSunMove.FormMouseDown(Sender: TObject; Button: TMouseButton;
   Shift: TShiftState; X, Y: Single);
begin
   if FReady then
   begin
     FDown := PointF(X, Y);
     FMoving := True;
   end;
end;

procedure TFormSunMove.FormMouseUp(Sender: TObject; Button: TMouseButton;
   Shift: TShiftState; X, Y: Single);
begin
   if FMoving then
   begin
     circleSun.Position.X := circleSun.Position.X + (X - FDown.X);
```

```
        circleSun.Position.Y := circleSun.Position.Y + (Y - FDown.Y);
        FMoving := False;
      end;
  end;
```

If we run the app now, moving does not work. Touch events do not reach the form, which is completely occupied by the *sky* rectangle. If we change its `HitTest` properties of sky rectangle, sun's circle and ray lines to `False`, then the app works as expected.

Our app has become interactive.

# Gestures

Another standard way to interact with a mobile app is to use more then one finger at a time. FireMonkey supports handling standard and interactive gestures. Let's add to our sun demo app support for interactive rotation.

Make sure that the form is selected in the Object Inspector and expand its **Touch** property. Check the **Rotate** gesture under the **Interactive Gestures** subproperty. See the following screenshot:

Now we can respond to the selected gestures. Double-click on the `OnGesture` event of the form. In the generated event handler, there are two parameters. The first parameter is `EventInfo: TGestureEventInfo`, which contains all the information about the gesture that was detected. Inside the `FMX.Types` unit, we can find the declaration of the `TGestureEventInfo` record and the corresponding types:

```
type
  TInteractiveGestureFlag = (gfBegin, gfInertia, gfEnd);
  TInteractiveGestureFlags = set of TInteractiveGestureFlag;
```

```
TGestureEventInfo = record
    GestureID: TGestureID;
    Location: TPointF;
    Flags: TInteractiveGestureFlags;
    Angle: Double;
    InertiaVector: TPointF;
    Distance: Integer;
    TapLocation: TPointF;
  end;

  TGestureEvent = procedure(Sender: TObject; const EventInfo:
TGestureEventInfo;
    var Handled: Boolean) of object;
```

The first field, **GestureID**, identifies what gesture it is and the remaining fields give information about the location of the gesture and other properties. An interactive gesture is happening over time. The **Flags** field is a set of TInteractiveGestureFlag values that can be used to process the gesture differently when the gesture has just started or ended.

In our OnGesture event handler implementation, we will first check whether it is a rotate gesture. If this is the case, then we will change the RotationAngle property of the sun's circle. We will also need a new FLastAngle: double private field in the form's class to store the last rotation angle:

```
procedure TFormSunGestures.FormGesture(Sender: TObject;
  const EventInfo: TGestureEventInfo; var Handled: Boolean);
begin
// ...
    if EventInfo.GestureID = igiRotate then
    begin
      if (TInteractiveGestureFlag.gfBegin in EventInfo.Flags) then
        FLastAngle := circleSun.RotationAngle
      else if EventInfo.Angle <> 0 then
        circleSun.RotationAngle := FLastAngle - (EventInfo.Angle * 180) /
Pi;
    end
  // ...
end;
```

If we run the app now, we can verify that the sun is now responding to rotation gestures.

There are also other gestures that we can handle in FireMonkey. Inside the `Touch` property of the form, we are instructed to use **Gesture Manager**. Drop `TGestureManager` on the form and point the `GestureManager1` property to the newly added component. Notice that next to the `Gestures` property appears the plus sign, and now it is possible to check which standard gestures we would like to handle. See the following screenshot:

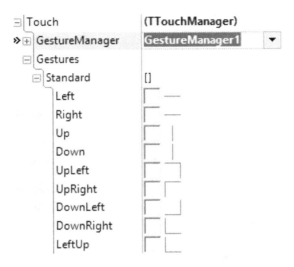

There are 34 standard gestures that we could add to our demo app.

# Multitouch

Sometimes, users touch the app with multiple fingers at the same time. With multitouch, we can provide a really nice user experience.

Let's create a new multidevice Delphi project. Drop `TPaintBox` on the form, and align it to `Client`. Save the app as `TouchApp` and the form as `uFormTouch`. Instead of drawing directly on the paint box canvas, we can also draw on the offline bitmap and draw the whole bitmap in one operation. This setup can be useful to achieve more complex animations.

Double-click on the OnTouch event of the form in the Object Inspector to generate an empty event handler. We are getting a dynamic array of locations of individual touch points as a parameter to this event. Let's just draw lines connecting all the touch points using the FireMonkey canvas helper that we defined earlier. Here is the code:

```
type
  TFormTouch = class(TForm)
    PaintBox1: TPaintBox;
    procedure PaintBox1Paint(Sender: TObject; Canvas: TCanvas);
    procedure FormCreate(Sender: TObject);
    procedure FormTouch(Sender: TObject; const Touches: TTouches;
      const Action: TTouchAction);
  private
    FBitmap: TBitmap;
  public
    { Public declarations }
  end;

var
  FormTouch: TFormTouch;

implementation

{$R *.fmx}

uses uFmxCanvasHelper;

procedure TFormTouch.FormCreate(Sender: TObject);
begin
  FBitmap := TBitmap.Create;
  FBitmap.SetSize(self.ClientWidth, self.ClientHeight);
  FBitmap.Clear(TAlphaColors.White);
end;

procedure TFormTouch.FormTouch(Sender: TObject; const Touches: TTouches;
const Action: TTouchAction);
var i, count: integer;
begin
  FBitmap.Canvas.BeginScene;
  try
    FBitmap.Clear(TAlphaColors.White);
    count := Length(Touches);
    if count > 1 then
    for i := 0 to count-2 do
      FBitmap.Canvas.Line(
        Touches[i].Location,
        Touches[i+1].Location,
```

```
                TAlphaColorRec.Red);
    finally
      FBitmap.Canvas.EndScene;
    end;
    PaintBox1.Repaint;
  end;

  procedure TFormTouch.PaintBox1Paint(Sender: TObject; Canvas: TCanvas);
  var R: TRectF;
  begin
    R := TRectF.Create(0, 0, FBitmap.Width, FBitmap.Height);
    PaintBox1.Canvas.DrawBitmap(FBitmap, R, R, 1, True);
  end;
```

When you run the app, it will show touch points connected with red lines.

It is not the most useful multitouch demo, but it is intentionally simple to illustrate how to handle multitouch information.

# Game of Memory

Let's put together the things that you have learnt about FireMonkey architecture so far, and let's build a complete, but simple, game. In the process, we will look at how to handle images with the `TImageList` component and some basics of building FireMonkey 2D user interfaces.

# Designing the game

*Game of Memory* is a board game. Player is presented with a grid of tiles. Every tile has an image, but all images are initially hidden. When the user touches a tile, its image is revealed. When the next tile is touched, the image of the currently visible tile is made hidden again, and the image of the new tile is shown. So, at every moment during the game, only one image is shown. The number of tiles has to be even, because every image is used twice. The objective of the game is to remove all the tiles in the minimum possible time, by touching the tiles with the same image one after another. If a user touches another tile with the same image as the currently visible tile, both tiles are removed from the grid. This process continues until there are no more tiles in the grid and the game ends. The score is the time that elapsed from the beginning of the game to the moment when the last two tiles where removed. The shortest time is the best.

In order to make our game more interesting, we are going to let the player choose the initial size of the grid, from a really small one, which should only take a couple of seconds to complete, to bigger ones, which will take longer. We are also going to keep track of the top scores for each grid size.

We have already started building this game in Chapter 2, *Mind Your Language*, there is a main form called FormMain, which we are going to use to display the game tiles. We will also add buttons to control starting, pausing, and stopping the game. The second form is FormSettings, which is displayed from within the main form. This form is created in a *lazy fashion*. Not at app startup but at the moment when the player clicks on the Settings *menu* button for the first time. On this form, we are going to change the current difficulty level and display the best times for each size of the grid.

# Working with images

The key asset of our game are images to be used on the back of every tile. There will be at least as many images as the number of pairs at the highest difficulty level, plus two additional images. The first image in the list will be completely white and will be used for removed tiles. The second special image will be used as a *cover* for every hidden tile. Before every new game is started, we are going to randomly assign image pairs to tiles, so the board layout is different every time.

FireMonkey comes with the TImageList component, designed to efficiently manage all the images used across the whole app. It is good practice to put images and all other *global* game assets not on a form but on a dedicated data module. This way, we can easily access them from all app forms or even reuse them across different projects.

Add a new data module to the game project. Save the file as uDMGameOfMem and change its **Name** property to just DMGameOfMem. A naming convention that you might want to follow involves starting the names of data modules with **DM** and their unit names with **uDM**. In the end, every programmer can have a different naming scheme, but once you adopt one, you should try to consistently use it.

This data module will always be needed by all the other forms in the app, so we are not going to lazy-create it, but we will make sure that it is always created before all the other forms in the app. Select **Options** in the **Project** menu, and in the **Forms** tab drag the data module to the top of the list of autocreated forms. See the following screenshot:

Drop TImageList on the data module and change its Name property to ImageListMain. The Delphi Help system documents the functionality of the TImageList component in a detailed way. There are two collections of images defined in the component: Source and Destination. The Source list contains all the images added to the image list components. They can be in different formats, such as BMP, PNG, JPEG, GIF, TIFF, and a few others. The images from this collection are used to construct images available in the Destination collection, which is used across the application. If you double-click on the image list component, you will be presented with the image list editor, which can be used to work with both lists of images. Images in the Destination list can be created by combining different parts of images from the Source list, using layers and transparent colors. The most frequently used images are stored in the built-in buffer for faster access. See the following screenshot:

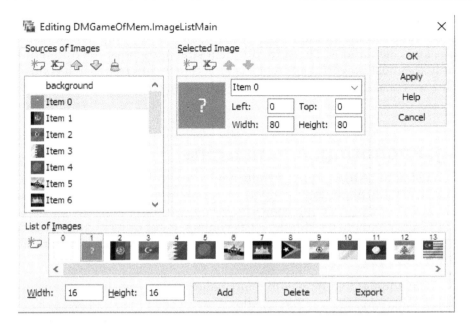

I have added eighteen randomly chosen images of national flags downloaded from one of the public domain web sites. The images are all roughly 80 by 80 pixels large. The list in the top-left corner contains `Sources` and the list at the bottom has the `Destinations` images. First you need to add images to `Sources` and then add the currently selected image in `Sources` to the `Destinations` list. The first two images in the list are special. The first image is completely white. It has the same color as the background on the main form, so we can display it in places where a tile has been removed. The second image contains the *back* of the tile, which is displayed for all hidden images. It has a white question mark on it.

Image lists are very flexible and can be very useful in situations where different visual FireMonkey controls need to efficiently display many small images.

# Designing a user interface

We now have a set of images ready to be used in the visual part of the app. Let's move to building the main form of the *Game of Memory*, where the end user will be spending most of his time unhiding tiles and removing them from the grid.

The key consideration in building mobile user interfaces with FireMonkey is the fact that our app can be compiled for different targets and it should run properly on displays with different sizes and orientations. There are different strategies to handle different screen sizes. Probably the most powerful approach is to organize different visual controls on the form in such a way that they always work properly on screens of all possible sizes, from small mobile phones to large tablets.

## Aligning, anchoring, and margins

We have been using the **Align** property quite a lot already. Regardless of a given control size, we can instruct it to align itself to a portion (or to the entire area) of its visual container. This is where FireMonkey parenting comes in. When designing user interfaces, we have to decide which visual components should act as containers for other components. The relative position of the children components can be controlled with the **Alignment**, **Anchors**, and **Margins** properties.

TAlignment is an enumerated type with many values, but in practice we mostly just use alignment to Client, Top, Bottom, Left, and Right.

The TAnchors property is a set of Top, Bottom, Left, and Right Boolean values that can be used to *snap* a given side of the control to its visual container. By default, a control is anchored to the top and left sides of its parent. Anchors control how a visual component reacts to the resizing of its visual container. For example, if we set the Right anchor to True and make the container wider, the child control will get wider as well, preserving the original distance between the right side of the control and its container. Setting just the Bottom and Right anchors to True and the others to False can be useful for buttons in dialog screens, where we always want them to be in the bottom-right corner of the form, regardless of its size. Examine the following screenshot:

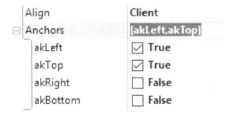

The `Anchors` property has `Top`, `Bottom`, `Left`, and `Right` values, which can be used to indicate the distance between a given side of the control and its visual container. It is typically used when a child control is *aligned* with its parent container.

## Layouts

During the user interface design in FireMonkey, we typically group controls in visual containers. FireMonkey comes with different components in the **Layouts** category in the **Tool Palette** that do not have a visual representation at runtime, but their sole purpose is to act as containers for other visual and non-visual controls. Examine the following screenshot:

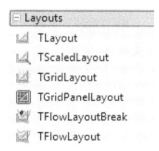

The most generic component is the `TLayout` component. It is just a simple container for other controls and is most commonly used to organize FireMonkey user interfaces.

## Building the games main form

In our game, we have a visual grid of tiles. The most natural component to use in this context is the `TGridLayout` component. Drop it on the main form of our app, change its **Name** property to `GridLayoutTiles`, and align it to **Client** so that it occupies the whole screen of the main form under the toolbar. Now, we can add other visual controls to the grid layout. The size of each item in the grid layout can be controlled with its `ItemHeight` and `ItemWidth` properties.

We are going to use the `TGlyph` component to display bitmaps from our image list in the data module. There is also the `TImage` component that we could have used, but in this case we would need to load bitmaps directly to every `TImage`, which is not as effective as using just one set of bitmaps.

Change the background color of the main form to **White**. Expand its **Fill** property, and change **Color** to **White** and **Kind** to **Solid**.

Add the `uDMGameOfMem` unit to the `uses` clause of the form and drop the `TGlyph` control onto the grid layout. Point its **Images** property to `DMGameOfMem.ImageListMain` and its **ImageIndex** to 1. Now, we should see the second image from the **Destination** collection of the image list displayed in the glyph control that symbolizes a *hidden* tile. Change all four **Margins** of the **Glyph** control to 2, so there is a distance between the different tiles in the grid. Examine the following screenshot:

| ⊟ Margins | (TBounds) |
|-----------|-----------|
| Bottom    | 2         |
| Left      | 2         |
| Right     | 2         |
| Top       | 2         |

Drop a speed button component on the toolbar, change its **Name** to `spdbtnPlay`, align it to **Left**, and change its **StyleLookup** property to `playtoolbutton`. Resize the button horizontally to make it smaller. It should just resize so its **Width** will be fixed, the same as its **Height**. Now drop the `TLabel` component on the toolbar. Change its **Name** to `lblScore`, `Text` to `Game of Memory`, and the `Align` property to `Client`.

Drop the `TComboBox` component on the toolbar. Align it to `Right`. Here, we are going to control the size of the grid. Change the **Name** property of the combo to `cmbbxLevel`. In its **Items** property, enter eight levels of difficulty, starting from *4 pairs* up to *18 pairs*. We do not want this list to be too long, so the difficulty levels are incremented by two pairs. Examine the following screenshot:

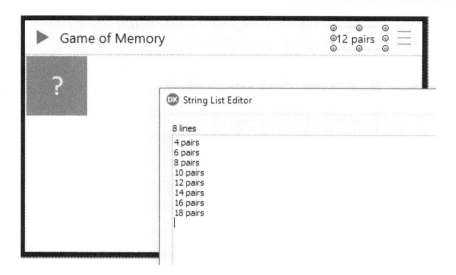

Change the **ItemIndex** property of the combobox to 4, so the initial selection will be *12 pairs*. Later on, we will store the currently selected difficulty level in a configuration file, so it would be handy to define a property on the form class called CurrPairsCount, which could be used to set and get the current selection in the difficulty level combo:

```
type
  TFormMain = class(TForm)
  private
  // ...
    procedure SetCurrPairsCount(const Value: integer);
    function GetCurrPairsCount: integer;
    property CurrPairsCount: integer
      read GetCurrPairsCount write SetCurrPairsCount;
  // ...
  end;
// ...
implementation
// ...
function TFormMain.GetCurrPairsCount: integer;
begin
  Result := 4 + cmbbxLevel.ItemIndex * 2;
end;

procedure TFormMain.SetCurrPairsCount(const Value: integer);
begin
  cmbbxLevel.ItemIndex := (Value - 4) div 2;
end;
```

We need a way to calculate the time that elapsed from starting the game. Drop the `TTimer` component on the form and change its name to `TimerGame`. Change **Interval** to `50`. When the timer is enabled, this will mean that the game is running; when it is not enabled, the game is stopped. In the **Score** label, we will be displaying the time of the game. We will need a function to nicely format the elapsed time. Add a new unit to the project, save it as `uGameUtils`, and enter the following code:

```
unit uGameUtils;

interface

function GameTimeToStr(Value: TTime): string;

implementation

uses
  System.SysUtils;

function Pad3Zeros(Value: string): string; inline;
var i: integer;
begin
  i := Length(Value);
  if i = 3 then
    Result := Value
  else if i = 2 then
    Result := '0' + Value
  else if i = 1 then
    Result := '00' + Value
  else
    Result := '000';
end;

function GameTimeToStr(Value: TTime): string;
var h,min,sec,msec: word; s: string;
begin
  DecodeTime(Value,h,min,sec,msec);
  s := 'Time: ';
  if h > 0 then
    s := s + h.ToString + 'h ';
  if min > 0 then
    s := s + min.ToString + 'min ';

  s := s + sec.ToString + '.' + Pad3Zeros(msec.ToString) + 's';
```

```
    Result := s;
  end;

end.
```

Let's add a new private field, FGameStart: TTime, to the form class to store the time when the current game starts. Add the following code to the OnTimer event:

```
procedure TFormMain.TimerGameTimer(Sender: TObject);
var delta: TTime; s: string;
begin
  delta := Now - FTimeStart;
  s := GameTimeToStr(delta);
  lblScore.Text := s;
end;
```

Now we are going to implement the heart of the game logic. Delete this one glyph that we have added to the grid layout, because we are going to add all the glyphs in code.

Let's implement the GameStart method that will be called when a player touches the start button and the corresponding GameEnd:

```
procedure TFormMain.spdbtnPlayClick(Sender: TObject);
begin
  if not TimerGame.Enabled then
    GameStart
  else
    GameEnd;
end;
```

We will read the current number of pairs count and dynamically add an appropriate number of tiles to the grid. We will also need an OnGlyphClick event handler, which will be programmatically attached to every glyph control, so it can react to end user touches. For this, every glyph needs to have its **HitTest** property set to **True**. We will also need a way to associate a given tile with its image. For this, we will use the **Tag** property, which is just an integer value, is available for all the descendants of the TComponent class, and can be used by a programmer in situations like this. FireMonkey and the VCL libraries do not use the Tag property at all.

The first two indices in the underlying image list component are reserved for displaying either a removed or hidden tile. Depending on the number of tiles, we can create a local dynamic list of indices and write some code to randomize their order.

In the form class, we will also need a counter with the number of pairs of tiles left on the board. When this number reaches zero, then the game ends. We will also need a reference to the currently visible glyph component:

```pascal
procedure TFormMain.GameStart;
var g: TGlyph; i,j,k, pairsCount, tilesCount, temp: integer;
   indices: array of integer;
begin
  // remove all glyphs from the grid,
  // if there are any left
  grdltTiles.DeleteChildren;

  pairsCount := CurrPairsCount;
  tilesCount := pairsCount * 2;

  FVisibleGlyph := nil;
  FPairsLeft := pairsCount;

  // initialize the list of indices
  SetLength(indices, tilesCount);
  for i := 0 to pairsCount-1 do
  begin
    indices[i] := i;
    indices[i + pairsCount] := i;
  end;

  // randomize indices list
  for j := 0 to 3 do
    for i := 0 to tilesCount - 1 do
    begin
      k := random(tilesCount);
      temp := indices[k];
      indices[k] := indices[i];
      indices[i] := temp;
    end;

  // add "2" to every index
  // because "0" and "1" are special
  for i := 0 to tilesCount-1 do
    indices[i] := indices[i] + 2;

  for i := 0 to tilesCount-1 do
  begin
```

```
      g := TGlyph.Create(grdltTiles);
      g.Parent := grdltTiles;
      g.Images := DMGameOfMem.ImageListMain;
      g.ImageIndex := 1; // hidden tile
      g.Tag := indices[i]; // image index
      g.HitTest := True;
      g.OnClick := OnGlyphClick;
      g.Margins.Top := TILE_MARGIN;
      g.Margins.Left := TILE_MARGIN;
      g.Margins.Bottom := TILE_MARGIN;
      g.Margins.Right := TILE_MARGIN;
    end;

  AdjustTileSize;

  FTimeStart := Now;
  TimerGame.Enabled := True;

  spdbtnPlay.StyleLookup := 'stoptoolbutton';
  cmbbxLevel.Enabled := False;
end;

procedure TFormMain.OnGlyphClick(Sender: TObject);
var g: TGlyph;
begin
  if Sender is TGlyph then
  begin
    g := TGlyph(Sender);

    if g.ImageIndex > 0 then // it is not a "removed" tile
    begin
      // if clicked on currently visible tile, do nothing
      if g <> FVisibleGlyph then
      begin
        g.ImageIndex := g.Tag; // show touched tile

        if FVisibleGlyph <> nil then // there is one other visible tile
        begin
          // there is match, remove both tiles
          if g.Tag = FVisibleGlyph.Tag then
          begin
            g.ImageIndex := 0;
            FVisibleGlyph.ImageIndex := 0;
            FVisibleGlyph := nil;

            dec(FPairsLeft);
            if FPairsLeft = 0 then
              GameEnd;
```

```
        end
        else // there is no match, hide previously visible tile
        begin
          FVisibleGlyph.ImageIndex := 1;
          FVisibleGlyph := g;
        end;

      end
      else
        FVisibleGlyph := g; // there is no other visible tile, make this
current

      end;
    end;
  end;
end;

procedure TFormMain.GameEnd;
const EL = #13;
var gameTime, bestTime: TTime; s: string;
begin
  TimerGame.Enabled := False;
  gameTime := Now - FTimeStart;
  spdbtnPlay.StyleLookup := 'playtoolbutton';
  cmbbxLevel.Enabled := True;

  if FPairsLeft = 0 then // game was completed
  begin
    bestTime := DMGameOfMem.ReadScore(CurrPairsCount);
    if (bestTime > 0) and (gameTime < bestTime) then
      s := 'GAME FINISHED!' + EL + 'Your time: ' + GameTimeToStr(gameTime)
    else
    begin
      s := 'YOU WON! BEST TIME!' + EL
        + 'New best time: ' + GameTimeToStr(gameTime);
      DMGameOfMem.SaveScore(gameTime, CurrPairsCount);
    end;
    ShowMessage(s);
  end;
end;
```

A nice thing about using glyphs is the fact that they easily scale. After all the tiles are loaded into the grid, we need to adjust their sizes. First of all, there could be a different number of image pairs and, also, we could be running our game on different display sizes. The logic to calculate the size of the glyph has been implemented in a separate `AdjustTileSize` method, which is also called from the `OnFormResize` events. On mobile targets, this event is fired when the end user changes the orientation of the screen, and on the desktop every time the form size changes:

```
procedure TFormMain.AdjustTileSize;
const ADJUST_FACTOR = 0.9;
var tileArea, tileSize: double;
begin
  // adjust the size of every tile in the grid
  tileArea := grdltTiles.Width * grdltTiles.Height / CurrPairsCount / 2;
  tileSize := (sqrt(tileArea) - 2 * TILE_MARGIN) * ADJUST_FACTOR;
  grdltTiles.ItemHeight := tileSize;
  grdltTiles.ItemWidth := tileSize;
end;
```

# Storing the game's configuration

The last part is to implement the functionality to remember the currently selected difficulty level and to keep track of top scores. We are going to add to the game's data module the `FIniFile: TIniFile` private fields from the `System.IniFiles` unit. In the `OnCreate` event of the data module, we will instantiate this class and will free it in the `OnDestroy` event. The constructor of the `INI` file object requires us to specify the path and filename; in our case, this will be the `Documents` folder on a given target platform.

Storing the app configuration information in an `INI` file is very convenient. The `TIniFile` class has the `read` and `write` methods for getting and setting the values of different types, such as strings, numbers, time, and so on. An `INI` file is a plain text file with key-value pairs organized into sections.

We are going to declare two public methods on the data module class for reading and writing the top times for different difficulty levels. If there is no top score, we will enter −1 as a special value. There will also be the `ClearAllScores` method to remove all the top scores.

The last two methods will be for remembering the currently selected difficulty level, so the end user does not need to change it every time the app is started:

```
unit uDMGameOfMem;

interface

uses
  System.SysUtils, System.Classes, System.ImageList, FMX.ImgList,
  System.IniFiles, System.IOUtils;

const
  MEM_GAME_CONFIG = 'MemGameConfig.ini';

type
  TDMGameOfMem = class(TDataModule)
    ImageListMain: TImageList;
    procedure DataModuleCreate(Sender: TObject);
    procedure DataModuleDestroy(Sender: TObject);
  private
    FIniFile: TIniFile;
  public
    procedure SaveScore(gameTime: TTime; aPairsCount: integer);
    function ReadScore(aPairsCount: integer): TTime;
    procedure ClearAllScores;
    procedure SaveCurrLevel(aPairsCount: integer);
    function ReadCurrLevel: integer;
  end;

var
  DMGameOfMem: TDMGameOfMem;

implementation

{%CLASSGROUP 'FMX.Controls.TControl'}

{$R *.dfm}

const
  StrSCORES = 'SCORES';
  StrLEVEL = 'LEVEL';
  StrSETTINGS = 'SETTINGS';
  StrCURRLEVEL = 'CURR_LEVEL';

procedure TDMGameOfMem.DataModuleCreate(Sender: TObject);
var filename: string;
begin
  filename := TPath.Combine(TPath.GetDocumentsPath, MEM_GAME_CONFIG);
```

```
  FIniFile := TIniFile.Create(filename);
end;


procedure TDMGameOfMem.DataModuleDestroy(Sender: TObject);
begin
  FIniFile.Free;
end;


procedure TDMGameOfMem.SaveScore(gameTime: TTime; aPairsCount: integer);
begin
  FIniFile.WriteTime(StrSCORES, StrLEVEL + aPairsCount.ToString, gameTime);
  FIniFile.UpdateFile;
end;


function TDMGameOfMem.ReadScore(aPairsCount: integer): TTime;
begin
  Result := FIniFile.ReadTime(StrSCORES, StrLEVEL + aPairsCount.ToString,
  -1);
end;


procedure TDMGameOfMem.ClearAllScores;
begin
  FIniFile.EraseSection(StrSCORES);
  FIniFile.UpdateFile;
end;


procedure TDMGameOfMem.SaveCurrLevel(aPairsCount: integer);
begin
  FIniFile.WriteInteger(StrSETTINGS, StrCURRLEVEL, aPairsCount);
  FIniFile.UpdateFile;
end;


function TDMGameOfMem.ReadCurrLevel: integer;
begin
  Result := FIniFile.ReadInteger(StrSETTINGS, StrCURRLEVEL, 4);
end;

end.
```

Changes to an INI file are kept in memory. In order to save them into the file, we need to call the UpdateFile method.

In the main form's `OnCreate` event, we are going to add code to read the last used difficulty level, and in the combobox `OnChange` event we are going to save the currently selected difficulty level:

```
procedure TFormMain.FormCreate(Sender: TObject);
begin
  CurrPairsCount := DMGameOfMem.ReadCurrLevel;
end;

procedure TFormMain.cmbbxLevelChange(Sender: TObject);
begin
  DMGameOfMem.SaveCurrLevel(CurrPairsCount);
end;
```

# The game's settings form

Our game is almost complete. We are storing the top scores for different levels, but there is no place to see them. This is the purpose of the game's *settings* form.

Drop a label component on the `FormSettings` toolbar and align it to `Client`. Change its **Text** property to **Top Scores**.

Drop the `TButton` component on the tool bar and align it to `Right`. Change its **Name** property to **btnClear** and its **Text** property to **Clear All**.

Drop `TComboBox` on the form. Align it to `Client`. Change its `Margins` properties to `8`, so there is a nice border around it. Right-click on the list box and select the **Add TListBoxItem** option to add the first item to the list box. Change its **StyleLookup** property to `listboxitemrightdetail`. Expand the `ItemData` property and enter into the **Text** property **4 Pairs**. The `Detail` property is where we are going to display the best time for a given difficulty level. Right-click on the list box item and select **Copy** from the **Edit** menu. Paste the list box item seven times into the list box and adjust the **Text** property of every item. Change their names so they correspond with the number of pairs: `lbi04`, `lbi06`, `lbi08`, and so on until `lbi18`.

List boxes are great for all kinds of static information. At design time, you can easily set them up. For dynamic information, coming from a database, for example, it is much better to use the `TListView` components.

Add the uDMGameOfMem unit to the uses clause of the **Settings** form. Implement the ReadTopScores private method in the form class to display all the top scores in the list box. Double-click on the OnShow event of the form and enter a call there to the ReadTopScores method. In the OnClick event of the button, we will call the method to clear all the scores:

```
uses
  uFormMain, uDMGameOfMem, uGameUtils;

procedure TFormSettings.FormShow(Sender: TObject);
begin
  ReadTopScores;
end;

procedure TFormSettings.btnClearClick(Sender: TObject);
begin
  DMGameOfMem.ClearAllScores;
  ReadTopScores;
end;

procedure TFormSettings.ReadTopScores;

procedure ShowScore(lbi: TListBoxItem; level: integer);
var t: TTime;
begin
  t := DMGameOfMem.ReadScore(level);
  if t > 0 then
    lbi.ItemData.Detail := GameTimeToStr(t)
  else
    lbi.ItemData.Detail := '';
end;

begin
  ShowScore(lbi04, 4);
  ShowScore(lbi06, 6);
  ShowScore(lbi08, 8);
  ShowScore(lbi10, 10);
  ShowScore(lbi12, 12);
  ShowScore(lbi14, 14);
  ShowScore(lbi16, 16);
  ShowScore(lbi18, 18);
end;

procedure TFormSettings.spdbtnBackClick(Sender: TObject);
begin
  FormMain.Show;
end;
```

Here is how the game looks on iPhone 6:

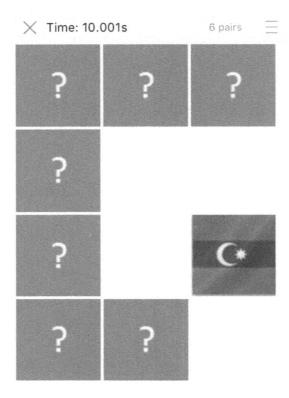

That's it! We have just implemented our first mobile game in Delphi. Congratulations!

# Summary

In this chapter, you learned the fundamentals of FireMonkey 2D programming. Starting from writing low-level code for drawing on canvas, we have quickly got to the fundamentals of rapid app development with reusable shapes, animations, effects, and timers. This is where Delphi shines and you are well on the path to becoming a developer superhero who writes less code to achieve better results.

In the next chapter, we are going to add an additional dimension to what we have seen so far. We will go into the realm of FireMonkey 3D.

# 5
# FireMonkey in 3D

3D programming is where the Delphi mobile development shines. With **FireMonkey**, we can create fully cross-platform GPU-powered graphical user interfaces using different 3D APIs on different platforms. In this chapter, we are going to add the third dimension to our FireMonkey projects.

This chapter will cover the following points:

- Using the TViewport component
- Working with camera and lights
- Using the TDummy component as a convenient non-visual 3D container
- Simple 3D shapes
- 3D controls and material components
- Using the TModel3D component for importing 3D data from third-party 3D graphics modeling tools

The objective of this chapter is to learn FireMonkey 3D programming and building of interactive cross-platform 3D GUIs.

## Cross-platform 3D rendering

Abstracting away the underlying 3D API from the programmer is the foundation of the FireMonkey graphics architecture. On top of this basis there is the second pillar, rapid application development with components. The FireMonkey framework comes with pre-built, reusable 3D components that make it easy to write complex 3D applications.

In FireMonkey it is very easy to create sophisticated, GPU-powered 3D user interfaces using reusable visual components that let you focus on your business application logic instead of spending time on writing low-level 3D API code.

There are different 3D APIs available on different operating systems supported by the FireMonkey library. Standard APIs for rendering 3D graphics on mobile targets is a cut down version of the OpenGL library called **OpenGL ES**. On desktop targets, FireMonkey supports DirectX on Windows and full OpenGL on Mac. All these APIs have different interfaces and abstractions, but the FireMonkey library provides one common denominator for writing cross-platform 3D apps using just one codebase. Have a look at the following figure:

The key abstraction in FireMonkey 3D graphics is the abstract `TContext3D` class that declares virtual drawing methods that are implemented differently on different targets. This is a similar architecture to FireMonkey 2D rendering, where the abstract `TCanvas` class has different implementations on all supported operating systems.

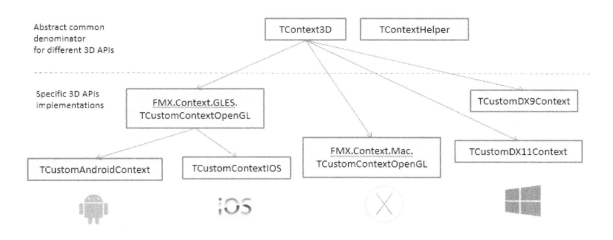

Writing 3D apps is considered a domain for professional developers, because it involves understanding low-level 3D mathematics and interacting with the **Graphical Processor Unit** (**GPU**). The component-based development of Delphi hides the underlying complexity of 3D coding and you can create highly interactive, visually rich 3D apps with very little to no coding at all.

FireMonkey provides a 3D material system that is based on GPU shader programs. You do not have to be an expert in writing DirectX HLSL or OpenGL shader code to create high-performance 3D graphics applications. In the FireMonkey framework, applying a different shading model is a matter of using a dedicated material component that can just be attached to a 3D object control that represents a specific geometry.

# Using Context3D

Similarly to FireMonkey 2D architecture, there are two possible approaches to 3D rendering. We can render in code or use reusable components. The first path is what is used by many other programming languages and development environments. The more complex and sophisticated our 3D visualization, the more complex our 3D rendering code becomes. Using **Rapid Application Development** (**RAD**) with components very quickly pays off as we typically do not need to write too much code to build a great user experience with interactive 3D worlds.

The main interface for calling into 3D APIs in a cross-platform way in FireMonkey is the TContext3D class. Let's build a simple project that is going to use the TContext3D class directly in code.

Create a new Delphi multi-device project and make sure to select **3D Application** as the application template.

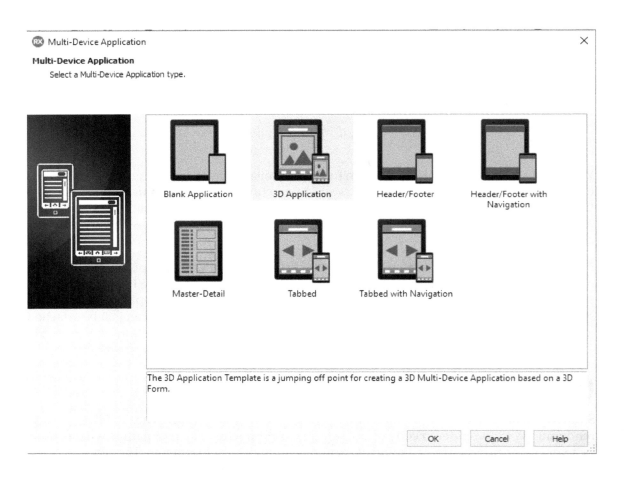

Save the main form unit as uFormCubeInCode and the whole project as CubeInCode. Change the Name property of the form to FormCubeInCode. Save all.

When we look into the source of the form, we will see that this time, the main form class is derived from TForm3D and not TForm. One of the best things about Delphi is that we can quickly inspect the source code of classes and types that come with it. Just right-click on the **TForm3D** identifier and select **Find Declaration**. You will jump to the FMX.Forms3D unit where this class is defined. The ancestor of the 3D form class is TCustomForm3D, which implements the IViewport3D interface. This interface, among other members, has a Context: TContext3D property that we can use to access the underlying 3D context of the form in code. An even more straightforward way to access the 3D context is to use the OnRender event of the TForm3D class that passes the context as one of its arguments.

Double-click on the OnRender event of the form. Typically, we enclose all rendering code with calls to BeginScene and EndScene. Enter the following code into the event handler:

```
procedure TFormCubeInCode.Form3DRender(Sender: TObject; Context:
TContext3D);
begin
  Context.BeginScene;
  try
    // access context 3D methods and properties here
  finally
    Context.EndScene;
  end;
end;
```

Right-click on the Context3D parameter and select the option to find its declaration. This time, we will jump to FMX.Types3D where we can find the TContext3D class. It is defined as **abstract**, because it serves as the interface to the functionality that is implemented by different platform-specific classes inherited from it that override its abstract virtual methods. There are quite a lot of low-level functions here for drawing different geometries, dealing with states, shaders, materials, and more. It has to be like this, because 3D APIs, such as OpenGL and DirectX, are relatively complex. Luckily, if we do not need to, we do not have to write code on such a low level. If we want to do something beyond what FireMonkey 3D classes provide, we can do it here, but most of the time, we will be dealing with higher level abstractions for doing 3D.

Just after the TContext3D class declaration in the source code, there is a helper class for it that offers some convenience methods for common drawing operations:

```
TContextHelper = class helper for TContext3D
public
  procedure FillCube(const Center, Size: TPoint3D; const Opacity: Single;
    const Color: TAlphaColor);
  procedure DrawLine(const StartPoint, EndPoint: TPoint3D;
    const Opacity: Single; const Color: TAlphaColor);
  procedure DrawRect(const TopLeft, BottomRight: TPoint3D;
    const Opacity: Single; const Color: TAlphaColor);
  procedure DrawCube(const Center, Size: TPoint3D; const Opacity: Single;
    const Color: TAlphaColor);
  procedure FillPolygon(const Center, Size: TPoint3D; const Rect: TRectF;
    const Points: TPolygon;
    const Material: TMaterial; const Opacity: Single;
      Front: Boolean = True; Back: Boolean = True;
      Left: Boolean = True);
end;
```

We can use them to quickly render typical geometries such as lines, rectangles, polygons, or cubes in 3D.

For starters, let's draw a cube. Enter this line of code between the BeginScene and EndScene calls in the OnRender event of the form:

```
Context.DrawCube(Point3D(0,0,0), Point3D(10,10,10), 1,
TAlphaColorRec.Black);
```

If we run the application now, there will be just empty white space. This is because the OnRender event has not been called. We need a mechanism to call it. Drop the TTimer component and, in its OnTimer event, call the Invalidate method of the form to force its re-rendering. You will see the following code:

```
procedure TFormCubeInCode.Timer1Timer(Sender: TObject);
begin
  self.Invalidate;
end;
```

If we keep the default timer's `Interval` value as `1000` milliseconds, the black cube should show up just exactly one second after the app starts:

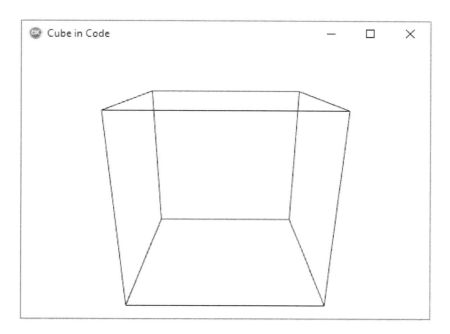

Now remove all code from the `OnRender` and `OnTimer` events and click on **Save**. The empty event handlers should disappear. Drop the `TStrokeCube` component on the form. Change its **Color** property to **Black** and its **Width**, **Height**, and **Depth** properties to `10`. If we run the app now, we should see exactly the same Wireframe of a cube, but this time with no code, but with a component that encapsulates the call to the `DrawCube` method of the 3D context. If we jump to the declaration of the `TStrokeCube` class, we could find its `Render` method implemented almost identically to our code. See the following code snippet:

```
procedure TStrokeCube.Render;
begin
  Context.DrawCube(TPoint3D.Zero,
    TPoint3D.Create(Width, Height, Depth), AbsoluteOpacity, FColor);
end;
```

Using components for 3D rendering makes you a more productive programmer.

# Custom Wireframe component

The source code of FireMonkey is very helpful in understanding how the library works, but we can also use it as a template to build our own custom components. Rendering a cube is not a lot of code but using a similar approach, we could create a custom wireframe component that is similar to TStrokeCube. We can just implement the Render method differently and paint arbitrary lines, the coordinates of which are stored internally within our component.

Create a new Delphi multi-device application and select **3D Application** as the application type. Save the main form unit as uFormWireframe and the whole project as WireframeTest. Rename the form as FormWireframe. Save all.

Add a new unit to the project and save it as uWireframe. Here we are going to implement a custom component called TWireframe that, similarly to TStrokeCube, inherits from the TControl3D class and renders an arbitrary wireframe by drawing lines.

Drawing a wireframe is based on just two data structures. We need a list of vertices that are locations in 3D space and a list of edges, which represents lines to be drawn. Each edge contains two indices in the list of vertices for the starting and ending point of a line. Let's define these two data structures in the uWireframe unit. Have a look at the following code snippet:

```
unit uWireframe;

interface

uses
  System.Math.Vectors, // TPoint3D
  System.Generics.Collections; // TList<T>

type
  TPoints3D = class(TList<TPoint3D>);

  TEdge = record
    A, B: integer;
  end;

  TEdges = class(TList<TEdge>)
    procedure AddEdge(pStart, pEnd: integer);
  end;

implementation

{ TEdges }
```

```
procedure TEdges.AddEdge(pStart, pEnd: integer);
var edge: TEdge;
begin
  edge.A := pStart;
  edge.B := pEnd;
  self.Add(edge);
end;

end.
```

The TEdges list class has a convenience method, AddEdge, for simplifying code that adds a new edge to it.

The rest of the code is similarly easy. We just declare a new TWireframe class derived from TControl3D. It will have the Points3D: TPoints3D and Edges: TEdges read-only public properties for accessing the wireframe. In the class constructor, we need to instantiate these lists and free them in the destructor. The actual drawing happens in the overridden virtual Render method. In the for...in...do loop, we draw all lines defined in the Edges list using a color defined by the DrawColor property.

Here is the actual source code that does this:

```
uses
  // ...
  FMX.Controls3D, // TControl3D
  System.UITypes, // TAlphaColor
  System.Classes, // TComponent
  FMX.Types3D; // TContext3D

type
// ...
  TWireframe = class(TControl3D)
  private
    FDrawColor: TAlphaColor;
    FEdges: TEdges;
    FPoints3D: TPoints3D;
    FDisplayed: boolean;
  public
    constructor Create(AOwner: TComponent); override;
    destructor Destroy; override;
    procedure Render; override;
    property DrawColor: TAlphaColor read FDrawColor write FDrawColor;
    property Points3D: TPoints3D read FPoints3D;
    property Edges: TEdges read FEdges;
    property Displayed: boolean read FDisplayed write FDisplayed;
  end;
```

```
implementation

constructor TWireframe.Create(AOwner: TComponent);
begin
  inherited Create(AOwner);
  FPoints3D := TPoints3D.Create;
  FEdges := TEdges.Create;
  FDrawColor := TAlphaColorRec.Red;
end;

destructor TWireframe.Destroy;
begin
  FEdges.Free;
  FPoints3D.Free;
  inherited;
end;

procedure TWireframe.Render;
var edge: TEdge;
begin
  if Displayed then
    for edge in Edges do
      Context.DrawLine(Points3D[edge.A], Points3D[edge.B], 1, DrawColor);
end;
```

Now we need to test if this class is actually working. Instead of creating a new package, installing this component in the IDE, and so on, we can quickly test the wireframe class by declaring it in the `FormWireframe` as a field. Now we need the code to create and free the wireframe instance in the form's `OnCreate` and `OnDestroy` events. In order to properly display this control, we need to make a call to assign its `Parent` property to the form itself:

```
unit uFormWireframe;

interface

uses
  System.SysUtils, System.Types, System.UITypes, System.Classes,
System.Variants,
  FMX.Types, FMX.Controls, FMX.Forms3D, FMX.Types3D, FMX.Forms,
FMX.Graphics,
  FMX.Dialogs, uWireframe, System.Math.Vectors;

type
  TFormWireframe = class(TForm3D)
    procedure Form3DCreate(Sender: TObject);
    procedure Form3DDestroy(Sender: TObject);
  private
```

```pascal
    FWireframe: TWireframe;
    procedure CreatePyramid;
  public
    { Public declarations }
  end;

var
  FormWireframe: TFormWireframe;

implementation

{$R *.fmx}

procedure TFormWireframe.Form3DCreate(Sender: TObject);
begin
  FWireframe := TWireframe.Create(self);
  FWireframe.Parent := self;
  FWireframe.RotationAngle.Point := Point3D(75, 10, 15);

  CreatePyramid;
end;

procedure TFormWireframe.Form3DDestroy(Sender: TObject);
begin
  FWireframe.Free;
end;

procedure TFormWireframe.CreatePyramid;
begin
  with FWireframe do
  begin
    Points3D.Add(Point3D(-2,-2,0)); // 0
    Points3D.Add(Point3D(2,-2,0));  // 1
    Points3D.Add(Point3D(-2,2,0));  // 2
    Points3D.Add(Point3D(2,2,0));   // 3
    Points3D.Add(Point3D(0,0,6));   // 4

    Edges.AddEdge(0,1);
    Edges.AddEdge(1,3);
    Edges.AddEdge(3,2);
    Edges.AddEdge(2,0);
    Edges.AddEdge(0,4);
    Edges.AddEdge(1,4);
    Edges.AddEdge(2,4);
    Edges.AddEdge(3,4);
```

```
    end;
  end;

  end.
```

We have also written some code to build a simple pyramid wireframe, so there is something to display on the form:

There is also a call in the `OnCreate` event, after the wireframe is created, to slightly rotate it so it looks better.

# Objects 3D

There are different 3D objects that we can use in our Delphi FireMonkey apps. From really simple ones, such as `TStrokeCube` or `TGrid3D`, that just render a few lines in 3D space, to more complex components that maintain their own vertex and index buffers for drawing complex geometries with triangles. This is a typical approach for rendering arbitrary geometries in 3D apps, for example mobile games, and it requires quite a lot of coding.

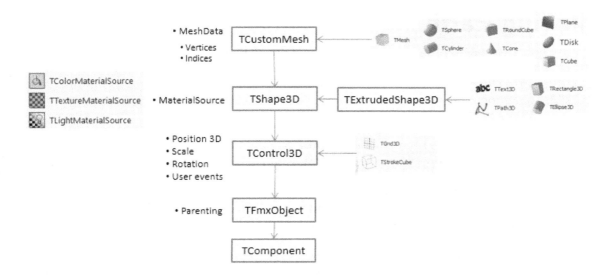

At the lowest level, all 3D objects inherit from the TControl3D class that introduces location and transformations in 3D space. It also adds interactivity to all 3D controls by implementing different mouse events that are translated to touch events on mobile targets. These user events have different parameters that give to application code the information about where such an event happened in 3D space, which can be very useful.

One level up in the 3D objects hierarchy, the TShape3D class is defined that introduces support for material components. All classes derived from 3D shapes have the MaterialSource property that can be used to connect any component that inherits from the TMaterialSource class. Material components implement different shading models used for rendering. Classes such as TText3D, TPath3D, TEllipse3D, or TRectangle3D inherit from TShape3D and can work with materials.

At the highest level of the hierarchy, there are 3D objects derived from the TCustomMesh class that introduces the MeshData property that is used for holding vertices and indices information for rendering with DrawTriangles calls using the underlying 3D context.

# Moving Earth

We are going to start with something simple and create an interactive 3D visualization of the rotating Earth in deep space. To make it interactive, we will implement a 3D touch event to move Earth closer and further from the viewer. This first example will be as minimal as possible to demonstrate how quickly you can build a 3D app with FireMonkey.

Create a new Delphi multi-device project and select **3D Application** as the application type. Save the form unit as uFormEarth and the project as *MovingEarth*. Change the Name property of the form to FormEarth and its **Color** to Black.

The next step is to add a TDummy component to the form. This component acts as a container for other 3D components and is very useful for applying common transformations to a group of 3D objects. It does not have any visual representation at runtime. In the FireMonkey 2D world, the TLayout component plays a similar role. In the world of FireMonkey 3D, the concept of parenting is also very important. Most FireMonkey components can own other components, and owned components inherit different properties from their owners including geometrical transformation, such as moving, scaling, and rotations. It is a common pattern to use one TDummy component as a parent for all other visual and non-visual 3D objects. In this way, we have one central point for manipulating the 3D scene as a whole, changing its position, rotation, and so on.

Drop the TDummy component on the form. Change its Name property to DummyScene. Drop the TSphere component on the form and make sure that it belongs to the root dummy control. Rename the sphere to SphereEarth. Let's make Earth bigger. Select the root dummy component in the **Object Inspector**. Expand its Scale property and change all three **X**, **Y**, and **Z** values to 5. Notice that the contained sphere changed its size. In this way we control the scale, rotation, and position of all 3D objects that make up the scene.

Drop TTextureMaterialSource components on the form and connect it with the sphere using the SphereEarth.MaterialSource property. Click on the ellipsis button next to the Texture property and click on **Edit**.

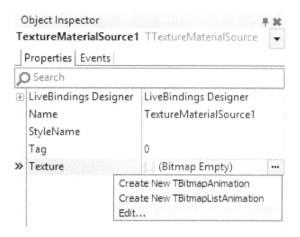

This will show a dialog where we can load a bitmap to be used as texture. There are some free textures of Earth available for download on the internet. I have downloaded one from the `http://visibleearth.nasa.gov/` website and saved it locally as `Earth.jpg`.

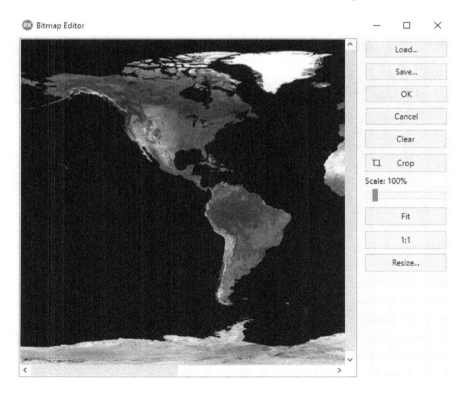

Click on the **Load** button. Select the texture image and click on **OK**. You should now see the sphere object with a nice Earth texture applied.

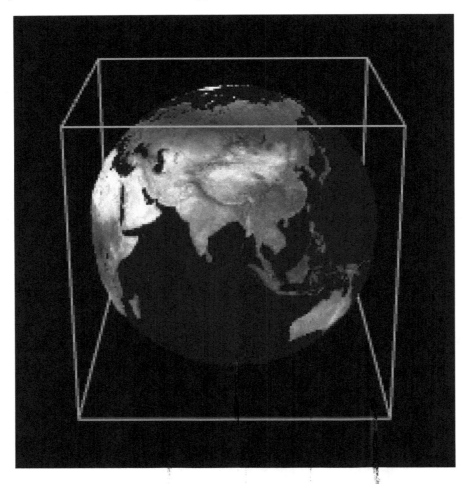

It already looks nice, but let's add some movement and interactivity to this visualization.

Drop the `TFloatAnimation` component on the form. Under **Structure** view, drag it onto the **SphereEarth** component.

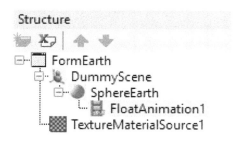

Now expand its `PropertyName` property and you will see all the float properties that belong to the `TSphere` class. Select the `RotationAngle.Y` property, because we want Earth to rotate around its vertical axis.

Make sure that the float animation is selected in the Object Inspector and change some of its properties. Set **Enabled** and **Loop** to **True**. Change **Duration** to 1 second and **StopValue** to -360. Save all and run the application. We have a spinning Earth and, so far, we have not written a single line of code.

The last step will be adding some basic interactivity to our app. When the end user touches Earth on the screen, it will move either closer or further in space. By default, when we drop 3D objects onto the 3D view, their position is in the beginning of the coordinate system. In FireMonkey, the X axis increases to the right side of the screen, the Y axis increases down the screen, and Z goes into the screen. We will be changing the `Position.Z` property in code. Change the `Position.Z` property of the sphere to -1 and note that Earth moved closer. If we would change it to a positive value, it would go further into the screen.

Double-click on the sphere's `OnClick` event. This will be translated to a touch event on a mobile target. In order to achieve a better visual effect, we will not be changing the Z position immediately, but with an animation. Enter the following code into the `OnClick` event handler:

```
procedure TFormEarth.SphereEarthClick(Sender: TObject);
begin
  if SphereEarth.Position.Z < 0 then
    TAnimator.AnimateFloat(SphereEarth, 'Position.Z', 1, 0.2)
  else
    TAnimator.AnimateFloat(SphereEarth, 'Position.Z', -1, 0.2);
end;
```

That's another way of using animations in FireMonkey. We can use either animation components or we can use different `Animate` class methods of the `TAnimator` class and specify the object and its property we want to animate, the target value, and the duration of the animation. This class is declared in the `FMX.Ani` unit, but it was already automatically added to the *uses* clause of the form, because we added the `TFloatAnimation` component earlier.

Run the application. If you touch the spinning Earth, it will move either further away or closer to you. We can now deploy this app to an iOS device and an Android device to verify that it works as expected on these targets.

This is the power of cross-platform FireMonkey 3D development. We have quickly created an interactive 3D app with a custom texture with almost no coding that can be natively compiled for all supported mobile and desktop platforms.

# Building an interactive 3D scene

In the first example, we wanted to keep things simple. This time, we are going to build an interactive visualization of three 3D arrows marking the beginning and orientation of the 3D coordinate system used in FireMonkey. For this we will just use some cylinder and cone 3D objects, color materials, lights, and an explicit `TCamera` component. We will also see how to implement looking at the scene from different points of view and distances.

Create a new Delphi multi-device project. This time, make sure to select **Blank Application** template and not **3D Application**. Save the form unit as *uFormArrows3D* and the project as *Arrows3D*. Change the `Name` property of the form to `FormArrows3D`.

Now, drop on the form, `TViewport3D` component and align it to `Client`. This component can be found in the special **Viewports** category on the **Tool Palette**.

This represents another way of building 3D visualizations. We can use either a 3D form that out-of-the-box implements the `TViewport3D` interface or we can use the `TViewport3D` component placed on a traditional 2D form. This second approach is more common and gives more possibilities. Specifically, the `TForm3D` class does not support multi-touch and gesture events that are critical for delivering proper user experience on mobile targets.

This time, we are going to use an explicit `TCamera` component that will allow us to view the scene from different locations. Drop the `TDummy` component on the form and change its `Name` to DummyCamera. Drop the `TCamera` component on the form. Change its `Name` property to CameraZ. In the Structure view, drag it onto the `DummyCamera`. By default, a camera component has position `0,0,-5` and looks along the Z axis. Change the camera's `Position.Z` property to `-10` to move it closer to the edge of the form. Now by changing the `RotationAngle` of the dummy component that the camera belongs to, we will be changing the location of the camera in 3D space and it will be constantly looking at the beginning of the coordinate system where we are going to place our scene. By changing the Z position of the camera we will be able to look at the scene from a closer or further distance, effectively making the visualization appear smaller or bigger. It is kind of a selfie stick that our camera is attached to. When the user is going to move their finger horizontally across the screen, we will be changing the `DummyCamera` rotation angle along the Y axis. Moving the touch point vertically will be changing the rotation along X axis. The interactive zoom gesture will be increasing and decreasing the `Position.Z` property of the camera.

Drop the `TLight` component on the form and drag it onto the camera in the Structure view. It is a common practice to put at least one light component onto the camera, so it is always in the same position as the camera. There are three different light types that can be used. We will keep the default `LightType` property to `Directional`. The other two possible values are **Point** and **Spot**.

In general, there could be more then one camera component. The one that is used for rendering needs to be connected to the `Camera` property of the viewport or a 3D form. There is also the built-in design camera that we have used so far. Set the `UsingDesignCamera` property of the viewport to `False` and change its `Camera` property, so it is pointing to our explicit camera component.

Now we are going to build the scene. Drop the `TDummy` component on the form and change its name to `DummyScene`. Let's add three colored arrows representing three space dimensions. Drop the `TCylinder` component on the form. Make sure that it belongs to the dummy scene component. Change its `Name` to `CylX`. We need to make it a bit longer and thinner and correctly orientated in space. Change its `Height` property to `4` and its `Width` and `Depth` values to `0.1`. Change its `RotationAngle.Z` property to `270`, so it is located along the X axis. Now drop, the `TCone` component on the form and make sure it belongs to the `CylX` component. Change its `Name` to `ConeX`. Change its `Height` property to `0.5` and its `Width` and `Depth` properties to `0.2`. Set the `Position.Y` property to `2` and `RotationAngle.X` to `180`. Now we have a really nice arrow! Make sure that the `CylX` component is selected on the form and copy and paste it into the `DummyScene` component. Rename the cylinder as `CylY` and the cone as `ConeY`. Change the `RotationAngle.X` of the new cylinder to `180` and its Z part to `0`. We have the second arrow. Paste the cylinder with the cone one more time into the dummy scene component. Rename both new components as `CylZ` and `ConeZ` and change the cylinder `RotationAngle.X` to `90`.

We have the geometry right, but all components are red. We need to attach some materials to the 3D objects. Every arrow will have a different color. Drop three `TLightMaterialSource` components on the form. Change their names to `MaterialSourceX`, `MaterialSourceY`, and `MaterialSourceZ`. Change the `DiffuseColor` property of the first one to **Red**, the second one to **Green**, and the third one to **Blue**. Now, set the `MaterialSource` properties of cylinders and cones to their respective materials. Immediately we should see that our arrows now have different colors. That looks much better!

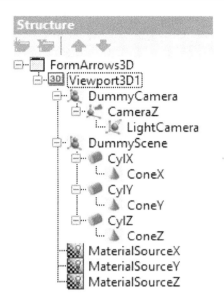

The last step is to add code to move the camera. We are going to use `OnMouseDown` and `OnMouseMove` events to achieve the illusion of rotation. In fact, the scene will remain in the same position, but we will be changing the position of the camera in 3D space.

Double-click on the `OnMouseDown` and `OnMouseMove` events of the viewport component. Add the `FDown: TPointF` private field to the form class. Here, we are going to remember the location of the last touch point on the screen.

Enter the following code into the event handlers:

```
const ROTATION_STEP = 0.3;

procedure TFormArrows3D.Viewport3D1MouseDown(Sender: TObject;
  Button: TMouseButton; Shift: TShiftState; X, Y: Single);
begin
  FDown := PointF(X, Y);
end;

procedure TFormArrows3D.Viewport3D1MouseMove(Sender: TObject;
  Shift: TShiftState; X, Y: Single);
begin
  if (ssLeft in Shift) then
  begin
    DummyCamera.RotationAngle.X := DummyCamera.RotationAngle.X - ((Y -
```

```
        FDown.Y) * ROTATION_STEP);
      DummyCamera.RotationAngle.Y := DummyCamera.RotationAngle.Y + ((X -
      FDown.X) * ROTATION_STEP);
      FDown := PointF(X, Y);
    end;
  end;
```

Save all and run the application. The orientation of the arrows changes when we use the mouse on Windows or touch on a mobile target.

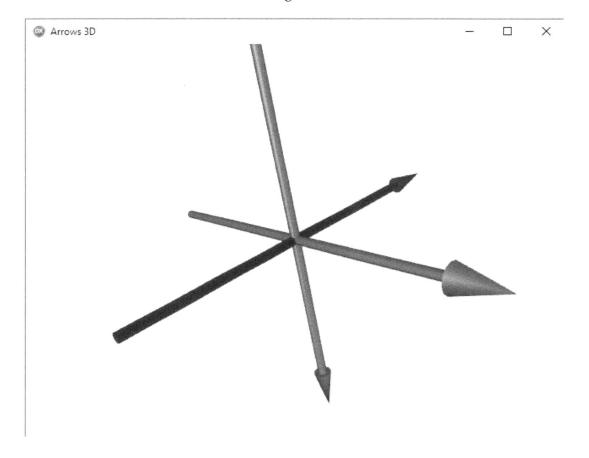

The very last thing is to implement zooming. It works differently on desktop and on mobile. On desktop we can use the `OnMouseWheel` event and on mobile, an interactive zoom gesture.

Let's centralize the actual zooming code in one method that we are going to call from different event handlers, depending on the platform:

```
const
  ZOOM_STEP = 2;
  CAMERA_MAX_Z = -2;
  CAMERA_MIN_Z = -102;

procedure TFormSimpleCamera.DoZoom(aIn: boolean);
var newZ: single;
begin
  if aIn then
    newZ := CameraZ.Position.Z + ZOOM_STEP
  else
    newZ := CameraZ.Position.Z - ZOOM_STEP;

  if (newZ < CAMERA_MAX_Z) and (newZ > CAMERA_MIN_Z) then
    CameraZ.Position.Z := newZ;
end;
```

There are `CAMERA_MIN_Z` and `CAMERA_MAX_Z` declared, because we do not want the camera to move into the positive Z values and we want to avoid being able to move the camera too far away from the scene.

The implementation of the mouse wheel event is very straightforward. We either zoom in or out, depending on the wheel move direction:

```
procedure TFormArrows3D.Viewport3D1MouseWheel(Sender: TObject;
  Shift: TShiftState; WheelDelta: Integer; var Handled: Boolean);
begin
  DoZoom(WheelDelta > 0);
end;
```

On mobile platforms, there is no mouse and no wheel. The most natural way of handling zoom is through an interactive gesture event. As one of the event parameters, we will get the distance between the two touch points. If this distance decreases, we want to zoom in, otherwise we will zoom out. That's why we will need a new private field declared in the form class `FLastDistance: integer` where we are going to store the last distance to compare the current one and decide if it is a zoom in or out.

Expand the `Touch` property of the form in the Object Inspector and check the `Zoom` event that we want to handle in our code.

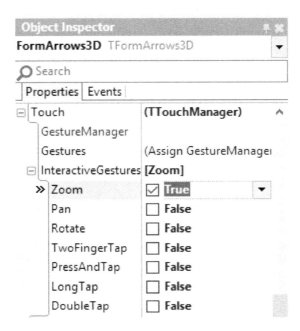

Double-click on the **OnGesture** event of the form and enter there the following code:

```
procedure TFormArrows3D.FormGesture(Sender: TObject;
  const EventInfo: TGestureEventInfo; var Handled: Boolean);
var delta: integer;
begin
  if EventInfo.GestureID = igiZoom then
  begin
    if (not (TInteractiveGestureFlag.gfBegin in EventInfo.Flags))
      and (not (TInteractiveGestureFlag.gfEnd in EventInfo.Flags)) then
    begin
      delta := EventInfo.Distance - FLastDistance;
      DoZoom(delta > 0);
    end;
    FLastDistance := EventInfo.Distance;
  end;
end;
```

Save all and run on both Windows and a mobile target to verify that rotations and zooming work as expected.

We have just built an interactive 3D visualization using the "camera on the selfie stick approach". This code is a good starting point for an interactive display of arbitrary geometries. You can remove all 3D objects from the `DummyScene` and replace them with any other geometries that you want to display in 3D.

# Using 3D models

Until now, we have been using different out-of-the-box 3D objects that come with built-in geometries. The FireMonkey library provides the `TModel3D` component that makes it possible to use geometries defined outside of Delphi, typically using a 3D modeling software and importing mesh data from one of the supported 3D file formats.

FireMonkey supports importing 3D models from OBJ, DAE, and ASE file formats. These are standard formats supported by many 3D modeling software packages.

If you have 3D modeling artistic skills then you can create your own models. Many programmers don't, so they need already existing models for their 3D apps. There are many websites offering free and commercial 3D models. One of them is `www.turbosquid.com` where I found a nice royalty-free OBJ model of a medieval helmet (`https://www.turbosquid.com/3d-models/free-3ds-model-medieval-helmet/681191`).

That's what we want to import into a 3D Delphi app.

Instead of rebuilding the 3D visualization logic, copy the source code of the *Arrows3D* demo into a new `HelmetApp` folder. Open the project and rename it as *HelmetApp*. Save the main form as `uFormHelmet` and change the form's `Name` property to `FormHelmet`. Delete all material components from the form and also cylinders and cones from the `DummyScene` component. We have a clean slate. Just the 3D visualisation code and an empty scene.

Drop the `TModel3D` component on the form and make sure that it is parented under the `DummyScene` in the **Structure** view. In the Object Inspector, click on the ellipsis button next to the `MeshCollection` property to display the Mesh Collection Editor. Click on the **Load** button and select the `Helmet.obj` downloaded file. Click on **OK**. The helmet should show up inside the scene. Change all the X, Y, and Z sub-properties of the `DummyScene.Scale` property to make the helmet bigger. Save all and run the app. Change `OrientationAngle.X` to `180`, so the helmet is initially not upside down.

We can see the geometry, rotate and zoom it, but it is all red now, without any materials applied.

Drop the `TLightMaterialSource` component on the form and change its `Diffuse` color to `Slategray`. Unfortunately, the `TModel3D` component does not have a `MaterialSource` property that we could use to connect the material component. We need to do it in code. Double-click on the `OnCreate` event of the form and enter the code that will assign our new light material to every mesh in the model's mesh collection:

```
  procedure TFormHelmet.FormCreate(Sender: TObject);
var mesh: TMesh;
begin
  for mesh in Model3D1.MeshCollection do
    mesh.MaterialSource := LightMaterialSource1;
end;
```

If we run the app now, we should see that it looks much better now with the helmet properly shaded.

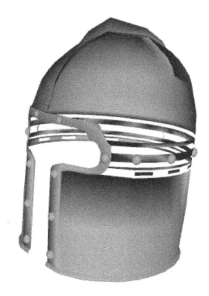

Different 3D modeling software packages output different types of information into exported files. The TModel3D component imports just the basic geometry information necessary to build its internal vertex and index buffers.

The support for importing different file formats is implemented in different FMX.*.Importer units that you might need to include manually in the project's uses clause if you want to load the model from a file in code and not at design time like we did.

# Starfield simulation

In this section, we will be looking into building efficient 3D visualizations that use multiple geometries. We will create a starfield simulation using TSphere and TObjectProxy components for sharing mesh data.

If we look into the source code of TSphere, TCone, TCylinder and other components in the FMX.Objects3D unit, we will see that their vertices and indices are hardcoded. If we want to build a 3D scene with many different objects, every object will occupy quite a lot of space in memory.

FireMonkey comes with a special TProxyObject 3D object. It does not hold its geometry, but instead has the SourceObject property that can be used to connect to any other 3D object which is used for rendering. In this way, we have just one copy of geometry data in memory and multiple objects rendered.

To illustrate this concept, let's build a starfield simulation with many sphere objects moving in space. That's similar to a classic Windows screensaver. We will just use one instance of a TSphere component and all other spheres will be rendered with proxy objects.

Create a new Delphi multi-device application and select **Blank Application** from the application templates gallery. Save the form's unit as uFormStars and project as *Starfield*. Change the Name property of the main form to FormStars. Save all.

Drop the TViewport3D component on the form. Align it to Client and change its color to Black. This is the deep space. Drop the TCamera component on the viewport and TLight component on the camera. Connect the Camera property of the viewport to point to Camera1 and set its UsingDesignCamera property to False. Drop the TDummy component on the viewport and change its Name to DummyScene. Now drop TSphere component on the dummy scene component. Change its Name to SphereStar. It will serve as the main holder of the sphere geometry. Change its Position.Z property to -10, so it is behind the camera. Drop the TLightMaterialSource component on the form and set the sphere's MaterialSource property to point to the material component. We should see the sphere turning from red to nice shades of gray.

This time, instead of moving the camera, we will be moving the Z position of all stars using a timer component. Drop one TProxyObject component on the form and set its SourceObject property to point to SphereStar. You should see the second sphere on the form. You can now safely delete the TProxyObject component from the form. We will be creating proxy spheres in code. First, let's implement a method for getting a random location within a cube defined by MAX_X, MAX_Y, and MAX_Z constants:

```
function TFormStars.RandomLocation: TPoint3D;
const
  MAX_X = 50;
  MAX_Y = 50;
  MAX_Z = 200;
begin
  Result.X := -MAX_X + random * 2 * MAX_X;
  Result.Y := -MAX_Y + random * 2 * MAX_Y;
  Result.Z := random * MAX_Z;
end;
```

Double-click on the form's **OnCreate** event in the Object Inspector and enter there the following code that will create a hundred of spheres in random locations in front of the camera:

```
procedure TFormStars.FormCreate(Sender: TObject);
const STARS_COUNT = 100;
var i: integer; star: TProxyObject;
begin
  Randomize;
  for i := 0 to STARS_COUNT-1 do
  begin
    star := TProxyObject.Create(DummyScene);
    star.SourceObject := SphereStar;
    star.Parent := DummyScene;
    star.Position.Point := RandomLocation;
  end;
end;
```

Save all and run the application. You should see a starfield. Now, we need to add movement. Drop the TTimer component on the form. Set its Interval property to 50 milliseconds. In the OnTimer event, we will be decreasing the Z position of 3D objects contained within the DummyScene component. If the value gets smaller then 0, then the object is moved again to a random place within a virtual cube:

```
procedure TFormStars.Timer1Timer(Sender: TObject);
const DELTA_Z = 2;
var i: integer; ctrl: TControl3D; obj: TFmxObject;
  begin
```

```
for i := 0 to DummyScene.ChildrenCount-1 do

  begin

    obj := DummyScene.Children[i];
if obj is TControl3D then

  begin

    ctrl := TControl3D(obj);
    ctrl.Position.Z := ctrl.Position.Z - DELTA_Z;

if ctrl.Position.Z < 0 then
      ctrl.Position.Point := RandomLocation;
end;
end;
end;
```

Save all and run the application.

You should see the illusion of moving through the starfield in space!

# Mixing 3D and 2D

In FireMonkey, you can mix 2D with 3D. In a 3D form we can use 2-dimensional user interface controls, or we can embed the special `TViewport3D` component in a standard FireMonkey 2D form to do some 3D rendering.

In this example, we are going to add some special visual effects by building a 2D user interface in 3D space. This will allow the user to interact with the app in a traditional way, but we could do some extra things like rotating or moving the whole user interface in 3D space for a surprising user experience.

Create a new multi-device Delphi project and select **Blank Application** as the application type. Save the main form's unit as `uFormTwistMe` and the whole app as `TwistMe`. Change the `Name` property of the form to `FormTwistMe`. Drop the `TViewport3D` component on the form and align it to **Client**.

On the Tool Palette, we can find the **3D Layers** category with different 3D controls for using normal 2D controls. In this demo we will use the `TLayer3D` component to pretend that the user interface is 2D, but at any moment in time we can do something in 3D to achieve an interesting user experience. Have a look at the image below:

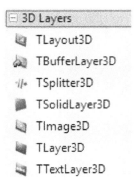

Drop the `TLayer3D` component on the viewport. Change its `Projection` property from `Camera` to `Screen` and its `Align` property to `Client`. Drop the `TButton` component on the layer and change its `Text` property to `Click me to twist!`. When the user touches the button, the whole layer will be animated in 3D space.

Add the `FMX.Ani` unit to the *uses* clause of the form, double-click on the button, and enter the following code inside the **OnClick** event handler that will animate the `RotationAngle.X` property of the `Layer3D1` component:

```
procedure TFormTwistMe.Button1Click(Sender: TObject);
begin
   TAnimator.AnimateFloat(Layer3D1, 'RotationAngle.X', 360, 1);
end;
```

When the user touches the button, the whole form makes a full rotation around the X axis.

The result can be seen in the screenshot:

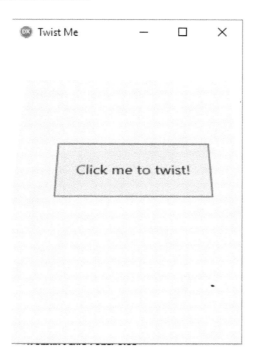

This is a super simple example that just shows the possibilities of using 3D in 2D user interfaces for making an interesting visual effect.

# Summary

In this chapter, we have explored the world of FireMonkey 3D programming.

With components, the FireMonkey parenting architecture, and cross-platform rendering it is possible to build stunning 3D interactive visualizations with little or no code that can be natively compiled for all major mobile and desktop platforms. That's a unique capability in the market today!

In the next chapter, we are going to see one of the most important aspects of FireMonkey architecture: styling!

# 6
# Building User Interfaces with Style

If you ever need to choose the single most important concept to understand in Delphi cross-platform programming that would probably be the concept of styles. Styling is the cornerstone of the cross-platform FireMonkey architecture. Styles are used at different levels. There are platform-specific, built-in styles that you use when you create a multi-device project and switch between styles in the form designer. FireMonkey controls on a form have a `StyleLookup` property, which can use a specific style for a given component. You can also apply a custom style using the `TStylebook` component. Finally, with the built-in style editor you can visually customize a given style item in the stylebook as easily as you would customize a component on the form. The goal of this chapter is to give you a solid understanding of FireMonkey styles to build stunning graphical user interfaces.

This chapter will cover the following points:

- Using built-in styles and style lookups
- Using custom styles with the stylebook component
- Customizing styles with Style Editor
- Using Frames
- Using inherited views for specific form factors
- Previewing forms on devices

The objective of this chapter is to understand how to create great looking user interfaces with custom styling.

# Working with built-in styles

The look and feel of every FireMonkey control depends on a style. There is only one codebase of your app, but when you compile it for a given platform, there is a different style used to render any control. In this way the *magic* is possible. The same app running on iOS will look like a regular iOS app, and when compiled for Android, it will look like an Android app. You can also compile the project for desktop targets and then an appropriate Windows or Mac style will be used.

Delphi comes with built-in styles. When you create a new multi-device application, during the design-time, you can preview how a given form will look with a different style applied.

Let's give it a try. Create a new multi-device blank application. Save the main form unit as `uFormStylesTest` and the whole project as `StylesTest`. Above the form designer area there is a **Style** combo-box where you can change the style that is used to preview the form you are working with. See the following screenshot:

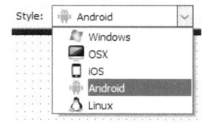

Style selection combo-box in FireMonkey Form Designer

The selection of a style in the **Style** combo applies different styles to the form we are working with, so we can see how a given form will look when it is compiled for the selected platform. Drop a `TToolbar` component on the form and then a `TSpeedButton` on the toolbar. Align the speed button to `Left` and make it slightly wider, so the whole caption is visible.

When we change the style in the **Style** combo from **Android** to **iOS**, we can see that the look-and-feel of the speed button changes accordingly to match selected platform design guidelines.

Here is how the speed button looks with the iOS style selected:

TSpeedButton control with iOS style applied

Here is the same speed button, but with the Android style chosen:

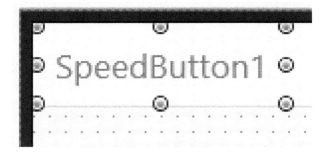

TSpeedButton control with Android style applied

Within a style there could be more than one definition of how a given control could look. FireMonkey controls have a `StyleLookup` property that we can use to apply a different style definition. Click on the drop-down button next to the `StyleLookup` property in the Object Inspector to see different styles that can be applied to a `TSpeedButton` control. Depending on the selected platform the choices can be different.

Here are the choices for Android styles for the TSpeedButton control:

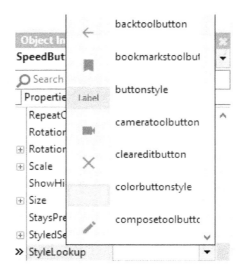

TSpeedButton built-in styles for Android

If the selected style in the **Form Designer** is **iOS,** then the choices are different:

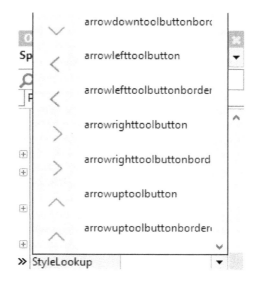

TSpeedButton built-in styles for iOS

Select `drawertoolbutton` from the list of available choices for the `StyleLookup` property. Notice that the speedbutton size changed and it is now a square. It looks like a proper **menu** button that you'll recognize from many mobile apps! If we now switch between styles in the **Style** combo, we can see how our app would look like on an Android target:

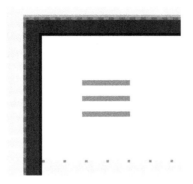

TSpeedButton with the drawertoolbutton style on Android

Here is the same `drawertoolbutton` style applied to a `TSpeedButton`, but on iOS:

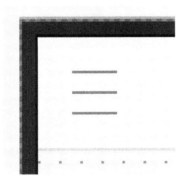

TSpeedButton with the drawertoolbutton style on iOS

Obviously everything here also applies to desktop platforms, but we are focusing in this book on mobile development, which is why only iOS and Android styles are demonstrated.

Let's add some more controls to the form to play with. Drop a TLabel component on the toolbar, align it to Client, and change its StyleLookup property to toollabel. Add the TTabControl component to the form and align it to Client. Right-click on the tab control and click three times on the **Add TTabItem** option from the context menu to add three tabs to the form. **Tab Control** is one of the most useful user interface elements and something that end users find very intuitive to use. It also illustrates differences in how styles are handled across different platforms. On iOS tabs are located at the bottom of the screen and on Android on top. This is because of the different design guidelines on different platforms. FireMonkey handles these differences in an elegant way. If you really want to have the tabs at the bottom or at the top regardless of the platform, you can change the **TabPosition** property. By default, it is set to PlatformDefault, but you can make it Top or Bottom. You can also choose not to display tabs at all and change the currently visible tab in code, which in many scenarios can be useful.

If we expand the **TabPosition** property, we see **PlatformDefault** listed in the combobox:

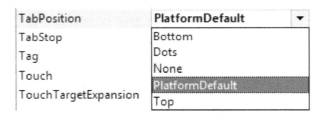

TabPosition property choices for TTabControl

It is important to be aware of the differences in the look-and-feel of a given control on different platforms, for example, the styling for individual tab items. On iOS there are many different style lookup choices and on Android there are hardly any. Make sure that **iOS** is the currently selected style in the **Form Designer** and change **StyleLookup** properties of individual tabs to styles that you like, for example to tabitemfeatured, tabitemhistory, and tabitemmore. Luckily if we select a style lookup for a tab on iOS, it would simply not have any effect on Android. The style engine would try to find the matching style specified in the **StyleLookup** property and if it fails, the built-in style will be used.

Drop a **TArcDial** control on the first tab. Change its **Height** and **Width** properties to **100**. Copy and paste this control twice, so there are three arc dial controls next to each other on the form. In order to have a sample of different controls, drop **TCheckBox**, **TSwitch**, and **TButton** components on the form as well.

Here is how our form looks with iOS style selected:

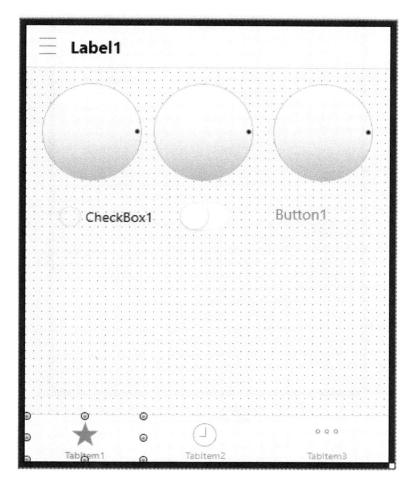

Test form with sample controls using iOS styles

Here is the same form, but previewed with Android styling:

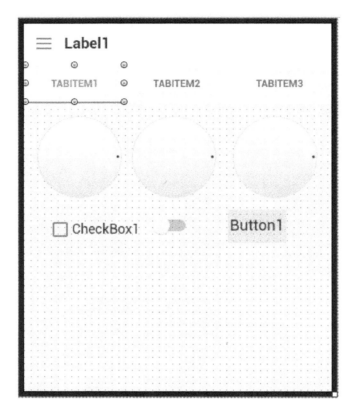

Test form with sample controls using Android styles

# Using custom styles

If we do not want to use a built-in style, we can always use a custom style. The Delphi installation comes with a number of custom styles. In Delphi 10.2 on Windows 10, FireMonkey custom styles are installed into the `C:\Users\Public\Documents\Embarcadero\Studio\19.0\Styles` directory. FireMonkey styles are files with the `*.style` extension. If we preview a FireMonkey style file with a text viewer, we will see that its content looks very much like a form file that we design with **Form Designer** inside the IDE.

It is good practice not to put non-visual components such as stylebooks directly on the form, but on a dedicated data module instead. Select **File | New | Other** from the main menu. In the **New Items** dialogs, select the **Delphi Files** category and choose to add a new **Data Module** to the project:

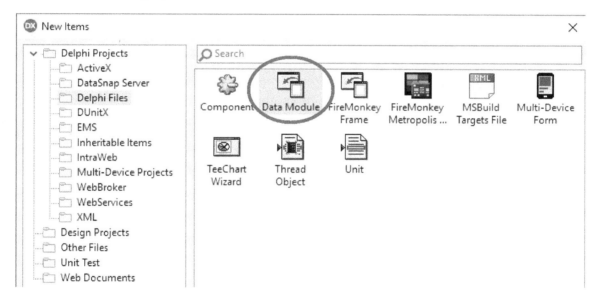

New Data Module in New Items dialog

Save the unit as uDMStyles. Change the **Name** property of the data module to DMStyles. Make sure that the data module is created before the application main form. You can do it in the **Forms** tab in the **Options** dialog for the current project, by moving DMStyles to the top of the list of auto-created forms. Add the new data module to the implementation uses clause of the application main form.

Drop a **TStylebook** component on the data module. It can be used to load custom styles for different platforms. See the following screenshot:

StyleBook1

TStyleBook component on the form

Double-click on the style book component. This will open the integrated FireMonkey Style Designer. Click on the second button at the top left corner of the style designer and load the Transparent.style file. Save and close the editor, answering **Yes** in the dialog message asking whether to save changes to the stylebook. Change the name of the stylebook component to StyleBookTransparent. Add another TStylebook component to the form. Load into it the **AquaGraphite** style and rename the component to StyleBookAquaGraphite. In order to apply a custom style to the form, we need to connect the stylebook component with the Stylebook property of the form. Have a look at the following screenshot. Both stylebook components are listed as choices to be applied to the form:

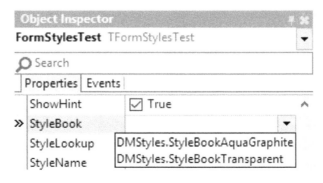

Options for the Stylebook property of the FormStylesTest form

Pointing this property to a given stylebook component will immediately load the style.

It would look as follows:

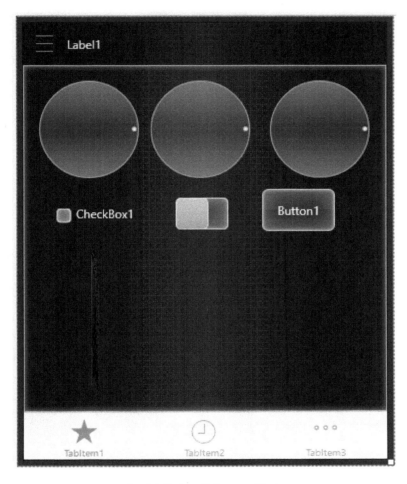

FormStylesTest form with Transparent iOS style

Take a look at the following screenshot:

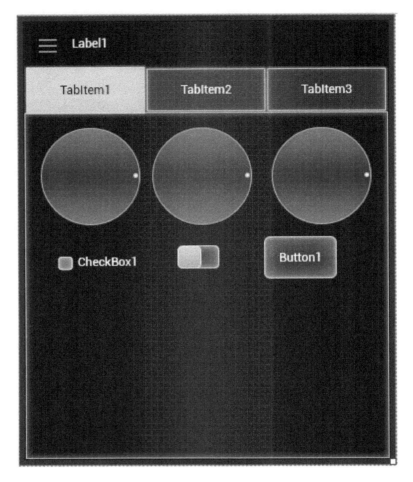

FormStylesTest form with Transparent Android style

This is how our form will look like after loading the Transparent style on iOS and on Android. I really like it. It has a nice gradient and the controls look a little like those on a space ship dashboard from science-fiction movies.

It is a good practice to put stylebook components on a dedicated data module. In this way we could have multiple forms reusing the same styles, and also we could possibly reuse this data module across different projects.

Another option to load a custom style is to use the `TStyleManager` class defined in the `FMX.Styles` unit. It has different public class methods for loading styles from a file or from a resource. The advantage of this approach is the fact that a style is loaded globally for the whole application and applied to all forms, but the disadvantage is the hassle of deploying custom styles with a mobile app. This can be done either by compiling the style into the app as a resource or deploying it as a separate file with the Deployment Manager.

# Embedding styles as resources

Let's have a look at the process of embedding custom styles into an app as a resource. Using custom resources is not limited to embedding. We can embed arbitrary files, for example, video, audio, custom graphics, data, or anything.

Remove the data module with style book components, because now we are going to load a custom style differently. In order to verify that the custom is loaded globally for all forms, we are going to add an additional form to the **StyleTest** app. Add an empty FireMonkey HD form to the project. Save the form's unit as `uFormExtra` and change the **Name** property of the new form to `FormExtra`. Add the new form to the `uses` clause of the main form. In the `OnClick` event of the `menu` speedbutton of the main form, add one line of code to display the new form.

The code will display `FormExtra` when the end user clicks on the button:

```
uses uFormExtra;

procedure TFormStylesTest.SpeedButton1Click(Sender: TObject);
begin
  FormExtra.Show;
end;
```

We will leave the form completely blank. A form itself will have a custom `backgroundstyle` applied. If we preview the `transparent` style definition from the previous example, we will see that the `backgroundstyle` definition is just a rectangle with a custom gradient fill.

In the **Project** menu click on the **Resources and Images...** option. This will display the **Resources** dialog. Click on the **Add...** button in the dialog and choose the file with a custom style that you want to embed. In the dialog we need to enter the **Resource identifier**. Using this identifier we can reference individual resources in code.

This could be anything. For example, we can add the `Transparent.style` file as a resource and use `TransparentStyle` as the **Resource identifier**:

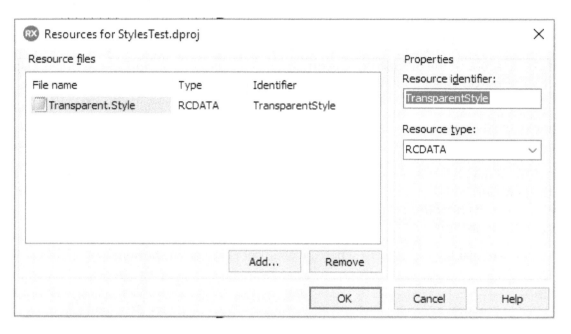

Transparent style added to the project as a resource

Click on **OK** to close the **Resources** dialog. The next step is to write code that will read the custom style from the resource and set it as a style for the whole application. Because this is global to all forms, a logical place to enter this code is in the project file itself. Click on the **View Source...** in the **Project** menu. Add to the project's `uses` clause `FMX.Styles` and a call to the `TStyleManager` class to try to load a custom style from the resource:

```
program StylesTest;

{$R *.dres}

uses
    System.StartUpCopy,
    FMX.Styles,
    FMX.Forms,
```

```
  uFormStylesTest in 'uFormStylesTest.pas' {FormStylesTest},
  uFormExtra in 'uFormExtra.pas' {FormExtra};

  {$R *.res}

begin
  TStyleManager.TrySetStyleFromResource('TransparentStyle');
  Application.Initialize;
  Application.CreateForm(TFormStylesTest, FormStylesTest);
  Application.CreateForm(TFormExtra, FormExtra);
  Application.Run;
end.
```

Adding a custom resource to a file has added some additional files to the project. Automatically an additional {$R *.dres} compiler directive has been included in the project file.

Build an app and deploy it to an iOS and Android device to verify that a custom style has been globally loaded for all forms in the application.

# Customizing styles

FireMonkey styling gives us a lot of flexibility. We can use built-in styles. Within a built-in style there could be multiple style definitions for a given control. There is also the possibility of using a custom style. But what if we want to apply a really special look to our styled control? We can go one step further and customize built-in or custom styles.

Remove custom resources and a call to load the style from the project's source.

On our test form there are three `TArcDial` components. If we right-click on any styled control at the bottom of the context menu there will be two options, one to edit custom styles and one to edit the default style. Refer to the following screenshot:

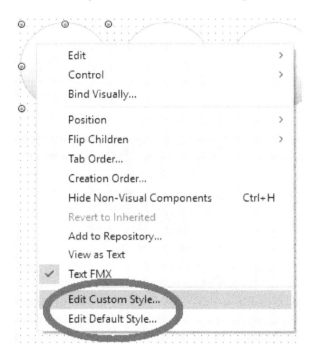

Options in the context menu of a control to edit styles

If we select the **Edit Default Style...** option we will be modifying the default style used by all controls of a given type. The option to **Edit Custom Style...** will only change the style for a given control, without changing the style for all other controls.

Right-click on the **ArcDial1** control and select **Edit Custom Style...** from the context menu. This will open the FireMonkey Style Designer and in the Structure View we can see the individual components that a **TArcDial** control is made of. It feels very much like editing a form, but we are editing a style here. The Object Inspector can be used to modify properties of all sub-elements of a style and we can also modify them visually in the designer.

Let's change something to see the effect in the running app. Let's change the size and color of the indicator ellipse. Change its **Width** property to **30** and its **Height** to **10**. Now it is bigger. Expand its **Brush** property and change the **Color** property to **Cornflowerblue**. Refer to the following screenshot:

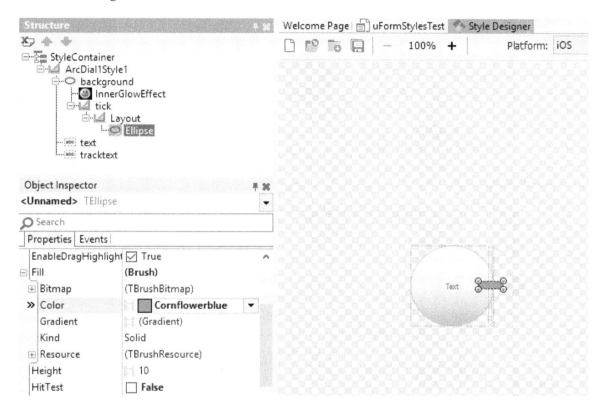

Editing custom styles in FireMonkey Style Designer

Now you can close the FireMonkey Style Designer. You will prompted to save the changes made to the style. Click on **Yes**. Now you should see the form again.

There are a few things to notice now. First a new `TStylebook` component has been added to the form. It contains the **ArcDial1Style1** style definition and this value is also already set in the **StyleLookup** property of the **ArcDial1** control. If we expand the **StyleLookup** property of any of the *arc dials* on the form, we see the additional choice that we could use to change the style of any of the other **TArcDial** controls on the form:

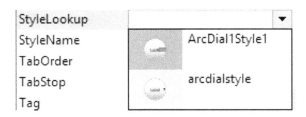

Custom ArcDial1Style1 style listed in the StyleLookup property

Now we can apply this style to other controls as well:

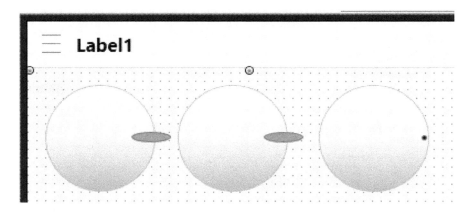

Custom style applied to other ArcDial controls

If we expand the `Stylebook1` component in the **Structure** view we will see that the style that we have created is for **iOS** only. There is only a **Default** and **iOS** option. If we change the current style for the form from **iOS** to **Android** our custom indicator will not show up. If we want to be truly cross-platform we need to make sure that our custom style has an **Android** version too. Make sure that **Android** is selected in the **Style** combobox and double-click on the style book component. We are back in the Style Designer. The new **Android** option has been added to the already listed **Default** and **iOS** styles:

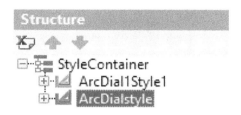

We can now make the same or similar modifications to the **Android** version of the custom **ArcDial1Style1** style. When we close the style designer, we can see that an **Android** version of our custom style has also been applied:

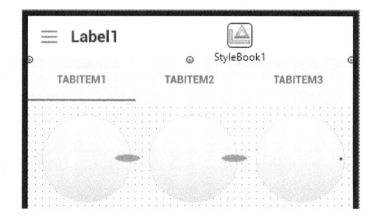

What would happen if we choose to edit the **default** style? Right-click on any of the **TArcDial** controls on the form and select the **Edit Default Style...** option from the context menu. The Style Designer window opens again. In the **Structure** view there is a new node. This time we are modifying the **ArcDialstyle** style definition:

This is a naming convention that the FireMonkey styling uses. The default style for a given class is the name of the class, without the preceding T but with `style` appended at the end. If such a style is found, then it is applied if there is no style specified in the **StyleLookup** property.

Let's introduce some modifications to the default style for **TArcDial** controls. Change the **Width** and **Height** of the *indicator* ellipse to **10** and its **Brush.Fill** color to **Cadetblue** for both **Android** and **iOS** styles. Save and close the style editor. Now the **ArcDial3** control uses a new style. Go to the **StyleLookup** property for **ArcDial1** and **ArcDial2** and clear their **StyleLookup** properties:

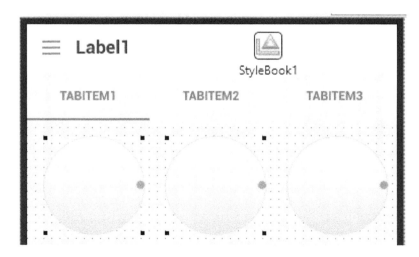

Notice that now all three controls are using the modified default **ArcDialstyle**.

This is the difference between editing custom styles and default styles. It all depends on the specific app that we are building. If we just want to modify a given control, it makes sense to edit a custom style and apply it to this one control. If it is desired to customize the look and feel of all controls of a given type on the form, it is easier to just modify the default style and it is automatically used by all controls.

# Using frames

Certain combinations of controls can be reused easily with frames.

Developer productivity often relies on being able to reuse previous work. Delphi projects consist of forms, data modules, and source code units. If you have an existing unit, it can always be added to a new project. On a smaller scale there are occasions when it is desirable to reuse certain combinations of components. This is where *frames* come in. If you have a few controls working together that you would like to reuse multiple times in the same or multiple forms then you can use frames.

Frames cannot exist on their own. They always need to be embedded in a form. They can contain controls and code.

Let's consider address information. Imagine we are designing a form with different controls for storing contact data. Our *contact* can have a home and office address. We can simplify our form and make it more user-friendly by defining a custom frame for address information and using it twice in the same form.

Create a new Delphi multi-device project. Save the main form as uFormContact and the whole project as Contacts. Change the **Name** property of the form to **FormContact**. Save everything. Now click on **File | New | Other...** menu, and inside the **New Items** dialog select the **Delphi Files** category and double-click on the FireMonkey Frame icon as shown in the following screenshot:

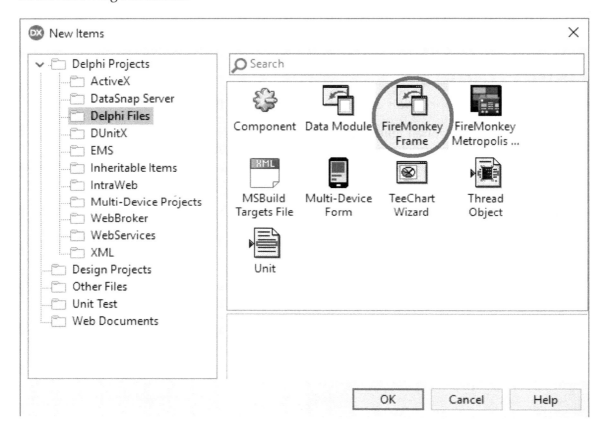

Save the new unit as uFrameAddress and change the **Name** property of the new frame to **FrameAddress**. At first the frame looks very much like a form. If we look into the source code, we will see that our **TFrameAddress** is derived not from **TForm**, but from the TFrame class. The process of designing the frame is the same as in the case of a form. Drop five edits and six labels on the frame. In the Structure view drag five labels onto edits, so they become their *children*. Position labels above the top left corner of every edit. In this way, when we move edits labels will go with them.

Here is our frame in the **Structure** view :

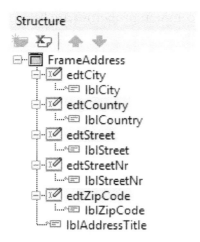

This is how the frame looks in the **Form Designer**. With the **Control** button we can select more than one component at a time:

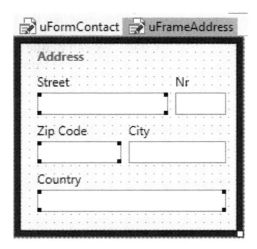

In the Object Inspector we can see that 3 *items are selected*. In one operation we can change properties of multiple components. That's a very useful trick. If you select components of different types, then only their common properties are listed in the Object Inspector as shown in the following screenshot:

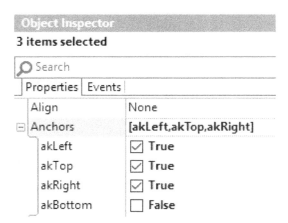

Rename the edits to `edtStreet`, `edtStreetNr`, `edtZipCode`, `edtCity`, and `edtCountry`. Make the frame as small as possible and have the controls occupy most of its space. We can use anchors to automatically adjust widths of all edits when the frame is resized.

In order to make our frame easier to use in code, we can define `Street`, `StreetNr`, `ZipCode`, `City`, and `Country` properties to read and write from the corresponding edit components:

```
unit uFrameAddress;

interface

uses
  System.SysUtils, System.Types, System.UITypes, System.Classes,
    System.Variants, FMX.Types, FMX.Graphics, FMX.Controls,
    FMX.Forms, FMX.Dialogs, FMX.StdCtrls, FMX.Controls.Presentation,
    FMX.Edit;

type
  TFrameAddress = class(TFrame)
    edtStreet: TEdit;
    lblStreet: TLabel;
    edtStreetNr: TEdit;
    lblStreetNr: TLabel;
    edtCity: TEdit;
    lblCity: TLabel;
```

```
      lblAddressTitle: TLabel;
      edtCountry: TEdit;
      lblCountry: TLabel;
  private
    procedure SetCity(const Value: string);
    procedure SetCountry(const Value: string);
    procedure SetStreet(const Value: string);
    procedure SetStreetNr(const Value: string);
    procedure SetZipCode(const Value: string);
    function GetCity: string;
    function GetCountry: string;
    function GetStreet: string;
    function GetStreetNr: string;
    function GetZipCode: string;
  public
    property Street: string read GetStreet write SetStreet;
    property StreetNr: string read GetStreetNr write SetStreetNr;
    property ZipCode: string read GetZipCode write SetZipCode;
    property City: string read GetCity write SetCity;
    property Country: string read GetCountry write SetCountry;
  end;

implementation

{$R *.fmx}

{ TFrameAddress }

function TFrameAddress.GetCity: string;
begin
  Result := edtCity.Text;
end;

function TFrameAddress.GetCountry: string;
begin
  Result := edtCountry.Text;
end;

function TFrameAddress.GetStreet: string;
begin
  Result := edtStreet.Text;
end;

function TFrameAddress.GetStreetNr: string;
begin
  Result := edtStreetNr.Text;
end;
```

```
function TFrameAddress.GetZipCode: string;
begin
  Result := edtZipCode.Text;
end;

procedure TFrameAddress.SetCity(const Value: string);
begin
  edtCity.Text := Value;
end;

procedure TFrameAddress.SetCountry(const Value: string);
begin
  edtCountry.Text := Value;
end;

procedure TFrameAddress.SetStreet(const Value: string);
begin
  edtStreet.Text := Value;
end;

procedure TFrameAddress.SetStreetNr(const Value: string);
begin
  edtStreetNr.Text := Value;
end;

procedure TFrameAddress.SetZipCode(const Value: string);
begin
  edtZipCode.Text := Value;
end;

end.
```

In this way, even if the internal structure or names of components change, the form's code would remain unchanged.

It is worth noting that frames do not have `OnCreate` and `OnDestroy` events. Their initialization and finalization code needs to go into the corresponding event handlers of a form that contains them.

In order to place the frame on the form, we need to go to the first item in the first tab of the **Tool Palette**:

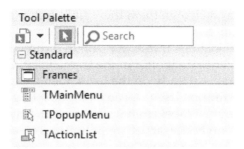

Click on **Frames** and select the frame you want to add from the list of frames contained in the project. In our case we have only one *address* frame:

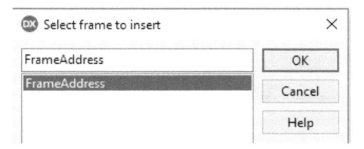

Drop two frames on the contact form. Change their names to `FrameAddressHome` and `FrameAddressOffice`. Change the **Text** property of the **lblTitle** on each frame to **Home Address** and **Office Address**.

In order to make our form more realistic let's additionally add a toolbar with a label and two edits with two labels for a contact's `Firstname` and `Lastname`.

If we now switch the style from Windows to iOS or Android, we will see that the vertical distances between edits on frames are too small and labels overlap edits above them. We have two choices here. We can either modify the positions and sizes of controls directly on the form, or go to the frame and change them there, so the change is automatically propagated to all frame instances already embedded in forms. It really depends on the scenario. If we want to adjust just one frame, we can do it directly on the form. If we want to change all frames, it is easier to do it once in the frame itself. Once we change a property of a component in a frame that is already on the form, then this change overrides any change made in the frame definition itself. As an example let's go to the frame design and change the font color or the title label from Black to Red. If we now switch to the form, we will see that title labels on both frames are now *Red*. The change has propagated to both of them. If we now change the color of the lblAddress on the FrameAddressHome to for example *Blue*, then any subsequent changes to the font color on the frame itself will not be propagated. The connection has been broken. A local value for the font color property *overrides* the inherited value.

Here is how the form with two *address* frames looks in the Form Designer. First with the **iOS** style applied:

And here is the same form, but previewed with **Android** styling:

With frames we can be more productive, because we can reuse big chunks of the form design across the same form, or different forms in the same project, or even across different projects. Not only can the visual design be reused, but also the logic. We could easily add to the form some logic to look up the street in the backend service based on the value entered into the zip code edits.

# Working with inherited views

When we design the form, it is the same for all platforms, form factors, and orientations. We can preview how the form is going to look on different platforms, but the design is the same. FireMonkey Form Designer lets us define inherited views that are specific to a given platform and the form factor. Next to the **Style** combo box at the top of the Form Designer there is another combo box, **View**. Here we can add to our form additional form files that are specific to a given platform and a form factor.

Every form always has a built-in **Master** view. From the list we can add additional views.

Available inherited views in the FireMonkey Form Designer

Let's add the **iPhone 4"** and **Android 7" Tablet** views to the **FormContact** design. The selected choices will now be listed in the **Created** category:

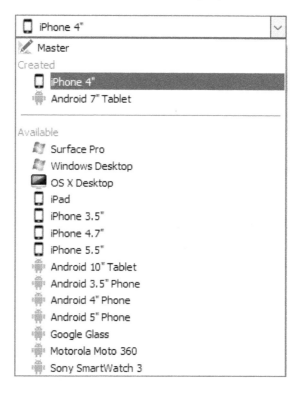

Available inherited and created views in the FireMonkey Form Designer

Inherited views are similar to frames. Instead of reusing a part of a form, now we are reusing the whole form. Changes made to the main form are propagated to inherited views, unless they are locally overridden on a given view specific form.

If we now switch to the Code Editor, we will see that there are two new additional compiler directives for compiling into the executable new device-specific form files.

In addition to a standard `{$R *.fmx}` directive that connects to the **Master** view, there are two new ones in the following snippet, which we have just added from the combo box:

```
// ...
var
   FormContact: TFormContact;

implementation

{$R *.fmx}
{$R *.iPhone4in.fmx IOS}
{$R *.LgXhdpiTb.fmx ANDROID}

end.
```

Fear not! If we have views defined for multiple platforms, only views for a specific platform will be compiled into the resulting executable. In our case the **Android 7'** view will not be included if we build for iOS, and vice versa. If we compile for Android, the **iOS 4'** view will not be included.

When we use frames, then we have both a form file and a unit with source code. In the case of "inherited views" there is only one source code file for a form, and multiple form files. These inherited views can be used to adjust the form to a given form factor. In our case we could for example modify the location of *address* frames so they are on top of one another.

On the right side of the **View** combo there are buttons to remove added views, switch between **portrait** and **landscape** views, and hide or show the custom image of any device that is displayed by default for an inherited view.

We can also preview current forms on all different form factors and devices inside the **Multi-Device Preview** tab in the top right corner of the IDE. In the default layout this view is located under the **Project Manager**. Have a look at the following screenshot:

Multi-Device Preview IDE window

This is very useful because we can quickly see how the current form is going to look on screens of different sizes. By default, *created* views are checked in the list of forms to preview, but we can also see additional forms, even if there is no inherited view created for them. These form factors that have inherited views are marked with a yellow check icon in their top left corner. See the following screenshot:

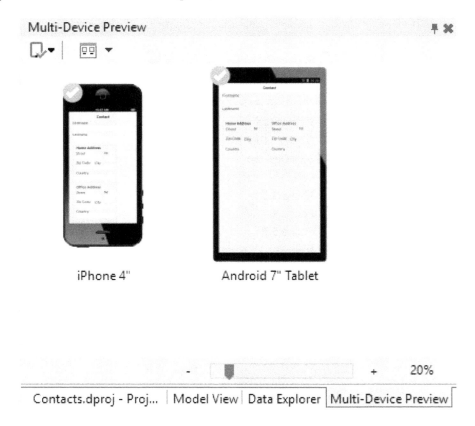

If you have more screens it is probably a good idea to move the **Multi-Device Preview** onto an additional screen to constantly preview the form you are designing on other devices.

Depending on the app that we are designing, it could be useful to be able to specify that our design, for example, works in **Portrait** orientation only. Or maybe we are building an arcade game and we only want to support **Landscape** orientation.

In the **Project Options** there is a special **Orientation** tab that we can use to specify custom orientations for our app:

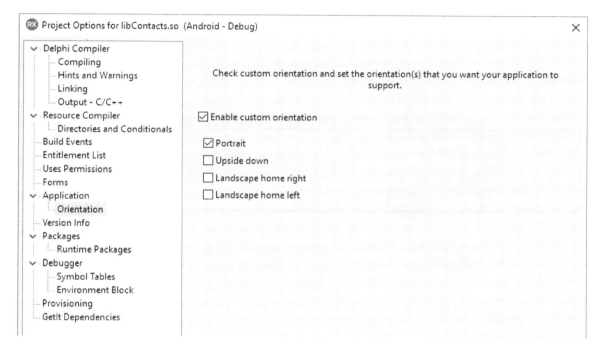

This information is then stored in a manifest file that the IDE generated for different supported platforms and embedded in the final executable file.

# Previewing forms on devices

Delphi Form Designer gives us the *what you see is what you get* functionality, but we can go one step further and use Delphi built-in functionality to preview the form we are designing live on a physical device. For this we will have to download a special mobile app published by Embarcadero Technologies called **FireUI App Preview**. It is available from both Apple App Store and Google Play Store. Refer to the following screenshot:

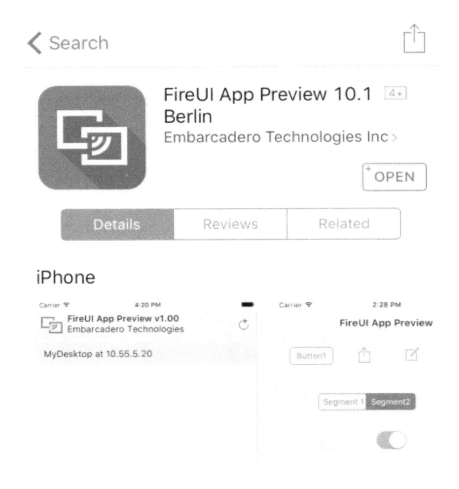

With the **FireUI App Preview** app you can preview an app as you are designing it live on a physical device. All changes made in the Form Designer are broadcasted to connected devices in real time. This app uses App Tethering technology available in Delphi, where arbitrary apps written in either Delphi or C++Builder, desktop or mobile, can communicate with each other over a Wi-Fi network or using Bluetooth. In this scenario, Delphi IDE runs on Windows desktop and communicates with a remote app running on any of the supported platforms. Installers for Windows and Mac versions of FireUI App Preview are located in the `LivePreview` directory in the main install folder of Delphi. It is also possible to build this app directly from source code, which is provided as part of the Delphi installation in the `source\Tools\FireUIAppPreview` folder.

In the Delphi **Options** dialog available from the **Tools** menu there is a special tab available from Environment **Options** | **Form Designer** | **FireUI Live Preview** where we can see all currently connected devices, the name under which the IDE is broadcasting, and an optional password to protect the communication between the IDE and preview devices.

If a FireUI Live Preview app running on a device does not see the IDE, it could be related to the wireless network configuration. App Tethering uses UDP broadcasting to make the connection, and this requires that both apps are running in the same subnet.

After establishing the connection to the IDE, the mobile app preview shows the form that is currently being designed inside the Form Designer. The form itself is interactive, so for example if you make edit, you would be able to enter a value into it, but the logic connected through events is not available through broadcasting. The ultimate goal is to preview the UI design and not the application logic. At any moment of time we can just run the app we are designing on the device itself.

The nice thing about **FireUI Live Preview** is the fact that it can broadcast the form to many different devices simultaneously in real time, so we can preview the UI design instantly.

# Summary

Building graphical user interfaces with Delphi and the FireMonkey library requires understanding the concept of a style. Styles in FireMonkey user interface design play a similar role to cascading style sheets in web development.

Every FireMonkey app uses a style. This could be a built-in style or a custom style loaded from the `TStylebook` component or from an embedded resource. The integrated FireMonkey Style Designer let us modify existing styles as easily as designing a form.

We have learnt a lot about building user interfaces with FireMonkey. In the next chapter, we will delve more deeply into the rich world of different frameworks available on the iOS and Android operating systems, and how FireMonkey helps us write cross-platform code that abstracts away the differences between different APIs.

# Working with Mobile Operating System

# 7

In this chapter, we are going to move from playing with FireMonkey to building useful cross-platform apps that are accessing mobile hardware and operating systems with high-level components, abstracting away underlying mobile APIs.

This chapter will cover the following points:

- Sensors
- Camera
- Share sheets
- Address book
- Embedding web browsers
- Using maps
- Creating and consuming Android services
- Using language bridges for accessing Java and Objective-C code

The objective of this chapter is to learn how to create native cross-platform apps that are using different frameworks and functionality provided by mobile operating systems.

# James Bond's toy

Contemporary mobile hardware does not significantly differ in capabilities from agent Bond's gadgets from just a few years ago. Your mobile phone is equipped with all kinds of sensors that you can use in your mobile apps, including location, orientation, motion, ambient light, microphones, speakers, cameras, and plenty of other hardware that you can control.

An app is immersed in the operating system, which is in charge of every aspect of an app execution. In your code, you can respond to different app lifecycle events such as start up, switching to background execution, moving back to the foreground, or app termination. In the end, it is all about responding to different events sent by the operating system and invoking operating system APIs. The FireMonkey library encapsulates access to common mobile operating system functionality through specialized types, classes, and components, but there is nothing that can stop you from invoking arbitrary APIs directly in your code. Sometimes this could be the only way to achieve certain things, like for example making your phone vibrate. Luckily most of the time, you can use cross-platform components and libraries that generalize common functionality such as accessing maps, contacts, embedding web browsers, and sharing data with other apps and services.

Different mobile operating systems provide functionality that might not exist on other platforms or in older versions of the same system. In such cases, we might want to write code against a specific feature on a specific platform. In this chapter, we are going to see how to invoke mobile APIs through Delphi language bridges. We will also see how to deal with features unique to iOS or Android, such as using and creating Android services.

# What I'm running on?

Building apps for multiple operating systems from the very same source code imposes unique challenges. Your code might be running on iOS or Android. It only takes two mouse clicks to recompile your app for a different target. Certain features might exist on a given platform and not be there on other platforms. Going further, new functionality is constantly being added to platforms, so we may want to know on which platform and operating system version your app is being executed.

This can be done with the `TOSVersion` record type defined in the `System.SysUtils` unit. It has a class constructor that instantiates all its fields. The `TOSVersion` record type has inner `TArchitecture` and `TPlatform` enumerated types and corresponding public class properties to read the current operating system architecture, platform, name, and major and minor numbers. Additionally, we can check major and minor numbers of the service pack level.

We can very quickly build a simple app that will log into a memo all information from the `TOSVersion` record. Create a new blank, multi-device project, save the main form as `uFormOSVer` and the whole project as `OSVersion`. Drop a toolbar on the form and add a label with a nice title, for example *What I'm running on?*. Change `TextSettings.HorzAlign` to `Center` and the `Align` property of the label to `Client`. Drop a `TMemo` component on the form, align it to `Client`, and rename it `MemoLog`. In order to simplify converting `TArchitecture` and `TPlatform` enumerated types to string, we can provide helper classes for these types. Add a new unit to the project and save it as `uOSVerHelpers`. Enter the following code there:

```
unit uOSVerHelpers;

interface

uses
  System.SysUtils;

type
  TOSArchitectureHelper = record helper for TOSVersion.TArchitecture
    function ToString: string;
  end;

  TOSPlatformHelper = record helper for TOSVersion.TPlatform
    function ToString: string;
  end;

function OSArchToStr(const Value: TOSVersion.TArchitecture): string;
function OSPlatToStr(const Value: TOSVersion.TPlatform): string;

implementation

function OSArchToStr(const Value: TOSVersion.TArchitecture): string;
begin
  case Value of
    arIntelX86: Result := 'IntelX86';
    arIntelX64: Result := 'IntelX64';
    arARM32: Result := 'ARM32';
    arARM64: Result := 'ARM64';
```

```
      else Result := 'Unknown OS Architecture';
    end;
end;

function TOSArchitectureHelper.ToString: string;
begin
  Result := OSArchToStr(self);
end;

function OSPlatToStr(const Value: TOSVersion.TPlatform): string;
begin
  case Value of
    pfWindows: Result := 'Windows';
    pfMacOS: Result := 'MacOS';
    pfiOS: Result := 'iOS';
    pfAndroid: Result := 'Android';
    pfWinRT: Result := 'WinRT';
    pfLinux: Result := 'Linux';
    else Result := 'Unknown OS Platform'
  end;
end;

function TOSPlatformHelper.ToString: string;
begin
  Result := OSPlatToStr(self);
end;

end.
```

Add this unit to the `uses` clause of the main form. We can additionally define in the form class a simple `Log(s: string)` method that will just display a given string in the memo. Now in the `OnCreate` event of the form, we can log all OS version information into the memo. Have a look at the following code:

```
procedure TFormOSVer.Log(s: string);
begin
  MemoLog.Lines.Add(s);
end;

procedure TFormOSVer.FormCreate(Sender: TObject);
begin
  Log('OS Architecture: ' + TOSVersion.Architecture.ToString);
  Log('OS Platform: ' + TOSVersion.Platform.ToString);
  Log('OS Name: ' + TOSVersion.Name);
  Log('OS Build: ' + TOSVersion.Build.ToString);
  Log('Version: ' + TOSVersion.Major.ToString + '.' +
TOSVersion.Minor.ToString);
  Log('Service Pack: ' + TOSVersion.ServicePackMajor.ToString + '.' +
```

```
    TOSVersion.ServicePackMinor.ToString);
end;
```

This could be a useful piece of code for troubleshooting apps running on unknown or exotic mobile device:

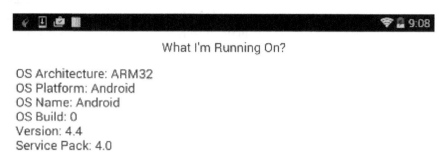

"OS Version" app running on an Android tablet

The second, more common option for dealing with different underlying operating systems is to use conditional compilation. Somewhere deep in the FireMonkey source there must be ultimately places where there is different code accessing different operating systems. A typical pattern is to have one header unit with type declarations in the interface section, and then platform-specific implementation units enclosed with ifdefs listed in the uses clause of the implementation section of the unit. Let's consider the FMX.Platform unit. It has different interface and class declarations in its interface part, and its implementation part has the following uses clause:

```
unit FMX.Platform;
interface
// ...
implementation
uses
{$IFDEF IOS}
  FMX.Platform.iOS,
  // ...
{$ENDIF IOS}
  // ...
{$IFDEF ANDROID}
  FMX.Platform.Android,
{$ENDIF}
  // ...
end.
```

This is a very common pattern used in the FireMonkey library. The FMX.Something unit provides an interface to the cross-platform application code, and FMX.Something.iOS and FMX.Something.Android units contain platform-specific implementation code.

In the FMX.Platform unit there is the TPlatformServices class that is used as the common access point to different platform services. The TPlatformServices class provides the Current class property that is used to query whether a given service is available or not.

If a given service is implemented via a hypothetical IFMXAService interface, then we could use the following code snippet to access it:

```
var aFMXAService: IFMXAService;
  begin
    if TPlatformServices.Current.SupportsPlatformService(IFMXAService,
IInterface(aFMXAService)) then
      begin
      // call methods defined in the IFMXAService:
      // aFMXAService.AMethod;
    end
    else
    // FMXAService is not supported
```

In this way, we have clean code for cross-platform access to common services provided by the FireMonkey library.

# The life of an app

An app is not a lonely island. It is always executed by the operating system, within bounds that it imposes. Depending on the type of the app, we could be interested in responding to different application lifecycle events that the operating system sends to it. Every operating system has a slightly different app lifecycle model, but in the case of mobile the most tricky part could be properly handling the situation when our apps move from foreground execution to background, and back.

FireMonkey provides common abstraction for handling an application lifecycle through different types of application events defined in the FMX.Platform unit:

```
type
  TApplicationEvent = (FinishedLaunching, BecameActive, WillBecomeInactive,
EnteredBackground, WillBecomeForeground, WillTerminate, LowMemory,
TimeChange, OpenURL);
```

If we want to receive the app lifecycle events, we need to pass the reference to our event handler function to the SetApplicationEventHandler method that is available as part of the IFMXApplicationEventService. First, we need to check if this service is available from the TPlatformServices class. Our event handler can be any method that takes TApplicationEvent and TObject parameters and returns Boolean.

Let's create a test app that will be displaying app life cycle events on different platforms. Select the new **Multi-Device Application - Delphi** option in the IDE and choose the **Blank Application** template. Save the main form unit as uFormLifecycle, the whole project as AppLifecycle, and change the main form's Name property to FormLifecycle. Save All. Drop the TToolbar and TMemo controls on the form. Rename the memo to MemoLog and align it to Client. Declare the Log(s: string) method in the form's class to output a message to the memo.

Now we have a generic skeleton of the app. It's time to do something about app lifecycle events. Add FMX.Platform to the uses clause in the interface section of the form and implement the event handler method for logging app life cycle events:

```
function TFormLifecycle.HandleAppEvent(AAppEvent: TApplicationEvent;
  AContext: TObject): Boolean;
begin
  case aAppEvent of
    TApplicationEvent.FinishedLaunching: Log('App event:
      Finished Launching');
    TApplicationEvent.BecameActive: Log('App event:
      Became Active');
    TApplicationEvent.WillBecomeInactive: Log('App event:
      Will Become Inactive');
    TApplicationEvent.EnteredBackground: Log('App event:
      Entered Background');
    TApplicationEvent.WillBecomeForeground: Log('App event:
      Will Become Foreground');
    TApplicationEvent.WillTerminate: Log('App event:
      Will Terminate');
    TApplicationEvent.LowMemory: Log('App event: Low Memory');
    TApplicationEvent.TimeChange: Log('App event: Time Change');
    TApplicationEvent.OpenURL: Log('App event: Open URL');
    else Log('Unknown app event');
  end;
end;
```

The last step is to register the `HandleAppEvent` method with the app lifecycle service, so it gets invoked by the operating system when there are important things happening to the app. A good place to do so is in the `OnCreate` event of the form:

```
procedure TFormLifecycle.FormCreate(Sender: TObject);
var aFMXApplicationEventService: IFMXApplicationEventService;
begin
  if TPlatformServices.Current.SupportsPlatformService(
    IFMXApplicationEventService, IInterface(aFMXApplicationEventService))
then
aFMXApplicationEventService.SetApplicationEventHandler(HandleAppEvent)
  else
    Log('Application Event Service is not supported.');
end;
```

Save all and run the app. This is how the app looks on my iPhone:

AppLifecycle project running on iOS

And this is what this very same app looks like running on Android:

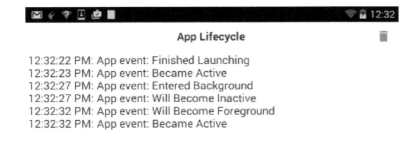

AppLifecycle project running on Android

When you switch to a different app on your phone or tablet, you will see that our app goes into the background execution and then, when it is selected again, it returns to the foreground.

Interestingly, the events on iOS and Android are not exactly the same. For example, on Android the very first app lifecycle event received is `Finished Launching`, while on iOS it is never received. It seems that `Became Active` and `Entered Background` are good choices for cross-platform handling of switching between the background and foreground.

There are also other interesting platform services that can be useful, for example, `IFMXSaveStateService` that is also surfaced as the event of a FireMonkey form. A mobile operating system may decide to suddenly kill your app and that could be a good place to preserve your app execution state.

# Sensing the world

Delphi comes with the `System.Sensors` unit, where all kinds of possible sensors are defined. Similarly to the `FMX.Platform` unit, the `System.Sensors` also has `ifdefs` in its implementation and a `uses` clause for different platforms including Android and iOS.

There is main `TSensorManager` class that acts as a gateway to all sensor information. It has a `Current: TSensorManager` class property that is used to reference all sensor information. At the top of the `System.Sensors` unit, you can find a `TSensorCategory` enumerated type that provides the top level categorization of all possible sensors:

```
type
    TSensorCategory = (Location, Environmental, Motion, Orientation,
  Mechanical, Electrical, Biometric, Light, Scanner);
```

Within each category there are different sensor types, so each category has its own enumerated type as well. All specialized sensor types derive from an abstract `TCustomSensor` class that provides basic functionality that is common to all sensors, for example, `Start` and `Stop` methods. In order to get access to individual sensors in code, you need to call the `GetSensorsByCategory` method of the `TSensorManager` class that takes as a parameter a sensor category and returns a dynamic array of available custom sensors.

At a level above the `System.Sensors`, there is the `System.Sensors.Components` unit that defines a generic `TSensor` class that is derived from `TComponent` and parameterized by the `TCustomSensor` type. This is a base class that provides basic functionality such as maintaining a reference to `TSensorManager`, calling its `GetSensorsByCategory` method, and access to specific properties of a given `TCustomSensor` descendant type. There are nine `TSensor` descendant types implemented in this unit, one for every `TSensorCategory` value, but only three of them are actually registered with the IDE and appear on the tool palette in the `Sensors` category.

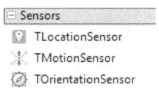

Sensor components on the tool palette

A lot of mobile apps depend on location information. The GPS sensor is a standard part of a typical smartphone or tablet. With the `TLocationSensor` component, it is very easy to add location awareness to an app.

There is nothing like building a test app and giving sensor components a try! Create a new multi-device Delphi app, select a **Blank Application** template, and then save the main form's unit as `uFormSensors` and the project as `Sensors`. You can also change the `Name` property of the form to `FormSensors`. Locate in the tool palette the `Sensors` category, or just use IDE Insight, and add `TLocationSensor` to the form. First of all, we need to switch the sensor on. There is an `Active` property that needs to be set to `True`. Drop the `TCheckBox` component on the form and align it to the `Top`. Change all its `Margin` subproperties to 8, so there is a distance from the border of the form. Change its `Name` to `chkbxLocSensor` and its `Text` property to `Location Sensor Active`. In its `OnChange` event, enter the following line of code:

```
procedure TFormLoc.chkbxLocSensorChange(Sender: TObject);
begin
  LocationSensor1.Active := chkbxLocSensor.IsChecked;
end;
```

The next step is to respond to location change events. Different readings from sensors are typically real numbers, so before proceeding, let's implement a small convenience function `DblToStr` that will be converting float numbers to strings to avoid calling just `ToString` methods that would display 14 digits after the decimal point. We just need a few:

```
uses System.Math; // IsNan
// ...
function TFormSensors.DblToStr(Value: Double): string;
begin
  if not IsNan(Value) then
    Result := Format('%3.5f',[Value])
  else
    Result := 'NaN';
end;
```

Add the `TLabel` component to the form. Align it to the `Top` and change its `Name` to `lblLocation`. Expand its `TextSettings` property in the `Object Inspector` and change the `HorzAlign` property to `Center`. Change the `Text` property to `(Location)`. Double-click on the `OnLocationChange` event of the location sensor and enter the following code to display the current geographical coordinates read from the GPS of our device:

```
procedure TFormLoc.LocationSensor1LocationChanged(Sender: TObject;
  const OldLocation, NewLocation: TLocationCoord2D);
begin
  lblLocation.Text := DblToStr(NewLocation.Latitude)
    + ' : ' + DblToStr(NewLocation.Longitude);
end;
```

Save all and run the app. First, on iOS. From the moment that we touch the checkbox to enable the location sensor, we should see the confirmation dialog from the iOS operating system asking if we want to allow our app to have access to location information.

Click on **Allow** and you should see the current latitude and longitude in the label.

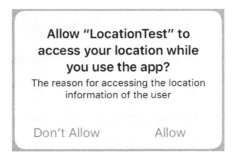

Confirmation dialog to allow app access to location information on iOS

In the case of Android, access to different operating system services can be configured in the **Project Options**. The first two options are there to access coarse and fine location information and they are checked by default, so we do not need to do anything. For other services, it could be necessary to adjust **Uses Permissions**.

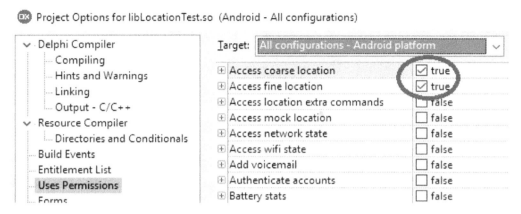

Uses permissions tab in project options for the Android platform

The TLocationSensor component also provides access to heading information. Drop another TLabel component on the form, align it to the Top, change its Height property to 34, its Name to lblHeading, Text to (Heading), and HorzAlign to Center. Now, double-click on the OnHeadingChange event of the location sensor component and enter one line of code to display the current heading:

```
procedure TFormLoc.LocationSensor1HeadingChanged(Sender: TObject;
  const AHeading: THeading);
begin
  lblHeading.Text := DblToStr(AHeading.Azimuth);
end;
```

Save all and run. Now, additionally to location, we should see the current azimuth in degrees.

In the `Sensors` category on the tool palette there are also `TMotionSensor` and `TOrientationSensor` components, but unlike the `TLocationSensor`, they do not provide change events and it is up to the application code to access their readings. Drop the `TTimer` component on the form so we can periodically update the user interface with current information. Set its `Enabled` property to `True`.

Drop `TMotionSensor` and `TOrientationSensor` on the form. They both have `Active` properties that need to be set to enable reading of information. Let's create two more sections on the form for motion and orientation information, similarly to location. Add two more checkboxes and four more labels to the form. Align all of them to the `Top` and adjust their margins. Something like this:

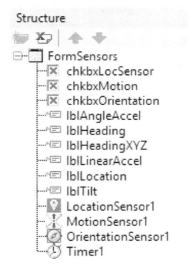

The sensors project's main form in structure view

Aligning visual controls to the `Top` and making sure that they have the proper `Height` and `Margins` can be a good strategy for designing user interfaces that adjust correctly to all screen sizes:

The sensors project's main form in form designer

Now we need to add `OnChange` events to, checkboxes to enable or disable respective sensors, depending on the `IsChecked` property. In the `OnTimer` event, we will be updating labels with readings from different properties of sensor components:

```
procedure TFormSensors.Timer1Timer(Sender: TObject);
begin
  lblLinearAccel.Text := DblToStr(MotionSensor1.Sensor.AccelerationX) +
    ', ' + DblToStr(MotionSensor1.Sensor.AccelerationY) + ', '
    + DblToStr(MotionSensor1.Sensor.AccelerationZ);

  lblAngleAccel.Text := DblToStr(MotionSensor1.Sensor.AngleAccelX) + ', '
    + DblToStr(MotionSensor1.Sensor.AngleAccelY) + ', '
    + DblToStr(MotionSensor1.Sensor.AngleAccelZ);

  lblTilt.Text := DblToStr(OrientationSensor1.Sensor.TiltX) + ', '
```

```
        + DblToStr(OrientationSensor1.Sensor.TiltY) + ', '
        + DblToStr(OrientationSensor1.Sensor.TiltZ);

    lblHeadingXYZ.Text := DblToStr(OrientationSensor1.Sensor.HeadingX) + ', '
        + DblToStr(OrientationSensor1.Sensor.HeadingY) + ', '
        + DblToStr(OrientationSensor1.Sensor.HeadingZ);
end;
```

If we look into the implementation of property readers for accessing sensor information in the `System.Sensors` unit, we will see that by default they return a `Not a Number` value. These getters are virtual and they are overridden in platform-specific implementations for a given sensor, so we do not need to worry. Anyway, it is just a good idea to check if a given value is not a `NaN` before converting it to a string.

# Taking photos

On many occasions, it is useful to be able to take a photo from an app. The programming model is very easy, but it is not the `TCamera` component that you need to use. In FireMonkey, taking photos is achieved by executing a special "take a photo from a camera" action.

Create a new multi-device FireMonkey blank application. Save the main form's unit as uFormCam, the project as CamApp, and change the `Name` property of the form to FormCam. Change the `Style` in the combobox above the form to `iOS` or `Android`. Drop `TToolbar` and `TImage` components on the form. Rename the image as `ImagePhoto` and align it to `Client` and drop `TSpeedbutton` onto the `Toolbar1`. Change its `Name` to spdbtnTakePhoto and the button's `Stylelookup` property to `cameratoolbutton`; align it to the `Left` and adjust the width so it becomes a square. Save all.

Drop the `TActionList` component on the form and double-click on it to display the `Action List Editor`. Right-click on the editor and select the **New Standard Action...** option from the context menu. Expand the **Media Library** category and double-click on the **TakePhotoFromTheCamera** action to add it to the list of actions.

We should see a **Standard Action Classes** dialog displayed in the IDE:

TakePhotoFromCameraAction in the Standard Action Classes dialog

There are all kinds of interesting actions here. We will have a look at more of them later.

Actions are just regular components with properties and events. Any action can be executed in code by calling its `Execute` or `ExecuteTarget` methods. A simpler way to invoke the action from a visual control is to attach it to the `Action` property. In this way, we do not need to write any code.

When the end user touches the button, the mobile device displays the view that would normally be displayed when clicking on the integrated camera app. The next step is to do something in code with the photo that has been taken with the camera. The **TakePhotoFromCameraAction1** component that was added to the form has different events, including **OnDidFinishTaking** that we can handle.

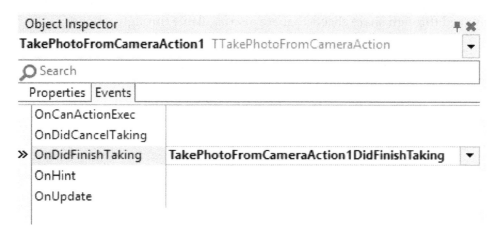

The OnDidFinishTaking event in the Object Inspector with an event handler

Double-click on it. The generated event handler has an `Image:  TBitmap` parameter that contains the bitmap with the photo that was just taken. We can do anything with it, for example display it in the image component already on our form. Enter one line of code to display the bitmap:

```
procedure TFormCam.TakePhotoFromCameraAction1DidFinishTaking(Image:
TBitmap);
begin
  ImagePhoto.Bitmap.Assign(Image);
end;
```

The first time you run the app on iOS, after touching the camera button, you will be presented with the message that your app would like to have access to the camera. Click on **OK** and take the photo. It is now displayed in the form. We have just built a camera app!

# Using share sheets

Our app is already very spectacular, but it is not very useful. The photo is displayed in the form, but it goes away when we stop the app or take another photo. It is a typical functionality in operating systems to be able to *share* things with other installed apps. For example, we might want to share a photo on social media or send it by email. This can be easily achieved through share sheets that are also available through actions.

Drop another `TSpeedButton` on the toolbar. Rename it to `spdbtnSharePhoto`, change its `StyleLookup` property to `actiontoolbutton`, adjust its width and align it to the `Right`. Expand its `Action` property in the **Object Inspector** and, through the context menu, add the standard `TShowShareSheetAction` from the **Media Library** category.

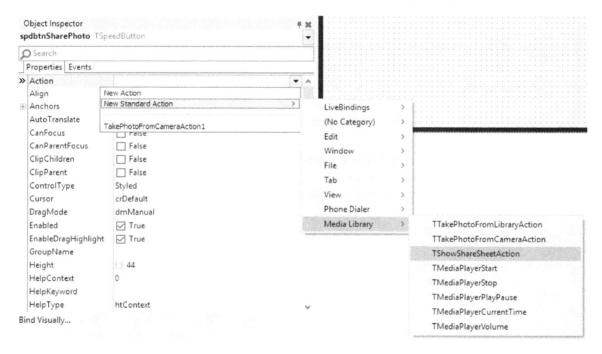

TShowShareSheetAction in the context menu in Object Inspector

That's a faster way of adding actions. We can do it directly from the **Object Inspector** without having to display **Action List Editor** and then hooking the action to a control.

The speed button will take care of executing the action, but we need to write some code to share this particular photo that we have just taken from the camera and which is now stored in the image component on the form. Select the ShowShareSheetAction1 component in the **Object Inspector**. It has a Bitmap property. It is a bitmap that is going to be shared to other apps. In the **Events** tab, double-click on the OnBeforeExecute event and enter this one line of code that assigns the bitmap from the image to the action:

```
procedure TFormCam.ShowShareSheetAction1BeforeExecute(Sender: TObject);
begin
   ShowShareSheetAction1.Bitmap.Assign(ImagePhoto.Bitmap);
end;
```

Now it is a much more useful app. We are just missing a nice title and then we can consider it ready. Just drop a TLabel component on the toolbar and align it to Client. Expand its TextSettings property and change HorzAlign to Center. Enter Delphi Camera into the Text property.

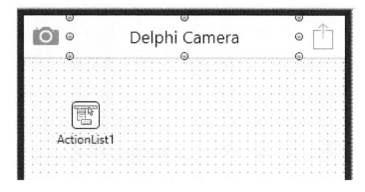

Main form of CamApp in form designer with iOS style

Save all and run the app on a device. Now we can take photos and share them through other apps installed on the device.

ShareSheet dialog on the iOS

Two lines of code for a fully functional cross-platform camera mobile app? Not bad!

# Camera, light, action!

We can take photos with special action components, so what is the purpose of the TCameraComponent component that can be found in the **Additional** category on the tool palette? A quick answer could be that it is the way to switch on and off the bright torch light that most phones are equipped with. A more elaborate answer would be that it can be used to make videos.

The source code for switching on and off the integrated camera light is simple. Create a new multi-device, blank application. Save the form's unit as uFormVideo and the whole project as VideoApp. Drop TToolbar on the form and then TCheckBox onto it. Rename the checkbox as chkbxTorchLight, change its Text property to Torch Light, and align it to the Right.

Drop TCameraComponent on the form. Not every device has a torch light, so first we want to check in the code if the torch light is present and enable or disable the checkbox. The natural place for such a check is in the OnCreate event of the form.

Add the following one line of code in the body of the OnCreate event handler:

```
procedure TFormVideo.FormCreate(Sender: TObject);
begin
   chkbxTorch.Enabled := CameraComponent1.HasTorch;
end;
```

In the OnChange event of the checkbox add the following code to turn the light on and off:

```
procedure TFormVideo.chkbxTorchChange(Sender: TObject);
begin
   if chkbxTorch.IsChecked then
     CameraComponent1.TorchMode := TTorchMode.ModeOn
   else
     CameraComponent1.TorchMode := TTorchMode.ModeOff;
end;
```

There are also very similar FlashMode and HasFlash properties. On my iPhone they seem to have exactly the same functionality as Torch.

The FireMonkey library has generic support for handling arbitrary types of cameras available on different hardware. The actual access to underlying video hardware is done through a non-visual `TCaptureDeviceManager` class defined in the `FMX.Media` unit. The programming model follows the same pattern as in other platform services. The class itself is abstract, but it has a `Current` public class property that returns a reference to the actual `TCaptureDeviceManager` implementation on a given platform. The `TCaptureDeviceManager` class has a `Devices` array property where we can access all available capture devices, but there are also `DefaultAudioCaptureDevice`: `TAudioCaptureDevice`, and `DefaultVideoCaptureDevice`: `TVideoCaptureDevice` properties.

We could have implemented a video recording app directly accessing the `DefaultVideoCaptureDevice`, but `TCameraComponent` provides a more convenient interface to this same functionality.

Drop the `TImage` component on the form, align it to `Client`, and rename it as `imgVideo`. Now, drop another `TCheckbox` component on the `Toolbar1`. Change its `Name` to `chkbxCamera`, its `Text` to `Camera Active`, and align it to the `Left`. In its `Margin.Left` property enter 8, so that the checkbox is not exactly at the edge of the form. In the `OnChange` event of the checkbox, add code to make the camera active or not:

```
procedure TFormVideo.chkbxCameraChange(Sender: TObject);
begin
  CameraComponent1.Active := chkbxCamera.IsChecked;
end;
```

In order to access video information from the camera, we need to handle its `OnSampleBufferReady` event, which is fired when there is a new image from the camera available in the buffer. The `TCameraComponent` class provides a special `SampleBufferToBitmap` method that can be used to easily display the contents of the buffer.

Enter the following code to the `OnSampleBufferReady` event handler:

```
procedure TFormVideo.CameraComponent1SampleBufferReady(Sender: TObject;
  const ATime: TMediaTime);
begin
  CameraComponent1.SampleBufferToBitmap(imgVideo.Bitmap, True);
end;
```

Save all and run on the device. It is similar to taking photos in Delphi.

Notice that making an augmented reality app is just one step away. Before we put the bitmap from the sample buffer into the image on the form, we could have done some pre-processing, for example, checking the orientation of a device in 3D space and drawing on the bitmap things that exist in augmented reality only.

# Working with address book

The most valuable information in our smartphone is arguably all our contact information. Before backing up a phone to a cloud was so common, when you lost a phone or got a new one, the first thing was to find a traditional paper address book and enter all your contacts again and again.

Luckily, this is not something that we need to worry about so much today. There is cloud storage and backup, but also it is possible to write an app that could manage our address book. FireMonkey comes with the TAddressBook component that makes it easy to add, modify, delete, or just list all contacts in our device.

The TAddressBook component on the tool palette

This component is declared in the FMX.AddressBook unit and its architecture follows the FireMonkey standard pattern for implementing a cross-platform service. Under the hood, the AddressBook component is just an easy to use wrapper on top of the IFMXAddressBookService service that has different platform-specific implementations.

Contact information is sensitive, so the app that is trying to access it must be granted proper privileges from the underlying operating system.

Let's play with the TAddressBook component to find out how to use it. Create a new multi-device, blank Delphi application. Save the form file as uFormContacts and the project as ContactsMgr. Drop a TAddressBook component on the form. You will need to change the target platform in the **Project Manager** to one of the mobile targets, because otherwise the TAddressBook choice is disabled in the tool palette.

Drop the `TTabControl` component on the form and align it to `Client`. Rename it as `TabControlMain`. Right-click on the tab control and add a new tab to it from the context menu.

The Add TTabItem option in the context menu for TTabControl

Contact information is a good example of hierarchical information. There will be at least two levels of detail. A list of contacts and selected contact's details. In such cases, the `TTabControl` component can be very useful. By default, its `TabPosition` property is set to `PlatformDefault`. This is a good choice for most cases. This means that on iOS tabs it will be shown at the bottom of the screen and on top on Android. The end user can randomly navigate through tabs by touching them. In some scenarios, we might not want the end user to move through tabs directly but to switch between tabs in code. That's what we want in this case. Change the `TabPosition` property of the `TabControl1` component to `None`. The tab has changed its appearance and is now just a dot. At runtime it would not be displayed at all. Add another tab to the tab control. Now we have two dots for two tabs. By clicking on dots, we can change between tabs at design-time. The `TTabControl` component has an `ActiveTab` property that we can use to programmatically control which tab is currently displayed. Change the `Name` property of the first tab to `tbiWelcome` and the second to `tbiContacts`. Add the `OnCreate` event to the form. We want to make sure that our app always starts from the **Welcome** tab.

Enter the following one line of code in the `OnCreate` event of the form:

```
procedure TFormContacts.FormCreate(Sender: TObject);
begin
  TabControlMain.ActiveTab := tbiWelcome;
end;
```

Drop `TButton` on the first tab. Change its `Name` property to `btnShowContacts` and its `Text` to **Show Contacts**. Align it to `Client`.

Before we can access contact information in code, we need to request permission to access it. There is a special `RequestPermission` method of the `AddressBook` that does it. If we receive the proper permission, we will display the second tab. This can be done just by setting the `ActiveTab` property of the tab control. A more elegant way is to use an animation. For this, we will need to use a special action. Drop the `TActionList` component on the form. Double-click on it to display the editor. Add a standard `TChangeTabAction` from the `Tab` category. Executing this action will change the current tab to the tab that is connected to its `Tab` property. Select `tbiContacts` in the `Tab` property and change the `Name` property of the action component to `ctaContacts`. `TChangeTabAction` has different properties that control how the change between tabs should be performed. By default, the `Transition` property is set to `Slide`, which will give us a nice sliding animation. There is also a `Direction` property that by default is set to `Normal`, but it could also be `Reverse` in case we want the sliding animation to be performed in the opposite direction.

Double-click on the `btnShowContacts`. First, we need to check if the address book is supported on a given device. If not, we will display an appropriate message; otherwise, we will request permission to access contacts:

```
procedure TFormContacts.btnShowContactsClick(Sender: TObject);
begin
  if AddressBook1.Supported then
    AddressBook1.RequestPermission
  else
    ShowMessage('Address book is not supported.');
end;
```

The `RequestPermission` will result with trying to obtain access permission. The `TAddressBook` component has an `OnPermissionRequest` event that is invoked after the access permission is granted or not. The `AAccessGranted` parameter can be used to check if we have got access. The `AMessage` parameter contains optional message information with a reason why the access request was rejected.

Before displaying the tab with contacts, we need to make sure that it already contains contact information. The logic to refresh contact information will be executed not only from this handler, but possibly also from other places in the app, so it is a good idea to centralize it in a custom action. Double-click on the action list component and add a new action. Change its `Name` to `actRefreshContacts`. Double-click on it to generate an empty `OnExecute` event handler. For now, let's leave it empty. We will implement it in a second. First, we need to write code that will be calling it. Double-click on the `OnRequestPersmission` event of the `AddressBook1` component and enter the following code:

```
procedure TFormContacts.AddressBook1PermissionRequest(ASender: TObject;
  const AMessage: string; const AAccessGranted: Boolean);
begin
  if AAccessGranted then
  begin
    actRefreshContacts.Execute;
    ctaContacts.Execute;
  end
  else
    ShowMessage(
      'You don''t have access to address book. The reason is: ' +
aMessage);
end;
```

Now we can move to implementing the logic for displaying contacts. In a general situation on a given mobile device there could be more than one source of contact information. For example, contacts could be stored additionally on an extra memory card. That is why when accessing contacts we also need to specify which `AddressBookSource` we want to use. `TAddressBook` has an `AllSources` method that can be used to retrieve a list of all available address book sources, but there is also the `DefaultSource` property that we will be using in our app.

Drop `TToolbar` on the contacts tab and a `TLabel` onto it. Change the label's `Name` property to `lblContacts`, its `TextSettings.HorzAlign` to `Center`, and `Align` to `Client`. Enter `Contacts` as the `Text` property. Now, drop the `TListView` component on the tab, rename it as `lstvwContacts`, and align it to `Client`.

`TListView` is one of the most flexible controls for working with dynamic data. The layout of an individual item in the list can be controlled with the `ItemAppearance` property that is also available through **Structure View**.

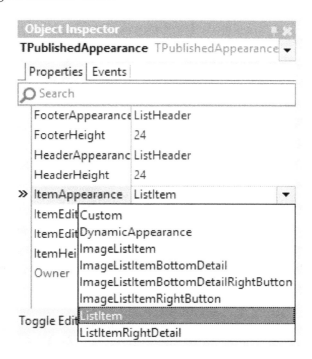

Available choices for the ItemAppearance property of TListView in Object Inspector

The default value is `ListItem` and, in order to keep this app simple, we will leave it like this.

Add the following code in the `OnExecute` event handler of the `actRefreshContacts` action:

```
procedure TFormContacts.actRefreshContactsExecute(Sender: TObject);
var i, aCount: integer; contacts: TAddressBookContacts; c:
TAddressBookContact;
  item: TListViewItem;
begin
  contacts := TAddressBookContacts.Create;
  try
    AddressBook1.AllContacts(AddressBook1.DefaultSource, contacts);
    aCount := contacts.Count;
    lblContacts.Text := 'Contacts (' + aCount.ToString + ')';
    lstvwContacts.BeginUpdate;
```

```
try
  lstvwContacts.Items.Clear;
  for i := 0 to aCount-1 do
  begin
    c := Contacts[i];
    item := lstvwContacts.Items.Add;
    item.Text := c.DisplayName;
    item.Tag := c.ID;
  end;
finally
  lstvwContacts.EndUpdate;
end;
finally
  contacts.Free;
end;
end;
```

The `AllContacts` method of the address book populates a generic list of `TAddressBookContact` objects. Adding items to a list view is done through calling the `Add` method of the `TListView.Items` property. Calls to clear the list view and to add individual items are enclosed with the `BeginUpdate` and `EndUpdate` methods. On the next tab we will be displaying contact details, so that is why we also store the contact's `ID` value in the `Tag` property.

Add another tab to the `TabControl` component and change its `Name` property to `tbiContactDetail`. Add another change tab action to the action list. Rename it as `ctaContactDetail` and set its `Tab` property of `tbiContactDetail`. Drop the `TToolbar` component onto the third tab. Add the `TSpeedButton` component to the toolbar. We will use it to provide a way for the end user to navigate back to the list of contacts. Change its `Stylelookup` property to `arrowlefttoolbutton`, its `Name` to `spdbtnBack`, and connect its `Action` property to the `ctaContact` change tab action.

Each contact can have a number of different information associated with it. We will just focus on the very basic information. Drop an edit on the tab and a label. Drag the label in the **Structure View** onto the edit and position the label on top of the edit. Change the `Name` property of the edit to `edtFirstname` and enter `Firstname` as the `Text` property of the label. Copy the edit and paste it below the first one. The label should be automatically copied as well. Change the `Name` property of the second edit to `edtLastname` and enter `Lastname` as the `Text` property. Now, drop the `TLabel` and `TButton` components on the toolbar. Change its `Name` to `spdbtnSave` and its `Stylelookup` property of the button to `listitembutton` and `Text` to `Save`. Align the button to the `Right` and enter 8 in the `Margins.Right` property, so there is a nice distance between the button and the edge of the form. Change the label's `Text` property to **Contact Info**, align it to `Client`, and change its `TextSettings.HorzAlign` property to `Client`.

We have the graphical user interface ready. Now we will need to implement the remaining functionality to add a new contact, delete a contact, and save changes made to a contact. We will also need code to navigate from the list of contacts to the **detail** tab.

Detail tab of the ContactsMgr app with iOS style

Double-click on the `OnItemClick` event of the list view. This event is fired when the end user clicks on any item in the list view. It has a parameter with a reference to the `TListViewItem` element that was clicked. First, we need to read the `ID` of the contact that is stored in the `Tag` property of the list view item, display contact information on the `ContactInfo` tab, and then execute the change tab action to show the last tab. We will also need to declare a private field in the `TFormContacts` class to keep reference to the currently displayed contact. Add `FCurrentContact: TAddressBookContact` as the private field of the form class. Now we can implement the `OnItemClick` event handler:

```
procedure TFormContacts.lstvwContactsItemClick(const Sender: TObject;
  const AItem: TListViewItem);
  var c: TAddressBookContact;
  begin
```

```
  c := AddressBook1.ContactByID(aItem.Tag);
  FCurrentContact := c;
  edtFirstname.Text := c.FirstName;
  edtLastname.Text := c.LastName;
  ctaContactDetails.Execute;
end;
```

Luckily, there is a handy `ContactByID` method on the `AddressBook` that we can use to retrieve `TAddressBookContact` using its integer `ID`.

Double-click on the `spdbtnSave` on the third tab and implement logic to save the current contact information:

```
procedure TFormContacts.btnSaveClick(Sender: TObject);
begin
  if FCurrentContact <> nil then
  begin
    FCurrentContact.FirstName := edtFirstname.Text;
    FCurrentContact.LastName := edtLastname.Text;
    AddressBook1.SaveContact(FCurrentContact);
    actRefreshContacts.Execute;
  end;
end;
```

After the current contact information has been updated, we also need to refresh the contact list by executing the `actRefreshContacts` action. Now we will want to be able to add and delete contacts. A natural place for this functionality is the second tab with the list of contacts. Add a new `TSpeedButton` to the toolbar on the `tbiContacts` tab. Change its `Name` property to `spdbtnAdd`, its `Stylelookup` to `addtoolbutton`, and `Align` to `Left`. Double-click on the button and enter the following code that will create a new contact and display the **contact detail** tab where the end user will be able to enter information for a new contact:

```
procedure TFormContacts.spdbtnAddClick(Sender: TObject);

begin

  FCurrentContact :=
AddressBook1.CreateContact(AddressBook1.DefaultSource);
  edtFirstname.Text := '';
  edtLastname.Text := '';
  ctaContactDetails.Execute;
end;
```

The last task is to add logic to delete contacts. We will do it using the `TListView` functionality **swipe to delete**. By default, when the user makes the swipe gesture on any of the list view items, the `Delete` button is displayed next to it. There are special events in the list view component that can be used to react to the deletion of an item. Double-click on the `OnDeletingItem` event. It has a `ACanDelete` boolean parameter that we can set to `True` or `False`, depending on if we want to allow deletion or not. An item will be deleted from the list view, but we also need to delete the contact itself in the `AddressBook1`. To avoid deleting important contacts by accident, we will also implement a confirmation message.

Add the following code in the `OnDeletingItem` event of the `lstvwContacts` list view:

```
procedure TFormContacts.lstvwContactsDeletingItem(Sender: TObject;
  AIndex: Integer; var ACanDelete: Boolean);
var aID: integer; aDisplayName: string; msg: string;
begin
  aID := lstvwContacts.Items[AIndex].Tag;
  aDisplayName := lstvwContacts.Items[AIndex].Text;
  msg := 'Do you really want to delete current contact: ' + aDisplayName +
'?';
  if MessageDlg(msg, TMsgDlgType.mtConfirmation, mbYesNo, 0) = mrOK then
  begin
    AddressBook1.RemoveContact(aID);
    actRefreshContacts.Execute;
  end
  else
    aCanDelete := False;
end;
```

We have a fully functional app for managing contacts! Save all and run it on your smartphone to find out if you can really see your phone contacts!

# Notify me!

One of the most common ways of attracting a mobile device user to a particular app is to display a notification. When a new email arrives or somebody posts something on social media, we are typically presented with a notification. Clicking on it displays the app that sends the notification.

Delphi provides the TNotificationCenter component that can be used to display and react to notifications and display badge numbers on the app icon itself. That's a very common use case. You see a number next to your app icon and you know that there are unread emails or missed calls.

The TNotificationCenter component in the tool palette

Create a new, blank, multi-device app. Save the main form as uFormNotify and the project as NotifyMe. Add a toolbar with a label aligned to Client with Delphi Notifications text. Now, drop the TNotificationCenter component on the form. As a side effect, the System.Notification unit will be added to the form's uses clause. The first class defined in this unit is TNotification, that is used as a lightweight object that represents a notification. If we want to display a notification, first we need to call the TNotificationCenter.CreateNotification method that returns a new TNotification instance. Then, we need to set desired public fields of the notification. The last step is to pass the notification object to one of the methods of TNotificationCenter to display the notification immediately or to schedule it to be displayed in the future or at given time intervals. There are also methods to cancel already scheduled notifications.

Drop a button on the form, change its Name to btnNotify, and Text to Notify Me. Double-click on the button and enter the following code to display a test notification from the app:

```
procedure TFormNotify.btnNotifyClick(Sender: TObject);
var n: TNotification;
begin
  n := NotificationCenter1.CreateNotification;
  try
    n.Name := 'MY_APP_NOTIFICATION_1';
    n.Title := 'Notify Me App';
    n.AlertBody := 'This is an important notification from Delphi!';
    NotificationCenter1.PresentNotification(n);
  finally
    n.Free;
  end;
end;
```

The Name field of the notification object is used to uniquely identify it within an application. It is used, for example, to cancel a specific notification.

If we would have added another button named `btnCancel` to the form, we could cancel the notification with the following line of code:

```
procedure TFormNotify.btnCancelClick(Sender: TObject);

begin
  NotificationCenter1.CancelNotification('MY_APP_NOTIFICATION_1');
end;
```

# Navigating the web

The debate about whether native or web mobile apps are better seems to be over. A native mobile app, like the ones built with Delphi, C++Builder, or Xcode are the most common choice. However, sometimes it would make a lot of sense to combine these two different worlds and create a hybrid solution where an app is still native, but it embeds a web browser.

Luckily, in FireMonkey there is a special `TWebBrowser` component that makes it easy to embed web browsing functionality in your app.

Create a blank, multi-device application. Save the form as `uFormWebBrowser` and the project as `WebBrowserApp`. Drop a toolbar component on the form. Drop the `TEdit` component on the toolbar and rename it as `edtURL`. It will contain a URL for the web browser component to navigate to. For convenience, you can already put a valid URL into the `Text` property of the edit so it is faster at runtime to see if our app is working correctly. This could be, for example, the web address of the Embarcadero community site at `https://community.embarcadero.com/`. Now, drop `TSpeedButton` on the toolbar. Change its `Name` property to `spdbtnGo`, `Stylelookup` to `refreshtoolbutton`, and its `Align` property to the `Right`. Drop another two speed buttons on the toolbar. Change their `Name` properties respectively to `spdbtnBack` and `spdbtnForward`. Change their `Stylelookup` properties to `arrowlefttoolbutton` and `arrowrighttoolbutton`. Align them both to the `Left`. Now change the `Align` property of the URL edit to `Client` and its `Margin.Top` property to 8, so there is a distance between the edit and the top of the form. Drop the `TWebBrowser` component on the form and align it to `Client`. Now, double-click on each speed button and enter the simple code for web browser navigation:

```
procedure TFormWebBrowser.spdbtnBackClick(Sender: TObject);
begin
  WebBrowser1.GoBack;
end;

procedure TFormWebBrowser.spdbtnForwardClick(Sender: TObject);
```

```
begin
  WebBrowser1.GoForward;
end;

procedure TFormWebBrowser.spdbtnGoClick(Sender: TObject);
begin
  WebBrowser1.Navigate(edtURL.Text);
end;
```

Save all and run on a iOS and Android device. We have just created a fully functional cross-platform mobile web browser app.

# Working with maps

One of the most useful components in mobile apps is a map. Delphi comes with the cross-platform TMapView component that makes it easy to embed a map in an app.

On Android, it uses the Google Maps Android API and on iOS it uses the Map Kit Framework. On Android, it is necessary to first obtain the Google Maps API key. There are different possible view types on each platform. A map can be displayed as **Normal**, **Satellite**, or **Hybrid**. On Android there is also an additional **Terrain** view mode.

Let's build a simple app to try out different TMapView features. Create a new multi-device, blank Delphi app. Save the main form as uFormMap and the project as MapApp. Change the Name property of the form to FormMap. Drop TToolbar on the form and a TMapView component. Align to Client.

Drop the TComboBox component onto the toolbar. Rename it as cmbbxMapType and add five items to its Items property that corresponds to five possible map types.

MapType choices in the items property of the cmbbxMapType

Change the ItemIndex property of the combo to 1, so the initial selection is Normal. Add the OnChange event to the combobox and enter the following code:

```
procedure TFormMap.cmbbxMapTypeChange(Sender: TObject);
begin
  MapView1.MapType := TMapType(cmbbxMapType.ItemIndex);
end;
```

At this stage, we could compile and run this app on iOS, but for Android we need to obtain a special Google Maps API Key.

The TMapView component supports different gestures, so it is already useful on its own. The key properties are Location: TMapCoordinates that controls the location that is displayed, Zoom that controls the scale of the map, and Bearing to control the orientation. The default Zoom value is 0 and this means the smallest possible scale with very little detail which is just continents. You cannot zoom out more, but you can zoom in. Depending on the app, we might want to start from a higher zoom value, for example, 10. An end user can control zoom level with interactive gestures.

Let's drop the TLocationSensor component on the form. Turn its Active property to True and, in the OnLocationChange event, add code to set the Location of the map view to the location reading from the sensor. We can also adjust Bearing to an Orientation value from the sensor:

```
procedure TFormMap.LocationSensor1HeadingChanged(Sender: TObject;
  const AHeading: THeading);
begin
  MapView1.Bearing := AHeading.Azimuth;
end;

procedure TFormMap.LocationSensor1LocationChanged(Sender: TObject;
  const OldLocation, NewLocation: TLocationCoord2D);
var mc: TMapCoordinate;
begin
  mc.Latitude := NewLocation.Latitude;
  mc.Longitude := NewLocation.Longitude;
  MapView1.Location := mc;
end;
```

Save all and run the app. It is already quite functional, but it would be nice to show the current location with a marker. The TMapView component makes it possible to add custom markers to the view and react to click events on markers. It is also possible to add circles, polygons, and polylines. In the FMX.Maps unit, there are record types that describe location and other values specific to different objects that can be added to a map. For example, if we would like to add a custom marker, we need to first initialize fields of the TMapMarkerDescriptor and pass it to the AddDescriptor method of the TMapView. This will return a reference to a newly added TMapMarker.

Let's add a marker to the map in the OnLocationChange event to show what the current location is. We also need to remove the already existing marker before adding a new one, that is why there is a FMe: TMapMarker private field added to the form class to keep track of the current marker. Add the following code in the OnLocationChanged event of the location sensor component:

```
procedure TFormMap.LocationSensor1LocationChanged(Sender: TObject;
  const OldLocation, NewLocation: TLocationCoord2D);
var mc: TMapCoordinate; mmd: TMapMarkerDescriptor;
begin
  mc.Latitude := NewLocation.Latitude;
  mc.Longitude := NewLocation.Longitude;
  MapView1.Location := mc;

  if FMe <> nil then
    FMe.Remove;

  mmd := TMapMarkerDescriptor.Create(mc, 'Me');
  FMe := MapView1.AddMarker(mmd)
end;
```

The process of adding polygons, polylines, and circles is very similar. If we run the app on a device, it will show the current location with the default red marker.

# Creating and consuming Android services

The key benefit of Delphi and C++Builder is to be able to create your app once, and from the very same source code, natively compile it for different operating systems. In this book, we are focusing on mobile operating systems, namely Android and iOS. Every system is different and has different concepts that might not exist elsewhere. A good example of something unique to a particular platform are Android services. This notion exists on Android only and as such it cannot be ported to iOS or other operating systems.

Delphi has a special project type and the IDE wizard for creating an Android service. It is also possible to use an Android service, created with Delphi or not, in a regular multi-device project, but only if it is targeting Android.

Services are intended to be used by different apps, so the same functionality does not need to be implemented over and over again, but it can be reused. In this way, certain logic needs to be coded just once. No duplication also means efficient utilization of system resources. Services do not have a user interface and can be used for executing long running operations in the background, while the host app is busy doing something else.

Let's have a look what it takes to create an Android service with Delphi. Click on **Create a New Project** in the **Welcome** page, or select **Other...** from the **File | New** menu, to display the **New Items** dialog. Click on the very first , which is **Android Service**.

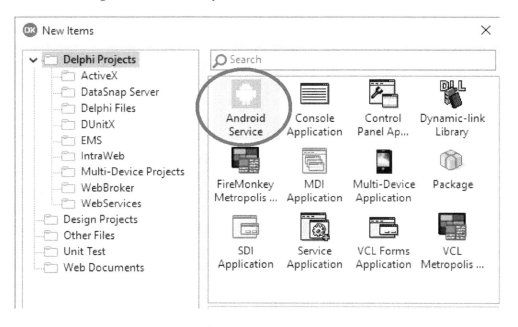

New Android Service wizard in the Delphi new items dialog

This will start the wizard. On the first screen of the wizard, we need to decide what kind of Android service to create. This could be a local or remote service.

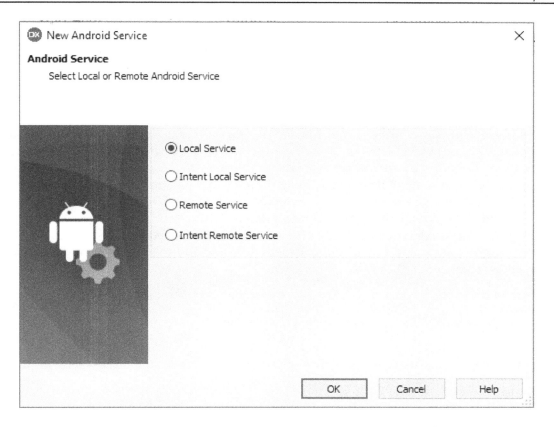

A local service is used by the host app only, while a remote service can be used by multiple apps running on the same device. Additionally, there is a variation to make this an intent service or not. Using intents means asynchronous communication between an app and a service.

In this example, we are going to create a service that will be periodically checking the light sensor and notifying the host app about the intensity of ambient light. The host app is going to just display the current reading, but in a more realistic example, it could adjust its color scheme to a more or less bright surrounding light or do something else.

There will be two projects created in the IDE. One for the service and one for the app. Create two folders for both projects. One named LightService and one named LightServiceApp.

Keep the default **Local Service** selection in the wizard and click on **OK**. An Android service project has been created. Click on **Save All**. In a service there is no user interface, only a data module class TDM that is derived from TAndroidService. Save the data module unit as uDMLightSensor and the project as LightSensorService. Make sure that they are both saved in the LightServiceApp folder. Change the Name property of the data module to DMLightSensor. Drop the TNotificationCenter component on the data module. It will be responsible for sending notifications to the host app with information about the current ambient light level. Drop a TTimer component on the form. Change its Interval property to 300 milliseconds and set its Enabled property to False. The last class to add is the light sensor component. It is not available from the tool palette, so we will have to create it in code. Add the System.Sensors.Components unit to the uses clause in the interface section of the data module unit and declare a private FLightSensor: TLightSensor member. We also need to make sure that the sensor class is created and destroyed. Add OnCreate and OnDestroy events to the data module and add calls to create and free the light sensor instance:

```
procedure TDMLightSensor.AndroidServiceCreate(Sender: TObject);
begin
  FLightSensor := TLightSensor.Create(self);
end;

procedure TDMLightSensor.AndroidServiceDestroy(Sender: TObject);
begin
  FLightSensor.Free;
end;
```

An Android service does not start automatically when it is created. There is a special OnStartCommand event that is used to execute any logic for starting the service. Here, we are going to start the light sensor and enable the timer. There is one additional line of code to add that will control the lifetime of the service. We want the service to start "sticky", which means that the system will try to recreate the service if it is killed. Add the following code into the event:

```
uses Androidapi.JNI.App;   // TJService
// ...
function TDMLightSensor.AndroidServiceStartCommand(const Sender: TObject;
  const Intent: JIntent; Flags, StartId: Integer): Integer;
begin
  FLightSensor.Active := True;
  Timer1.Enabled := True;
  Result := TJService.JavaClass.START_STICKY;
end;
```

We also needed to use the `Androidapi.JNI.App` unit, where the `TJService` type is declared. The last thing is to add the `OnTimer` event with the code to read the sensor ambient light level property and send the notification to the host app with this value. In the case that the ambient light sensor is not supported on a particular device, we will get the `Not a Number` value, so we need to check for that:

```
procedure TDMLightSensor.Timer1Timer(Sender: TObject);
var v: double; s: string; n: TNotification;
begin
  v := FLightSensor.Sensor.Lux;

  if IsNan(v) then
    s := 'NaN'
  else
    s := Format('%3.5f', [v]);

  n := NotificationCenter1.CreateNotification;
  try
    n.Name := 'LightSensorNotification';
    n.AlertBody := s;
    NotificationCenter1.PresentNotification(n);
  finally
    n.Free;
  end;
end;
```

That's it. Our service is ready. Right-click on it in the **Project Manager** and select **Compile**. Now we will create a host app that will be using the service. Still in the **Project Manager**, right-click on the **Project Group** and select **Add New Project**. Choose **Multi-Device Application** and a blank application template. Save the main form's unit of the project as `uFormLightLevel` and the project as `LightServiceApp`. Make sure they are both saved in the `LightServiceApp` folder. Now, the IDE will ask to save the project group. Save it as `LightServiceGrp`. Change the `Name` property of the form to `FormLightLevel`. Save All.

Before we can use the service, we need to add it to the project first. Our light service is already compiled. That is important. It needs to be compiled because we will need to have access to binary service files. Double-click on the `LightServiceApp` in the **Project Manager** to make it active. Expand its **Target Platforms** and double-click on the **Android** node. Now, right-click on this nod **Add Android Service**.

Add Android Service context menu option in the Project Manager

The first screen of the wizard for adding an Android service to a project lets you choose how you want to specify individual files to be added. The default choice is automatic, where the wizard will try to find appropriate files in a given directory. The other option is to select files manually. Let's keep the default automatic selection:

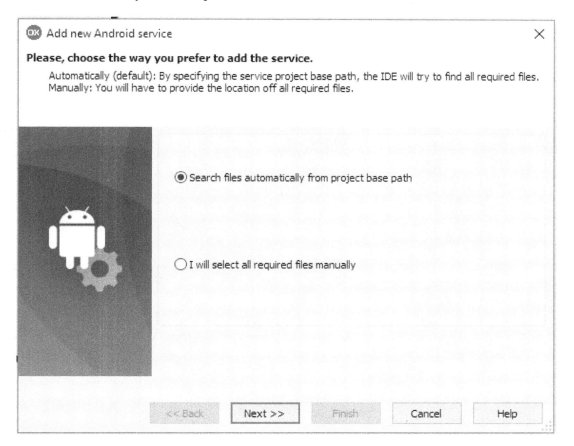

On the second screen, we need to specify the base path where all files belonging to the service project are stored. In our case, this is the `LightService` directory:

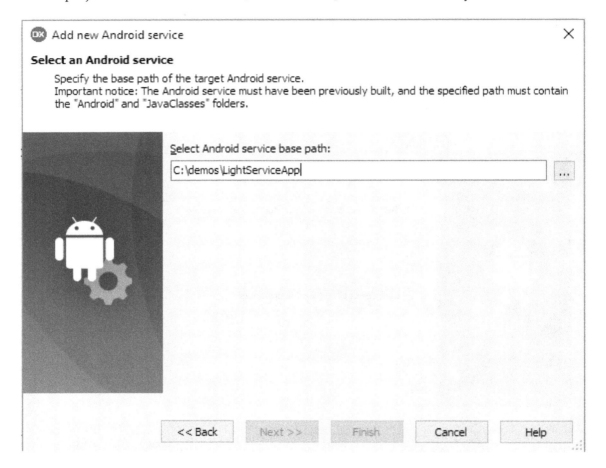

On the last screen, we can review which files are going to be added to the project:

There are three files added when we add an Android service to a project. There is the source file of the data module with Object Pascal implementation of the service (*.pas), a Java archive with the service (*.jar), and a natively compiled service library (*.so). These files need to exist, so that is why the service project needs to be compiled before it can be added.

Click on the **Finish** button and the service is added to the project. In the **Project Manager**, we can see that the uDMLightSensor unit has been added to the project, but also in the Libraries node under the Android target platform, there is a new LightSensorService.jar file listed.

Java libraries referenced by our Android project

The user interface of our host app will be super simple. Just drop a button on the form and enter Start Light Sensor Service as its Text property. Below the button drop, TLabel where we are going to display the ambient light value from the sensor. Change the Name property of the label to lblLux and Text to (Ambient Light). We also need a way to receive notifications from the service. Drop the TNotificationCenter component on the form. In the OnClick event of the button, we are going to start the service. It is implemented as a local service, so we are going to use a special TLocalServiceConnection class from the System.Android.Service unit that provides the class StartService procedure that takes the service name to start. This needs to match the name of the service specified in the generated Android Manifest file in the <service> tag.

Double-click on the `OnReceiveLocalNotification` event of the notification center component and add one line of code to display the `AlertBody` property of the received notification in the label:

```
uses
  System.Android.Service;

procedure TFormLightLevel.btnStartServiceClick(Sender: TObject);
begin
  TLocalServiceConnection.StartService('LightSensorService');
end;

procedure TFormLightLevel.NotificationCenter1ReceiveLocalNotification(
  Sender: TObject; ANotification: TNotification);
begin
  lblLux.Text := ANotification.AlertBody + ' [Lux]';
end;
```

Save all and run the host application. After clicking on the button, we should start seeing the value of ambient light surrounding our Android device.

# Delphi language bridges

So far, we have seen how to access cross-platform implementations of services such as sensors, address book, maps, and others. All of them come out of the box. Luckily, Delphi comes with the source code, so it is possible to inspect how Delphi itself is accessing the underlying mobile APIs on Android and iOS. All supported operating systems are different and there are different ways of accessing their raw APIs.

Let's consider a simple example of making your mobile device vibrate in code. That is not something that Delphi provides, but we can use this case to analyze the process of accessing any functionality that is not readily accessible in Android and iOS.

# Vibrating on Android

Android is based on Linux and Java. Accessing Android APIs requires being able to call from Object Pascal into Java code. This is the role of the Object Pascal to Java language bridge and this is how FireMonkey gets access to Android functionality. Before we can access certain functionality in Android, we need to find the documentation and know what Java class we want to access and what the methods we want to call are. Vibrations on Android are accessible through the `Vibrator` class declared in the `Android.os` namespace and derived directly from the base `java.lang.object`. The online documentation of this class can be found at `https://developer.android.com/reference/android/os/Vibrator.html`.

In the `source\rtl\Android` folder under the Delphi installation, we can find a number of Object Pascal units with names that start from `Android.JNI`. These are files already imported to Object Pascal. In the `Android.Jni.Os` unit, we can find Object Pascal interfaces for different Java classes imported from the `Android.os` namespace, including `JVibrator`. That's what we need, but how do we use it in code? Browsing through the source code we can find two interface declarations, `JVibratorClass` and `JVibrator`. The first interface represents class methods of the given Java type and the second is for instance methods. The `TJVibrator` class derived from the generic `TJavaGenericImport` glues these interfaces together. The `TJavaGenericImport` class is defined in the `Androidapi.JNIBridge` unit and it provides base functionality for importing all kinds of Java classes:

```
TJVibrator = class(TJavaGenericImport<JVibratorClass, JVibrator>) end;
```

We want to call the vibrate method declared in the `JVibrator` interface, but how do we get access to it? Different Java classes can be accessed through the `SharedActivityContext` function defined in the `Androidapi.Helpers` unit that returns Java application context. The documentation says that we need to call the `getSystemService` method and pass `VIBRATOR_SERVICE` as argument. The `TJavaGenericImport` class declares a handy `Wrap` method that lets us typecast from a raw pointer into the proper interface type.

In this way, we can make our Android device vibrate using the following code. It has to be surrounded with IFDEFs for Android:

```
uses
    Androidapi.JNI.Os, Androidapi.JNI.GraphicsContentViewText,
    Androidapi.Helpers, Androidapi.JNIBridge;

procedure TForm1.Button1Click(Sender: TObject);
var aVibrator: JVibrator;
begin
  aVibrator :=
TJVibrator.Wrap((SharedActivityContext.getSystemService(TJContext.JavaClass
.VIBRATOR_SERVICE) as ILocalObject).GetObjectID);
  aVibrator.vibrate(300); // Vibrate for 300 milliseconds
end;
```

Before running this code, make sure to set `Vibrate` to `True` in Project Options **Uses Permissions**.

This is just a simple example. There are also Java classes without already imported Object Pascal interfaces. In these cases, you can use a command-line `Java2OP` tool that is available in the `bin\converters\java2op` subdirectory in Delphi installation.

# Vibrations on iOS

Making an iOS device vibrate requires completely different steps as compared to Android. Vibrations on iOS are available as part of the `AudioToolbox` framework. In order to make an iOS device vibrate, one needs to call the AudioServicesPlaySystemSound API function, which is documented at

`https://developer.apple.com/reference/audiotoolbox/system_sound_services`.

Similarly to Android, there are already a number of pre-imported units with interfaces to iOS APIs in the `source\rtl\ios` directory. The model is similar. Different frameworks have their own import units with names starting from `iOSapi`. There is also a generic class for importing arbitrary `ObjectiveC` classes defined in the `Macapi.ObjectiveC` unit called `TOCGenericImport` that serves a similar role as `TJavaGenericImport`, for Android.

Delphi installation comes with a number of iOS frameworks already imported. Go to the **Tools** dialog and find **SDK Manager**. Scroll down in the listbox. Unfortunately the `AudioToolbox` framework is not imported to Delphi out of the box, so it is not listed as an available framework and there is no `iOSapi.AudioToolbox` unit in the source directory.

If we want to write code that is using certain framework functionality, we need to first import it to Delphi. Click on the **Add Remote Path Item** button next to the **Remote paths** list and enter the path to the `AudioToolbox` framework to import it. Leave **Path Type** choices unchecked.

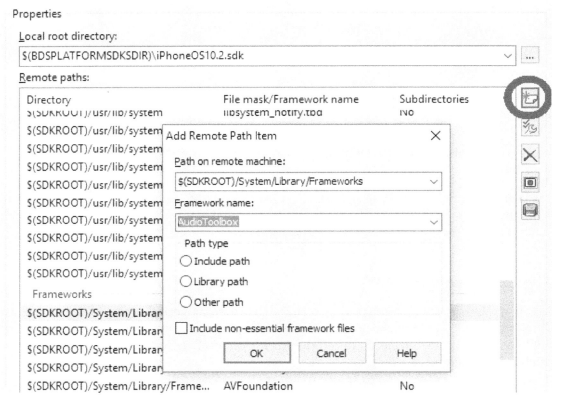

Add Remote Path Item dialog in the SDK Manager tab for iOS

The second step is to click on the **Update Local File Cache** button. This will update all files needed for compilation against different iOS frameworks, including the new `AudioToolbox` framework that we have added.

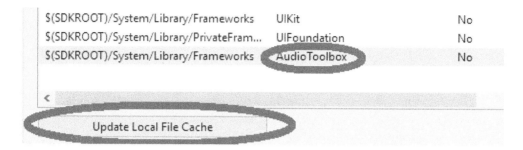

$(SDKROOT)/System/Library/Frameworks      UIKit                     No
$(SDKROOT)/System/Library/PrivateFram...   UIFoundation              No
$(SDKROOT)/System/Library/Frameworks      AudioToolbox              No

Update Local File Cache

The Update Local File Cache button in SDK Manager

OK. How can we call the `AudioServicesPlaySystemSound` function from the imported framework?

In the `bin` directory of Delphi there is an `SdkTransform` tool that can help with importing ObjectiveC frameworks into Object Pascal.

```
Command Prompt

C:\>sdktransform
Usage: SdkTransform [cmds] [options]

Options:
--out:<output_dir> - directory where the output .pas files should be placed.
--task:<xml file> - file with descrption of the task.
--unit:<Unit name> - transform only framework with the specified name.
--fmt - perform formatting of the output files after translation.
--comments - copy the block comments from Obj-C code to the output Delphi files
```

Output from the sdktransform tool executed with no parameters

Once we know the signature of our API method, we can call it in code. Again, the following code should be surrounded with IFDEFs for iOS to be able to compile it:

```
uses
  IOSapi.MediaPlayer, IOSapi.CoreGraphics, FMX.Platform, FMX.Platform.IOS,
  IOSapi.UIKit, Macapi.ObjCRuntime, Macapi.ObjectiveC, iOSapi.Cocoatypes,
  Macapi.CoreFoundation, iOSapi.Foundation, iOSapi.CoreImage,
iOSapi.QuartzCore,
  iOSapi.CoreData;

const
  libAudioToolbox =
'/System/Library/Frameworks/AudioToolbox.framework/AudioToolbox';
  kSystemSoundID_vibrate = $FFF;

procedure AudioServicesPlaySystemSound(inSystemSoundID: integer); cdecl;
  external libAudioToolbox Name _PU + 'AudioServicesPlaySystemSound';

procedure TForm1.Button1Click(Sender: TObject);
begin
  AudioServicesPlaySystemSound(kSystemSoundID_vibrate);
end;
```

Luckily, Delphi and FireMonkey come with most of the commonly used functionality already available in the form of components and libraries, so we do not need to go into such low-level programming very often.

# Summary

In this chapter, we have learnt how to work with functionality provided by different mobile operating systems. Every system is different, but we can use high-level components and cross-platform abstractions that make it possible to just recompile your project to a different system from the very same source code.

# 8
# Extending to the Internet of Things

The possibility to integrate apps running on mobile devices with the world of Internet of Things gadgets and wearables opens new and exciting possibilities for mobile developers. In this chapter, we are going to see how easy it is to use Delphi to integrate with the IoT using **Bluetooth Low Energy** (**BLE**) communication. We are going to use specialized `ThingConnect` components available with the **GetIt Package Manager** for working with devices such as heart rate monitors. The special type of BLE devices are beacons that you can use to add precise indoor and outdoor location awareness to your mobile app. At the end of this chapter, we are going to learn how to use the `BeaconFence` framework for building complete mobile microlocation solutions. We are also going to play with *App Tethering* technology that makes it super easy for two arbitrary apps to communicate with each other over Bluetooth or TCP/IP.

This chapter will cover the following points:

- Bluetooth Low Energy
- ThingConnect components
- Beacons
- BeaconFence
- App Tethering

The objective of this chapter is to teach you how to integrate your Delphi apps with different IoT devices, work with beacons, and use app tethering.

# Communication protocols

The **Internet of Things** (**IoT**) is based on the fact that a computer program can interact with all kinds of devices, gadgets, and sensors. At the lowest level, interacting with a remote *thing* needs to be done through a communication protocol.

The world of IoT is very interesting because it is a relatively new concept. When technology is not yet mature, it evolves very quickly and there are many competing solutions and only a few standards. There is still nobody to dominate the IoT market. If you try to look up IoT on the internet, you will find a lot of different answers. Every hardware and software vendor will have a different opinion about what IoT is and how to do it.

It always starts from a problem at hand, and how it can be solved. At one side of the IoT landscape, there are systems based on long-range protocols, such as LoRa, which provide bi-directional communication with sensors located within a radius of many kilometers, possibly covering the whole city. On the other side of the IoT spectrum, there are protocols such as NFC, which enables wireless communication between devices located only a few centimeters away.

# Understanding BLE

One of the most important communication protocols for IoT is Bluetooth. In fact, there are two different Bluetooth technologies. The *classic* Bluetooth and the newer, BLE, sometimes called *smart* Bluetooth; Bluetooth LE, or just BLE for short. The classic Bluetooth is useful for data streaming and provides data transfer rates up to 2 Mbps. It is commonly used in cars, especially in hands-free headsets. It has much higher data transfer rates as compared to BLE, but also much higher energy consumption.

BLE protocol has been designed with very low power consumption in mind, and uses a different set of radio techniques than classic Bluetooth. Data transfer rates in Bluetooth LE are relatively low, less than 100 Kbps. A big advantage of smart Bluetooth is the very fast connection time, typically just a few milliseconds, because there is no *pairing* process involved, like in classic variant. BLE communication is based on the **Generic Attribute Profile** (**GATT**) model. The whole GATT specification can be found at `https://www.bluetooth.com/specifications/generic-attributes-overview`. The GATT model defines how two BLE devices send and receive standard messages. Each GATT profile describes a use case, roles, and general behaviors based on the GATT functionality. At `https://www.bluetooth.com/specifications/adopted-specifications` you can find a list of different adopted GATT specifications for connecting to different types of devices.

For example, you can find profiles such as *Heart Rate Profile, Weight Scale Profile, Glucose Profile,* or *Proximity Profile.* In this way, we can build a mobile app that communicates over BLE with heart rate monitors from different vendors in a standard way.

The Bluetooth LE GATT profile describes a number of services. Each service is a collection of characteristics. Each characteristic includes different attributes. A GATT profile defines if a certain characteristic is mandatory or optional. For example, in the *Heart Rate Service,* the *Heart Rate Measurement* characteristic is mandatory, while *Body Sensor Location* and *Heart Rate Control Point* are optional. Each characteristic is basically data that you can write, read, or subscribe to in a BLE device of a certain kind. In BLE, one party participating in communications acts as a **GATT server** and another as a **GATT client**. The server exposes a set of attributes to a client that are accessible using the attribute protocol. An attribute is the actual data. It could be anything. It could be a heart rate value measured in beats per minute, the state of a light switch, temperature, or something else.

Not every version of mobile operating systems and not every mobile device type supports BLE and the specification itself is evolving too. That is why it is important to pay attention if your combination of software and hardware supports what you want to build.

The key types and classes for working with Bluetooth in Delphi are defined in the `System.Bluetooth` unit. With Delphi, it is not only possible to build GATT clients, but also to implement GATT servers. Similar to other frameworks in Delphi, there are two levels of Bluetooth support. You can do things in code, with types defined in `System.Bluetooth`, or you can use reusable components, `TBluetooth` and `TBluetoothLE`, defined in the `System.Bluetooth.Components` unit, that can make your life easier and act as a wrapper to non-visual classes. In this chapter, we are going to focus primarily on BLE, because this is the key protocol for IoT.

Bluetooth components on Tool Palette

The access to BLE functionality on a given platform is managed by the `TBluetoothLEManager` class in the `System.Bluetooth` unit. The application code does not need to instantiate this class, because the reference to platform-specific implementation of the BLE manager can be obtained through its `Current` class property.

The BLE manager class is also the way to obtain the reference to GATT server implementation. Before calling `GetGattServer: TBluetoothGattServer`, it is a good idea to check first with the `SupportsGattServer: boolean` method if this capability is supported on a given platform and hardware combination.

In most scenarios, our mobile app is going to act as a GATT client and will be connecting to a GATT server implemented by an IoT device. In order to connect with a device, after obtaining a reference to `TBluetoothLEManager`, we need to call one of its overloaded versions of the `StartDiscovery` function. They return a `true` Boolean value if the discovery process has been successfully initiated. The parameters are `Timeout` in milliseconds and a list of UUID of services to be discovered.

The BLE specification uses 16-bit identifiers for services and characteristics. In order to construct a full 128-bit BLE GUID, you have to combine a given 16-bit number from a GATT specification with the base Bluetooth LE UUID that can be found at `https://www.bluetooth.com/specifications/assigned-numbers/service-discovery` and is the following:

```
00000000-0000-1000-8000-00805F9B34FB
```

Let's consider the *Heart Rate Measurement* profile. This service has assigned number 0x180D. Consequently, the full 128-bit UUID for this service is:

```
0000180D-0000-1000-8000-00805F9B34FB
```

This is the value that needs to be passed to the `StartDiscovery` method in order to discover available devices that provide the *Heart Measurement* service.

There is nothing like building a test app and giving things a try. For this test, you would need a BLE-compatible heart rate monitor device. I have got one from a sport shop and there are many different models and vendors available. There are also a number of apps that are advertised to work with BLE heart monitors. Let's build another one.

We could code directly against the non-visual `TBluetoothLEManager` class, but it is easier to use the `TBluetoothLE` component that encapsulates the BLE manager. Create a new multidevice Delphi blank app, and save the main form's unit as `uFormHRM` and the project as `HeartRateApp`. Change the **Name** of the form to `FormHRM` and save all. Drop the `TBluetoothLE` component on the form. The user interface will be super simple. Just drop `TCheckBox` on the form, change its **Name** property to `chkbxHRM`, and its **Text** to **Heart Rate Monitor Enabled**. Drop the `TLabel` component as well on the form, change its **Name** property to `lblHeartRate`, and its **Text** to **Heart Rate: ? BPM**.

In the OnChange event of the checkbox, add the following line of code that will enable the BLE component and start the discovery for available heart rate monitors:

```
const
  HRM_SERVICE: TBluetoothUUID =
    '{0000180D-0000-1000-8000-00805F9B34FB}';
  HR_MEASUREMENT_CHARACTERISTIC: TBluetoothUUID =
    '{00002A37-0000-1000-8000-00805F9B34FB}';
  A_TIMEOUT = 3000;

procedure TFormHRM.chkbxHRMChange(Sender: TObject);
begin
  BluetoothLE1.Enabled := chkbxHRM.IsChecked;
  if BluetoothLE1.Enabled then
    BluetoothLE1.DiscoverDevices(A_TIMEOUT, [HRM_SERVICE]);
end;
```

The first parameter to the StartDiscovery call is the timeout in milliseconds. If we skipped the second parameter, we would find all BLE devices visible to our app. That could be useful, if we would like to build a generic BLE scanner, but in most cases we are just interested in connecting to a particular device and getting from it a particular data.

Now we need to add code to the OnEndDiscoverDevices event that is triggered when the discovery process is finished. The ADeviceList parameter holds a list of all discovered devices. There could be zero, one, or more devices found. Let's assume that we have only one heart device monitor to connect to, so we would be interested in the first device in the list, if there are any. The next step is to call DiscoverServices on the discovered device, and then we can use the GetService method of the BluetoothLE1 component and pass the device info and the UUID of the heart rate service. This call should return a reference to the heart rate measurement service. When we have a reference to the heart service, we can call the GetCharacteristic method of the BLE component passing the service reference and the identifier of the heart rate measurement service. The last thing is to subscribe to the desired service.

After successful subscription to a characteristic, we can read its data in the `OnCharacteristicRead` event of the BLE component. The data from the characteristic is passed as a dynamic array of bytes, so we need to know how to convert these bytes into a meaningful number to be displayed in the label. The heart rate service GATT specification provides information about the meaning of individual bytes in the characteristics data. The first bit of the first byte of data indicates if the heart rate measurement is encoded as UINT8 or UINT16. If this bit is zero, then the heart rate value is encoded in the next byte, if the flag is set to one, then the next two bytes represents the value encoded as an unsigned 16-bit integer:

```
procedure TFormHRM.BluetoothLE1EndDiscoverDevices(const Sender: TObject;
  const ADeviceList: TBluetoothLEDeviceList);
var device: TBluetoothLEDevice; service: TBluetoothGattService;
  characteristic: TBluetoothGattCharacteristic;
begin
  if ADeviceList.Count > 0 then
  begin
    if aDeviceList[0].Connect then
    begin
      device := aDeviceList[0];
      ShowMessage('Connected to HRM device');
      device.DiscoverServices;
      service := BluetoothLE1.GetService(device,
        HR_MEASUREMENT_CHARACTERISTIC);
      if service <> nil then
      begin
        characteristic := BluetoothLE1.GetCharacteristic(service,
          HR_MEASUREMENT_CHARACTERISTIC);
        if characteristic <> nil then
        begin
          if BluetoothLE1.SubscribeToCharacteristic(device,
            characteristic) then
            ShowMessage('Subscribed to HRM characteristic')
          else
            ShowMessage('Failed to subscribe to HRM characteristic');
        end
        else
          ShowMessage('Failed to get characteristic');
      end
      else
        ShowMessage('Failed to get HRM service');
    end
    else
      ShowMessage('Failed to connect to HRM device');
  end
  else
    ShowMessage('No HRM devices discovered');
```

```
end;

procedure TFormHRM.BluetoothLE1CharacteristicRead(const Sender: TObject;
  const ACharacteristic: TBluetoothGattCharacteristic;
  AGattStatus: TBluetoothGattStatus);
var bytes: TBytes; v: integer;
begin
  if aGattStatus = TBluetoothGattStatus.Success then
  begin
    bytes := ACharacteristic.Value;
    if bytes[0] and $1 = 0 then // 8 bits
      v := bytes[1]
    else // 16 bits
      v := bytes[1] + (bytes[2] * 16);
    lblHeartRate.Text := 'Heart Rate: ' + v.ToString + ' BPM';
  end
  else
    ShowMessage('Gatt status is not SUCCESS. Cannot read
                characteristic.');
end;
```

If you plan to run this app on Android, you will need to go to **Uses Permissions** in **Project Options** and set **Bluetooth** and **Bluetooth admin** permissions to **true**. Otherwise, you will get a security error when you try to enable BLE as shown in the following screenshot:

Bluetooth-related options in Uses Permissions tab in Project Options for Android target

Save all and run the app on the device. Place the heart rate monitor on your chest. Tick the enable checkbox and in a moment you should see your current heart rate. Do some push ups and your heart rate should go up!

# Connecting to things with ThingConnect

We have seen the steps to connect to an arbitrary BLE device using the `TBluetoothLE` component. For certain popular services, this can be even easier. Delphi comes with a number of components that simplify working with standard services such as, heart rate monitors, blood pressure monitors, and proximity sensors. There are also components available in GetIt for working with specific devices from specific vendors using not only BLE, but also other IoT protocols, such as Z-Wave.

Under the **Tools** menu, you can find the **GetIt Package Manager**. In order to use GetIt, you will need to have an internet connection. Over time, more and more new and updated software is available in GetIt. One of the available components in the IoT category is generic **Heart Rate Monitor** as shown in the following screenshot:

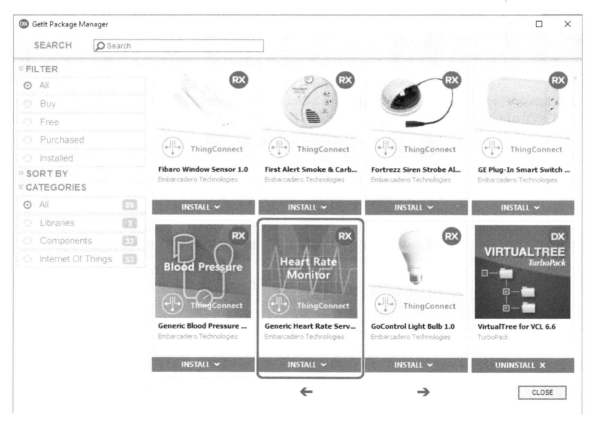

Heart Rate Monitor component available in the GetIt Package Manager

Similar to other component packages, after clicking the **Install** button, you are presented with the **End User License Agreement** that you need to accept in order to proceed. In case of the generic **Heart Rate Monitor**, you will need to accept two EULAs--one for the component itself, and one for the whole **ThingConnect IoT Device Component Pack** that this component belongs to. Click on **Agree All** to proceed. The whole installation process is very straightforward and only takes a couple of seconds to complete. First the IoTDevices library package is downloaded, compiled, and installed into the IDE. Then the actual Generic Heart Rate Service library is downloaded, compiled, and installed as well. The associated help file and demo projects are downloaded too. Refer to the following screenshot:

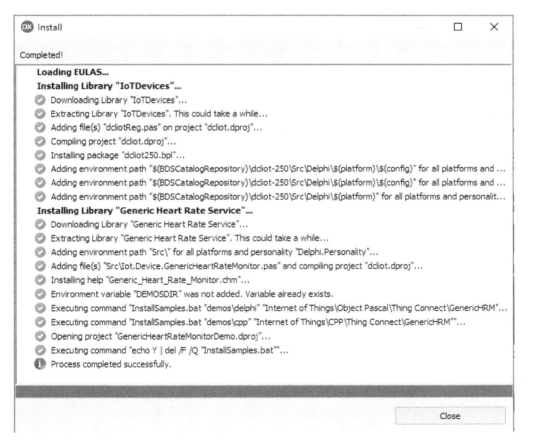

Log information from installing the Heart Rate Monitor component in the IDE

If we now install additional `ThingConnect` components, the `IoTDevices` library will not be downloaded, because it is already installed.

In the **Tool Palette,** a new **Internet of Things** category of components appears and there are currently two non-visual components: **TBluetoothDeviceDiscoveryManager** and **TGenericHeartRateMonitor**. Take a look at the following screenshot:

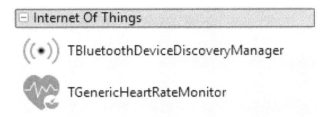

The contents of Internet of Things category in the Tool Palette after installing the Heart Rate Monitor component

These two components are already in the form of the demo project. The **TGenericHeartRateMonitor** component has a **DiscoveryManager** property that needs to be connected to the discovery manager component on the form.

Different BLE services can have a number of characteristics that can be read, written to, or subscribed to. The generated IoT component exposes characteristics directly as properties and events, but we can consult the downloaded help file to see how to deal with different characteristics. In the case of **Heart Rate Monitor**, there are three characteristics, and the following table from the help topic explains how to work with them:

| Service | Characteristic | Property | Event | Read | Subscribe | Write |
|---|---|---|---|---|---|---|
| Heart Rate | Body Sensor Location | `BodySensorLocation` | `OnBodySensorLocationUpdate` | ✔ | | |
| | Heart Rate Control Point (*) | `HeartRateControlPoint` | | | | ✔ |
| | Heart Rate Measurement | | `OnHeartRateMeasurementUpdate` | | ✔ | |

Information about Heart Rate service characteristics from the downloaded help file

If we want to get access to a heart rate measurement, we need to subscribe to this characteristic and implement the `OnHeartRateMeasurementUpdate` event handler to find out the current heart rate value.

With the prebuilt components, we do not need to work at the level of the plain BLE and GATT specification. This information is already embedded in the component, and we can write code on the higher level of abstraction. Instead of receiving just a generic `OnCharacteristicRead` event, we receive the `OnHeartRateMeasurementUpdate` event with heart rate information already properly decoded.

Let's build the same heart rate monitor app, with just one checkbox and label for displaying the heart rate, but this time, instead of using generic **TBluetoothLE**, we are going to use specialized IoT components from GetIt.

Create a new blank, multidevice app. Save the main form as `uFormHRMGetIt`, the project as `HRMGetIt`, and rename the form as `FormHRMGetIt`. Add `TCheckBox` and `TLabel` controls to the form and rename them as, respectively, `chkbxHRM` and `lblHeartRate`. Drop the `TBluetoothDeviceDiscoveryManager` and `TGenericHeartRateMonitor` components on the form. Select the `GenericHeartRateMonitor1` component in the **Object Inspector** and choose `BluetoothDeviceDiscoveryManager1` from the dropdown.

In the `OnChange` event for the checkbox, we are going to call the `DiscoverDevices` method on the discovery manager component. In the `OnDeviceConnected` event of the generic **Heart Rate Monitor**, we need to make a call to start subscribing to the heart rate value characteristic, and in the `OnHeartRateMeasurementUpdate`, we can display the current heart rate value in the label.

Make sure to add to the interface uses clause `IoT.Family.BluetoothLE.GattTypes` and `System.Bluetooth` units. Don't forget to add Bluetooth permissions to the *Android* build configuration in the **Project** option:

```
procedure TFormHTMGetIt.chkbxHRMChange(Sender: TObject);
begin
  if chkbxHRM.IsChecked then
    BluetoothDeviceDiscoveryManager1.DiscoverDevices;
  end;

procedure TFormHTMGetIt.GenericHeartRateMonitor1DeviceDiscovered(const
  Sender: TObject;
  const ADevice: TBluetoothLEDevice);
begin
  GenericHeartRateMonitor1.SubscribeHeartRateMeasurement;
end;

procedure TFormHTMGetIt.GenericHeartRateMonitor1HeartRateMeasurementUpdate(
  Sender: TObject; const Value: TGattHeartRateMeasurement);
begin
  lblHeartRate.Text :=
```

```
        'Heart Rate: ' + Value.HeartRateMeasurement.ToString + ' BPM';
    end;
```

This is so much easier. With specialized IoT components from **GetIt Package Manager**, we can write code on a higher level of abstraction.

# Getting close with beacons

One of the most popular Bluetooth LE devices are beacons. With beacons it is possible to add precision location awareness to mobile apps. They are becoming increasingly popular, and more and more apps are using them. A *beacon* is any device that provides a standard Bluetooth LE *proximity* service. Beacons are a very important IoT technology. Different vendors offer beacons with different capabilities. Some of them are battery-powered, and others are using a USB connection for charging. Beacons do not use a lot of energy, so a small, watch-sized battery can last for more than a year or even longer.

The support for Bluetooth beacons in Delphi is very similar to other supported cross-platform frameworks. The key beacons related types and classes are defined in the System.Beacon unit. There is a non-visual TBeaconManager class with many virtual abstract methods that are implemented by its platform-specific descendants that are available through the GetBeaconManager class method. There is also the System.Beacon.Components unit where TBeacon and TBeaconDevice components are implemented.

The key two things about beacons are their identification and the signal strength that is used to judge how far a beacon is away from a mobile device. A beacon device, depending on its configuration, sends out a couple of bytes of data a few times a second just to identify itself. You can think about it as a kind of a radio QR code. The only thing that a beacon does is tell the whole world--*I'm here and my identification number is the following*. A mobile app can detect the presence of a beacon and, based on the strength of the signal, determine how far the beacon is from the device. This is different as compared to GPS positioning. With GPS the positioning accuracy is up to a few meters and the GPS does not work well indoors. Beacons are different. They are just tiny radio transmitters advertising their presence. Suddenly, the logic of your app has more input. I'm receiving signals from a beacon *XYZ*, so I must be at a specific location where this particular beacon is installed.

Beacons are no longer an exotic technology. They have become mainstream, and more and more companies are using them to deliver better services. Ok. My app can detect the presence of a beacon and know how far it is from a mobile device with the accuracy of centimeters. Now what? What can we do with this information? It really depends on the technology and the particular use case. Proximity-enabled apps are used in stores, stadiums, museums, restaurants, and many other places. Beacons can be installed at fixed locations or attached to movable objects.

The operating system is only going to tell your app that it senses radio signals from a number of beacons with specific identifiers, and it is up to your app logic to do something with this information.

There are a number of different beacon device manufactures and there are different standards to communicate with beacons. One of the first beacon standards on the market was *iBeacon* from Apple. Another very similar open standard is **AltBeacon** ( `http://altbeacon.org/`) proposed by Radius Networks. With these standards, beacons identify themselves using a UUID number, and two additional integer values: **Major** and **Minor**. Typically, the UUID is the same for the whole beacon solution, or beacon vendor, and individual beacons have different major and minor values. A newer beacon standard is **Eddystone** from Google. Here, different types of data can be advertised by a beacon. There are different payloads that can be transmitted by an Eddystone beacon. The first type of data is **Eddystone-UID**, which is similar to the iBeacon standard. Eddystone beacons can also broadcast compressed URLs in the **Eddystone-URL** frame or special **Eddystone-TLM** frame that contains information about the beacon itself, such as its battery level or readings from additional sensors. The TLM payload is useful for beacon administrators or people responsible for beacon installations.

# Beacons in a museum

The `System.Beacon` unit defines key types and classes to work with beacons, using any of the supported standards. In order to get some practical knowledge of building beacon-enabled apps with Delphi, we are going to create a simple app for a museum. Imagine that behind every piece of art there is a beacon installed. When we get closer to an item in the exhibition, our app gets information from a particular beacon, looks up its identification, and displays a web page in the embedded web browser window about a piece of art that we are next to.

In this demo, we are going to use the iBeacon standard, so every beacon in a museum is identified by its UUID, and major and minor numbers.

Create a new Delphi multidevice app and use a blank application template. Save the main form as `uFormMuseum` and the project as `MuseumApp`. Change the **Name** property of the form to `FormMuseum`. Drop the **TBeacon** component on the form.

TBeacon component on the form

The key property of the **TBeacon** component is the enumerated scanning **Mode** value that controls which types of beacons can be detected by this component. The possible values are: Alternative, Eddystone, Extended, and Standard. The default value is **Extended**, which is the most flexible option where we can scan for all beacon types simultaneously, as shown in the following screenshot:

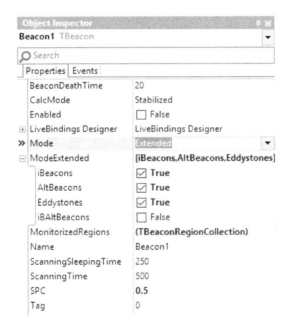

Beacon component Mode property set to Extended in the Object Inspector

The second key property is **MonitorizedRegions**. With this, we can specify the identification numbers of beacons we are interested in receiving signals from.

For our simple beacon museum demo, let's assume that we have just three beacons behind famous paintings of Vincent Van Gogh--**The Potato Eaters** (`https://en.wikipedia.org/wiki/The_Potato_Eaters`), **Bedroom in Arles** (`https://en.wikipedia.org/wiki/Bedroom_in_Arles`), and **Almond Blossoms** (`https://en.wikipedia.org/wiki/Almond_Blossoms`). All three beacons have the same UUID `74278BDA-B644-4520-8F0C-720EAF059935`, the same `Major` number `1973`, and they only differ in `Minor` numbers that are, respectively, `1001`, `1002`, and `1003`. These identification numbers need to be added to the **MonitorizedRegions** property. We do not need to specify all three entries. A value of **-1** for **Major** and **Minor** will scan for any beacons that have matching UUIDs, as shown in the following screenshot:

Properties of the first item in the MonitorizedRegions collection property of the Beacon1 component

Let's build a simple user interface for our app. Drop **TToolbar** on the form. Drop **TCheckBox** on the tool bar, rename it as chkbxActive, and its **Text** as Museum Tour Started. Add **TLabel** to the form. Change its **Name** property to lblInfo and Text to (Information). Expand its **Margins** property and enter 4 for each sub-property. Align it to **Top**. Drop **TWebBrowser** on the form and align it to **Client**.

The **TBeacon** component has a number of events that are triggered in response to changes in the beacon's proximity. Double-click on the OnBeaconProximity event. This will generate an empty event handler with two parameters: ABeacon: IBeacon and Proximity: TBeaconProximity. This event is executed when a change in proximity of one of the monitored beacons is detected. TBeaconProximity is an enumerated type defined in the System.Beacon unit and has four possible values: Immediate, Near, Far, and Away. Immediate means a distance of less than half a meter, Near is a distance between half and one and a half meters, Far is more than one and a half meters, and Away means we cannot determine the distance. The first parameter is a reference to the IBeacon interface that we can use to read the information about the beacon, including its identifiers, the *RSSI* value (relative signal strength), and proximity. We will need some way of looking up the URL to be displayed in the web browser, based on the detected beacon's identity. In a more realistic scenario, we would probably read this data from a database or from a service, but for simplicity, we are going to hardcode this information in the app itself. Add a new unit to the project, save it as *uBeaconInfo*, and enter there the following code:

```
unit uBeaconInfo;

interface

type
  TBeaconInfo = record
    UUID: TGUID;
    Major: integer;
    Minor: integer;
    Name: string;
    URL: string;
  end;

const
  AUUID = '{74278BDA-B644-4520-8F0C-720EAF059935}';
  BEACON_COUNT = 3;
  BEACONS: array[0..BEACON_COUNT-1] of TBeaconInfo = (
  (UUID: AUUID; Major: 1973; Minor: 1001; Name: 'The Potato Eaters';
    URL: 'https://en.wikipedia.org/wiki/The_Potato_Eaters'),
  (UUID: AUUID; Major: 1973; Minor: 1002; Name: 'Bedroom in Arles';
    URL: 'https://en.wikipedia.org/wiki/Bedroom_in_Arles'),
  (UUID: AUUID; Major: 1973; Minor: 1003; Name: 'Almond Blossoms';
```

```
      URL: 'https://en.wikipedia.org/wiki/Almond_Blossoms')
   );

function GetBeaconInfo(aUUID: TGUID; aMajor, aMinor: integer;
   out aName: string; out aURL: string): boolean;

implementation

function GetBeaconInfo(aUUID: TGUID; aMajor, aMinor: integer;
   out aName: string; out aURL: string): boolean;

var i, index: integer;
begin
   index := -1;
   for i := 0 to BEACON_COUNT-1 do
   if (BEACONS[i].UUID = aUUID) and (BEACONS[i].Major = aMajor)
     and (BEACONS[i].Minor = aMinor) then
   begin
    index := i;
    break;
   end;

   Result := index > -1;
   if Result then
   begin
     aName := BEACONS[i].Name;
     aURL := BEACONS[i].URL;
   end;
end;

end.
```

That is just an example, and your beacons will have different identifiers and possibly names, and the URLs will be different, but this technique is very handy. Being able to declare and initialize a constant array of records is very verbose, readable, and efficient at the same time. We have a simple GetBeaconInfo function that will return true if a given beacon was found in the table, and in its out parameters we will get a description and URL associated with the beacon. The OnBeaconProximity event may fire quite frequently, so we will need to add some logic to the app to prevent currently displayed information from disappearing too quickly.

In the TFormMuseum class, let's add two private fields: FCurrentURL: string and FShowingStarted: TTime. We will also define the MIN_SHOWING_TIME = 10 constant. Before implementing the code in OnBeaconProximity, let's first implement two simple utility methods for showing and hiding the museum information:

```
uses
  uBeaconInfo, System.DateUtils;

const
  MIN_SHOWING_TIME = 10; // seconds

procedure TFormMuseum.chkbxActiveChange(Sender: TObject);
begin
  Beacon1.Enabled := chkbxActive.IsChecked;
  if not chkbxActive.IsChecked then
    HideInfo;
end;

procedure TFormMuseum.HideInfo;
begin
  FCurrentURL := '';
  lblInfo.Text := '';
  WebBrowser1.Visible := False;
end;

procedure TFormMuseum.ShowInfo(aName, aURL: string);
begin
  // show current information for at least "MIN_SHOWING_TIME"
  if (FCurrentURL <> '') and
    (SecondSpan(Now, FShowingStarted) < MIN_SHOWING_TIME) then
    exit;

  if (FCurrentURL = '') or (FCurrentURL <> aURL) then
  begin
    lblInfo.Text := aName;
    WebBrowser1.Navigate(aURL);
    FShowingStarted := Now;
    WebBrowser1.Visible := True;
  end
end;
```

Now we just need to implement the OnBeaconProximity event and our simple beacon museum app will be ready, as shown in the following code snippet:

```
procedure TFormMuseum.Beacon1BeaconProximity(const Sender: TObject;
  const ABeacon: IBeacon; Proximity: TBeaconProximity);
var aName, aURL: string;
```

```
begin
  if Proximity in [Immediate, Near] then
  begin
    if GetBeaconInfo(aBeacon.GUID, aBeacon.Major, aBeacon.Minor,
      aName, aURL) then
      ShowInfo(aName, aURL)
    else
      HideInfo;
  end;
end;
```

We only display the information if the proximity is `Immediate` or `Near`. Save all and run. Refer to the following screenshot:

MuseumApp project running on iPhone

Using beacon events is the most natural solution for a beacon-enabled app.

Another possible approach is to have a timer component and periodically scan through the list of all the beacons visible to the beacon component using the **BeaconList** property.

# Emulating beacons with TBeaconDevice

Next to the **TBeacon** component in the **Tool Palette**, we can find **TBeaconDevice**. With this component, we can turn our mobile device into a programmable beacon that will be advertising the proximity data.

That's a very cool ability. Our device can pretend to be any of the supported beacon types, including newer Eddystone beacons. If you do not have physical beacons for developing and testing beacon projects, this component could be very useful. Just turn one or more of your mobiles to act as test beacons, when you need beacons to develop your brand new beacon app.

TBeaconDevice component on the form

The **BeaconType** property controls what kind of beacon we want to emulate. Possible choices are **Alternative, EddystoneUID, EddystoneURL** and **Standard**. Depending on which beacon type we want to use, other properties are used, as shown in the following screenshot:

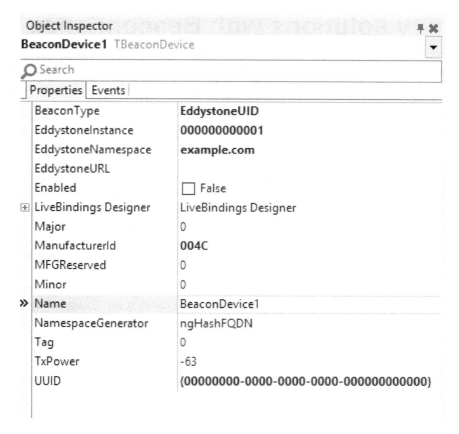

Properties of TBeaconDevice component in the Object Inspector

If we set the **Enabled** property of the **BeaconDevice** component, then it will start to advertise proximity data using Bluetooth LE.

Delphi installation comes with the `BeaconDeviceDemo` project that demonstrates emulating different types of beacons on different platforms.

# Proximity solutions with BeaconFence

A simple beacon-based proximity system can just detect the presence of a beacon and trigger some actions based on *seeing* it. Another interesting use case is to build a positioning system, where our app would know the precise location of the device on which it is running.

It is very similar to **Global Positioning System (GPS)**, a system of satellites that can provide the app with geographical coordinates where it is currently located. GPS is great, but it has its limitations. First of all, the accuracy of GPS is only up to a few meters. The second limitation is that it only works outdoors. With beacons it is possible to build much more precise systems, with location accuracy below one meter, and which work both outdoors and indoors. A good example of such a location tracking use case would be to find your way in the underground parking garage, or inside a big office building.

When an app receives proximity advertisements from a beacon, it only knows which beacon it is and approximately how far away it is located. It cannot tell from which direction the beacon radio signal is coming. In order to a build localization system, we need to have more beacons and use similar trigonometry as sailors were using on the sea to calculate the position of their ship using stars or light signals from traditional light beacons broadcasting their location.

Delphi comes with **BeaconFence**, which is a developer proximity solution that builds on top of the beacon support. BeaconFence is not installed out-of-the-box, but it needs to be downloaded and installed through GetIt. It is also licensed separately from Delphi, so before deploying a BeaconFence-based system into production, you need to get an appropriate license from Embarcadero, or one of its partners.

The first step is to download and install BeaconFence. Go to the **Tools** menu and select **GetIt Package Manager**. Find **BeaconFence** and click on the **Install** button:

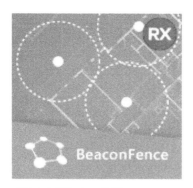

**BeaconFence 1.2**

Embarcadero Technologies

BeaconFence entry in the GetIt Package Manager

After accepting the end user license agreement, BeaconFence will be downloaded, compiled, and installed into the IDE. The `BeaconFence.chm` help file and demo projects will be downloaded as well. On the **Tool Palette**, in the **Internet of Things** category, you should find two new components: **TBeaconZonesFencing** and **TBeaconMapFencing**:

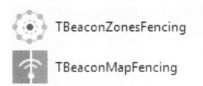

BeaconFence components in the Tool Palette

In your BeaconFence solution, you can use either of these components, or both of them. The second has an integrated map editor, while the first one allows defining zones only.

In the default Windows 10 and Delphi 10.2 installation, you should find a new `BeaconFence-250-1.2` folder installed in the `CatalogRepository` directory in the user documents. On my machine, the full path to this folder is `C:\Users\Pawel\Documents\Embarcadero\Studio\19.0\CatalogRepository\BeaconFence-250-1.2`. Here you can find the help file and demo projects. The fastest way to become familiar with BeaconFence is to have a look into an existing demo, the open `FencingGeneric` project from the `demo` directory.

BeaconFence is based on the `TBeaconManager` class from the `System.Beacon` unit. It adds an interactive map editor where you can specify the location of beacons, define zones, and add walking paths. Double-click on the **BeaconMapFencing1** component in the demo project to open the BeaconFence map editor. In the toolbar, click on the **Show Object Tree** to see the list of all the elements of the map in the window at the left of the screen:

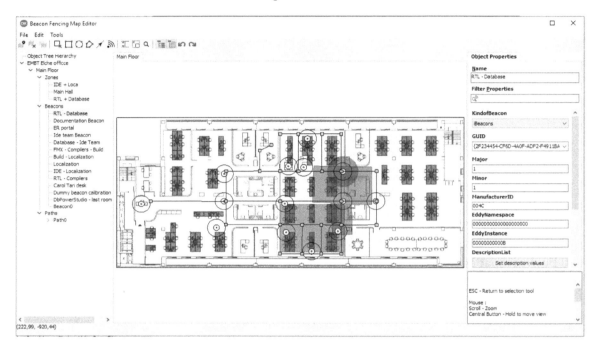

Integrated BeaconFencing Map Editor

Typically, we start a new map from loading a plan as a graphic image. Then we need to set up the scale. This is done interactively be selecting two points horizontally and vertically on the map, selecting units, and entering the numeric value of the distance between them. Then we can start to define zones and paths and place individual beacons on the map.

In your app, you no longer need to work at the level of individual beacons, but additionally you can get proximity zone events, such as `OnZoneEnter` and `OnZoneExit`. The `TBeaconMapFencing` component has a **PaintControl** property that you can connect to a visual control which you want to use for rendering the map and selected information from the beacon fence, such as beacons, zones, and so on.

BeaconFence is internally implemented using a **particle filter** algorithm optimized for localization tasks, which is based on the **Monte Carlo Localization** algorithm.

One important thing to remember when running the BeaconFence solution on iOS is to enable it to run in background mode. For this, you would need to modify the Info.plist file of your project and include the **bluetooth-central** value in the **UIBackgroundModes** key. This setting can be changed in **Project Options** in **Version Info**, as shown in the following screenshot:

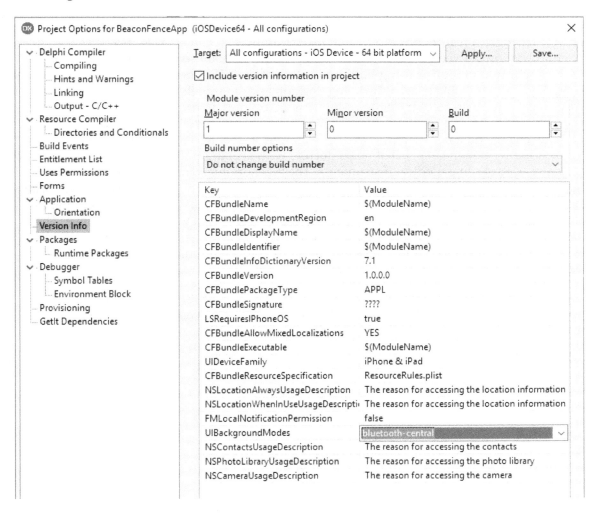

UIBackgroundModes bluetooth-central option selected for iOS target in Project Options

BeaconFence is a really powerful technology to easily create a complete beacon-positioning app that offers much better accuracy than GPS and that works indoors.

# App tethering

IoT is about apps talking to all kinds of devices, gadgets, and sensors. In this same vein, we can fit **app tethering** technology, where an app can easily communicate over Bluetooth or just plain TCP/IP protocols with other apps.

App tethering is a feature of Delphi, and also C++Builder. It can be used to set up communication between different types of applications, mobile or desktop, running on any of the supported platforms using FireMonkey, and also VCL. The original use case for app tethering was to be able to *extend* existing desktop apps to mobile devices and easily create *companion* apps. Instead of trying to re-implement existing desktop apps on mobile devices, the idea was to be able to either control a desktop app from a mobile app or to be able to easily exchange data between the two. For example, we could have an existing desktop application written in Delphi that helps doctors with keeping track of patients' data and possibly control some medical instruments. There is nothing wrong with this desktop application; it has stood the test of time and is very useful. But now, mobile approach brings new possibilities. It would be cool to use a mobile device with a camera and send images to the existing desktop app. With app tethering, such a use case is very easy to achieve. The Delphi IDE itself is using app tethering for the **Live Preview** feature. In this scenario, the IDE, which is a good example of a Delphi desktop app, communicates with the Live Preview app running on iOS or Android.

Using app tethering in your apps is relatively straightforward. Both apps that need to communicate with each other need to have two app tethering components on the form: **TTetheringManager** and **TTetheringAppProfile**:

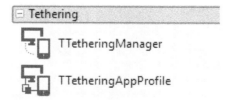

App tethering components available in the Tool Palette

These two components work together. **TTetheringAppProfile** has a **Manager** property that is used to connect the associated **TTetheringManager**.

App tethering can use either Wi-Fi or Bluetooth for communication. The **TTetheringManager** component has the **AllowedAdapters** property where we can specify the communication protocols to be used. By default, it is set to **Network**, which means using the standard TCP/IP network protocol for communication, but we can also choose **Bluetooth**. It is also possible to specify more than one communication protocol by separating their names with | or ; characters.

The communication in app tethering starts from discovering other tethering managers available in the network or via Bluetooth. The app that acts as a client needs to call the `DiscoverManagers` method on the app tethering manager component. There are different overloaded variations of this method. We can specify the discovery timeout and, if we want to connect to a specific manager, also a list of targets. When the discovery process is finished then the `OnEndDiscovery` event is triggered and a list of discovered managers is passed to this event in the `ARemoteManagers: TTetheringManagerInfoList` parameter. The next step is to *pair* a remote manager. In order to pair a remote manager we need to call the `PairManager` method of the `TAppTetheringManager` class passing as a parameter a reference to one of the discovered managers from the list. When the *pairing* process is finished then the `OnEndProfileDiscovery` event is executed. A list of remote profiles is passed in the `ARemoteProfiles: TTetheringProfileInfoList` parameter of this event. The last step is to establish a connection with a remote profile component. This can be done by calling the `Connect` method of the `TTetheringAppProfile` component, passing as a parameter a reference to a selected remote profile from the list.

When a connection is established, we can either send data to a remote application or execute remote actions on the server application. This second option is useful in the scenarios when we use app tethering to implement a *remote control* app to an existing, typically desktop app. On the server, or *controlled* application, we need to decide which actions should be exposed to remote applications. The `TTetheringAppProfile` component has an **Actions** collection property. For every exposed regular action, there should be an item added to the **Actions** property, which has an **Action** property that needs to be connected to the actual action component to be executed. These action items in the **Actions** collection in the tethering app profile have a **Name** property that is used to identify an action to be executed. The *remote controller* app can execute remote actions by calling the `RunRemoteAction` method of the tethering app profile component passing the reference to a remote profile and the action name.

Let's have a look at app tethering through implementing a simple system. We will be using a mobile app that will take photos and a second app that can be run on a desktop and its job will be to display a received photo.

First, let's implement the app for taking and sending photos. Create a new Delphi, multidevice blank app, save the main form as uFormPhotoTake, and save the whole project as PhotoTake. Change the **Name** property of the form to FormPhotoTake. Drop **TToolbar** on the form and drop **TSpeedButton** onto the toolbar. Change its **Name** property to spdbtnSendPhoto and its **Align** property to **Right**. Drop another **TSpeedButton** on the form. Align it to **Bottom** and change its **Name** property to spdbtnTakePhoto. Now drop the **TImage** component on the form, align it to **Client**, and change its **Name** to ImagePhoto. The user interface is ready. Drop the TActionList component on the form. Double-click on it and add **TakePhotoFromCameraAction**. Change the **CustomText** property of the action to **Take Photo**. Double-click on the OnDidFinishTaking event of the action and enter a line of code to display the photo from the camera in the image on the form:

```
procedure TFormPhotoTake.TakePhotoFromCameraAction1DidFinishTaking(
  Image: TBitmap);
begin
  ImagePhoto.Bitmap.Assign(Image);
end;
```

Select **spdbtnTakePhoto** in the **Object Inspector** and connect the TakePhotoFromCameraAction1 component to the **Action** property button.

Now we have the logic to take a photo, the next step will be to send it to another app with app tethering technology. Drop **TTetheringManager** and **TTetheringAppProfile** on the form. Select the **Manager** property in **TetheringAppProfile** component and select **TetheringManager1** from the drop-down list.

To avoid connecting to random app tethering apps in the network that are visible to our app, we are going to provide a password in both applications. In the **Password** property of the **TetheringManager1**, enter an arbitrary password, as shown in the following screenshot:

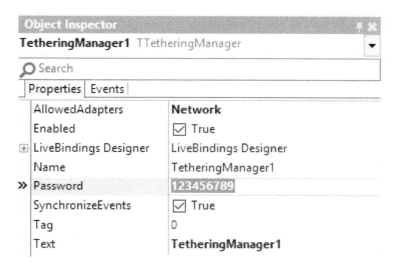

Properties of the TetheringManager component in the Object Inspector

Implement the `OnRequestManagerPassword` event to use the password stored in the **Password** property. As you can see:

```
procedure TFormPhotoTake.TetheringManager1RequestManagerPassword(const
  Sender: TObject;
const ARemoteIdentifier: string; var Password: string);
begin
  Password := TetheringManager1.Password;
end;
```

Add a new action to the action list. Change its **Name** to **actSendPhoto** and its **CustomText** to **Send Photo**. Attach this action to the **spdbtnSendPhoto** and implement its `OnExecute` event. Take a look the following code:

```
procedure TFormPhotoTake.actSendPhotoExecute(Sender: TObject);
begin
  if not ImagePhoto.Bitmap.IsEmpty then
    TetheringManager1.DiscoverManagers(1000)
  else
    ShowMessage('Take a photo before sending');
end;
```

First, we are checking if there is a bitmap to be sent, and if this is the case, we initiate communication with the receiver app through a call to `DiscoverManagers` specifying the timeout of 1 second. When remote managers are discovered then the `OnEndManagersDiscovery` event is executed. Have a look at the following code:

```
procedure TFormPhotoTake.TetheringManager1EndManagersDiscovery(const
    Sender: TObject; const ARemoteManagers: TTetheringManagerInfoList);
begin
  if aRemoteManagers.Count > 0 then
    TetheringManager1.PairManager(ARemoteManagers[0])
  else
    ShowMessage('Cannot find any photo receiver app.');
end;
```

Here, we just pair with the first manager on the list. When pairing is done, the `OnEndProfilesDiscovery` event is executed. Here, we connect to the first profile in the list, and if the connection is successful, the bitmap is sent to a remote app profile using the `SendStream` method. See the following code:

```
procedure TFormPhotoTake.TetheringManager1EndProfilesDiscovery(const
    Sender: TObject; const ARemoteProfiles: TTetheringProfileInfoList);
var
  memstr: TMemoryStream;
begin
  if ARemoteProfiles.Count > 0 then
  begin
    if not TetheringAppProfile1.Connect(ARemoteProfiles[0]) then
      ShowMessage('Failed to connect to remote profile.')
    else
    begin
      memstr := TMemoryStream.Create;
      try
        ImagePhoto.Bitmap.SaveToStream(memstr);
        if TetheringAppProfile1.SendStream(ARemoteProfiles[0],
          'Photo', memstr) then
```

```
        ShowMessage('Image sent')
      else
        ShowMessage('Failed to send image');
      finally
        memstr.Free;
      end;
    end;
  end
  else
    ShowMessage('Cannot find any remote profiles to connect to.');
end;
```

The nice thing about app tethering is the fact that the whole discovery process reduces a lot of complexity typically involved with network communication. We do not need to specify remote host addresses and port numbers; however, it is also possible to specify the exact IP address of the machine where the server app is running. By default, the network discovery is done through UDP broadcasting, so that is the reason that both apps need to be running in the same subnet to be properly discovered.

The photo receiving app is even simpler. Add to the **Project Group** a new multidevice blank Delphi app, save the main form unit as uFormPhotoDisplay, and the project as PhotoDisplay. Drop **TToolbar** on the form and then drop a **TLabel** onto it. Align the label to **Client**, change its **HorzAlign** property in **TextSettings** to **Center**, and enter **Photo Display** in the **Text**. Now drop **TImage** on the form, align it to **Client**, and rename it as ImageDisplay. Drop the **TTetheringManager** and **TTetheringAppProfile** components on the form as well. Connect the two components through the **Manager** property of the app profile component. In the **Password** property of TetheringManager1, enter the same password that was entered in the **PhotoTake** app. The only thing left except for providing the password, is to handle the OnResourceReceived event of the TetheringAppProfile1 component. This event has the **AResource: TRemoteResource** parameter that contains received information. In our case, we know that this is a stream with bitmap data, so we can just access the information AsStream and directly load into the image with the LoadFromStream method. See the following code:

```
procedure TFormPhotoDisplay.TetheringAppProfile1ResourceReceived(
  const Sender: TObject; const AResource: TRemoteResource);
begin
  ImageDisplay.Bitmap.LoadFromStream(AResource.Value.AsStream);
end;
```

That's it. Now we can run the **PhotoTake** app on a mobile device equipped with a camera, take a photo, and send it over with app tethering to a remote app running on another mobile or desktop machine.

Before deploying to the mobile, it is always good to test both apps on Windows. Typically, you won't have a camera on Windows, but we can load a test image into the **ImagePhoto** at design time and just try out the actual sending.

# Summary

The IoT is a brand new world to explore for mobile developers. There is still no clear market leader, and different companies do the IoT their own way. One aspect of IoT that everybody agrees on is the fact that it is all about communicating with *things*, sometimes very far from a traditional computer or a mobile device. Those devices, gadgets, and sensors sometimes communicate using a traditional internet TCP/IP protocol, but in most cases they use protocols optimized for low energy consumption and IoT use cases. One of the key communication protocols that enables IoT today is Bluetooth Low Energy.

Delphi comes with very good support for building both mobile and desktop apps that are using Bluetooth LE. You can build Bluetooth LE clients, but it is also possible to implement GATT servers that emulate Bluetooth LE devices.

In this chapter, we have learned about interacting with the Internet of Things. We have started from using plain Bluetooth LE protocol with the TBluetoothLE component and then moved to specialized support for standard Bluetooth devices, such as heart monitors and beacons for building proximity apps. We have also looked into BeaconFence technology for building complete GPS-free positioning solutions and the app tethering framework for having two arbitrary Delphi apps exchange data over Bluetooth or TCP/IP with almost no coding required.

In the next chapter, we will learn how to embed a database on a mobile device and use it from a Delphi FireMonkey app.

# 9
# Embedding Databases

The majority of mobile apps work with data. Building database applications has always been one of the strongest features of Delphi. In this chapter, we will learn how to build data-driven mobile user interfaces, use the FireDAC database access framework, and embed databases on mobile devices. As an example, we are going to build a simple mobile app for managing a To-Do list.

This chapter will cover the following points:

- Embedding mobile databases
- Using the FireDAC framework for database access
- TListView designer
- Visual live bindings
- Using TPrototypeBindSource

The objective of this chapter is to learn how to build data-driven GUI interfaces.

# Architecting data-driven apps

On the following pages, we will go through the steps of building a simple mobile app with an embedded database for managing a list of To-Do items. Before jumping into coding, let's first look into the overall application architecture. The more complex the system we are going to build is, the more important it is to properly structure it. The typical approach is to *divide and conquer*. Break a big problem into smaller problems that are simpler to solve. The most common approach in software development is to break the whole system into clearly separated tiers. In a data-driven app, we should be able to identify at least two logical parts: the user interface and the data access logic. Clear separation of these two tiers enables pluggable architecture, where the user interface can connect to different data access *blocks* in a standard way.

In the context of a Delphi app, we can split our project into three independent entities--a visual form that will serve as the graphical user interface, a data module with non-visual components for working with a database, and a standalone unit, with common types and utility functions used by both tiers of the application. Take a look at the following diagram:

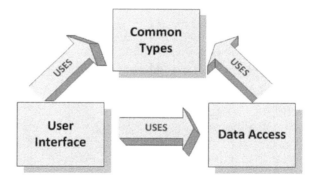

Two-tier app architecture

Create a new multi-device, blank Delphi project. Save the main form unit as `uFormToDo` and the whole app as `ToDoList`. Change the **Name** property of the form to **FormToDo**. Select **File | New | Other...** from the Delphi main menu and add to the project a new data module, which can be found in the **Delphi Files** category. Change its **Name** property to **DMToDo** and save it as `uDMToDo`. Now, from the same **Delphi Files** category, add a blank unit to the project. Save it as `uToDoTypes`. This is how our project looks right now in the Project Manager:

Main blocks of two-tier architecture mapped to units in a Delphi project

Our project consists of three different units that represent three major building blocks of our data-driven app. Now let's create dependencies between these three units. The unit uToDoTypes does not depend on any other unit in the project, so there is nothing to add to its uses clauses. This unit needs to be used by both user interface and data access logic. Select **File** | **Use Unit**, add the uToDoTypes unit to the uses clauses in the interface parts of the form and of the data module. Now add the data module uDMToDo to the uses clause in the implementation part of the main form's unit.

# Modeling data

The uToDoTypes unit is where we can add data types that are shared between the user interface and the data access module. To achieve a proper level of separation between the user interface and the data access logic, we should define the interface for communication between the two tiers of the application. The data module will implement it and the main form of the application should use this interface as the only way to communicate with the data module. In this way, we have a truly pluggable architecture. The user interface can be developed independently and we can provide different implementations of data access logic without affecting the rest of the application. Our data-driven app could be using different types of embedded databases, a different data access framework, or maybe we would want later to switch to storing our data in a plain file or in cloud storage.

The ToDoList app will be dealing with To-Do items, so it makes perfect sense to declare in the common types unit a type that will represent a single To-Do item. We need to decide if this type should be a record or a class. With records we do not need to worry about memory management and typically, records are more performant then objects. On the other hand, defining our *data wrapper* type as an object is also an option. Record types cannot be inherited. In more complex scenarios, the flexibility that comes from using objects could justify using them rather than records.

What attributes should a To-Do item have? To keep the demo simple, let's just add `Title` and `Category` string fields. In databases it is also handy to have an identifier for a given item; typically this is an integer value. Here is how we could represent a To-Do item in code:

```
unit uToDoTypes;

interface

uses
  System.Generics.Collections;

  type
    TToDo = record
    Id: integer;
    Title: string;
    Category: string;
end;

TToDos = TList<TToDo>;

implementation

end.
```

Notice that we have also implemented a generic list of To-Do items. It will be very useful to return the list of all To-Do items from the data module.

The next step is to define standard operations that the data module should provide. In the database world these are typically referred to as **CRUD** or sometimes **CRUDL** operations. This abbreviation stands for **Create, Read, Udpdate, Delete, and List**. We just have one entity in our data model, so these operations should be implemented by five different methods. Let's declare a new interface type called `IToDoData` that will define what functionality our data module should offer:

```
IToDoData = interface
  function ToDoCreate(aValue: TToDo): integer;
  function ToDoRead(id: integer; out aValue: TToDo): boolean;
  function ToDoUpdate(aValue: TToDo): boolean;
  function ToDoDelete(id: integer): boolean;
  procedure ToDoList(aList: TToDos);
end;
```

This is a fairly common way of representing CRUDL operations. The `ToDoCreate` function takes the To-Do item, optionally checks if the data is correct, and returns the identifier of the new item in the underlying data store. If the operation was not successful, it returns a special value, such as, for example *-1*. The identifier for the new data item could be generated by the underlying database or created in code. The `ToDoRead` function could return the item as the function result, but it is also practical to return it as the `out` parameter and indicate with a Boolean value if it contains valid data. The `Update` and `Delete` functions are self-explanatory. The last procedure for retrieving all the items takes the list as a parameter. The underlying code would check if the pointer to the list is not nil, optionally clear the list, and populate it with the underlying data.

The data module class in our app needs to implement this interface.

# Choosing a database

The majority of mobile apps work with data. If you are not building a calculator app, or an arcade game, the possibility to store the data that your app is using can be very valuable. When designing your app, you need to make some architectural choices up front. Where and how is my data stored? One obvious solution is to store your data in the cloud. This approach is the most common, but what if you do not have network access? You still want to be able to work with your app, and with the latest version of your data. This is the main reason why you also want to store your data locally on the device.

In many cases, storing data as plain files, text or binary, is sufficient. However, it is also possible to embed a complete database system locally on the device. There are many relational and non-relational embedded databases available. If we think about an arbitrary database as just another mobile framework available from the mobile operating system, then it should be possible to integrate your Delphi mobile app with pretty much any database. However, that could require a deep understanding of the inner workings of your particular database. In most cases, we just want to have the job done, and it is the most productive approach to use databases that Delphi already provides support for. The key database access framework for mobile Delphi apps is FireDAC. It provides connectivity to all major databases, and also includes support for working with embedded databases. There are two main databases that you can embed:

- InterBase
- SQLite

Depending on your app, you may want to choose one or the other.

**InterBase** is the SQL relational database management system from **Embarcadero** (`https://www.embarcadero.com/products/interbase`). It is one of the best available SQL databases on the market and is very popular, primarily in embedded applications. The InterBase Developer Edition is installed as part of the Delphi installation and comes with the development license. InterBase runs on all major platforms, both mobile and desktop. It has a very light footprint and is self-tuning, and requires almost no administration. Internally, it is based on unique, transactional **Multi-Generational Architecture**. It provides very high performance and referential integrity. The database file format is the same across different platforms, so the same database file can be used in the standalone installation and in an embedded mobile app. There are two mobile, embeddable variants of InterBase: IBLite and IBToGo. IBLite is a free SQL engine and a database file can be up to 100 MB in size. The commercial, embeddable IBToGo version has no database size limits and a very important feature, especially on mobile, is that it provides strong (AES) database, table, and column-level encryption. Only one application is allowed to connect to the database and the application exclusively locks the database file. However, this application is allowed to make multiple connections to the database, so a multi-threaded application can make a single connection or multiple connections and access the database simultaneously. In order to embed the InterBase database, you need to additionally deploy the database engine library and the database file with your application. Delphi **Deployment Manager** makes it easy to quickly add required libraries to your mobile app when deploying to a desired platform:

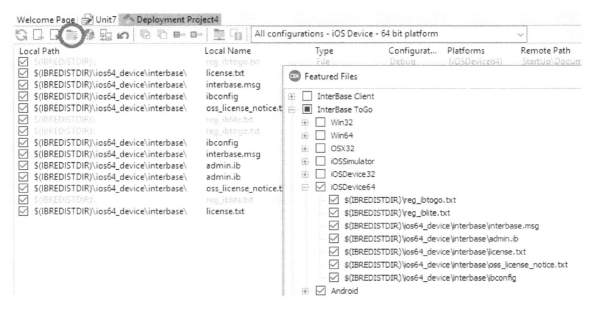

Add featured files option in the IDE Deployment Manager window

A simpler alternative to InterBase is SQLite (`https://www.sqlite.org/`). It is a relational database engine, which belongs to the public domain. The deployment of apps that are using SQLite is very simple, because the engine itself is part of the iOS and Android operating systems. SQLite does not have all the power of InterBase and does not provide referential integrity. In fact, with SQLite, you do not need to deploy anything with your mobile Delphi app, because the database and its structure can be created by the application on-the-fly. SQLite does not have a separate server process. SQLite reads and writes directly to plain disk files. A complete SQL database with multiple tables, indices, triggers, and views, is contained in a single disk file. The SQLite file format is similar to InterBase, offering portability across different operating systems and processor architectures.

# Accessing databases with FireDAC

To keep the demo app simple, we are going to use SQLite as the database engine and our *To-Do List* app will have just one database table, called `ToDos`. SQLite has a simple type system and effectively, a column can store null, integer, real, text, or blob values.

In our design, we are going to use as a primary key an integer `Id` value. We will also need `Title` and `Category` text fields. The key FireDAC component that we will need is the FireDAC database connection. There will also be query components connected to the database connection. Drop the `TFDConnection` component onto the data module. Change its `Name` property to `fdconnToDos`. Now double-click on the connection component to display the FireDAC database connection editor window. Select **SQLite** in the **Driver ID** combo-box. This should display the list of different parameters specific to working with SQLite.

First we will have to enter the name of the database file. It is important to realize that the location of the database file on our development Windows machine, where we have Delphi installed, will be different to the location on a mobile device where our app will be deployed. During development of our application, we will be running it on Windows for testing, and when the app is finished then we will deploy and run it on an Android or iOS device. On your Windows machine, create a directory for the SQLite database file (for example, `C:\Data`). The name of the database file will be `ToDos.db`. The extension of the database file can be anything and it is a matter of convention. There is no need to enter a username and password and we can leave all the default parameter values. The default **OpenMode** parameter is set to **CreateUTF8**. This means that the database file will be created automatically on the first attempt to connect to it. This simplifies the deployment to a mobile device, because the database file can be created the first time the mobile app runs.

Click on the **Test** button in the connection editor. Leave the password blank and you should get the message that the connection has been successful. If you now go to the C:\Data folder, you should find there a new, empty SQLite database file:

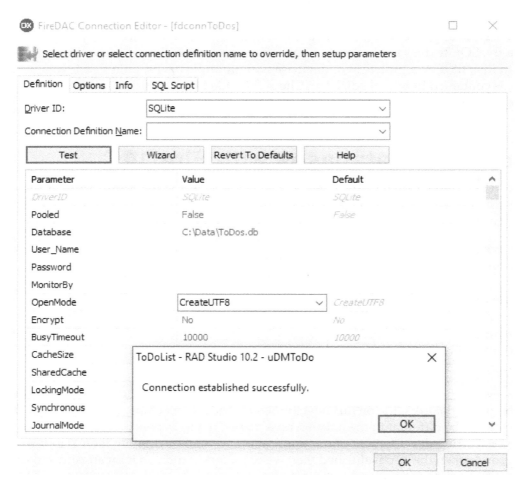

TFDConnection integrated IDE component editor

The connection editor is very handy. On the second tab, there are different options that can control how FireDAC works. The third tab provides all kinds of information about the database connection. The last tab is called **SQL Script** and can be used to execute arbitrary SQL statements against the connected database.

SQLite has a nice SQL construct, `CREATE TABLE IF NOT EXIST...`, which can be used to create the database table directly after the opening the database.

Click on the **SQL Script** tab and enter the following code into the query window to create the `ToDos` database table. Click on the green arrow button to execute the query. You should get the message that the query has been successfully executed:

Running the SQL script for creating the ToDos table from within the TFDConnection component editor

Right now we have got the database file with the `ToDo` table created. There are two possible approaches to deploying the database to a mobile device. We could use the Deployment Manager and add an existing database file to the list of files to be deployed. The other, simpler option is to create the database file and the database table on-the-fly.

Change the `LoginPrompt` property of the connection component to `False` and double-click on its `OnBeforeConnect` and `OnAfterConnect` events. Before opening the connection to the database, we are going to specify in the code the location and name of the database file. The only practical location on a mobile device is the `Documents` folder. The database file will be created when the app is run for the first time. After the connection is established and the database file created, we are going to execute the SQL code to create the `ToDos` table, if it does not already exist:

```
uses System.IOUtils;

function TDMToDo.IsMobilePlatform: boolean;
begin
  Result := (TOSVersion.Platform = pfiOS) or (TOSVersion.Platform =
pfAndroid);
end;

procedure TDMToDo.fdconnToDosBeforeConnect(Sender: TObject);
begin
  if IsMobilePlatform then
    fdconnToDos.Params.Values['Database'] :=
      TPath.Combine(TPath.GetDocumentsPath, 'ToDos.db')
end;

procedure TDMToDo.fdconnToDosAfterConnect(Sender: TObject);
const
  sCreateTableSQL = 'CREATE TABLE IF NOT EXISTS ToDos ('
    + 'Id INTEGER NOT NULL PRIMARY KEY,'
    + 'Title TEXT, Category TEXT)';
begin
  if IsMobilePlatform then
    fdconnToDos.ExecSQL(sCreateTableSQL);
end;
```

For convenience, a simple `IsMobilePlatform` function has been added as well. Alternatively, we could use a conditional compilation, but using the `TOSVersion` record for checking if the app executes on a mobile platform is more elegant.

Now we can move on to implementing the functionality defined in the `IToDoData` interface. Add `IToDoData` to the class declaration of the `TDMToDo` ancestor class, which is `TDataModule`, and copy the signatures of the interface methods to the public section of the data module class. Now press the *Ctrl + Shift + C* key combination to invoke the class completion and generate empty method implementations stubs. Drop six `TFDQuery` components on the form and change their names to, respectively: `fdqToDoMaxId`, `fdqToDoInsert`, `fdqToDoSelect`, `fdqToDoUpdate`, `fdqToDoDelete`, and `fdqToDoSelectAll`:

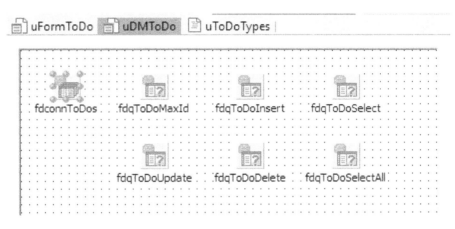

FireDAC components on the data module

The first method in the data access interface will be responsible for adding a new record to the table. In our data model, we have defined the `Id` integer primary key for storing identifiers. There are different strategies for generating unique identifiers. Some databases, such as, for example InterBase, provide generators that can efficiently generate primary keys. In our design, we are going to calculate the new value for an identifier using an additional query that will return the maximum value stored in the `Id` column. The new identifier will be the maximum value increased by 1. If there are no records in the table, we can return an arbitrary positive value that will serve as the starting point for consecutive inserts. In the private section of the data module class, declare a new `GetNewId: integer` function.

At this point, the declaration of the `TDMToDo` data module class is now complete. Now we can move to implementing all the declared methods:

```
type
  TDMToDo = class(TDataModule, IToDoData)
    fdconnToDos: TFDConnection;
    fdqToDoMaxId: TFDQuery;
```

```
    fdqToDoInsert: TFDQuery;
    fdqToDoSelect: TFDQuery;
    fdqToDoUpdate: TFDQuery;
    fdqToDoDelete: TFDQuery;
    fdqToDoSelectAll: TFDQuery;
    procedure fdconnToDosBeforeConnect(Sender: TObject);
    procedure fdconnToDosAfterConnect(Sender: TObject);
  private
    function IsMobilePlatform: boolean;
    function GetNewId: integer;
  public
    // IToDoData
    function ToDoCreate(aValue: TToDo): integer;
    function ToDoRead(id: integer; out aValue: TToDo): boolean;
    function ToDoUpdate(aValue: TToDo): boolean;
    function ToDoDelete(id: integer): boolean;
    procedure ToDoList(aList: TToDos);
  end;
```

Double-click on the `fdqToDoMaxId` query component. This will display the query editor where we can enter the SQL code of the query:

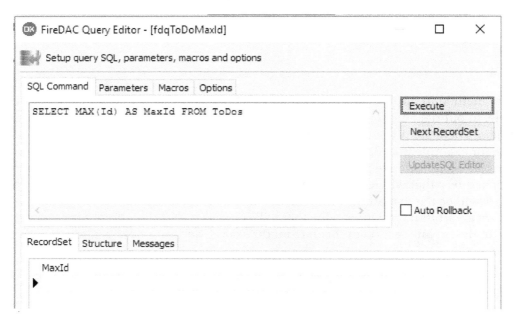

SQL query for getting the maximum Id value from the ToDos table

Working with FireDAC is very comfortable. In the query editor, there is also the **Execute** button, which we can use to test our queries. At this stage, there are no records in the database, so the query returns an empty dataset, but this is very useful. By executing the query at design-time, we can check that there are no errors in the SQL statement.

Enter the following code in the body of the GetMaxId method:

```
function TDMToDo.GetNewId: integer;
var fld: TField;
begin
  fdqToDoMaxId.Open;
  try
    fld := fdqToDoMaxId.FieldByName('MaxId');
    if fld.IsNull then
      Result := 1
    else
      Result := fld.AsInteger + 1;
  finally
    fdqToDoMaxId.Close;
  end;
end;
```

The local variable fld is here to simplify the code and make it more readable. Otherwise, we would need to make the FieldByName call two times. It is probably more efficient too.

Double-click on the fdqToDoInsert query component. The INSERT statement will be responsible for the Create operation and adding a new To-Do item to the table. Enter the following parameterized SQL code there:

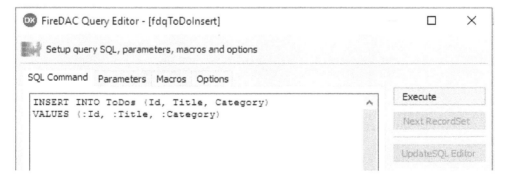

Parameterized SQL query for inserting a new ToDo record

In the second tab of the query editor, we need to specify parameter directions and their data types. All three parameters have the **ptInput** direction. The **ID** has the **ftInteger** type, and **Title** and **Category** are both of the **ftString** type.

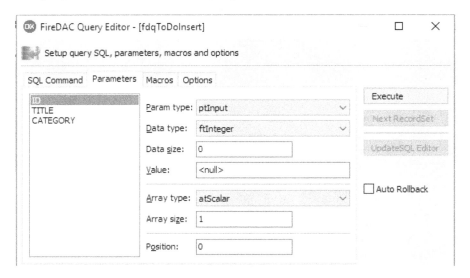

Insert query parameter properties in the query editor

In the `ToDoCreate` method, we are going to calculate a new identifier for a To-Do record, assign values to parameters, execute the query, and return the new identifier if the query was successful, or −1 otherwise:

```
function TDMToDo.ToDoCreate(aValue: TToDo): integer;
var id: integer;
begin
  id := GetNewId;
  fdqToDoInsert.ParamByName('Id').AsInteger := id;
  fdqToDoInsert.ParamByName('Title').AsString := aValue.Title;;
  fdqToDoInsert.ParamByName('Category').AsString := aValue.Category;
  try
    fdqToDoInsert.ExecSQL;
    Result := id;
  except
    Result := -1;
  end;
end;
```

The next method to implement in our CRUDL list is reading a To-Do item. Double-click on the `fdqToDoSelect` query component and enter the following simple parameterized SQL statement:

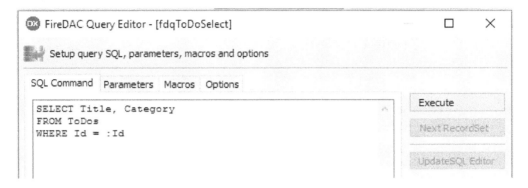

Parameterized SQL query to retrieve a ToDo record by its Id

On the next tab, specify the **ptInput** as the **ID** parameter type and **ftInteger** as the data type. The implementation of the `ToDoRead` method is relatively simple:

```
function TDMToDo.ToDoRead(id: integer; out aValue: TToDo): boolean;
begin
  fdqToDoSelect.ParamByName('Id').AsInteger := id;
  fdqToDoSelect.Open;
  try
    if fdqToDoSelect.RecordCount > 0 then
    begin
      Result := True;
      aValue.Id := id;
      aValue.Title := fdqToDoSelect.FieldByName('Title').AsString;
      aValue.Category := fdqToDoSelect.FieldByName('Category')
                         .AsString;
    end
    else
      Result := False;
  finally
    fdqToDoSelect.Close;
  end;
end;
```

The next method to implement is responsible for updating an existing To-Do record. Double-click on the `fdqToDoUpdate` query component and enter the following SQL code. On the second page, set the types and data types of parameters in the same way as we did for the insert query:

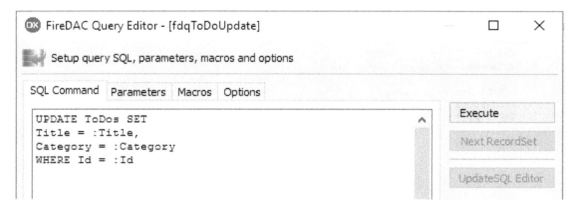

SQL query to modify a ToDo record

The implementation of the update method is simple as well:

```
function TDMToDo.ToDoUpdate(aValue: TToDo): boolean;
begin
  fdqToDoUpdate.ParamByName('Id').AsInteger := aValue.Id;
  fdqToDoUpdate.ParamByName('Title').AsString := aValue.Title;
  fdqToDoUpdate.ParamByName('Category').AsString := aValue.Category;
  try
    fdqToDoUpdate.ExecSQL;
    Result := True;
  except
    Result := False;
  end;
end;
```

The method responsible for deleting To-Do items is the simplest. Double-click on the `fdqToDoDelete` query component and enter the following SQL. Set the `Id` parameter on the second tab in the query editor as `ptInput` and `ftInteger`:

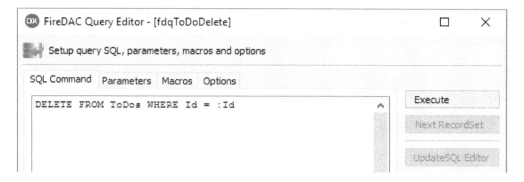

SQL query to delete a ToDo record

Again, the implementation of the corresponding method is not difficult at all:

```
function TDMToDo.ToDoDelete(id: integer): boolean;
begin
  fdqToDoDelete.ParamByName('Id').AsInteger := id;
  try
    fdqToDoDelete.ExecSQL;
    Result := True;
  except
    Result := False;
  end;
end;
```

The last method of the data module is going to return the list of all To-Do items in the database. Double-click on the `fdqToDoSelectAll` and enter the following SQL code:

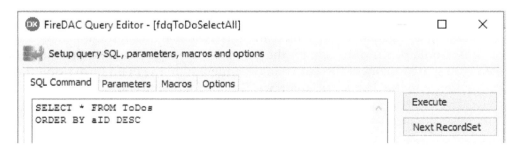

SQL query to return the list of all ToDo records

Enter the following code in the body of the ToDoList method:

```
procedure TDMToDo.ToDoList(aList: TToDos);
var item: TToDo;
begin
  if aList <> nil then
  begin
    aList.Clear;
    fdqToDoSelectAll.Open;
    try
      while not fdqToDoSelectAll.Eof do
      begin
        item.Id := fdqToDoSelectAll.FieldByName('Id').AsInteger;
        item.Title := fdqToDoSelectAll.FieldByName('Title').AsString;
        item.Category := fdqToDoSelectAll.FieldByName('Category')
                         .AsString;
        aList.Add(item);
        fdqToDoSelectAll.Next;
      end;
    finally
      fdqToDoSelectAll.Close;
    end;
  end;
end;
```

In the ToDoList method, we are checking first if the aList parameter is not nil and then populating the list with To-Do items retrieved from the table.

# Building data-driven user interface

The data access logic has been implemented and it is available through the IToDoData interface. This should be the only way for the user interface logic to access the data. That is why we are going to implement the GetToDoData method in the main form's unit that will return the reference to the data access interface. See the following code:

```
uses uDMToDo;

function TFormToDo.GetToDoData: IToDoData;
begin
  if DMToDo = nil then
    DMToDo := TDMToDo.Create(Application);
  Result := DMToDo;
end;
```

In this way, we have achieved a truly pluggable architecture. If we decide to change the underlying database access logic, database access framework, or the database platform, we only need to make sure that the new implementation implements the IToDoData interface that is available to the GUI code through the GetToDoData method.

The user interface for the database will be simple. Drop the TTabControl component on the form, align it to Client, and rename to tbctrlMain. Right-click on the tab control and add two tabs. The first tab will contain the list of all To-Dos and the second one will be used for editing the selected To-Do item. Drop two TToolBar components. One on each tab. The navigation between tabs will be happening in the code, so we do not want to see the tabs. Change the TabPosition property of the tab control to None. Rename the individual tabs to, respectively, tbiList and tbiEdit. Drop TActionList on the form, double-click on it, and add two ChangeTabActions. Change their names to ctaList and ctaEdit, and connect their Tab properties to the correct tabs.

Double-click on the OnCreate and OnDestroy events of the form. Here we are going to create and free a global list of all To-Dos. Declare a generic list of To-Do items as a private field in the class declaration of the form. We are going to pass it to the ToDoList method of the data module to get all the records:

```
procedure TFormToDo.FormCreate(Sender: TObject);
begin
  FToDos := TToDos.Create;
  tbctrlMain.ActiveTab := tbiList;
  RefreshList;
end;

procedure TFormToDo.FormDestroy(Sender: TObject);
begin
  FToDos.Free;
end;
```

Additionally, in the OnCreate event, we are also making sure that the tab with the list is always displayed at the start of the application. There is also a call to the RefreshList method responsible for displaying all To-Dos.

The best control for displaying a list of data in FireMonkey is TListView. Drop a TListView component on the first tab, rename it to lstvwToDos, and align it to Client. TListView is very flexible and performant. It has been designed for building data-driven user interfaces and has a number of properties that control the layout of data and how this control operates.

Expand the `ItemAppearance` node under `lstvwToDos` in the Structure View and click on the item node. Here we can see the elements that will make up a single row in the list view. There are also separate nodes for setting header, footer, and, additionally, the layout of the item in the edit mode. By default, the `Appearance` property of a list view item is `ListItem` and the height of a single row is 44. The default `ListItem` appearance will display just a line of text and the greater than sign at the right side of the item as an `Accessory`. By selecting different elements of the list view in the structure view, we can easily adjust their properties in the object inspector.

In our app, a single To-Do item consists of `Title` and `Category`. Change the `Appearance` property of a list view item to `ListItemRightDetail`. Notice that changing the `Appearance` property changes the number of items under the item node. Suddenly, we have not only `Text`, but also a `Detail` element inside the individual item:

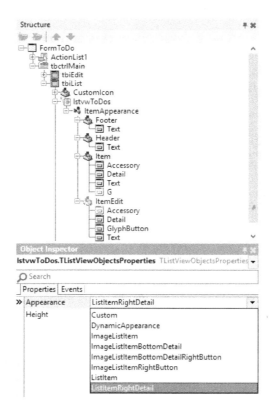

Changing the value of the Appearance property of a list view item

The default properties of `Text` and `Detail` could have been good for our app, but we want a more powerful approach. The most flexible `Appearance` option is `DynamicApperance`, where we do not need to select from the list of predefined appearances, but we can add our own elements and control their arrangement with the integrated list view designer. Let's give it a try and change the `Appearance` of the item node to `DynamicApperance`. That's very interesting. In the Object Inspector, we now have the plus sign at the bottom of the property list, where we can add visual elements of different types available from the drop-down list. By default, we already have one text element, called `Text1`. Let's add one more text object and an accessory to indicate that touching a row would allow editing a single To-Do item.

Change the `AppearanceObjectNames` to `Title`, `Category` for text items, and to `More` for accessory items. We will be able to use these names in the code. Now let's adjust the layout of a To-Do row. Change the `Height` property of an item to 64 and click on the **Toggle DesignMode** in the object inspector. Alternatively, we could switch to the design mode from the list view context menu:

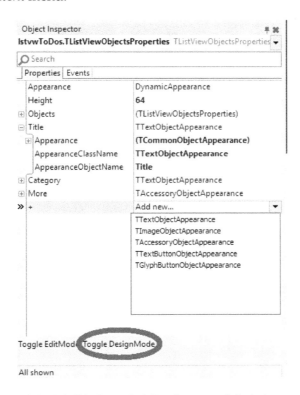

Options in the Object Inspector for the Dynamic appearance of a list view item

The list view control in the form designer has changed and now we can design the layout of the individual list view item. Initially, all three elements are in the middle of the row, all of them one on top of another. Carefully reposition them and adjust their sizes. It is up to your artistic preferences. The `Title` item can be displayed on top of the row in bold font and the category in italics, just below it:

Toggle DesignMode context menu option for the TListView component

When we are done with designing an item, we can switch back to the normal view by unchecking the **Toggle DesignMode** option from the context menu.

Now we can implement the `RefreshList` method that will be responsible for reading data from the underlying database and displaying it in the list view:

```
procedure TFormToDo.RefreshList;
var todo: TToDo; item: TListViewItem;
begin
  GetToDoData.ToDoList(FToDos);
  lstvwToDos.BeginUpdate;
  try
    lstvwToDos.Items.Clear;
    for todo in FToDos do
    begin
      item := lstvwToDos.Items.Add;
      item.Tag := todo.Id;
      item.Objects.FindObjectT<TListItemText>('Title').Text := todo.Title;
      item.Objects.FindObjectT<TListItemText>('Category').Text :=
todo.Category;
    end;
  finally
    lstvwToDos.EndUpdate;
  end;
end;
```

Note that `FindObjectT` is a generic method that accepts the type of the element that we want to find inside the item.

Let's add functionality to add, delete, and edit To-Do items from the list. Drop a `TSpeedButton` component on the toolbar on the first tab, where the list view is located. Rename it to `spdbtnAdd`, change its `StyleLookup` to `addtoolbutton`, and its `Align` property to `Left`. Now drop `TLabel` on the toolbar, change its `Text` property to To-Do list, its `StyleLookup` to `toollabel`, and align it to `Client`.

On the second tab, we are going to provide the way for the user to add, save, or delete a single To-Do item. Drop three speed buttons and one label on the toolbar. Change the `StyleLookup` of the first button to `arrowlefttoolbutton` and its `Name` to `spdbtnBack`. Align it to `Left`. Set its `Action` property to point to the `ctaList` change tab action. Change the `Name` of the second speed button to `spdbtnSave`, its `StyleLookup` property to `composetoolbutton`, and align it to the right. The third speed button will be responsible for deleting items. Change its `Name` property to `spdbtnDelete`, its `StyleLookup` to `thrashtoolbutton`, and align it to `Right`. Change the `Text` property of the label to `To-Do Edit` and align it to `Client`.

Add two edits and two labels to the tab. Change their names to edtTitle and edtCategory. Check the akRight option in the Anchors property of both edits, so they will automatically adjust their width to different screen sizes:

Detail tab for editing a single ToDo item

The functionality of the **Save** button will be either Insert or Update. Let's declare a private integer field, FCurrentId: integer; in the form class, to indicate if we are adding or editing a To-Do item. If this value is -1 then it means that we are adding a new item; otherwise, it will contain the identifier for the currently edited item.

Double-click on the action list component and add two actions with the **New Action** option. Rename the first one to actAdd and the second one to actDelete. Connect both actions to appropriate speed buttons on both toolbars through their Action properties. Now double-click on the actAdd action to implement its OnExecute event handler:

```
procedure TFormToDo.actAddExecute(Sender: TObject);
begin
  FCurrentId := -1;
  edtTitle.Text := '';
  edtCategory.Text := '';
  ctaEdit.ExecuteTarget(self);
end;
```

Let's add another action to the action list. Rename it to `actSave` and in its `OnExecute` method, write the following code:

```
procedure TFormToDo.actSaveExecute(Sender: TObject);
var todo: TToDo;
begin
  todo.Title := edtTitle.Text;
  todo.Category := edtCategory.Text;
  if FCurrentId < 0 then
    GetData.ToDoCreate(todo)
  else
  begin
    todo.Id := FCurrentId;
    GetToDoData.ToDoUpdate(todo);
  end;
  RefreshList;
  ctaList.ExecuteTarget(self);
end;
```

Right after inserting or updating a To-Do item, we are refreshing the list and jumping back to the first tab with the list of all to-dos. Connect the `actSave` action to the `spdbtnSave` speed button through its `Action` property.

The last functionality to implement is deleting the item. Double-click on the `OnExecute` event of the `actDelete` action and enter the following code:

```
procedure TFormToDo.actDeleteExecute(Sender: TObject);
begin
  if FCurrentId > 0 then
  begin
    GetToDoData.ToDoDelete(FCurrentId);
    RefreshList;
  end;
  if tbctrlMain.ActiveTab <> tbiList then
    ctaList.ExecuteTarget(self);
end;
```

It only makes sense to delete an existing To-Do if we are in the middle of adding it. If the current identifier is negative then there is nothing to delete. We just switch to the list tab. The last `if` is here to check if we are not in the **list** tab. This is because we are also going to provide the way to delete items directly from the list view. It is a common mobile user interface feature to be able to swipe to delete. This functionality is built into the list view component. There is the `CanSwipeDelete` property, by default set to `True`, and the `DeleteButtonText` property with the default `Delete` value. Double-click on the `OnDeleteItem` event and enter the following code:

```
procedure TFormToDo.lstvwToDosDeleteItem(Sender: TObject; AIndex: Integer);
begin
  FCurrentId := FToDos[AIndex].Id;
  actDelete.Execute;
end;
```

Before executing the delete action, we need to make sure that the `FCurrentId` field has the correct value of the To-Do item to be deleted.

The very last thing to implement is navigation between the list and the edit tab. Double-click on the `OnItemClick` event of the list view and type in the following code:

```
procedure TFormToDo.lstvwToDosItemClick(const Sender: TObject;
  const AItem: TListViewItem);
var todo: TToDo;
begin
  FCurrentId := AItem.Tag;
  GetToDoData.ToDoRead(FCurrentId, todo);
  edtTitle.Text := todo.Title;
  edtCategory.Text := todo.Category;
  ctaEdit.ExecuteTarget(self);
end;
```

That's it! You can try out the app by running it on Windows. If it works OK, you can switch to one of the mobile targets and deploy the app to a mobile device. Unfortunately, every time we save the data module unit, the IDE keeps adding the `FireDAC.VCLUI.Wait` unit to the `uses` clause of the data module, which prevents the whole project from compiling. The solution is to place the `TFDGUIxWaitCursor` component on the data module and change its `Provider` property to `FMX`. You can now safely remove the `FireDAC.VCLUI.Wait` unit from the `uses` clause. Now you should be able to build and deploy the app to a mobile device.

Our app architecture is very sound. There is true separation between the user interface and the database access logic.

# Using visual live bindings

There are many tools for developers on the market. What makes Delphi one of the most productive development environments is the **Rapid Application Development (RAD)** paradigm, where you can use reusable components and very quickly assemble them together to create a working application. In Delphi there is hardly any prototyping phase of the project. When you are building an app, it very quickly starts to look like the final product. Most applications work with data. Graphical user interfaces that we design typically display information coming from a database or from a service in the cloud. In Delphi you can preview the data at design time.

There are two visual frameworks in Delphi for building graphical user interfaces. There is the Visual Component Library, the VCL, which is arguably the best library for building native applications for Windows. There is also the FireMonkey multi-device library for building cross-platform graphical user interfaces for all supported mobile and desktop operating systems. The VCL has a concept of data-aware control that can be connected with the `IDataSource` component to a non-visual dataset component representing a database query, table, or a stored procedure. In FireMonkey there is no concept of data-aware controls. If you want to quickly build data-driven graphical user interfaces in FireMonkey you can use Visual Live Bindings. This technology is much more capable then just connecting controls to data. It can be used in FireMonkey, VCL, or even a console project. Visual Live Bindings are components themselves and can be used to connect properties of two arbitrary objects.

Let's start from a very simple example of connecting properties of visual controls on the form. Create a new multi-device and a blank Delphi project. Save the main form's units as `uFormVLB` and the whole project as `VLBTest`. Change the `Name` property of the form to `FormVLB` and save all. Drop the `TEdit` and `TLabel` components on the form. Right-click on the label component and select the **Bind Visually...** option from the context menu. That will display the **LiveBindings Designer** window. Alternatively, we could have displayed this window from the **Tool Windows** menu in the **View** main menu option.

Here we can visually create live bindings between different properties, so they can get automatically synchronized. Let's connect the `Text` properties of both controls, so when we change the text in the edit box, it gets automatically updated in the label. Click on the `Text` property of the `Edit1` control. Drag this property onto the other property that you wish to connect to. This will automatically create a binding between these two properties:

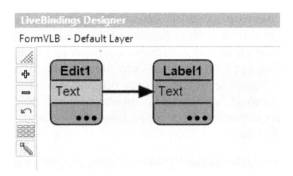

Visual LiveBindings Designer IDE window

Notice that the `BindingList1` component has been automatically added to the form. This is where all bindings are stored. If you double-click on this component, you can preview all existing bindings, which are just regular components with properties and events that can be set with the Object Inspector:

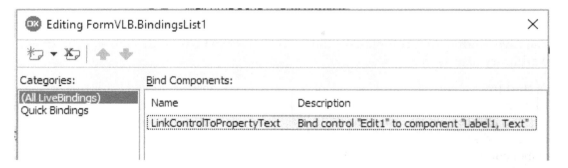

LinkControlToPropertyText live binding component in the integrated TBindingsList component editor

The **LiveBindings Designer** automatically created for us the `TLinkControlToProperty` binding, but there are other types of bindings that can be used to connect different types of properties and objects together.

There is also the **LiveBindings Wizard**, which can be invoked from the `TBindingsList` component or using the magic wand button at the bottom of the menu in the **LiveBindings Designer** window:

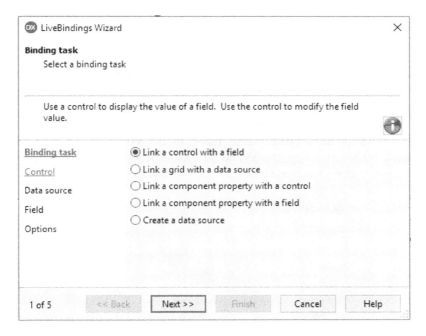

The first screen of the IDE LiveBindings Wizard

With the wizard, you can automatically create bindings and optionally add new objects.

If we run our test app at this stage, we can see that the value of the label gets updated every time we change the text in the edit. In this way, we can build complex user interfaces, with multiple controls connected to each other with live bindings, with virtually no coding required.

# Fast user interface prototyping

Live bindings are not limited to string properties. You can bind different simple and complex data types. One of the really cool components that you can use to quickly design a data-driven user interface is `TPrototypeBindSource`. This component can emulate a data table and generate test data for display. In this way, we can very quickly prototype graphical user interfaces.

Let's look at how we could use live bindings to quickly prototype the user interface of our *To-Do List* app. Reopen the `ToDoList` project in the IDE, right-click on the Project Manager, and select the option to add a new project to the project group. Create a separate folder for the new project and save the main form's unit as `uFormToDoTest`, the project as `ToDoTest`, and the whole project group as `ToDoGrp`. Change the `Name` property, the main form of the new project, to `FormToDoTest`. Now copy the list view control from the `FormToDo` form onto `FormToDoTest`. We have our dynamic list view design in the new test form. Let's imagine that we have just started prototyping our app. It would be cool to preview what the To-Do list would look like without going through the process of implementing a proper data access logic. Drop the `TPrototypeBindSource` component onto the form. Change its `Name` to `PrototypeBindSourceToDo` and double-click on it. Here we can add fields of different types to the prototype bind source and preview sample test values that would be generated for us. In our case, we just need two fields with random string values. There are some interesting generators to create test contacts, lorem ipsum strings, bitmaps, or colors:

Add Field dialog for the PrototypeBindSource1 component

Add one **BitmapNames** and one **ColorNames** field. Change the names of two test fields to
`TestTitle` and `TestCategory`:

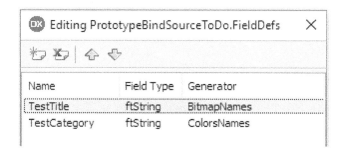

Fields added to the PrototypeBindSource1 component

Open the **LiveBindings Designer** window and make connections between `Title` and
`Category` fields in both components:

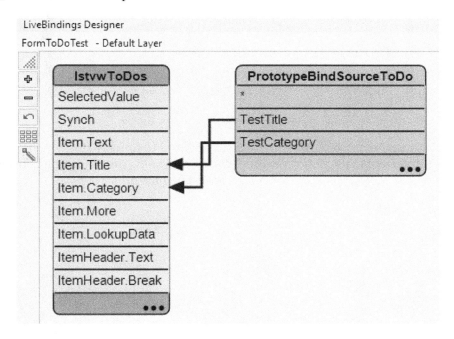

Visual LiveBindings connecting the list view with the prototype bind source

Immediately, we can see our list view populated with some test data:

List view with random data generated by the prototype bind source

Visual live bindings are very powerful. They can be used to quickly prototype data-driven graphical user interfaces, but also as the underlying technology for building complete applications and to build interactive user interfaces even faster!

A good example of a complete app that uses Visual live bindings can be found as one of the multi-device project templates. Select an option to create a new Delphi multi-device project and, instead of the usual blank template, select the **Master-Detail** template:

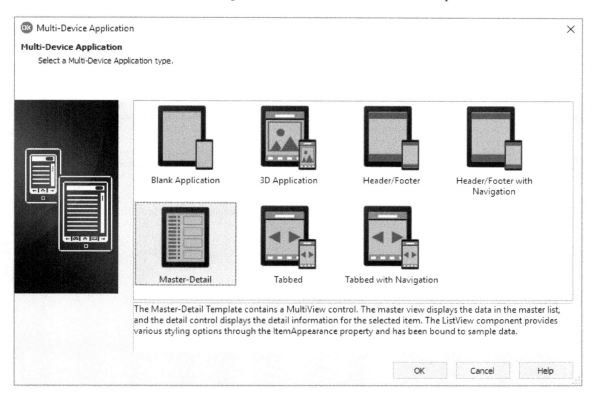

Master-Detail multi-device application template

You will need to provide a folder name for the wizard to generate the complete project with a list view and prototype bind source emulating contacts information:

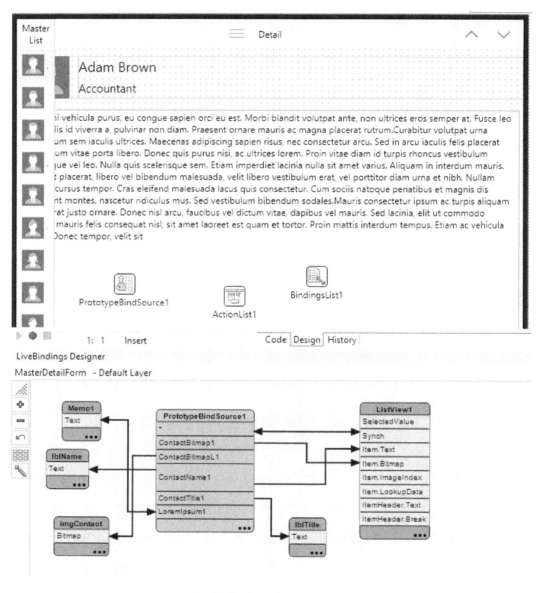

Master-Detail project template created in the IDE

That could be a nice starting point for a complete app with flexible `TMultiView` control for displaying master information in the menu and also using special actions for navigating through the data.

# Summary

In this chapter, we have learned how to build data-driven apps and embed a database on mobile devices.

In the next chapter, we are going to reuse the visual part of our *To-Do List* app and use cloud data storage as the underlying implementation of the `IToDoData` interface.

# 10
# Integrating with Web Services

No mobile app is a lonely island. You can create standalone mobile apps with Delphi, but most of the time developers want to integrate with backend services to provide access to data and add the whole social dimension to the mobile user experience. In this chapter, we are going to have a tour of different technologies available in Delphi to integrate with mobile backends running in the cloud, including the HTTP native client library, accessing REST APIs, and using the Cloud API framework for integrating with cloud web services available in Amazon and Azure clouds.

This chapter will cover the following points:

- HTTP native client library
- SOAP clients
- REST clients
- BaaS clients
- Cloud API

The objective of this chapter is to learn how to build mobile HTTP clients and connect to web services and data in the cloud.

# Understanding web services

Not so long time ago and not in a galaxy far, far away, Sir Timothy John Berners-Lee invented the World Wide Web. In his vision for an information management system, individual documents should be hyper-linked with each other through special **Uniform Resource Locators** (**URL**) and anyone reading a document inside of a web browser program would be able to jump directly to a referenced hyper-text document. He was also the one who designed the **Hypertext Transfer Protocol** (**HTTP**) and implemented the first versions of web server and web browser programs, that used the HTTP protocol for communication. The fact that his ideas were from the very beginning open, public and *for everyone* contributed to the enormous, global success of the World Wide Web and something that nowadays we take for granted when opening our favorite web browser and searching for information or reading news.

The HTTP is a simple protocol for exchanging text documents over the underlying TCP/IP protocol. It is very scalable, because from the very design, servers and clients do not need to maintain the state of communication and every HTTP request is independent. The HTTP specification defines different request types that a client can send to a server, sometimes referred to as *verbs*, that specify the type of action that a client wants to perform on a referenced *resource*. There are many HTTP methods, but the most common ones are GET, HEAD, POST, PUT, and DELETE. An HTTP server performs requested actions and returns response codes and optionally returns data. When the request is successful, the server returns the OK status code 200. The other popular standard HTTP response code is 404, which indicates an error *not found*.

In the original WWW design from 1989, Tim Berners Lee created the **Hypertext Markup Language** (**HTML**). Documents in this format can be displayed by web browsers. A few years later, the concept of web services was born from the realization that the HTTP protocol does not need to be limited to exchanging HTML documents. Any other document format can be returned from a web server and web client applications do not necessary need to be web browsers. The first popular web services implementation was based on the **Extensible Markup Language** (**XML**) document format. The XML was the natural evolution of HTML. In this new format, the types of markup *tags* were not defined by a specification, but anybody could define their own tags. The XML-based web services defined a set of XML tags for encoding **Simple Object Access Protocol** (**SOAP**) messages that were exchanged between XML SOAP web services clients and servers. The key tag was envelope and web services request messages were sent by clients with information which web service method needs to be invoked and what the parameters are. A web server would return an XML envelope with the results of a web method call.

Delphi 6 was the first developer tool on the market to support building SOAP web services servers and clients. This support is still there in the current Delphi versions, but over time the popularity of SOAP XML web services decreased. Instead of SOAP and XML, it is more common to use JSON as the document exchange format and REST as the communication protocol. **Representational State Transfer** (**REST**), builds on the weaknesses of SOAP. In SOAP, the main focus is on the XML syntax of a request `envelope` and the SOAP messages can be exchanged over any protocol, which does not necessarily need to be HTTP, although this is the most common implementation. REST-ful web services are simpler and take full advantage of the underlying HTTP protocol with its different request methods and response codes. The REST specification is not as formalized and rich as SOAP web services. The XML specification over time became very complex and XML parsing is no longer a trivial process. As with any new technology, the main adoption driver is simplification. REST web services are typically using a very simple JSON text format for exchanging data. REST became the main way for integrating with any remote functionality through an **Application Programming Interface** (**API**). The *REST API* became synonymous for *REST web services*.

# Native HTTP client

Arguably the most important contemporary network communication protocol is HTTP and its secure HTTPS version. Every operating system typically has its own HTTP client functionality built-in. In the cross-platform world of Delphi programming, there is the HTTP `native client` library, which provides uniform access to HTTP client implementations available on different platforms.

Similar to other cross-platform libraries in Delphi, you can either work with HTTP entirely in code using the types defined in `System.Net.HttpClient` and `System.Net.URLClient` units, or you can rely on reusable components declared in the `System.Net.HttpClientComponents` unit that are available from the **Tool Palette** in the **Net** category:

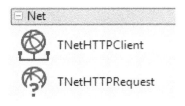

Native HTTP client components in the Tool Palette

Let's give them a try and build a simple app that will allow us to enter the URL into an edit box, download data using the HTTP GET request, and display the result in the memo.

Create a new blank Delphi multi-device project, save the main form unit as uFormHTTP, and the whole app as HTTPApp. Change the **Name** property of the form to FormHTTP. Drop the **TNetHTTPClient** component on the form.

Drop the **TToolbar** component on the form and drop the **TSpeedButton** and **TEdit** components onto the toolbar. Change the **Name** property of the speed button to spdbtnDownload, its **StyleLookup** property to arrowdowntoolbutton, and **Align** to **Right**. Change the **Name** property of the edit control to edtURL. Expand its **Margins** property and enter **8** as a margin value for all four sides of the control. Now align it to **Client**. Drop the **TMemo** control on the form. Rename it to MemoData and align to **Client**. The user interface is ready. As a nice twist, we can optionally set the SystemStatusBar.Visibility property of the form to "Invisible" to hide the system toolbar on iOS and have more space on the screen.

The **TNetHTTPClient** component has different methods for executing different types of HTTP requests that correspond to their names. For example, if we want to make a GET request, we need to use the Get method. For a POST request, there is Post method, and so on. Double-click on the speed button and enter the following code in its OnClick event handler:

```
procedure TFormHTTP.spdbtnDownloadClick(Sender: TObject);
var memstr: TMemoryStream; resp: IHTTPResponse;
begin
  memstr := TMemoryStream.Create;
  try
    resp := NetHTTPClient1.Get(edtURL.Text, memstr);
    if resp.StatusCode = 200 then
      MemoData.Lines.LoadFromStream(memstr)
    else
      ShowMessage(resp.StatusCode.ToString + ': ' + resp.StatusText);
  finally
    memstr.Free;
  end;
end;
```

That's probably the simplest way of using the HTTP client component. Here we are assuming that the content in the response stream can be displayed as text in the memo. The response type can also be binary. Let's imagine that we want to build a viewer for the chemical molecules. In this case, we might want to download to our app molecule information in the specialized PDB text file format. Here is a sample *Hemoglobin* data downloaded from the **Protein Data Bank** (www.rcsb.org). At the end, it is just a text file. Refer to the following screenshot:

```
https://files.rcsb.org/download/4hhb.pdb                              ∨

HEADER    OXYGEN TRANSPORT            07-MAR-84   4HHB
TITLE     THE CRYSTAL STRUCTURE OF HUMAN DEOXYHAEMOGLOBIN AT 1.74 ANGSTROMS
TITLE    2 RESOLUTION
COMPND    MOL_ID: 1;
COMPND   2 MOLECULE: HEMOGLOBIN (DEOXY) (ALPHA CHAIN);
COMPND   3 CHAIN: A, C;
COMPND   4 ENGINEERED: YES;
COMPND   5 MOL_ID: 2;
COMPND   6 MOLECULE: HEMOGLOBIN (DEOXY) (BETA CHAIN);
COMPND   7 CHAIN: B, D;
COMPND   8 ENGINEERED: YES
SOURCE    MOL_ID: 1;
SOURCE   2 ORGANISM_SCIENTIFIC: HOMO SAPIENS;
SOURCE   3 ORGANISM_COMMON: HUMAN;
SOURCE   4 ORGANISM_TAXID: 9606;
SOURCE   5 MOL_ID: 2;
SOURCE   6 ORGANISM_SCIENTIFIC: HOMO SAPIENS;
SOURCE   7 ORGANISM_COMMON: HUMAN;
SOURCE   8 ORGANISM_TAXID: 9606
```

Contents of a sample "PDB" file downloaded with a native HTTP client component

The HTTP client can work with both HTTP and HTTPS protocols. It can also execute requests asynchronously. If there is a lot of data to return from a server then the user interface gets temporarily frozen. It will only start again after the Get method is completed. Let's modify our example to make the request asynchronously. Change the Asynchronous property of the HTTP client component to True. If we executed our app again, we would get an error. This is because the method Get would not block, but the execution would continue immediately to the next command and the data from the response stream is not yet available. The request will execute in a different thread and when it is completed then the appropriate event is fired. Double-click on the OnRequestCompleted event of the HTTP client component. Modify the code in the OnClick event of the speed button and implement the logic for displaying the response data.

**Check the following code:**

```
procedure TFormHTTP.spdbtnDownloadClick(Sender: TObject);
begin
  NetHTTPClient1.Get(edtURL.Text);
  MemoData.Lines.Clear;
  MemoData.Lines.Add('Downloading...');
end;
procedure TFormHTTP.NetHTTPClient1RequestCompleted(const
  Sender: TObject;
  const AResponse: IHTTPResponse);
begin
  if AResponse.StatusCode = 200 then
    MemoData.Lines.LoadFromStream(AResponse.ContentStream)
  else
    ShowMessage(AResponse.StatusCode.ToString + ': ' +
    AResponse.StatusText);
end;
```

Now it works better. The user interface stays responsive during the download operation that is happening in a different thread.

The HTTP client library is the foundation for other specialized web services client components including SOAP, REST, BaaS, and Cloud API clients, which are discussed next.

# Consuming XML SOAP web services

The starting point for implementing the SOAP web service client is the **Web Services Description Language** (**WSDL**) document, which specifies what web methods a given web service implements and what are the names and types of the expected parameters. Delphi provides the **WSDL Importer** wizard that takes as input a WSDL file and generates the Object Pascal unit with types and methods that correspond with the functionality exposed by a SOAP web service. The main application logic can use these generated classes in order to issue web services requests and receive results returned from the remote web services server app.

Let's have a look at the process of integrating with a SOAP web service on the example of the *WHOIS* service. This is a test service hosted by www.webservicesx.net. It provides the interface to the WhoIs internet service, where you can check who is the registered owner of a given domain. This web service is very simple. It takes as a parameter a string value with a hostname and returns a string with information about the domain owner.

Create a new Delphi multi-device blank project. Save the main form as `uFormWhoIs` and the whole project as `WhoIsApp`. Change the **Name** property of the form to `FormWhoIs` and save all. Drop the **TPanel** control on the form and align it to **Top**.

Drop **TLabel** in the top left corner of the panel and in its **Text** property enter the **Domain Name**. Just below the label, drop the **TEdit** control. Change its **Name** to `edtHostName`. Below the edit, drop **TButton**, change its **Name** to `btnWhoIs`, and its **Text** property to `WHOIS`. Drop **TMemo** below the panel and align it to **Client**. Change its **Name** property to **MemoInfo**. Change the **WordWrap** property of the memo in the `TextSettings` to `True`. Our simple user interface is ready.

The starting point for importing the SOAP web service into an app is the location of its WSDL document. Typically, WSDL information is generated dynamically from a running web service. In the case of the `WhoIs` web service, the WSDL URL is `http://www.webservicex.net/whois.asmx?WSDL`.

Go to the **File** menu and select **Other...**. In the **New Items** dialog, click on the **WebServices** category in **Delphi Projects** and double-click on the **WSDL Importer** wizard:

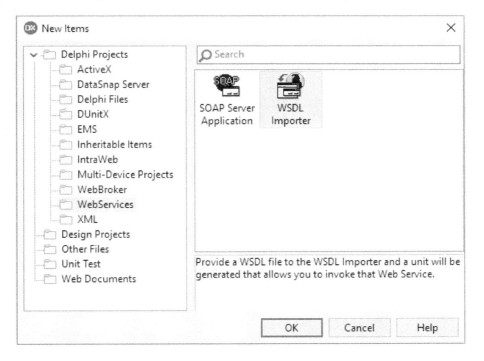

WSDL Importer wizard icon in the Delphi New Items dialog

In the first screen, we need to enter the WSDL file location:

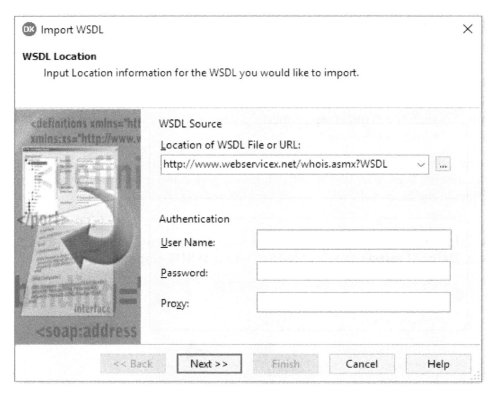

WSDL Location tab in the WSDL Importer wizard

On the next tab of the wizard, we can choose which SOAP version to use. Keep the default **Automatic SOAP versioning** option:

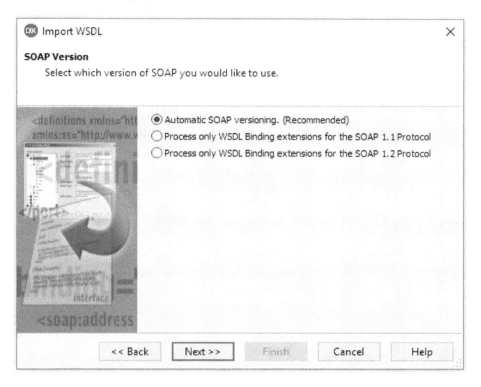

SOAP Version tab in the WSDL Importer wizard

On the next tab, we can fine tune the WSDL import option. Let's keep the default choices and click on **Finish**:

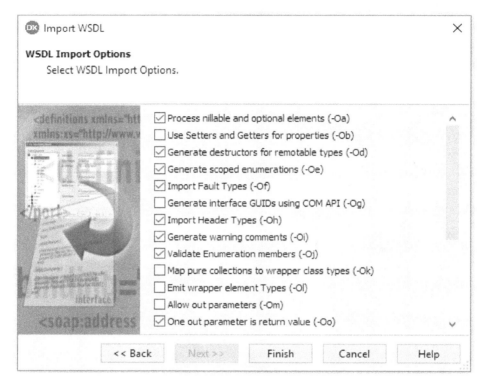

WSDL Import Options tab in the "WSDL Importer" wizard

The wizard will generate a new unit with a name derived from the web service and will automatically add it to the current project. In our case, the name of the generated unit is `whois`. Click on **Save All** to save the new unit. In the **File** menu, select the **Use Unit...** option and add the new unit to the `uses` clause in the implementation part of the main form unit.

The **WSDL Importer** wizard generates among other things the interface type whoisSoap that encapsulates the functionality of the imported web service. In the case of this simple web service, there is only one GetWhoIS method defined in the interface, but there could be more. The GetWhoIS method takes a string parameter and returns a string result. There is also a global function, GetwhoisSoap, which returns the reference to this interface:

```
type
  whoisSoap = interface(IInvokable)
  ['{67C5AD14-8EFA-64B7-66E7-4AE2D3725530}']
  function  GetWhoIS(const HostName: string): string; stdcall;
end;

// ...

function GetwhoisSoap(UseWSDL: Boolean=System.False; Addr:
  string=''; HTTPRIO: THTTPRIO = nil): whoisSoap;
```

In the client app code, we need to use the generated global function to obtain the web service interface reference. From this moment, we can start calling remote web service methods. Under the hood, the call to our local method will be encapsulated in a proper XML SOAP request envelope and sent to the web service server for processing. The resulting package will be received, unpacked, and the result will be passed back as the result of the GetWhoIS function.

Double-click on the **WHOIS** button on the form and enter the following code in the OnClick event handler:

```
uses whois;

procedure TFormWhoIs.btnWhoIsClick(Sender: TObject);
var s: string;
begin
  s := GetwhoisSoap.GetWhoIS(edtHostName.Text);
  MemoInfo.Lines.Clear;
  MemoInfo.Lines.Add(s);
end;
```

Very simple, isn't it? Now save all and run the app. You can enter an arbitrary domain and check to whom it is registered:

Information about the example.com domain from the WHOIS web service

This is how our WhoIsApp looks like on an iPhone.

# Integrating with REST services

Technology does not like to stand still. It keeps evolving. Nowadays, SOAP web services are not so frequently used compared to their newer REST-ful variant.

Over time, the XML file format became harder and harder to process. Initially, the simple XML specification went through many improvements and became more complex. The addition of XML Namespaces, XSLT, XQuery, and a couple of other specifications made XML processing much more demanding. In the meantime, much simpler **JavaScript Object Notation (JSON)** became the most popular format for exchanging structured data.

The new REST architecture for implementing web services is not as standardized as XML SOAP web services. **Representation State Transfer (REST)**, fully utilizes the underlying HTTP protocol and makes use of its different request methods and response codes. On the other hand, the SOAP specification was primarily focused on the content of the standard XML envelope. In fact, you do not necessarily need to exchange a SOAP message using HTTP. You could imagine sending it using other transport such as email or even a homing pigeon.

In REST there is more freedom. Inside the REST server, there are different resources identified by their URL paths. Typically, these resources, or *endpoints*, can be accessed using different HTTP verbs, such as GET, POST, DELETE, and PUT. In many cases, these different verbs correspond to different CRUD operations on the underlying resource. In the case of GET requests, parameters to web service calls are encoded inside the URL. Other HTTP verbs may take parameters inside the request header. The most common data format for returning information from REST services is JSON, but that could be XML or anything else.

Delphi provides a number of components for integrating with REST services. They are available in the **Tool Palette** under the **REST Client** category and internally they are implemented using the Native HTTP client library discussed earlier:

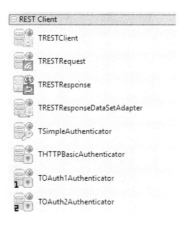

REST Client components in the Tool Palette

There are many free and paid public and private REST APIs out there to integrate with. Wikipedia has a nice list of open APIs at https://en.wikipedia.org/wiki/List_of_open _APIs. Let's have a look at what it takes to integrate with a REST API with the example of the INQStats service (inqubu.com) that provides demographic and statistical data of all the countries of the world. This API can be used publicly and free by everyone. The first thing to do is to obtain the API key at http://blog.inqubu.com/inqstats-open-api-published -to-get-demographic-data.

When integrating with a REST service, you need to know its *base URL*. What follows is the list of parameters. In the case of INQStats APIs, you always need to provide the API key as the api_key parameter. Then you need to pass other parameters to specify what information you want to get from the service.

For example, you could issue the following HTTP GET request to retrieve information about the population of Poland and Portugal:

```
http://inqstatsapi.inqubu.com?api_key=ADDYOURKEYHERE&data=population&co
untries=pl,pt
```

We could have entered this URL into the web browser, but there is a useful utility program that comes with Delphi called **REST Debugger** that you can find in the **Tools** menu. It comes with the source code and is a great place to learn how to use different REST components. Enter the preceding URL into the request edit box and click on the **Send Request** button. You can preview the response as plain JSON, but you can also view it in the tabular format, as shown in the following screenshot:

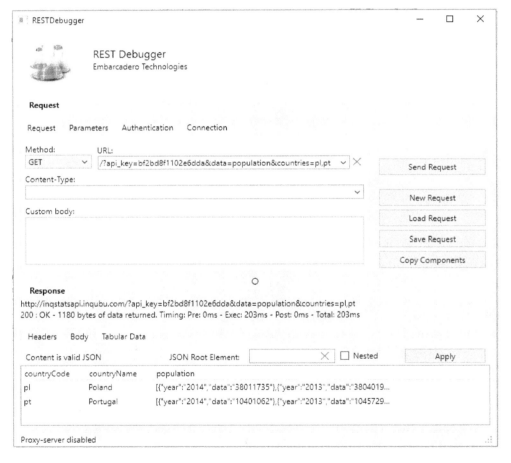

REST Debugger tool testing the INQStats service

Let's build a simple app to try the INQStats service out! Create a new multi-device, blank Delphi project. Save the main form unit as uFormStats and the whole project as INQStatsApp. Drop the **TTabControl** component on the form. Align the tab control to **Client** and add two tabs to it. Rename the first tab to **tbiCountries** and the second to **tbiPopulation**. Change the **TabsPosition** property of the tab control component to None. Drop the **TActionList** component on the form. Add two **TChangeTabAction** actions to the list. Change their names to ctaCountries and ctaPopulation and connect their **Tab** properties to the correct tabs. Drop the **TToolbar** control on the **Countries** tab. Drop the **TEdit** component on the toolbar. Change its **Name** property to edtCountryCodes and enter the pl, pt, nl string into its **Text** property. Add the TLabel component to the toolbar and enter **Country codes:** into its **Text** property. Drop **TSpeedButton** on the toolbar, change its **StyleLookup** property to refreshtoolbutton, rename it spdbtnRefresh, and align it to **Right**. Drop the **TListView** component on the first tab. Change its **Name** property to lstvwCountry. Add the **TToolbar** component to the second tab. Add the **TSpeedButton** control to it. Change its **StyleLookup** to arrowlefttoolbutton and its **Name** to **spdbtnBack**. Align it **Left** and connect its **Action** property to the ctaCountries change tab action. Drop the **TLabel** component on the toolbar and change its **Name** property to lblCountry. Align it to **Client**. Drop the **TListView** component on the second tab. Align it to **Client**. Change its **Name** property to lstvwPopulation. Expand the **ItemAppearance** property and select **ListItemRightDetail**. Expand the **Item** node in the **Structure** view and change the **Visible** property in the **Accessory** sub-node to False. Add the OnCreate event to the form and enter code to make sure that the Country tab is always displayed first:

```
procedure TFormStats.FormCreate(Sender: TObject);
begin
  TabControl1.ActiveTab := tbiCountries;
end;
```

That's the starting point for the user interface. Now let's integrate with the REST service. It is a good practice to keep non-visual, data access components in a separate unit. Add a new data module to the project and save it as uDMStats. Change its **Name** property to DMStats. Add the data module unit to the uses clause in the implementation part of the main form's unit.

Drop the **TRESTClient**, **TRESTRequest**, and **TRESTResponse** components onto the data module:

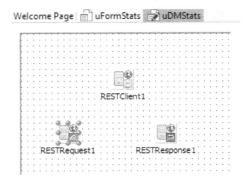

TRESTClient, TRESTRequest, and TRESTResponse components on the data module

All three REST components are connected to each other through the **Client** and **Response** properties of the **RESTRequest1** component:

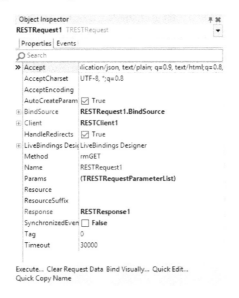

Properties of the TRESTRequest component

Enter `http://inqstatsapi.inqubu.com/` into the **BaseURL** property of the
**RESTClient1** component. Click on the **Params** property of the **RESTRequest1** component
and add three properties to the collection. Change the **Name** property of the first parameter
to `api_key` and enter your API key into the **Value** property. The second parameter **Name** is
`data` and the **Value** is `population`. In the third parameter, enter `countries` and `pl,pt`.
Right-click on the **RESTRequest1** component and select **Execute** to make the request. You
should see the message with the HTTP response code 200:

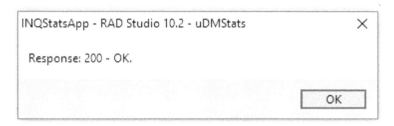

The response result message from the REST request executed at design time

If you now click on the **RESTResponse1** component, you should see that the **Content**
property is filled with data returned from the service. It is exactly the same JSON as in the
REST debugger. What can we do with this data? At this point, we could start writing some
code to put different values into the **Value** properties of the REST request component, call
its `Execute` method, and retrieve JSON text from the REST response component `Content`
property. The other option is to convert the response into a dataset and use visual live
bindings to quickly create a user interface. Drop `TRESTResponseDataSetAdapter` on the
data module. Set its **ResponseJSON** property to point to the **RESTResponse1** component.
Drop the **TFDMemTable** component on the data module. Set the **Dataset** property of the
adapter component to point to the **FDMemTable1** component. Change the **Active** property
of the adapter to `True` and select the **Update Dataset** option from the adapter context menu.

If you now expand the **FieldDefs** property of the **FDMemTable1** component, you should see that there are now three fields defined that correspond to JSON data in the REST response component:

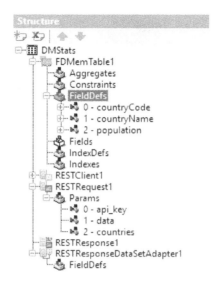

DMStats data module in the Structure View

Right-click on the memory table component and select **Edit Dataset** option. You should see the population data inside of the component. Now it is just a matter of connecting this data with the user interface controls. Switch to the main form of the application and select the **LiveBindings Designer** option from the **Tool Windows** menu in the main **View** menu. The data module is already in the `uses` clause of the form, so you should be able to see all components from the data module in the visual live binding designer window.

Connect the * field of the memory table component with the **Synch** property of the **lstvwCountries** control. Also connect the **countryName** field with the `Item.Text` property and also with the **Text** property of the **lblCountry** label in the toolbar of the second tab:

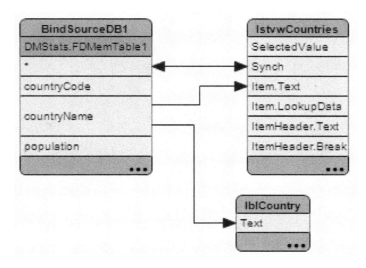

Visual Live Bindings connecting visual controls on the FormStats form with the data FDMemTable1 in the data module

If you now ran the app, you would see the list of countries in the list view, but that would be static. Add the following code to the `OnClick` event of the `spdbtnRefresh` button:

```
procedure TFormStats.spdbtnRefreshClick(Sender: TObject);
begin
    DMStats.FDMemTable1.Active := False;
    DMStats.RESTResponseDataSetAdapter1.Active := False;
    DMStats.RESTRequest1.Params[2].Value := edtCountryCodes.Text;
    DMStats.RESTRequest1.Execute;
    DMStats.RESTResponseDataSetAdapter1.Active := True;
    DMStats.FDMemTable1.Active := True;
end;
```

Run the app. Click on the **Refresh** button and you should see the names of countries in the list view:

Country names in the first tab of the INQStats app

Now we need to display the `population` JSON field in the second list view component. For this we are coding to write a utility function to convert the JSON array of population objects into a generic list of population records. Add a new unit to the project and save it as `uINQStatsUtils`. Enter there the following code:

```
unit uINQStatsUtils;
interface
uses
  System.Generics.Collections;
type
  TPopulation = record
  Year: integer;
  Value: integer;
end;
TPopulationList = TList<TPopulation>;
procedure JsonToPopulationList(json: string; aList:   TPopulationList);
implementation
uses
  System.SysUtils,
  System.Classes,
  System.JSON.Readers,
  System.JSON.Types;
procedure ReadItem(aList: TPopulationList; jtr: TJSONTextReader);
var item: TPopulation;
begin
  while jtr.Read do
  begin
    if jtr.TokenType = TJsonToken.PropertyName then
    begin
      if jtr.Value.ToString = 'year' then
```

```
      begin
        jtr.Read;
        item.year := StrToInt(jtr.Value.AsString);
      end
      else if jtr.Value.ToString = 'data' then
      begin
        jtr.Read;
        item.Value := StrToInt(jtr.Value.AsString);
      end
    end
    else if jtr.TokenType = TJsonToken.EndObject then
    begin
      aList.add(item);
      exit;
    end;
  end;
end;

procedure JsonToPopulationList(json: string; aList:   TPopulationList);
var jtr: TJsonTextReader; sr: TStringReader;
begin
  if aList <> nil then
  begin
    aList.Clear;
    sr := TStringReader.Create(json);
    try
      jtr := TJsonTextReader.Create(sr);
      try
        while jtr.Read do
          if jtr.TokenType = TJsonToken.StartObject then
            ReadItem(aList, jtr);
      finally
        jtr.Free;
      end;
    finally
      sr.Free;
    end;
  end;
end;

end.
```

Add this unit to the main form `uses` clause and add the following code in the `OnItemClick` event of the `lstvwCountries` list view. See the following code:

```
procedure TFormStats.lstvwCountriesItemClick(const Sender: TObject;
  const AItem: TListViewItem);
var aList: TPopulationList; rec: TPopulation; json: string; item:
TListViewItem;
begin
  DMStats.FDMemTable1.RecNo := AItem.Index;
  json := DMStats.FDMemTable1.FieldByName('population').AsString;
  aList := TPopulationList.Create;
  try
    JsonToPopulationList(json, aList);
    lstvwPopulation.Items.Clear;
    for rec in aList do
    begin
      item := lstvwPopulation.Items.Add;
      item.Text := rec.Value.ToString;
      item.Detail := rec.Year.ToString;
    end;
  finally
    aList.Free;
  end;
  ctaPopulation.ExecuteTarget(self);
end;
```

If you now run the app, it should be fully functional. When you click on the item in the list of countries, you should see the population information:

Population information for Poland from the INQStats service in the second tab of the app

# Backend as a service client

Only the simplest mobile apps can operate on their own. In most scenarios, a typical mobile app architecture can be divided into two pieces. A backend and a frontend. Both architectural layers can be very complex and may require different programming skills. It is becoming more common to see on a business card titles such as *backend developer, frontend developer*, or *full stack developer*. Specialization grows. As a Delphi super hero, you do not need to limit yourself! You can develop from the same source code to different mobile frontends and easily architect mobile backends.

When building a complex app, you do not want to reinvent the wheel and spend your precious time on implementing things that already exist. What if we could just use an existing backend in our next mobile app, instead of building it from scratch? There are number of typical functions that a mobile backend provides. Things such as user management, data storage, mobile push notifications, analytics, and others are common to any full-featured mobile backend. This is where **Backend as a Service** (BaaS) offerings come into the picture. There is a growing number of services in the internet that provide paid BaaS services that your app can integrate to.

On top of the `REST Client` component library, the whole set of BaaS components for integrating with different BaasS providers has been built and is available from the **BAAS Client** category in the **Tool Palette**:

The first two are provider components that can be used to integrate with two existing Backend as a Service providers: **Kinvey** (www.kinvey.com) and Parse. The second company has been acquired by Facebook and is no longer available as a separate entity, but the provider component is still there on the **Tool Palette**. There is also the third BaaS provider component available. It is installed on the **Enterprise Mobility Services** tab for integrating with Embarcadero's own mobile backend solution: the RAD Server that is installed as part of the Delphi installation. Delphi itself comes with the developer license for developing and testing mobile backends built using the RAD Server product. In the next chapter, we are going to have a closer look into building mobile backends with the RAD Server and will discuss the functionality of different BaaS client components.

# Integrating with the cloud

Integrating with *cloud services* can be understood in different ways. It could mean to integrate with any remote service. It is a very broad term. There are different cloud web service providers that offer all kinds of services. The main players in this arena are Amazon Web Services, Google Cloud Services, and Microsoft with their Azure Cloud. There are also other vendors, but not as big as the top ones. Cloud services are typically accessible using the HTTPS protocol and as such they are just regular web services.

Delphi comes with the Cloud API framework for accessing different cloud services. On top of abstract types and classes that are common for any cloud service defined in the Data.Cloud.CloudAPI unit, there are two specialized units with types and classes specific for working with selected services available from Amazon and Azure declared in **Data.Cloud.AmazonAPI** and **Data.Cloud.AzureAPI**:

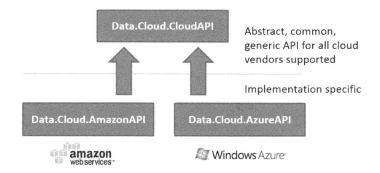

For both cloud vendors, there are implementations of blob storage, table, and queue services. The following table summarizes all the currently supported services in the Cloud API framework:

| | Amazon Web Services | Microsoft Azure |
|---|---|---|
| **Storage** | Simple Storage Service | Blobs Service |
| **Table** | Simple Database Service | Table Service |
| **Queue** | Simple Queue Service | Queue Service |

Cloud services from Amazon and Azure supported by the Delphi Cloud API

In this chapter, we are going to focus on Amazon Web Services **Simple StorageService** (S3) service. Amazon S3 allows us to store arbitrary amounts of data in the cloud at a very low cost and in a reliable and scalable way. It is one of the most popular and frequently used cloud services in the world.

# Moving ToDo List to Amazon S3

In the previous chapter, we built a simple **ToDo List** mobile app with a pluggable data access architecture. Here we are going to replace the data access logic. Instead of storing To-Do data in the local database, we are going to store them in the Amazon Simple Storage Service in the form of a JSON file. This is a very powerful and cost-effective solution. We will be able to access the same To-Dos from apps running on different mobile devices effectively implementing a serverless architecture.

The first step is to make sure that we have an account in the Amazon Web Services. If you do not have an AWS account, you can create one at `http://aws.amazon.com/free/`. In the first year, you can use certain services for free and try them out. In the case of the AWS Simple Storage Service, this allows for 5 GB of free storage and 20,000 Get and 2,000 Put requests to be used for 1 year from creating an AWS account.

After signing up to the Amazon Web Services, you have now access to the AWS Management Console web page where you can manage different services. The AWS Simple Storage Service lets you store arbitrary amounts of data in a secure, reliable way. All data objects are organized into buckets. A single user can have up to 100 buckets, but the amount of objects stored in a bucket is unlimited. An individual object can have a size up to 5 TB. Within a bucket, you can further organize files in a folder structure. Every AWS object may be accessed via a HTTP URL or programmatically from an app using a special API. Bucket names need to be unique and lower case. The identifier of an object within S3 cannot exceed 1,024 characters.

Log in to the AWS Management Console at https://console.aws.amazon.com/. Click on the **S3** link in the category of **Storage** services to enter the S3 management page:

Storage services available from Amazon Web Services

Here you can see the list of all your buckets. Initially the list is empty, so the first thing to do is to create a new bucket. Click on the **Create bucket** button and enter the name of your bucket. This name has to be unique across different AWS accounts, so you will have to be creative and select something that nobody else has already chosen. In my case, the name of the bucket will be **todostorage**, but you might want to choose a different identifier.

Amazon S3 can be used to efficiently share big files with other people. From within the S3 web console, you can upload files from your computer. By default, they are private to you, but if you select the option to make them public, anybody can access your files using the URL that you can see when you click on the selected object properties. Many big companies such as Dropbox, Netflix, and others are using Amazon S3 as their underlying storage infrastructure. In the case of our app, we are not going to access files stored in the S3 using their URLs, but we are going to work with them through AWS REST APIs that are accessible in Delphi through the Cloud API.

Let's start with a simple app to test if we are able to upload and download arbitrary string values to and from the Amazon S3 service. Later, we are going to plug in the existing To-Do List GUI form and connect it to through the IToDoData interface to the new data access implementation. Create a new blank, multi-device app, save the main form as uFormTestS3, and the whole project as TestS3. Add a data module to the project. Save it as uDMAmazon and change its **Name** property to DMAmazon. In the **Project Options**, in the **Forms** category, make sure that the data module is created before the main form of the application. Add the data module to the uses clause of the main form in its implementation section.

Now drop the **TAmazonConnectonInfo** component on the data module design surface from the **Cloud** category in the **Tool Palette**:

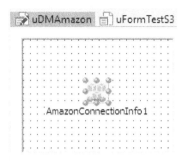

TAmazonConnectionInfo component on the data module

The **TAmazonConnectionInfo** component is responsible for storing credentials needed for accessing AWS. The first two properties of the connection component listed in the Object Inspector are **AccountKey** and **AccountName**. How do we get them?

Here we will have to dig into important concepts of the AWS security model. Go back to the AWS Management Console and click on the **IAM** from the list of services in the category of **Security, Identity & Compliance**:

Identity and Access Management (IAM) Amazon Web Service

The **Identity and Access Management** (**IAM**) service is used to manage users and groups that can access your account. After creating the account in AWS, the root user has been created for you. It has full access to all services. From a security point of view, you should never access Amazon Web Services on behalf of this user. Inside the IAM service web console, we can create new users and grant them access to specific resources. For our app, we will need to create a new user that will have access to the Simple Storage Service only. We could restrict this access even further, to just specific actions on objects inside of a specific bucket, but granting full access to just the S3 service with IAM will be simpler.

Click on the **Users** option in the IAM web page and click on the **Add user** button to add a new user. Enter the name for the new user. In the **Add user** page, enter the name of the user (for example, s3user), and check **Programmatic access** in the **Access type** section. In this way, we will be able to generate access keys that are needed in our app:

Add user

1 ——————— 2 ——————— 3 ——————— 4

Details        Permissions        Review        Complete

Set user details

You can add multiple users at once with the same access type and permissions. Learn more

User name*    s3user

⊕ Add another user

Select AWS access type

Select how these users will access AWS. Access keys and autogenerated passwords are provided in the last step. Learn more

Access type*   ☑   **Programmatic access**
                    Enables an **access key ID** and **secret access key** for the AWS API, CLI, SDK, and other
                    development tools.
               ☐   **AWS Management Console access**
                    Enables a **password** that allows users to sign-in to the AWS Management Console.

\* Required                                                    Cancel      Next: Permissions

AWS IAM Add User wizard first screen to create a user

Click on the **Next: Permissions** button to move to the next screen. Here we can add a new user to an existing group, copy permissions from other users, or directly attach security policies. Click on the **Attach existing policies directly** option and from the list of existing policies, check the **AmazonS3FullAccess** policy and click on the **Next: Review** button at the bottom of the page:

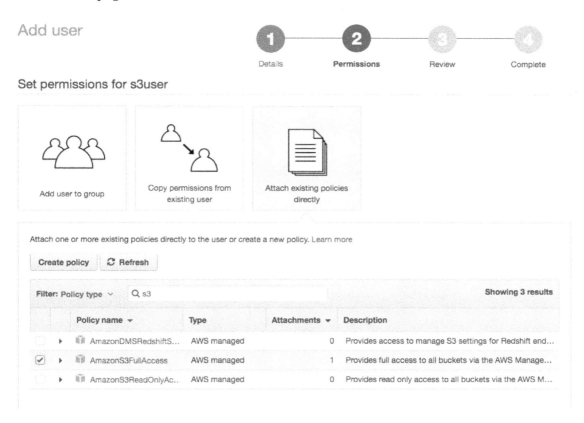

AWS IAM Add User wizard screen to add permissions to a new user

In the **Review** page, we can verify that all options are correctly set. Click on the **Create user** button to create the **s3user** with full access to the S3 service:

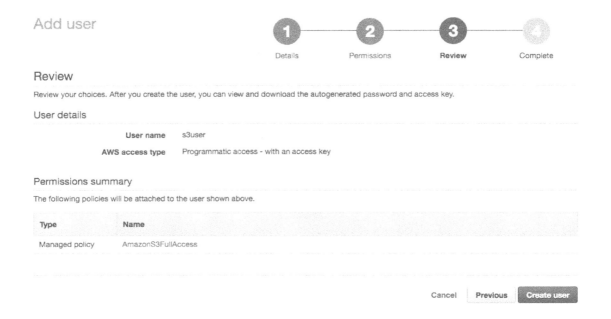

AWS IAM "Add User" wizard "Review" screen

**Complete** is the last page of the **Create user** wizard. This is our only opportunity to copy the credentials for our newly created user. They can be downloaded as a CSV file or copied directly to the clipboard from the web page. We can always create new credentials for any user. Refer to the following screenshot:

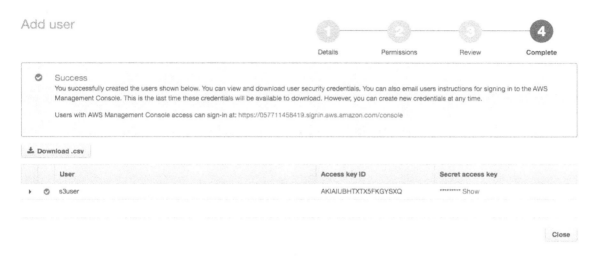

IAM Add User screen with newly created credentials

Copy the **Access key ID** and **Secret access key** to, respectively the **AccountKey** and **AccountName** properties of the **AmazonConnectionInfo1** component on the data module.

At this stage, it is not obvious, but there is also one additional property to be set. Change the **UseDefaultEndpoints** property to `False` and enter `s3-eu-west-1.amazonaws.com` as the value of the **StorageEndpoint** property. The S3 service would not be happy if we were to use default credentials which contain the *east* and not *west* value in the URL. Take a look at the following screenshot:

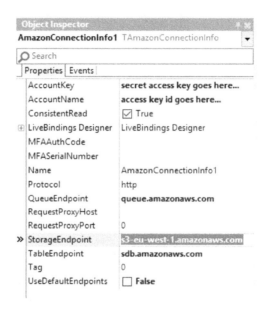

Properties of the AmazonConnectionInfo component in the Object Inspector

In `Data.Cloud.AmazonAPI`, there are different classes that provide access to different supported Amazon web services. In order to start working with S3, you will need to create an instance of the `TAmazonStorageService` class. As a parameter to its constructor, it takes the connection info component. Let's define the S3 public read-only property in the public section of the data module. This will be a handy way to access `TAmazonStorageService`. The service reference will be created in the *lazy* fashion inside of the property `getter` and destroyed in the data module overridden destructor.

Let's also define two methods for reading and writing to an object in a bucket: `S3ReadStr` and `S3WriteStr`. They will take the name of a bucket, an object name, and the string value to be saved or returned. Both methods will return Boolean results to indicate if the request was successful or not. An object in S3 is just an array of bytes, so we will need to convert the string to a bytes stream using arbitrary encoding, for example UTF8:

```
type
  TDMAmazon = class(TDataModule)
```

```pascal
    AmazonConnectionInfo1: TAmazonConnectionInfo;
  private
    FS3: TAmazonStorageService;
    function GetS3: TAmazonStorageService;
  public
    destructor Destroy; override;
    function S3WriteStr(bucket, obj, s: string): boolean;
    function S3ReadStr(bucket, obj: string; var s: string):    boolean;
    property S3: TAmazonStorageService read GetS3;
  end;

// ...

function TDMAmazon.GetS3: TAmazonStorageService;
begin
  if FS3 = nil then
    FS3 := TAmazonStorageService.Create(AmazonConnectionInfo1);
    Result := FS3;
end;

destructor TDMAmazon.Destroy;
begin
  FS3.Free;
  inherited;
end;

function TDMAmazon.S3ReadStr(bucket, obj: string; var s: string):
  boolean;
var bstr: TBytesStream;
begin
  bstr := TBytesStream.Create;
  try
    Result := S3.GetObject(bucket, obj, bstr);
    if Result then
      s := TEncoding.UTF8.GetString(bstr.Bytes)
    else
      s := '';
  finally
    bstr.Free;
  end;
end;

function TDMAmazon.S3WriteStr(bucket, obj, s: string): boolean;
var strstr: TStringStream;
begin
  strstr := TStringStream.Create(s, TEncoding.UTF8);
  try
    Result := S3.UploadObject(bucket, obj, strstr.bytes);
```

```
    finally
      strstr.Free;
    end;
  end;
end;
```

Now we can try out the data module code. Drop **TPanel** on the form and align it to **Left**. Drop **TMemo** on the form and align it **Client**. Rename it to MemoLog. Put a **TEdit** and two **TButton** components on the panel. Change the **Text** on the first button to Write and its **Name** to btnWrite. Rename the second button to btnRead and its **Text** to Read. Double-click on the **btnWrite** and enter the code to write the text from the edit box into the S3 storage. When we click on **btnRead**, we will read the test testobj object from the S3 todostorage bucket and display it in the memo to verify that it is the same as in the edit:

```
uses uDMAmazon;

const
  TODO_BUCKET = 'todostorage';
  TODO_OBJ = 'testdata';

procedure TFormTestS3.Log(s: string);
begin
  MemoLog.Lines.Add(s);
end;

procedure TFormTestS3.btnReadClick(Sender: TObject);
var s: string;
begin
  DMAmazon.S3ReadStr(TODO_BUCKET, TODO_OBJ, s);
  Log('Read: ' + s);
end;

procedure TFormTestS3.btnWriteClick(Sender: TObject);
var s: string;
begin
  s := Edit1.Text;
  DMAmazon.S3WriteStr(TODO_BUCKET, TODO_OBJ, s);
  Log('Written: ' + s);
end;
```

Run the test app to verify that writing and saving an arbitrary string to an S3 bucket works as expected. Here is what the test app looks like on Windows target:

Test app for writing and reading a string from the Amazon S3 service

The basic functionality for writing and reading strings from Amazon S3 is working, so now we can continue with moving the **To-Do List** app to the cloud storage. The first thing we will have to take care of will be serialization of the TDoLists generic list of TToDo records to and from JSON so it can be stored in the S3 bucket.

Locate the ToDoList source code files from the previous chapter and copy them to the current directory where the TestS3 project is in the uToDoTypes unit and add them to the project. Save the project as ToDoListS3. Now add an empty unit to the project and save it as uToDoUtils. Here is where we are going to implement two global procedures for converting the TToDos list to a string and back. Add uToDoTypes to the interface uses clause of the unit and enter there the following code:

```
unit uToDoUtils;

interface

uses
  uToDoTypes;

function ToDosToStr(aList: TToDos): string;
procedure StrToToDos(s: string; aList: TToDos);

implementation

uses
  System.SysUtils, System.Classes, System.JSON.Types,
  System.JSON.Writers, System.JSON.Readers;

procedure WriteItem(item: TToDo; jw: TJSONWriter);
begin
  jw.WritePropertyName('ID');
  jw.WriteValue(item.Id.ToString);
```

```
    jw.WritePropertyName('Title');
    jw.WriteValue(item.Title);
    jw.WritePropertyName('Category');
    jw.WriteValue(item.Category);
  end;

  function ToDosToStr(aList: TToDos): string;
  var
    item: TToDo;
    sw: TStringWriter;
    jtw: TJsonTextWriter;
  begin
    sw := TStringWriter.Create();
    jtw := TJsonTextWriter.Create(sw);
    try
      jtw.WriteStartArray;

      for item in aList do
      begin
        jtw.WriteStartObject;
        WriteItem(item, jtw);
        jtw.WriteEndObject;
      end;

      jtw.WriteEndArray;
      Result := sw.ToString;
    finally
      jtw.Free;
      sw.Free;
    end;
  end;

  function ReadStr(jtr: TJSONReader): string;
  begin
    jtr.Read;
    jtr.Read;
    Result := jtr.Value.AsString;
  end;

  procedure ReadItem(aList: TToDos; jtr: TJSONReader);
  var todo: TToDo;
  begin
    todo.Id := StrToInt(ReadStr(jtr));
    todo.Title := ReadStr(jtr);
    todo.Category := ReadStr(jtr);
    aList.Add(todo);
  end;
```

```
procedure StrToToDos(s: string; aList: TToDos);
var jtr: TJsonTextReader; sr: TStringReader;
begin
  sr := TStringReader.Create(s);
  try
    jtr := TJsonTextReader.Create(sr);
    try
      while jtr.Read do
        if jtr.TokenType = TJsonToken.StartObject then
          ReadItem(aList, jtr);
    finally
      jtr.Free;
    end;
  finally
    sr.Free;
  end;
end;

end.
```

We already know from Chapter 3, *Packing Up Your Toolbox*, how to process JSON arrays using readers and writers, so this code should be self-explanatory.

The next step it is to implement the IToDoData interface using the already tested functionality for storing strings in the cloud. Rename the **Name** property of the data module to DMToDoList and save the data module file as uDMToDoList. Add uToDoTypes ′ to the uses clauses in the interface section of the data module unit and add the IToDoData interface to the class declaration of the data module.

We could have started adding code to the DMAmazon data module, but it will be a cleaner design to inherit from the TDMAmazon data module class. Add a new unit to the project and save it as uDMToDoS3 and declare there the TDMToDoS3 class that inherits from the TDMAmazon class and implements the IToDoData interface. Copy the signatures of the interface methods into the public declaration section of the data module and press *Ctrl + Shift + C* for the class completion. In the implementation section of the data module, we will *use* the uToDoUtils unit and the To-Do items' serialization code and declare two constants for the bucket and the object name to be used for storing the list of To-Dos.

The method that returns the list of all To-Do items is very simple to implement:

```
uses uToDoUtils;

const
  TODO_BUCKET = 'todostorage';
  TODO_DATA = 'tododata';
```

```
// ...

procedure TDMToDoS3.ToDoList(aList: TToDos);
var s: string;
begin
  if aList <> nil then
  begin
    aList.Clear;
    if S3ReadStr(TODO_BUCKET, TODO_DATA, s) then
      StrToToDos(s, aList);
  end;
end;
```

Just read the JSON data from S3 and if the operation was successful, convert from the string to the list.

Reading a particular item from the list is slightly more completed because we need to iterate over the list looking for the particular identifier and then return the desired item:

```
function TDMToDoS3.ToDoRead(id: integer; out aValue: TToDo): boolean;
var aList: TToDos; i, index: integer; s: string;
begin
  aList := TToDos.Create;
  try
    Result := S3ReadStr(TODO_BUCKET, TODO_DATA, s);
    if Result then
    begin
      StrToToDos(s, aList);

      index := -1;
      for i := 0 to aList.Count-1 do
      if id = aList[i].Id then
      begin
        index := i;
        break;
      end;

      Result := index > -1;
      if Result then
        aValue := aList[i];
    end;
  finally
    aList.Free;
  end;
end;
```

Adding the To-Do item will require reading the list, adding the item, and saving it back. A nice side-effect of serialization is that we do not need to implement the special logic for calculating the new maximum identifier. We always insert new items at the beginning of the list, so the first item on the list will always have the highest identifier value. This time we will also have to convert the list back to the string and save it into the S3:

```
function TDMToDoS3.ToDoCreate(aValue: TToDo): integer;
var aList: TToDos; newId: integer; s: string; ok: boolean;
begin
  Result := -1;
  aList := TToDos.Create;
  try
    ok := S3ReadStr(TODO_BUCKET, TODO_DATA, s);
    if ok then
    begin
      StrToToDos(s, aList);

      if aList.Count > 0 then
        newId := aList[0].Id + 1
      else
        newId := 1;
      aValue.Id := newId;
      aList.Insert(0, aValue);

      s := ToDosToStr(aList);
      if S3WriteStr(TODO_BUCKET, TODO_DATA, s) then
        Result := newId;
    end;
  finally
    aList.Free;
  end;
end;
```

The implementation of `delete` involves reading items into the list, locating a given item, removing it, and then saving the modified list back:

```
function TDMToDoS3.ToDoDelete(id: integer): boolean;
var aList: TToDos; i, index: integer; s: string;
begin
  Result := False;
  aList := TToDos.Create;
  try
    if S3ReadStr(TODO_BUCKET, TODO_DATA, s) then
    begin
      StrToToDos(s, aList);
      index := -1;
      for i := 0 to aList.Count-1 do
```

```
          if id = aList[i].Id then
          begin
            index := i;
            break;
          end;

          if index > -1 then
          begin
            aList.Delete(index);
            s := ToDosToStr(aList);
            Result := S3WriteStr(TODO_BUCKET, TODO_DATA, s);
          end;
        end;
    finally
      aList.Free;
    end;
end;
```

The implementation of the update method is very similar to delete. The only difference is that we are not removing the item, but replacing it with the new value. Have a look at the following code:

```
function TDMToDoS3.ToDoUpdate(aValue: TToDo): boolean;
var aList: TToDos; i, index: integer; s: string;
begin
  Result := False;
  aList := TToDos.Create;
  try
    if S3ReadStr(TODO_BUCKET, TODO_DATA, s) then
    begin
      StrToToDos(s, aList);
      index := -1;
      for i := 0 to aList.Count-1 do
      if aValue.id = aList[i].Id then
      begin
        index := i;
        break;
      end;

      if index > -1 then
      begin
        aList[index] := aValue;
        s := ToDosToStr(aList);
        Result := S3WriteStr(TODO_BUCKET, TODO_DATA, s);
      end;
    end;
  finally
    aList.Free;
```

```
    end;
end;
```

The implementation of the data access logic is complete. Now we can plug it into the graphical user interface. Copy from the original ToDoList project folder both the files that make up the GUI: uFormToDo.pas and uFormToDo.fmx. Add the uFormToDo to the project and save. Now you can safely remove from the project the FormTestS3 test form. The only modification to make in the GUI is to change the code in the GetToDoData method. See the following code:

```
uses uDMToDoS3;

function TFormToDo.GetToDoData: IToDoData;
begin
  if DMToDoS3 = nil then
    DMToDoS3 := TDMToDoS3.Create(Application);
    Result := DMToDoS3;
end;
```

Save all and run locally on Windows. Change the target to iOS or Android and run again. You should see the same To-Do data on all the devices. This is a truly *serverless* design with no server logic. Everything is running on the client, so it is a very scalable solution.

# Summary

In this chapter, we have learned how to integrate mobile Delphi apps with different types of web services. In the next chapter, we will look into implementing mobile backends in Delphi.

# 11
# Building Mobile Backends

In the mobile development world, it is common to have dedicated developers and teams responsible for just building mobile frontend and backends. This time we are going to wear the backend developer hat and use Delphi to build modern scalable, secure, and fault-tolerant REST API web services with full database access. This chapter will cover the following points:

- Why multi-tier architectures?
- Creating mobile backends with:
  - WebBroker
  - DataSnap
  - RAD Server

The objective of this chapter is to understand different choices for backend technologies in Delphi and get practical knowledge on how to build scalable, fault-tolerant mobile backends in the cloud.

# Delphi and multi-tier architectures

In the previous chapter, we saw that you can use cloud web services to create an information system where apps running on different devices can connect to the same data store. Not only can you use Delphi to integrate with existing web services, but you can also build your own!

Why would you build mobile backend services? Multi-tier architectures, with client apps communicating with server apps to access underlying resources, have a lot of benefits. Additional tiers make the app architecture more complex, and they also bring benefits such as improved scalability and security. The multi-tier approach simplifies change management, because client apps are not tied to the underlying services and communicate with them through an abstraction layer provided by server APIs.

In multi-tier architectures, the actual server app is just one of the many pieces of the overall picture. It is very important to know how a server app is deployed. If scalability and high-availability of services is our primary concern, then we should think about using load-balancing technologies. One of the most popular deployment platforms is Amazon Web Services Elastic Cloud (`https://aws.amazon.com/ec2/`), which offers load-balancing functionality with auto-scaling groups. In this scenario, the server app that we are building is installed into a virtual machine (**Amazon Machine Image**). Depending on the number of incoming HTTP requests, the auto-scaling infrastructure can start and stop instances of this virtual machine image, adapting to the current load. In the following diagram, we can see that clients at the bottom read and write data to the database indirectly, through the server tier:

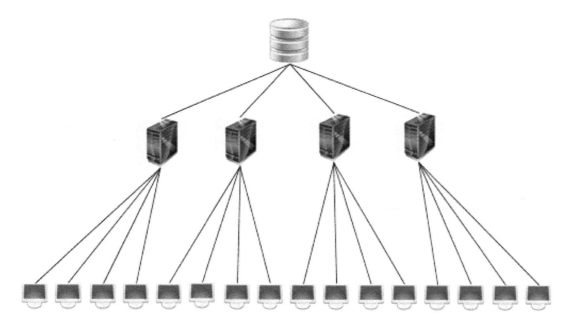

Three-tier architecture

In architectures like this, it is beneficial not to maintain the state of communication with a client app in the server tier, because different requests coming from the same client app might be received by different instances of the server.

There are many types of Delphi server apps that you can build with different IDE wizards. In this chapter, we are going to focus on web services accessible through HTTP and HTTPS protocols. Since version 10.2, Delphi supports compiling server apps to the Linux platform. That's one of the most popular and powerful deployment choices for web services, so it is nice to have this flexibility to either deploy to Windows or Linux.

In the previous chapter, we have moved our *To-Do List* app to the cloud. The *To-Do* items are stored in the Amazon Simple Storage Service and there is a clear interface to access this functionality. It is a common scenario to build REST API backends to provide uniform, controlled access to the underlying data access services like this. Over the following pages, we will move this simple mobile app to multi-tier architectures. Look at the following diagram:

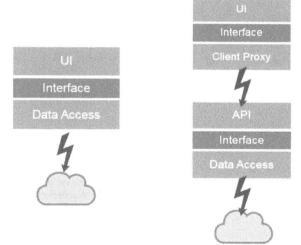

The user interface and data access logic will stay the same. In the client app, the data access layer will be replaced with logic responsible for communication with a remote service using the HTTP protocol. On the serverside, the existing code to work with Amazon S3 will be accessed by the API layer, which will expose the underlying service to HTTP clients.

# Getting low-level with WebBroker

The most simple and generic web server development framework in Delphi is **WebBroker**. It is the underlying technology for many specialized web service types that you can build with Delphi, such as SOAP XML Web Services and DataSnap. If you create a new web server app with the **New WebBroker App** wizard, you can implement arbitrary HTTP server functionality. In our case, that will be a simple web service that will provide REST API access to the *To-Do* data.

Click on the **File | New | Other...** menu items in the IDE and double-click on the **New Web Server Application** wizard in the **WebBroker** category, as shown in the following screenshot:

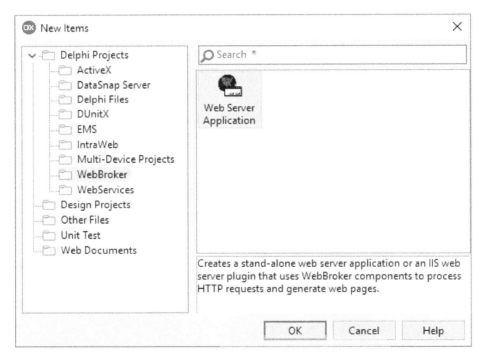

New Web Server Application wizard in New Items

Check the option to add Linux support to the project on the first page of the wizard:

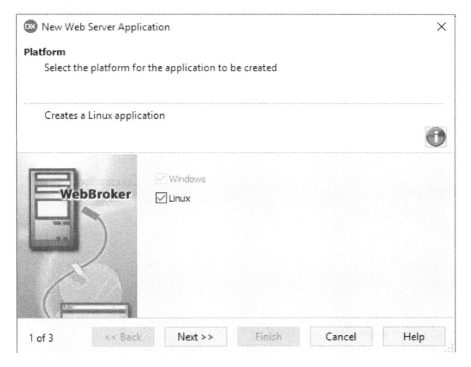

Platforms selection in the "New Web Server Application" wizard

On the second page of the new web server app wizard, we need to decide if our project should be an Apache module or a self-contained executable based on Indy web server technology. If we select **Apache** then the resulting binary will be a library with a web application that would need to be deployed to the Apache server. That's the right choice for scalable deployment. For development and testing, it is better to select **Standalone** as the project type. Later on, we will want to convert the standalone project into an Apache module for deployment. One possible solution is to create two WebBroker projects, one as an Apache module and the other as a standalone app, and attach them to the same project group. Within this project group, all units, except for those containing a project source, can be shared between both projects. During development, we can always select the **Build All** option to create test and production versions of the same web app.

For now, let's choose the **Standalone** option. Later on, we will add the second Apache project to the project group:

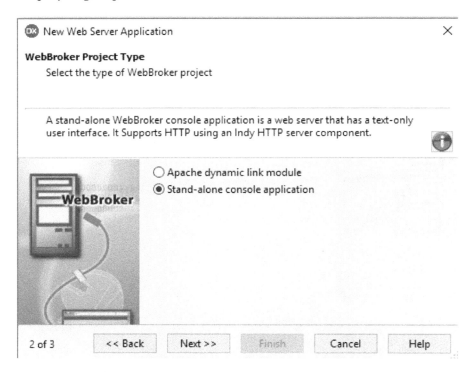

Project type choice in the "New Web Server Application" wizard

On the last page of the wizard, we can choose the communication protocol, HTTP or HTTPs, and the default port. In the case of a standalone web server, we can choose any port. If we were to deploy to Apache or IIS web servers then the communication protocol and port used would be a matter of web server configuration:

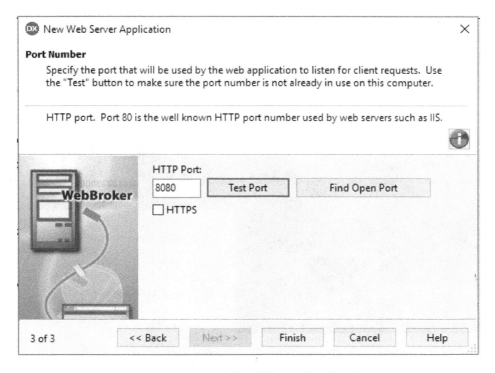

Port number selection in the "New Web Server Application" wizard

Click on the **Test** button to verify that the selected port is not in use and click on **Finish** to generate the WebBroker server project.

# Organizing your WebBroker projects

Let's make sure to have a good folder structure to properly organize our two WebBroker projects, **Standalone** and **Apache**. Create a new folder for both projects. Inside this folder, create three sub-directories: `apache`, `standalone`, and `shared`. Click on **Save All**. Save the `ServerConst1` unit into `standalone` and `WebModuleUnit1` into the `shared` folder. Save the project as `ToDoWebBrokerStandaloneHTTP` and make sure it is saved in the `standalone` folder.

Run the web server project on Windows. You should see the console window prompting you to enter one of the options. Type in `start` to start the web server. If you see the message from Windows Firewall, click on the **Allow Access** button to let client apps communicate with the server. If you now open any web browser and enter `127.0.0.1:8080` in the address box, you should see the default web page of our server:

Default output from a blank WebBroker application

Type in `exit` in the web server console to stop the web server project.

It is not very convenient to have to enter `start` after the web server starts. Let's make a small modification in the main program file to start the server automatically. Select **View Source** from the **Project** menu. Scroll towards the end of the file. In the `RunServer` procedure, copy the line of code with the `StartServer(LServer)` call and paste it just before the `while True do` statement. In this way, we will not have to enter the `start` command manually. Save all. You can run the app again and verify the server app is started automatically. The same code is given here:

```
procedure RunServer(APort: Integer);
var
  LServer: TIdHTTPWebBrokerBridge;  LResponse: string;
begin
  WriteCommands;  LServer := TIdHTTPWebBrokerBridge.Create(nil);
  try
    LServer.DefaultPort := APort;
    StartServer(LServer); // copied from the "while" loop below
    while True do
    begin
      Readln(LResponse);
```

```
      LResponse := LowerCase(LResponse);
      if LResponse.StartsWith(cCommandSetPort) then
        SetPort(LServer, LResponse)
      else if sametext(LResponse, cCommandStart) then
        StartServer(LServer) // here
      else if sametext(LResponse, cCommandStatus) then
        WriteStatus(LServer)
      else if sametext(LResponse, cCommandStop) then
        StopServer(LServer)
      else if sametext(LResponse, cCommandHelp) then
        WriteCommands
      elseif sametext(LResponse, cCommandExit) then
        if LServer.Active then
        begin
          StopServer(LServer);
          break
        end
        else
          break
      else
      begin
        Writeln(sInvalidCommand);
        Write(cArrow);
      end;
    end;
  finally
    LServer.Free;
  end;
end;
begin
  try
    if WebRequestHandler <> nil then
      WebRequestHandler.WebModuleClass := WebModuleClass;
      RunServer(8080);
  except
    on E: Exception do
      Writeln(E.ClassName, ': ', E.Message);
  end
end.
```

The block of code in the main program file of the web server console app is very simple. The whole functionality of our web server app is encapsulated inside `WebModuleClass`, which is implemented in `WebModuleUnit1`. The Indy standalone web server will instantiate a web module using the class reference provided and will route to it the incoming URL for processing. The web module is a specialized form of data module. You can put there different non-visual components to implement server logic. A web module class has an **Actions** collection property. These actions corresponds to different URL paths within the web server application:

"Default Handler" web action item properties in the Object Inspector

The wizard has generated for us a default action that is called in the response to any HTTP request arriving to the server. In the `OnAction` event of the web action item, we can enter code that will be executed when the HTTP request arrives. This event has `request` and `response` parameters. We can programmatically inspect values in the `request` object and put data into the `response` parameter to be returned to the HTTP client. This could be anything. In this case, the content that is sent back is HTML, but this could also be JSON, XML, or even binary data. We can modify the default handler to return information that it is our `To-Do REST API` service.

Here is what the modified code looks like. It is just returning a bit of static HTML markup:

```
procedure TWebModule1.WebModule1DefaultHandlerAction(Sender: TObject;
  Request: TWebRequest; Response: TWebResponse; var Handled: Boolean);
begin
  Response.Content :=
    '<html>' +
    '<head><title>To-Do REST API</title></head>' +
    '<body>Delphi "To-Do List" REST API</body>' +
    '</html>';
end;
```

Before starting to implement our web service, let's add the second Apache project. Right-click on the project group node in the **Project Manager** and select **Add New Project** option. Double-click on the **New Web Server Application** icon in the **New Items** dialog. On the first page of the wizard, select the option to add **Linux** support. On the second page make sure to select **Apache dynamic link module** as the project type:

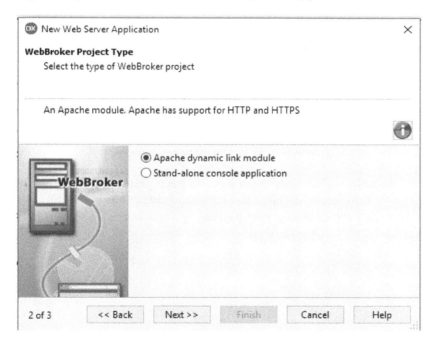

"Apache dynamic link module" option selected in the "New Web Broker Application" wizard

On the last page of the wizard, you can specify the Apache version you want to support:

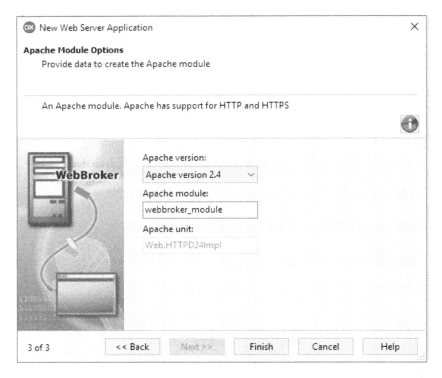

Apache version selection in the "New Web Server Application" wizard

Click on the **Finish** button. The Apache project has been generated. Now we need to carefully save it. Click on **Save All**. Save the web module unit as `WebModuleUnit2` in the `apache` folder and the project as `ToDoWebBrokerApache` in the `apache` folder as well. Save the project group as `ToDoWebBrokerGrp`.

Now we want both projects to use the same web module. Click on the `WebModuleUnit1` in the **Project Manager** and drag and drop it onto the `Apache` project node:

Confirmation dialog to add a new unit to the web project

Confirm that you would like to add this web module to the `apache` project. Now right-click on the `WebModuleUnit2` in the **Project Manager** and select **Remove from project** option. Now both projects are using the same web module code. Right-click on the **Project Group** node and select **Build All**. At any time, we can build our web server as a standalone app for testing and as the Apache module for deployment:

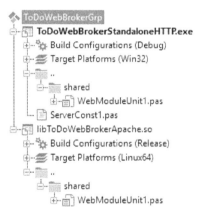

Both WebBroker projects in the Project Manager

Let's add the client app project to the group. Create a new `restclient` folder in the previously created folder that already contains three other folders for both server projects. Copy all files from the `ToDoListS3` to the newly created folder. Right-click on the project group node in the **Program Manager** and select the **Add Existing Project** option. Add the `ToDoListS3` project to the group. Save the project as `ToDoListRESTClient`. Save the main form unit as `uFormToDoRESTClient` and change the **Name** property of the form to `FormToDoRESTClient`. Add the `uToDoTypes`, `uToDoUtils`, and `uDMToDoS3` units to both server projects. The IDE will show the message that adding the data module to the WebBroker server projects is going to add the FireMonkey framework to them. Click on **OK**:

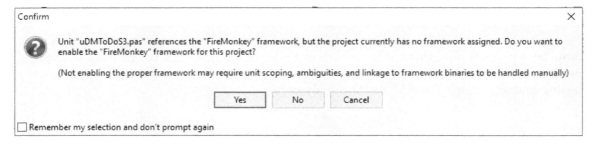

Confirmation dialog to add the FireMonkey framework to the project

Now right-click on the project and select `Build All`. All three projects should compile successfully.

There are different approaches for architecting REST APIs. In our case, we want to expose the CRUDL operations on the underlying To-Do data. Unlike SOAP, RESTful web services are just an architectural style and not a protocol, so you will see different ways of implementing REST APIs.

In our example, let's add to the **Action** collection of the web module five more web action items that will correspond to the underlying operations on the To-Do data. Rename them to `ActToDoCreate`, `ActToDoRead`, `ActToDoUpdate`, `ActToDoDelete`, and `ActToDoList`:

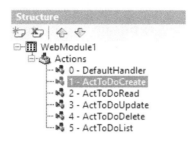

Web Module action items in the "Structure View"

In their **PathInfo** property, enter respectively, the **/ToDo/Create**, **/ToDo/Read**, **/ToDo/Update**, **/ToDo/Delete**, and **/ToDo/List** values:

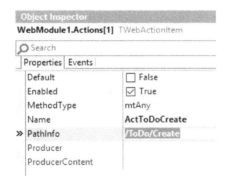

"PathInfo" property for the "ActToDoCreate" web action item

The first step to implementing their `OnAction` handlers is providing access to the underlying `IToDoData` interface exposed by the `DMToDoS3` data module. Add the `uToDoTypes` unit to the `uses` clause in the `interface` section of the data module, and `uDMToDoS3` and `uToDoUtils` in the implementation `uses` clause.

Declare the `FToDoData: IToDoData;` private field in the web module class declaration and the private function `GetToDoData` that will return the reference to the interface needed in the implementation of all web action items event handlers:

```
function TWebModule1.GetToDoData: IToDoData;
begin
  if FToDoData = nil then
    FToDoData := TDMToDoS3.Create(nil);
  Result := FToDoData;
end;
```

Double-click on the `OnAction` event of the `ActToDoCreate` web action item and enter the following code to add a new To-Do item in the underlying Amazon S3 storage:

```
procedure TWebModule1.WebModule1ActToDoCreateAction(Sender: TObject;
    Request: TWebRequest; Response: TWebResponse; var Handled: Boolean);
var aToDo: TToDo; id: integer;
begin
  aTodo.Title := Request.QueryFields.Values['title'];
  aToDo.Category := Request.QueryFields.Values['category'];
  id := GetToDoData.ToDoCreate(aToDo);
  Response.Content := id.ToString;
end;
```

Save all. Make sure that the standalone test web server project is active in the **Project Manager** and run it. Now go to the **Tools** menu and run the **REST Debugger** utility. In the **Request** tab, enter `http://127.0.0.1:8080/ToDo/Create` as the **URL** and in the **Parameter** tab add the **Title** and **Category** parameters with some test values. Click on the **Send Request** button.

Click on the **Body** tab in the **Response** section and you should see there the **ID** of the newly added To-Do item:

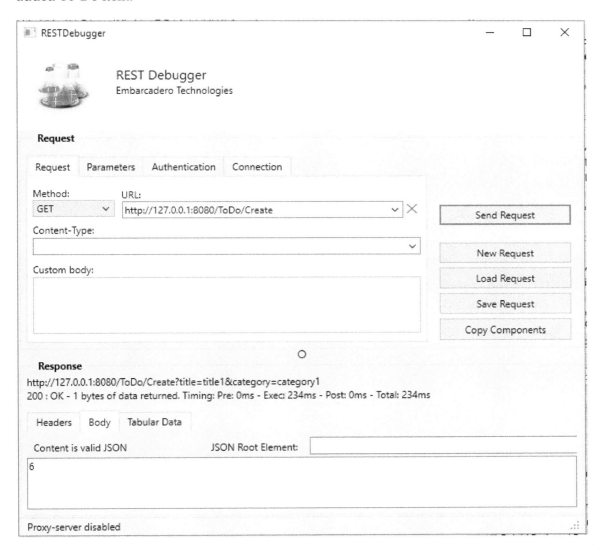

Testing "ToDo/Create" resource in the REST Debugger tool

The `ToDoRESTClient` project is still the original project from the previous chapter, so you can run it to verify that the new To-Do item has been successfully added:

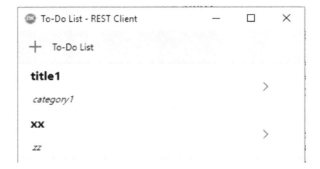

"To-Do List" REST client app after adding a dummy item

Now we can similarly implement the remaining web action items. In the `ActToDoRead` action, we are going to extract the `id` parameter from the request, invoke the underlying method of the data module, and return the To-Do item encoded as JSON.

Add the following procedure to the `uToDoUtils` unit that will allow you to convert a single `TToDo` record to its JSON representation:

```
function ToDoToStr(aToDo: TToDo): string;
var
  sw: TStringWriter;
  jtw: TJsonTextWriter;
begin
  sw := TStringWriter.Create;
  jtw := TJsonTextWriter.Create(sw);
  try
    jtw.WriteStartObject;
    WriteItem(aToDo, jtw);
    jtw.WriteEndObject;
    Result := sw.ToString;
  finally
    jtw.Free;
    sw.Free;
  end;
end;
```

Additionally, we are setting the response `ContentType` property to `application/json`:

```
procedure TWebModule1.WebModule1ActToDoReadAction(Sender: TObject;
  Request: TWebRequest; Response: TWebResponse; var Handled: Boolean);
var aToDo: TToDo; id: integer;
begin
  id := Request.QueryFields.Values['id'].ToInteger;
  if GetToDoData.ToDoRead(id, aToDo) then
    Response.Content := ToDoToStr(aToDo)
  else
    Response.Content := 'Failed';
  Response.ContentType := 'application/json';
end;
```

The implementation of the `update` web action is similar. We are extracting parameter values and passing them to the underlying method of the data module:

```
procedure TWebModule1.WebModule1ActToDoUpdateAction(Sender: TObject;
  Request: TWebRequest; Response: TWebResponse; var Handled: Boolean);
var aToDo: TToDo;
begin
  aToDo.Id := Request.QueryFields.Values['id'].ToInteger;
  aTodo.Title := Request.QueryFields.Values['title'];
  aToDo.Category := Request.QueryFields.Values['category'];
  if GetToDoData.ToDoUpdate(aToDo) then
    Response.Content := 'OK'
  else
    Response.Content := 'Failed';
end;
```

The **Delete** web action implementation is even simpler. Just extract the `id` value of the To-Do record to be deleted and call the `ToDoDelete` method:

```
procedure TWebModule1.WebModule1ActToDoDeleteAction(Sender: TObject;
  Request: TWebRequest; Response: TWebResponse; var Handled: Boolean);
var aToDo: TToDo; id: integer;
begin
  id := Request.QueryFields.Values['id'].ToInteger;
  if GetToDoData.ToDoDelete(id) then
    Response.Content := 'OK'
  else
    Response.Content := 'Failed';
end;
```

The last operation returns the list of all To-Do items. It does not expect any parameters. We are going to use the utility function, `ToDosToStr`, from the `uToDoUtils` unit to convert the generic list of To-Do items returned from the data module to JSON:

```
procedure TWebModule1.WebModule1ActToDoListAction(Sender: TObject;
  Request: TWebRequest; Response: TWebResponse; var Handled: Boolean);
var aList: TToDos; json: string;
begin
  aList := TToDos.Create;
  try
    GetToDoData.ToDoList(aList);
    Response.Content := ToDosToStr(aList);
    Response.ContentType := 'application/json';
  finally
    aList.Free;
  end;
end;
```

Our simple REST APIs based on WebBroker technology are ready. Right-click on the project group in the **Project Manager** and select **Build All** to build test and deployment versions of our web server app.

Now we need to convert our REST client project that is already in the project group to invoke the REST APIs that we have just built, instead of communicating directly with the Amazon Simple Storage Service. Run the *standalone* version of the web server project and double-click on the `ToDoListRESTClient` project in the **Project Manager** to make it active. Remove the uDMToDoS3 data module from the project and add a new data module. Change the **Name** property of the data module to DMToDoWebBrokREST and save its unit as uDMToDoWebBrokREST. Add uToDoTypes to the `uses` clause in the interface section of the data module and uToDoUtils in its implementation part. Add the IToDoData interface to the class declaration of the data module, copy the signatures of routines from the interface declaration to the public section of the data module class declaration, and press *Ctrl* + *Shift* + *C* to invoke the class completion:

```
type
  TDMToDoWebBrokREST = class(TDataModule, IToDoData)
  private
    { Private declarations }
  public
  // IToDoData
  function ToDoCreate(aValue: TToDo): integer;
  function ToDoRead(id: integer; out aValue: TToDo): boolean;
  function ToDoUpdate(aValue: TToDo): boolean;
  function ToDoDelete(id: integer): boolean;
  procedure ToDoList(aList: TToDos);
  end;
```

In the main form class of the client application, change the name of the unit in the `uses` clause in the `implementation` section to use the new data module and modify the implementation of the `GetToDoData` method accordingly:

```
uses uDMToDoWebBrokREST;

function TFormToDoRESTClient.GetToDoData: IToDoData;
begin
  if DMToDoWebBrokREST = nil then
    DMToDoWebBrokREST := TDMToDoWebBrokREST.Create(Application);
    Result := DMToDoWebBrokREST;
end;
```

That's the beauty of clear separation of application tiers. We have just plugged in a different implementation of the data access logic to the user interface.

Switch to the `uDMToDoWebBrokREST` data module and drop onto it `TRESTClient`, `TRESTResponse`, and five `TRESTRequest` components. Rename them to, respectively, `rclientToDo`, `rrespToDo`, `rreqToDoCreate`, `rreqToDoRead`, `rreqToDoUpdate`, `rreqToDoDelete`, and `rreqToDoList`:

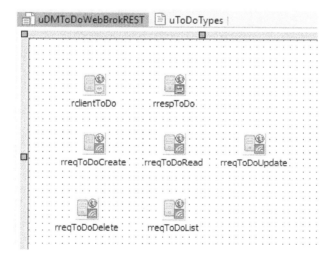

"REST Client" components on the data module

Enter `127.0.0.1:8080` into the **BaseURL** property of the REST client component. This is for testing. In the final version of the client app, this value should be updated to the actual IP address of the server where our REST API web server app is running.

In the **Resource** property of the `rreqToDoList` component, enter `ToDo/List`. Make sure that the test web server app is running. Right-click on the **List** request component and select **Execute** from the context menu. You should see the dialog form displayed with the message **Response: 200 - OK**. If you now click on the `rrespToDo` component, you should find the JSON data with the list of all To-Do items.

We need to set up properties of the remaining REST request components. In `rreqToDoCreate` enter `ToDo/Create` as the **Resource** property. Add two parameters to the **Params** property and set their **Name** properties to **title** and **category**. In the `rreqToDoDelete` component, enter `ToDo/Delete` as the resource and add one parameter named `id`. In the `rreqToDoUpdate` component, change the **Resource** property to **ToDo/Update** and add three parameters: `id`, `title`, and `category`. In the `rreqToDoDelete` request component, change **Resource** to `ToDo/Delete` and add one parameter. Change its **Name** property to **id**:

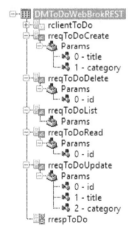

"DMToDoWebBrokREST" data module in the "Structure View"

The last element is to implement the data module methods. The `ToDoCreate` method is quite simple. We just need to assign parameter values in the `rreqToDoCreate` component, call its `Execute` method, and return the result from the `Content` property of the REST response component:

```
function TDMToDoWebBrokREST.ToDoCreate(aValue: TToDo): integer;
begin
  rreqToDoCreate.Params[0].Value := aValue.Title;
  rreqToDoCreate.Params[1].Value := aValue.Category;
  rreqToDoCreate.Execute;
  Result := rrespToDo.Content.ToInteger;
end;
```

The implementation of the `ToDoRead` method will require converting a JSON string to a `TToDo` record. To keep the code clean, let's add a new `StrToToDo` function to the `uToDoUtils` unit:

```
function StrToToDo(s: string): TToDo;
var jtr: TJsonTextReader; sr: TStringReader;
begin
  sr := TStringReader.Create(s);
  try
    jtr := TJsonTextReader.Create(sr);
    try
      while jtr.Read do
        if jtr.TokenType = TJsonToken.StartObject then
        begin
          Result.Id := StrToInt(ReadStr(jtr));
          Result.Title := ReadStr(jtr);
          Result.Category := ReadStr(jtr);
        end;
    finally
      jtr.Free;
    end;
  finally
    sr.Free;
  end;
end;
```

Now the implementation of the `ToDoRead` method becomes very simple:

```
function TDMToDoWebBrokREST.ToDoRead(id: integer;
  out aValue: TToDo): boolean;
begin
  rreqToDoRead.Params[0].Value := id.ToString;
  rreqToDoRead.Execute;
  Result := rrespToDo.Content <> 'Failed';
```

```
  if Result then
    aValue := StrToToDo(rrespToDo.Content);
end;
```

The `ToDoUpdate` method is also simple:

```
function TDMToDoWebBrokREST.ToDoUpdate(aValue: TToDo): boolean;
begin
  rreqToDoUpdate.Params[0].Value := aValue.Id.ToString;
  rreqToDoUpdate.Params[1].Value := aValue.Title;
  rreqToDoUpdate.Params[2].Value := aValue.Category;
  rreqToDoUpdate.Execute;
  Result := rrespToDo.Content = 'OK';
end;
```

Calling the API to delete a To-Do item is even simpler:

```
function TDMToDoWebBrokREST.ToDoDelete(id: integer): boolean;
begin
  rreqToDoDelete.Params[0].Value := id.ToString;
  rreqToDoDelete.Execute;
  Result := rrespToDo.Content = 'OK';
end;
```

The last method to implement is `ToDoList`. Here we are using the `StrToToDos` utility method to convert a JSON representation of the list and populate the list passed in the `aList` parameter with the received items:

```
procedure TDMToDoWebBrokREST.ToDoList(aList: TToDos);
begin
  aList.Clear;
  rreqToDoList.Execute;
  StrToToDos(rrespToDo.Content, aList);
end;
```

That's it. Save all and run the REST client application. It should just work!

The WebBroker framework is the underlying technology for other types of web server apps such as the SOAP web server application or different DataSnap server project types hosted in a web server. It is the simple form of HTTP server that you can build with Delphi.

# Do it yourself with DataSnap

WebBroker is good for really simple HTTP server functionality, but the more complex the system you want to build, the more you look into complete Delphi multi-tier frameworks such as DataSnap or RAD Server. They provide a lot more higher-level functionality than you can find in WebBroker.

The DataSnap framework has been part of Delphi since its early days and has been evolved over time. Delphi 3 introduced MIDAS technology to make it easy to build client/server database applications. In Delphi 6, this technology has been renamed to DataSnap and in Delphi 2009 it has been completely rewritten. In this new architecture, remote methods published by a DataSnap server look like database stored procedures that a typical SQL relational database system exposes. The dbExpress database access framework has been reused and a special DBX driver has been built to provide connectivity between DataSnap clients and servers. The DBX model is still there in the current DataSnap implementation, but a newer REST-based model has been added. In DBX you could have used TCP/IP or HTTP for communication between the client and the server. In DataSnap REST-based architecture, the only choice is to use HTTP or HTTPS.

When you open the **New Items** dialog in Delphi, there are three different wizards in the **DataSnap Server** category to create new server projects:

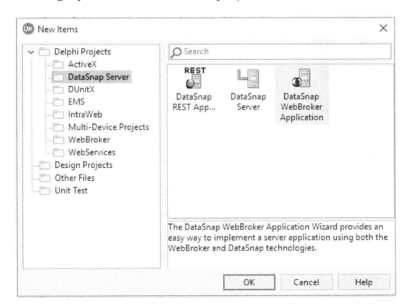

"DataSnap WebBroker Application" wizard in the Delphi "New Items" dialog

The **DataSnap REST Application** wizard generates the DataSnap web server project, including web pages and JavaScript files to invoke server methods. The **DataSnap Server** wizard supports creating old-style DBX-based DataSnap servers. The **DataSnap WebBroker Application** wizard generates the DataSnap server app hosted in a WebBroker web server.

In the context of building backends for mobile apps, the last choice seems to be the most useful. Let's give it a try and build a simple server and client projects to understand what the different building blocks of this framework are. Select the **DataSnap WebBroker Application** wizard and click on **OK**. On the first page of the wizard, check the option to add **Linux** support. On the third tab, we can choose which features will be added to a new project. Select all of them and click **Next**:

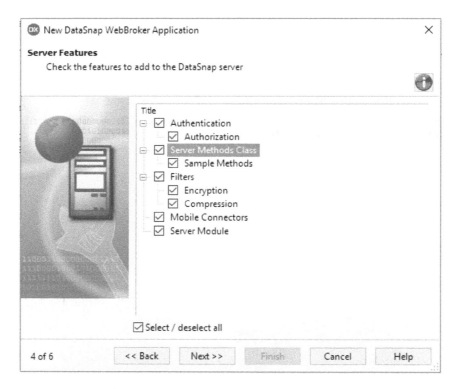

"Server Features" tab in the "New DataSnap WebBroker Application" wizard

In the next tab, we will have to choose the ancestor class for the server methods class. For simple projects, where we do not plan to use non-visual components in server implementation, we could have chosen TComponent. In most cases, it is best to choose TDataModule. The last choice can be ignored. The TDSServerMethods class is a specialized DBX specific data module with support for building old-style client/server database apps using the IAppServer interface from the MIDAS era:

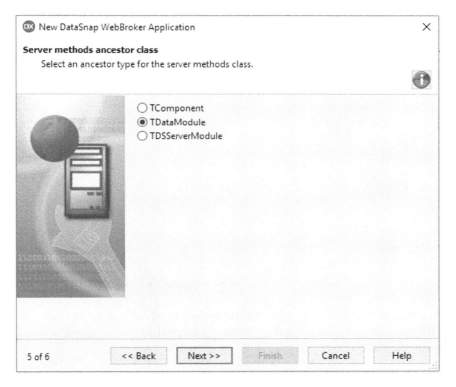

"Server methods ancestor class" selection in the "New DataSnap WebBroker Application" wizard

On the last tab, we need to specify the folder for the project files. The folder name needs to be a valid identifier for Delphi projects, because the last part of the path will be used by the wizard to generate the project name:

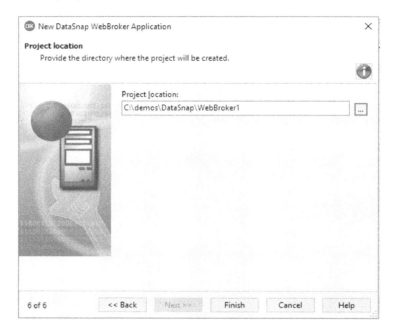

Choosing the location for the "New DataSnap WebBroker Application"

Because we have selected TDataModule as the server method's ancestor class, we are presented with the dialog to confirm that we want to enable the VCL framework. Click on the **OK** button:

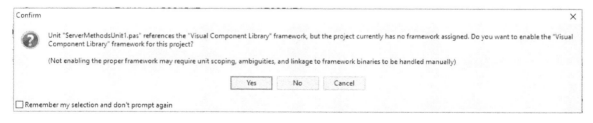

Adding "VCL" reference to the new DataSnap Web Broker Application

The wizard will generate for us the complete project. Click on **Save All** and accept default names for all new units.

The heart of the DataSnap server application is the DSServer1 component that you can find in the ServerContainerUnit1. It has the **AutoStart** property that is set to True, so at the moment that the application starts, it starts to wait for incoming requests from clients:

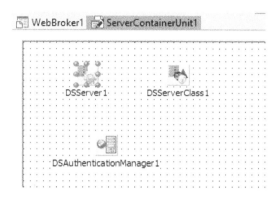

Key DataSnap components on the "ServerContainerUnit1" data module

The ServerMethodsUnit1 holds the actual APIs of the server. All public and published methods declared in this class are callable by clients. The DSServerClass1 component in the ServerContainerUnit1 connects the DSServer1 component with the server methods class. It has the **Server** property that points to DSServer1 and also the OnGetClass event that tells the DSServer1 components what the server class type is.

Notice that in the following code, we are assigning the *class* and not the *object reference*:

```
procedure TServerContainer3.DSServerClass1GetClass(
  DSServerClass: TDSServerClass; var PersistentClass: TPersistentClass);
begin
  PersistentClass := ServerMethodsUnit1.TServerMethods3;
end;
```

# Implementing DataSnap server functionality

In DataSnap architecture, a programmer does not write code to instantiate a server methods class inside the server app. The **LifeCycle** property of DSServerClass1 component controls the life cycle of the server class. By default, it is set to Session, which means that for every connected client there is one server methods class instance inside the server app. When the client connects, it is created and when the client disconnects, it is destroyed. If this property is set to Server then there is only one, single server class instance for all the connected clients. In this case, the server method implementation should be thread safe because its methods could be called from different threads. The most scalable **LifeCycle** option is **Invocation**. In this scenario, the server methods class is instantiated just for the duration of a server method call. It does not maintain a state across server method calls.

DataSnap servers are hosting agnostic. This means that DataSnap servers can be implemented as WebBroker web servers, console apps, VCL or FireMonkey forms applications, or as a Windows service.

Similarly to building clients for XML SOAP web services, there must be a client access unit generated that mimics the functionality available on the server. In the case of the SOAP web services, the starting point for generating client proxies is the WSDL document that typically is generated automatically from the running service. DataSnap client development is similar. The DataSnap proxy generator needs to have access to a running server. It queries the server and generates the DataSnap client class that exposes the same methods as are available on the server. There are client proxy generators for multiple programming languages, including Object Pascal, C++, PHP, JavaScript, C#, Java, and Objective C. On the client, you just need to instantiate this DataSnap client class passing the DataSnap connection component to the constructor.

The DataSnap framework uses RTTI to provide serialization functionality for many simple and complex Delphi data types. Consequently, we do not need to manually convert parameter and result types from their native Delphi representation to strings and JSON. This is done for us, but the choice of parameter types is important in DataSnap. If the proxy generator does not support certain parameter types, it just ignores a given server method and the proxy is not generated for it.

The server wizard has generated the `TServerMethods3` class in the `ServerMethodsUnit1`. It has just two sample server methods: `EchoString` and `ReverseString`. They take a string parameter and return a string. You can add other public methods to this class and they will automatically be available to clients. Note the `METHODINFO` compiler directive. It enforces generating full RTTI information about methods belonging to a server methods class, which is needed by the DataSnap framework:

```
type
{$METHODINFO ON}
  TServerMethods3 = class(TDataModule)
  private
      { Private declarations }
  public
      { Public declarations }
    function EchoString(Value: string): string;
    function ReverseString(Value: string): string;
  end;
{$METHODINFO OFF}
```

In general, there could be more server methods classes in the DataSnap server. Each class would require its own `TDSServerClass` component pointing to the `DSServer1` and returning in its `OnGetClass` event the type of a server methods class.

For now let's keep the server project *as is* and build a client application for it. The proxy generator will require access to the running server. Save all and click on the `Run` button to start the DataSnap server. Enter `start` in the console window and keep the server running. You can optionally enter the server URL in the web browser to verify that it listens on port `8080` specified in the wizard:

Default WebBroker DataSnap Application running

Right-click on the project group node in the **Project Manager** and select **Add New Project** from the context menu. Create a new Delphi multi-device and a blank application. Save the main form unit as `uFormDSClient` and the project as `DataSnapClient`. Change the **Name** property of the main form to `FormDSClient`. Now we will use a wizard to generate the DataSnap client code. In the **DataSnap Server** category in the **New Items** dialog, double-click on the **DataSnap REST Client Module** icon:

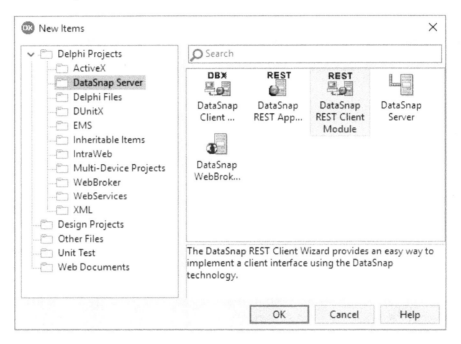

New "DataSnap REST Client Module" wizard in the "New Items" dialog

On the first screen of the wizard, select **Remote Server** as the server location. At the end, our mobile DataSnap client will be accessing a remote server:

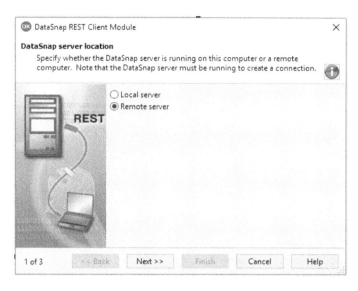

"DataSnap server location" tab in the new "DataSnap REST Client Module" wizard

On the second screen of the wizard, we can specify the DataSnap server project type. Right now we are building the client app against the standalone WebBroker server, but in production we will most likely be using the DataSnap server built as an Apache module and deployed to a Linux machine. It is OK to specify the **Do not know** option here:

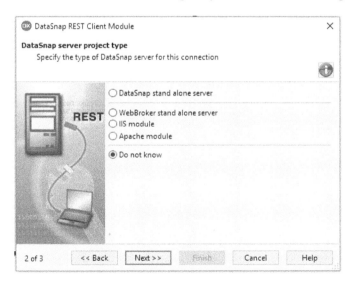

Choosing server project type in the new "DataSnap REST Client Module " wizard

On the last screen, we need to enter the URL of the server and test if the connection can be established. If the wizard cannot connect to the server, it will not be able to generate the DataSnap client code. Enter 127.0.0.1 as the hostname and 8080 as the port number. Click on the **Test Connection** button to verify that we can connect with the server and click on the **Finish** button:

Testing server connectivity in the "DataSnap REST Client Data Module" wizard

The wizard has generated two new units and added them to the client project:
`ClientClassesUnit1` and `ClientModuleUnit1`. Click on the `Save All` button to save
the new units:

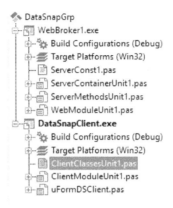

DataSnap server and client projects in the "Project Manager"

The `ClientClassesUnit1` is the actual DataSnap proxy code. You will find there the
`TServerMethods3Client` class generated. It has the same name as the server methods
class, but with the `Client` appended. It inherits from the `TDSAdminRestClient` class and
has the same method declarations as the server:

```
// Created by the DataSnap proxy generator.

unit ClientClassesUnit1;
interface
uses
  System.JSON, Datasnap.DSProxyRest, Datasnap.DSClientRest,
  Data.DBXCommon, Data.DBXClient, Data.DBXDataSnap, Data.DBXJSON,
  Datasnap.DSProxy, System.Classes, System.SysUtils, Data.DB,
  Data.SqlExpr, Data.DBXDBReaders, Data.DBXCDSReaders,
  Data.DBXJSONReflect;
type
  TServerMethods3Client = class(TDSAdminRestClient)
  private
    FEchoStringCommand: TDSRestCommand;
    FReverseStringCommand: TDSRestCommand;
  public
    constructor Create(ARestConnection: TDSRestConnection); overload;
    constructor Create(ARestConnection: TDSRestConnection;
      AInstanceOwner: Boolean); overload;
    destructor Destroy; override;
    function EchoString(Value: string; const ARequestFilter:
```

```
        string = ''): string;
    function ReverseString(Value: string; const ARequestFilter:
        string = ''): string;
end;
```

The second `ClientModuleUnit1` is a data module with the `DSRESTConnection1` component already added. In its `Host` and `Port` properties, there are values entered on the last page of the wizard. Right-click on the connection component and select `Test Connection` from its context menu to verify that the server is still running. See the following screenshot:

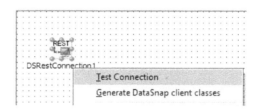

"Test Connection" context menu option for the "TDSRESTConnection" component

The second option, **Generate DataSnap client classes**, is very useful when we want to regenerate client classes with the proxy generator. That needs to be done every time we are adding or changing server methods declarations.

The wizard has added the private `FServerMethods3Client` field in the client module class and added the `GetServerMethods3Client` public method that is creating the `TServerMethods3Client` instance passing to its constructor the REST connection component and returning a ready-to-use class.

In the client app code, if we want to invoke any method of the remote DataSnap server, we can just call the corresponding method on the `TServerMethods3Client` class returned from `GetServerMethods3Client`, and our call will be forwarded to a remote server for execution and the result received from the server will be returned. If a remote method throws an exception, then it is intercepted on the server and re-raised on the client side.

Go to the main form of the client app and add `ClientModuleUnit1` to its `uses` clause in the `implementation` part of the unit. Drop `TButton` and `TEdit` on the form. Change the **Name** property of the button to `btnReverse` and its **Text** to **Reverse**. Rename the edit to `edtTest` and in its **Text** property enter any string, for example **Delphi**. Double-click on the button and enter just one line of code that will take the text from the edit, send it to the DataSnap `ReverseString` method, and display in the edit the reversed version of the original string:

```
uses ClientModuleUnit1;

procedure TFormDSClient.btnReverseClick(Sender: TObject);
begin
  edtTest.Text :=
    ClientModule1.ServerMethods3Client.ReverseString(edtTest.Text);
end;
```

Save the client app and run it. If you click on the button, you should see the original text from the edit reversed, as shown in the following screenshot:

DataSnap client app running on Windows

DataSnap is a very powerful and rich framework. It is a very good choice for implementing systems with a relatively small number of concurrent clients. It also supports authentication and authorization, where access to certain server classes or methods can be restricted to a certain group of users. There is also support for communication filters, where you can provide custom modifications to the raw stream of bytes that are exchanged between clients and servers. Out of the box, there are compression and encryption filters available, but it is possible to implement a custom filter. Another interesting feature of DataSnap is the callback functionality. Servers can notify selected or all connected client applications by sending information to callback channels that something interesting happened on the server. There is also FireDAC JSON reflection framework that simplifies building client/server database applications. Data from multiple FireDAC datasets on the server can be combined into one object and sent to the client to be loaded into local `TFDMemTable` components for processing. All changes to the data made on the client can be sent in one operation to the server for updating the underlying database.

DataSnap is a feature of Enterprise and higher versions of Delphi.

# Easy REST API publishing with RAD Server

Probably the most feature-rich and powerful architecture for building mobile backends is RAD Server. Unlike other types of Delphi server applications, RAD Server is pre-built and out of the box offers functionality typical for other **Backend as a Service (BaaS)** products.

RAD Server is installed as part of Delphi Enterprise or Architect. In Delphi `bin` and `bin64` directories, you can find two different RAD Server binaries. `EMSDevServer.exe` is the development version of RAD Server that can be run standalone. The `EMSServer.dll` is an ISAPI library that is intended to be deployed to Microsoft IIS web server for production. RAD Server is licensed separately, but the Delphi license includes a 5-user development license that can be used for the development and testing RAD Server solutions.

RAD Server is designed as a scalable REST API publishing framework. Its functionality is extended through building Delphi `bpl` packages that are loaded into the RAD Server at its startup. It also requires access to the Embarcadero InterBase SQL database where it keeps its system database. During Delphi installation, make sure to install the development version of InterBase. It comes with a special license for using it as a system database for RAD Server.

# RAD Server setup

Make sure that InterBase is installed and running on your system. In the Windows **Start** menu, locate and run **InterBase Server Manager**. If the server is not started, run it. In the default installation, the InterBase instance name is `gds_db`. The name of the database instance will be needed during the RAD Server setup:

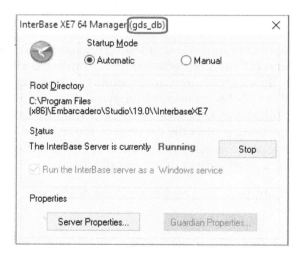

"InterBase instance name" in the caption of the InterBase Server Manager

Go to the Windows command line and enter the `EMSDevServer` command. The Delphi `bin` directory is on the path, so the RAD Server should start. In many places, you will see EMS. It stands for **Enterprise Mobility Services** and is the former name of RAD Server. The very first time when the `EMSDevServer` is run, or when it is run with the `-setup` parameter, you will see the installation wizard that will create the RAD Server system database, the configuration `ini` file. Optionally, the setup wizard may create a default user and a default group.

On the first page of the wizard, we need to enter the instance name of the InterBase server where the RAD Server database needs to be created. In the default installation, it is `gds_db`:

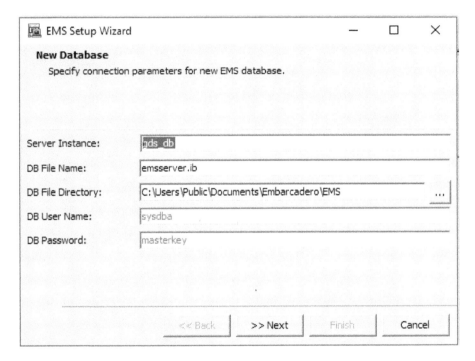

"New Database" tab in the RAD Server setup wizard

On the second screen, leave the default options to create sample users and groups:

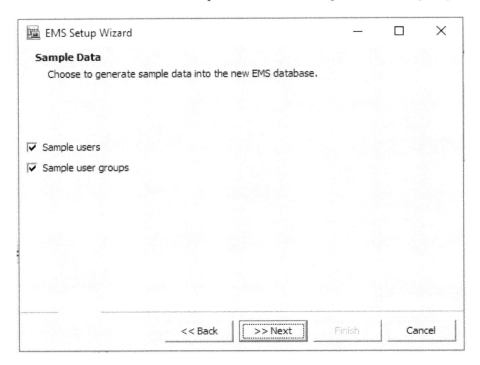

"Sample Data" tab in the RAD Server setup wizard

On the next page of the RAD Server setup wizard, we can specify the username and password for accessing the EMS Console. The EMS Console is a separate `EMSConsole.exe` executable file that is located in the `bin` and `bin64` directories. It is used to manage users, groups, and view REST API analytics:

Providing console user credentials in the RAD Server setup wizard

The last page of the wizard provides the setup summary. Click on **Finish** to run the RAD
Server setup:

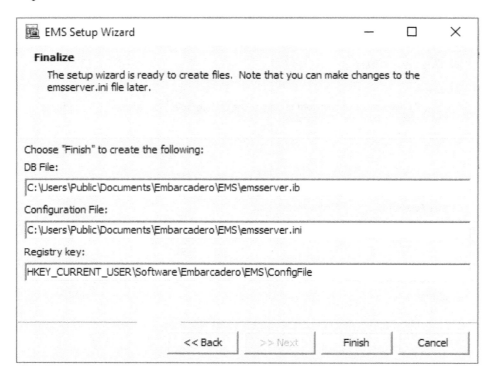

"Finalize" tab in the RAD Server setup wizard

In the default installation, you just have the development RAD Server license, so the
appropriate message is displayed. Click on **OK** to proceed:

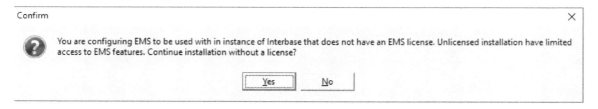

Confirmation dialog to use RAD Server with the "Development" license

After a moment, you should see the information about operations performed by the setup:

Summary message from the RAD Server setup

Click on **OK** and the EMS Development Server console should be displayed with the log window:

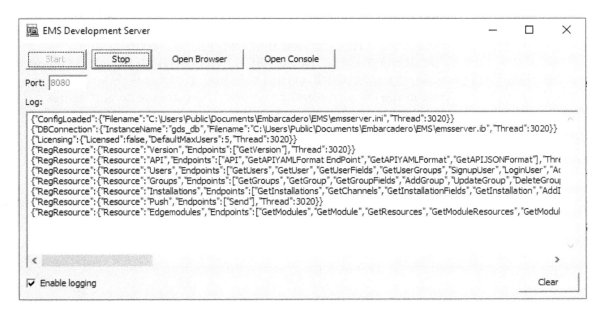

RAD Server "Development" window

In the first three lines of the log, we can see that the `emsserver.ini` configuration file has been loaded, the location and name of the RAD Server system database (`"emsserver.ib"`), and the licensing information. The following lines provide information about available resources, which can be accessed with the corresponding URLs and specific endpoints.

Click on the **Open Browser** button. The default web browser will be displayed pointing to the **Version** built-in RAD Server resource. In Delphi 10.2, the EMS version is 3.0:

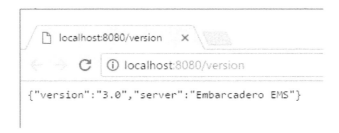

Built-in "version" RAD Server resource in a web browser

Notice that the request to the `version` resource has been logged in the console. You can try accessing other RAD Server built-in resources by replacing `version` with other resource names presented in the log window.

Click on the **Open Console** button. This will start the `EMSConsole` executable and automatically run the default web browser. By default, the EMS Server is using HTTP port `8080` and the EMS Console port `8081`. Click on the **Login** button and enter `consoleuser` and `consolepass` as the console username and password. These are the default values from the EMS setup:

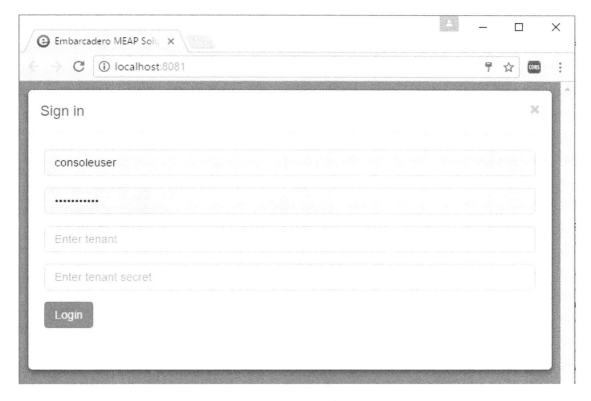

Logging into the RAD Server Console

There are two more fields for entering `tenant` name and `tenant secret`. These are used if RAD Server is running in the multi-tenancy mode. By default, it is not running in this mode, so we do not need to enter tenant information. The multi-tenancy mode is controlled by a setting in the EMS `.ini` file. In order to run the RAD Server in the multi-tenancy mode, you need to uncomment the `MultiTenantMode=1` line in the last section of the configuration file and restart the server.

After clicking on the **Login** button, you should see the EMS Console home page with links to different kinds of available information.

The RAD Server has been setup and we can start publishing our own APIs. Now you can safely close the EMS server and the EMS Console programs.

# Building resources

RAD Server architecture has been elegantly designed. You can add custom REST API resources through Delphi package library files that are loaded to RAD Server at startup. The location of packages to be loaded is stored in the `.ini` configuration file:

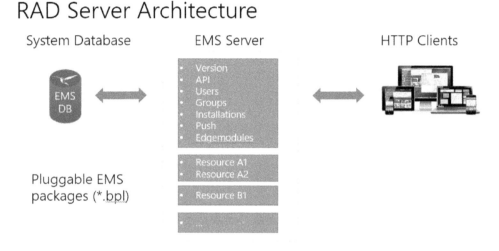

RAD Server architecture

Earlier in this chapter, we used WebBroker architecture to expose CRUDL operations on the underlying To-Do data stored in the Amazon Simple Storage Service as custom REST APIs. Here we are going to implement a similar solution, but this time we are going to expose the same functionality using RAD Server.

Let's start by creating a proper folder structure for our projects. Create a new folder for the RAD Server To-Do resource and client projects. Inside this folder, create three sub-folders: `resource`, `client`, and `shared`.

Select **File** | **New** | **Other...** from the Delphi main menu. Double-click on the **EMS Resource** icon in the **EMS** category:

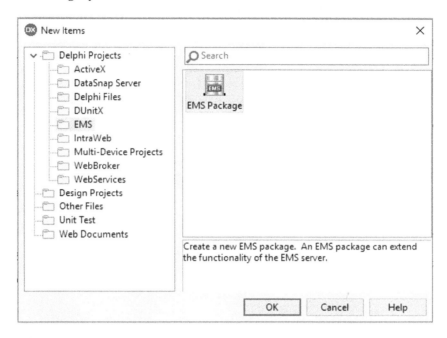

New "EMS Package" wizard in the "New Items" dialog

On the first page of the wizard, we have an option to create an empty package, or a package with a resource. Select the latter option. In general, in a single package there could be multiple resources. They can be added using the **EMS Module** wizard that is available in the **EMS** category when an EMS package project is opened in the IDE:

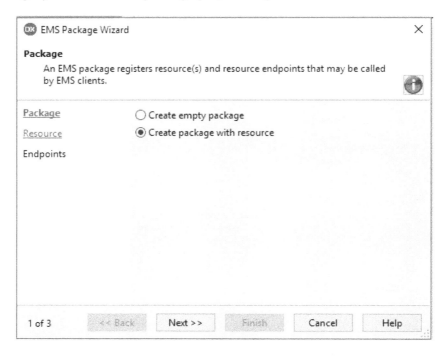

"Package" tab in the "EMS Package" wizard

On the second page of the wizard, we need to specify the resource name and the base class for the resource implementation. If we plan to add any components to a resource, then it is a good idea to choose **Data Module**, otherwise we can go for just plain `unit`:

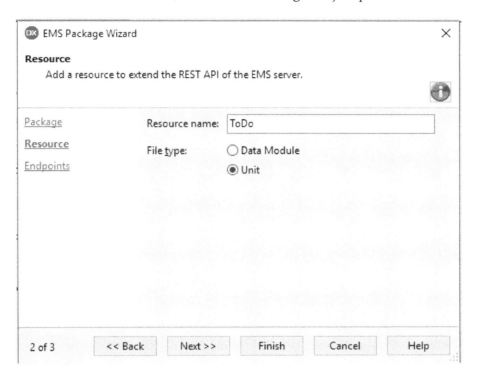

Choosing the resource name in the "EMS Package" wizard

On the last page of the wizard, we can specify which endpoints we want to add to the resource. These endpoints will translate to different HTTP request types and URLs. We want all of them, because there are five different CRUDL operations to expose on our ToDo resource:

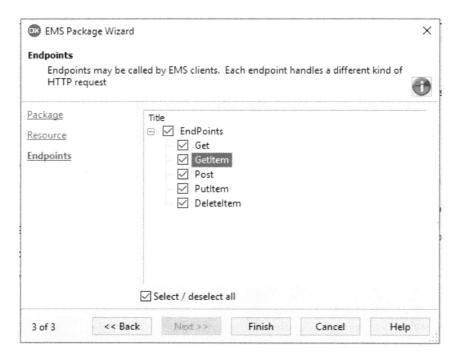

Endpoints selection in the "EMS Package" wizard

Click on the **Finish** button. The new package project has been generated for us. Click on the **Save All** button. Save the resource unit as uToDoRes and the project as ToDoPckg in the resource folder. Copy the uToDoTypes.pas and uToDoUtils.pas units from the WebBroker project to the shared directory and add them to the package project. Copy the uDMToDoS3.pas and uDMToDoS3.dfm files to the resource directory and the uDMToDoS3 unit to the resource project. Save all:

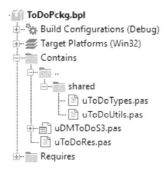

"ToDoPckg" EMS package" in the Project Manager

Open the uToDoRes unit in the code editor. You will find there a resource class declaration with five published methods that correspond to all the endpoints that we have selected in the wizard. The custom attribute decorating the class contains the actual resource name to be used in the URL pointing to this resource. Depending on the type and parameters of the HTTP request, a different method will be called for processing. This class is similar to the web module class from the WebBroker implementation.

Add the uToDoTypes unit to the uses clause in the interface section of this unit and the uToDoUtils and uDMToDoS3 units to the uses clause in the implementation part. Declare a private field, FToDoData: IToDoData, and a function, GetToDoData: IToDoData;. Press *Ctrl + Shift + C* to invoke the class completion. Implement the GetToDoData method in exactly same way as in the *web module* earlier:

```
unit uToDoRes;

// EMS Resource Module

interface

uses
  System.SysUtils, System.Classes, System.JSON,
  EMS.Services, EMS.ResourceAPI, EMS.ResourceTypes, uToDoTypes;
```

```
type
  [ResourceName('ToDo')]
  TToDoResource1 = class(TDataModule)

  private
    FToDoData: IToDoData;
    function GetToDoData: IToDoData;
  published
    procedure Get(const AContext: TEndpointContext;
      const ARequest: TEndpointRequest;
      const AResponse: TEndpointResponse);
    [ResourceSuffix('{item}')]
    procedure GetItem(const AContext: TEndpointContext;
      const ARequest: TEndpointRequest;
      const AResponse: TEndpointResponse);
    procedure Post(const AContext: TEndpointContext;
      const ARequest: TEndpointRequest;
      const AResponse: TEndpointResponse);
    [ResourceSuffix('{item}')]
    procedure PutItem(const AContext: TEndpointContext;
      const ARequest: TEndpointRequest;
      const AResponse: TEndpointResponse);
    [ResourceSuffix('{item}')]
    procedure DeleteItem(const AContext: TEndpointContext;
      const ARequest: TEndpointRequest;
      const AResponse: TEndpointResponse);
  end;

implementation

uses uDMToDoS3, uToDoUtils;

function TToDoResource1.GetToDoData: IToDoData;
begin
  if FToDoData = nil then
    FToDoData := TDMToDoS3.Create(nil);
  Result := FToDoData;
end;
// ...
```

Let's start from the implementation of the `Get` endpoint. It will be used to return the list of all To-Do items. The wizard has generated a sample code, which we need to modify.

EMS endpoint implementations are very similar to `OnExecute` events of web action items from the WebBroker framework. Here we also have HTTP `request` and `response` parameters. In RAD Server architecture, we need to put JSON into the `AResponse.Body` that will be returned from this endpoint. We have already got the code from retrieving the generic list of To-Do records from the cloud and converting it into a JSON string. Now we can use the `JSONWriter` property of the `body` object to put raw JSON into the response:

```
procedure TToDoResource.Get(const AContext: TEndpointContext; const
ARequest: TEndpointRequest; const AResponse: TEndpointResponse);
var aToDos: TToDos; s: string;
begin
  aToDos := TToDos.Create;
  try
    GetToDoData.ToDoList(aToDos);
    s := ToDosToStr(aToDos);
    AResponse.Body.JSONWriter.WriteRaw(s);
  finally
    aToDos.Free;
  end;
end;
```

Save all and click on the **Run** button. The EMS Server started and according to the log, it has loaded our package. How was this possible? The explanation is in the **Options** for the package project. If you click on **Debugger**, you will see that `EMSDevServer` is specified as the **Host** application that is called with a parameter that instructs RAD Server to load current EMS package projects:

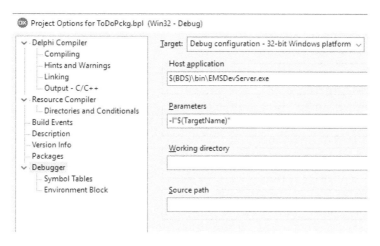

"Debugger" tab in the EMS package project options

In the **EMS Server Development Console**, click on the **Open in the Browser** button and replace the version with the todo resource. Refresh the page and you should see JSON with To-Do records:

"To-Do" records listed as JSON in a web browser

That's a good start. Now we can implement the remaining methods. The next one is GetItem that corresponds to Read functionality in our To-Do interface. This method is called if the HTTP request kind is GET and there is a parameter value after the slash:

```
procedure TToDoResource.GetItem(const AContext:
  TEndpointContext; const ARequest: TEndpointRequest;
  const AResponse: TEndpointResponse);
var aToDo: TToDo; id: integer; s: string;
begin
  id := ARequest.Params.Values['item'].ToInteger;
  if GetToDoData.ToDoRead(id, aToDo) then
    s := ToDoToStr(aToDo)
  else
    s := 'Failed';
  AResponse.Body.JSONWriter.WriteRaw(s);
end;
```

The next method to implement is Post and is invoked if the HTTP request kind is POST. This will be used for inserting new To-Do records. In the case of a POST request, we can pass parameters in its body. That will be just a JSON string with a new To-Do item to be inserted. We will need to implement one more utility function that will take the JSON string as a parameter and return a TToDo record. Add to the uToDoUtils unit the StrToToDo global function:

```
function StrToToDo(s: string): TToDo;
var jtr: TJsonTextReader; sr: TStringReader;
begin
  sr := TStringReader.Create(s);
  try
    jtr := TJsonTextReader.Create(sr);
```

```
try
  while jtr.Read do
    if jtr.TokenType = TJsonToken.StartObject then
  begin
    Result.Id := StrToInt(ReadStr(jtr));
    Result.Title := ReadStr(jtr);
    Result.Category := ReadStr(jtr);end;
  finally
    jtr.Free;
  end;
finally
  sr.Free;
end;
end;
```

Now we can implement the actual POST endpoint:

```
procedure TToDoResource.Post(const AContext: TEndpointContext;
  const ARequest: TEndpointRequest;
  const AResponse: TEndpointResponse);
var aStream: TStream; bstr: TBytesStream; s: string; aToDo: TToDo;
begin
  if not ARequest.Body.TryGetStream(aStream) then
    AResponse.RaiseBadRequest('no data');
  bstr := aStream as TBytesStream;
  s := TEncoding.UTF8.GetString(bstr.Bytes);
  aToDo := StrToToDo(s);
  GetToDoData.ToDoCreate(aToDo);
end;
```

Next on the list is the PUT method. We will use it for updating a To-Do record. The implementation is almost identical to the POST method. Only the last line of code is different. Instead of calling the ToDoCreate function, we are calling ToDoUpdate:

```
procedure TToDoResource.PutItem(const AContext: TEndpointContext;
  const ARequest: TEndpointRequest;
  const AResponse: TEndpointResponse);
var aStream: TStream; bstr: TBytesStream; s: string; aToDo: TToDo;
begin
  if not ARequest.Body.TryGetStream(aStream) then
    AResponse.RaiseBadRequest('no data');
  bstr := aStream as TBytesStream;
  s := TEncoding.UTF8.GetString(bstr.Bytes);
  aToDo := StrToToDo(s);
  GetToDoData.ToDoUpdate(aToDo);
end;
```

The last endpoint to implement is responsible for deleting the To-Do item. The identifier of the record to be deleted is passed to this method via the `item` parameter:

```
procedure TToDoResource.DeleteItem(const AContext: TEndpointContext;
  const ARequest: TEndpointRequest;
  const AResponse: TEndpointResponse);
var id: integer;
begin
  id := ARequest.Params.Values['item'].ToInteger;
  GetToDoData.ToDoDelete(id);
end;
```

Save all and click on **Run**. The RAD Server should start and load the ToDo REST API resource. Now we can move on to implementing the client app. We are going to reuse the main form unit and will only need to implement the data module that will be calling different ToDo endpoints.

Create a new, blank multi-device project and save it as `ToDoListEMS` in the `client` folder. Keep the default name of the main form. It does not matter because in a moment we are going to remove it from the project. Add to the project `uToDoTypes` and the `uToDoUtils` unit to the client project. Add a new data module to the client project. Save it as `uDMToDoEMS` and change its **Name** to `DMToDoEMS`. Add `uToDoTypes` to its `uses` clause in the `interface` section and copy the five `IToDoData` interface method declarations from the `uToDoTypes` unit to the public section of the data module, and press *Ctrl + Shift + C* to create empty implementations of all the methods. Also make sure to add `uToDoUtils` to the `uses` clause, but in the `implementation` part of the data module:

```
unit uDMToDoEMS;
interface
uses
  System.SysUtils, System.Classes, uToDoTypes;
type
  TDMToDoEMS = class(TDataModule, IToDoData)
  private
    { Private declarations }
  public
    // IToDoData
    function ToDoCreate(aValue: TToDo): integer;
    function ToDoRead(id: integer; out aValue: TToDo): boolean;
    function ToDoUpdate(aValue: TToDo): boolean;
    function ToDoDelete(id: integer): boolean;
    procedure ToDoList(aList: TToDos);
  end;
```

That's a start. Now copy the `uFormToDoRESTClient` unit and form files from the previous WebBroker project to the `client` folder. Add the form unit to the client project and save it as `uFormToDoEMS`. Also change the **Name** property of the form to `FormToDoEMS`. Remove the existing main form from the client project and save all. Now modify the `uses` clause of the main form unit and change the implementation of `GetToDoData` to use the `DMToDoEMS` data module:

```
uses uDMToDoEMS;

function TFormToDoEMS.GetToDoData: IToDoData;
begin
  if DMToDoEMS = nil then
    DMToDoEMS := TDMToDoEMS.Create(Application);
  Result := DMToDoEMS;
end;
```

That's the only modification that was needed to be made in the main form unit. The last task is to implement all five methods of the `IToDoData` interface in the `DMToDoEMS` module.

Drop on the "DMToDoEMS" data module the `TEMSProvider` component. It is responsible for connecting with the RAD Server. For testing, enter `127.0.0.1` in its `URLHost` property and `8080` in the `URLPort`. Right-click on the EMS provider component and click on the `Test Connection` item in the context menu. An information message should be displayed with the version of the RAD Server. That means the connection is **OK**:

RAD Server version information displayed from the "Test Connection" context menu option of the "TEMSProvider" component

Now drop five `TBackendEndpoint` components on the data module. Rename them to `beToDoCreate`, `beToDoRead`, `beToDoUpdate`, `beToDoDelete`, and `beToDoList`.

Drop `TRESTResponse` component on the data module and rename it `rrespToDo`. With the *Shift* key pressed, click on each backend endpoint component to select them all at once. Enter `ToDo` as the value of **Resource** property and connect the `rrespToDo` component to their **Response** property. In this way, we can change the properties of all five components in just one operation:

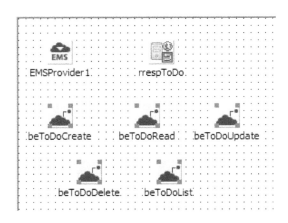

"BaaS" components on the data module

Already at design-time we can invoke backend methods. The first method to try will be GET that should return all To-Do records. Right-click on the `beToDoList` component and select **Execute** from its context menu. The message with response code **200 - OK** should be displayed. Click on the `rrespToDo` component and in the Object Inspector you should see that its **Content** property contains JSON text with the list of all To-Do items. In order to implement all methods of the interface, we need to optionally provide values for the expected parameters, call the `Execute` method of a given endpoint, and retrieve the result from the REST response component if a given method returns anything.

The implementation of all the `ToDoList` methods is straightforward. We will do the same thing, but in code:

```
procedure TDMToDoEMS.ToDoList(aList: TToDos);
begin
  aList.Clear;
  beToDoList.Execute;
  StrToToDos(rrespToDo.Content, aList);
end;
```

The second variation of the GET endpoint is the Read method that will return just a value of a given To-Do item. Enter item in the ResourceSuffix property of the beToDoRead component. In this way, we will be calling the right GET endpoint. We will also need to provide the identifier of a To-Do item to be retrieved. Click on the Params property of the beToDoRead backend endpoint component and add one parameter to the collection. Change its **Name** property to item. Now we can implement the ToDoRead method:

```
function TDMToDoEMS.ToDoRead(id: integer; out aValue: TToDo): boolean;
begin
  beToDoRead.Params[0].Value := id.ToString;
  beToDoRead.Execute;
  Result := rrespToDo.Content <> 'Failed';
  if Result then
    aValue := StrToToDo(rrespToDo.Content);
end;
```

Now let's move to the ToDoCreate method. It will correspond with the POST endpoint, so change the Method property of the beToDoCreate component to rmPOST. The code in this endpoint at the server is expecting to find JSON representation of the To-Do item to be added to the underlying storage in the request body. Enter the following code in the create method. Add the REST.Types units to the uses clause:

```
uses uToDoUtils, REST.Types;

function TDMToDoEMS.ToDoCreate(aValue: TToDo): integer;
var strstr: TStringStream;
begin
  Result := 0; // no response expected from POST request
  strstr := TStringStream.Create(ToDoToStr(aValue), TEncoding.UTF8);
  try
    beToDoCreate.Params.Clear;
    beToDoCreate.AddBody(strstr, TRESTContentType.ctAPPLICATION_JSON);
    beToDoCreate.Execute;
  finally
    strstr.Free;
  end;
end;
```

The next method to implement is ToDoUpdate. It will have a similar implementation to the Create method. Make sure to change the Method property of the beToDoUpdate component to rmPUT:

```
function TDMToDoEMS.ToDoUpdate(aValue: TToDo): boolean;
var strstr: TStringStream;
begin
  Result := True; // no response expected from PUT request
```

```
  strstr := TStringStream.Create(ToDoToStr(aValue), TEncoding.UTF8);
  try
    beToDoUpdate.Params.Clear;
    beToDoUpdate.AddBody(strstr, TRESTContentType.ctAPPLICATION_JSON);
    beToDoUpdate.Execute;
  finally
    strstr.Free;
  end;
end;
```

The last method to implement is the `ToDoDelete`. Change the `Method` property of the `beToDoDelete` component to `rmDELETE` and add a parameter to its `Params` property. Change its **Name** to `item` and enter the following code in the body of the `delete` method:

```
function TDMToDoEMS.ToDoDelete(id: integer): boolean;
begin
  beToDoDelete.Params[0].Value := id.ToString;
  beToDoDelete.Execute;
end;
```

That's it. Save all and run the client application. You should just run and display the To-Do data from the underlying Amazon Simple Storage Service received from a REST API resource hosted in the RAD Server mobile backend.

RAD Server is a very powerful product. It is the perfect backend for mobile apps written in Delphi. Publishing REST APIs is its core functionality, but it also has other features, including user and group management, API analytics, mobile push notifications, and support to build IoT solutions.

# Summary

In this chapter, we have looked at different options for building mobile backends with Delphi. There are many wizards to help you build all kinds of server apps from simple WebBroker HTTP servers, through SOAP XML Web Services, to DataSnap and RAD Server architectures providing a lot of reusable functionality to build great mobile backends for your cross-platform, mobile Delphi apps.

# 12
# App Deployment

Building and deploying your mobile app to an App Store is just the beginning. There is a lot more to successful app deployment. In this chapter, we are going to focus on all the nitty-gritty details of app deployment. We are going to discuss adding artwork, app monetization with ads, and in-app purchases. To be successful in mobile app development you need to constantly improve your app. For this you need to have good understanding of how users interact with your app. You also need to automate as many tasks as possible for reduced development and deployment times. That is why at the end of this chapter best practices for version control, testing, continuous integration, and deployment are discussed.

This chapter will cover the following points:

- Deploying to App Stores
- Monetizing with ads and in-app purchases
- Effectively using version control
- Unit testing
- Automating everything with continuous integration and deployment

The objective of this chapter is to teach how to successfully deploy mobile apps.

## Deploying to App Stores

You have built your app, tested it on multiple different devices, with different versions of supported mobile operating systems and now you feel that you are ready to make it available in an App Store.

Before submitting your app, you need to have artwork in place and a number of screenshots from different devices that you plan to support. Delphi developers are *full stack*, but typically they would ask a real graphic artistic to provide them with required app artwork including app icons and splash screens.

Let's go through the steps of publishing your app to different mobile App Stores. As an example, we are going to use the *Molecule Hero* demo app that I have written. It is built with Delphi and is available from different App Stores including the Apple iOS App Store and Android Google Play. The app is a 3D chemical molecule viewer that reads data from **Protein Data Bank** (**PDB**) file format and generates models made of spheres and cylinders that can be watched from different points of view using techniques described in `Chapter 5`, *FireMonkey in 3D*, of this book.

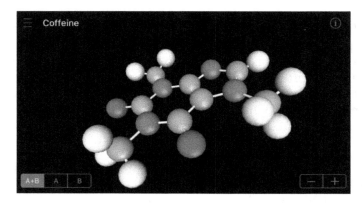

*Molecule Hero* Delphi app running on iOS

The app itself is called *Molecule Hero*. It is open source with an MIT License and is completely free to use and modify by anybody. You can download or fork it from `https://github.com/pglowack/MoleculeHero`.

# Publishing your apps to Apple iOS App Store

Before you can build your app for deployment to the App Store, you need to add to your project required artwork. This is a collection of images in PNG files for formats that are used as application icons, launch images, and spotlight search icons. When you create a new multidevice app in Delphi it is using default *FireMonkey* artwork that can be found in the standard Delphi installation in the `bin\artwork` directory. Delphi developers tend to have lots of these icons on their devices. Here is an icon for the *Molecule Hero* app:

*Molecule Hero* artwork

All the required graphic files can be configured in the **Application** tab in the **Project Options**. Select the **All Configurations - iOS Device - 64-bit platform** target to preview the default artwork. There are two tabs, one for iPhone and one for iPad. When you publish your app, you can specify if it is designed for iPhone, iPad, or both. You cannot use default the *FireMonkey* artwork for the App Store submission, but at least you can use it as a starting point for your own artwork. One trick to quickly start working on your own artwork is to copy the whole artwork folder from Delphi installation to the directory of your app project. If you just remove the $(BDS)\bin\ part from every path pointing to a given image, you will redirect it to your own copy. Now you can copy the whole project directory around and you will not need to adjust these paths. See the following screenshot:

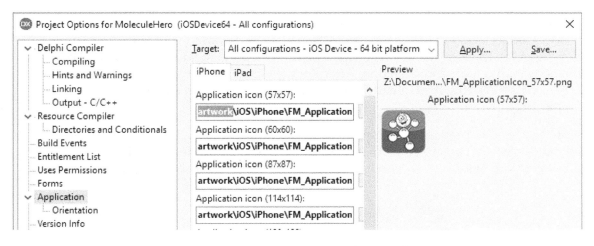

Application tab in Project Options where you can add custom artwork

In the **Orientation** tab of **Project Options** you can specify optional custom orientation. By default it is not enabled, and when you rotate a device your app form will adapt to the current orientation firing `OnFormResize` event. Sometimes, like in the case of certain games, you may want to disable resizing of the screen and specify that, for example, you only want your app to be displayed in landscape mode. Look at the following screenshot:

Orientation tab in Project Options

The first step to publishing your app at Apple iOS App Store is to create a developer account on the `https://developer.apple.com` website. Most likely you have one already created to be able to deploy Delphi apps to iOS phones and tablets for testing.

In order to submit an app to the iOS App Store you need to create an entry for your app on iTunes Connect. Go to `http://itunesconnect.apple.com` and log in with your Apple iOS developer ID. Click on the **My Apps** icon. Select the option to add a new app and complete the page with required information. After finishing the app entry configuration your app will have the **Waiting for Upload** status. You should also obtain an app ID for your application.

Now you need to prepare your app for deployment. Go to your **Project Options** of your app and select as **Target** at the top of the dialog **All Configurations - iOS Device - 64 bit**. iOS App Store requires your app to be compiled with an iOS 64-bit compiler.

Select the **Version Info** tab and make sure that **CFBundleIdentifier** matches the bundle ID that you have created on the *iTunes Connect* page. In the case of *Molecule Hero* that will be `com.superlolo.MoleculeHero`:

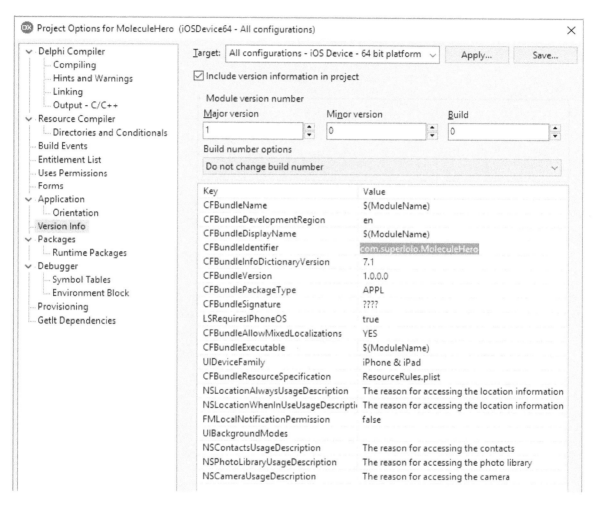

Setting the CFBundleIdentifier value in Project Options

The next step is to create an app archive file that you can submit to the App Store. In the **Project Manager** make sure to select the **Release** build configuration and under the **Configuration** in the iOS 64-bit target double-click on the **Application Store** node to make it active.

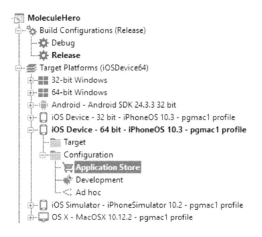

Application Store configuration selected in Project Manager

Make sure that the **Platform Assistant Server (PAServer)** is running on Mac. Right-click on the project node in **Project Manager** and select **Build** from the context menu. Now go to the **Deployment Manager** window and click on the **Deploy** button. Alternatively, you can deploy your app from the project menu. Follow the screenshot for the steps:

Deploy button in the Deployment Manager window

If everything has been configured correctly, you should be able to find the `.ipa` file in the `Release` folder of your project that is ready to be submitted to the App store.

To submit your iOS app you need to run the Application Loader application that comes with Xcode and select the **Deliver App** option. Select the app entry that you have created on iTunes Connect from the combo box, choose your app archive file `.ipa` and click `Send`. Now your app go to Apple for testing and eventually you will be notified by email if your app has been accepted to the App Store or rejected. It may take a couple of days or even weeks. At the end your app should be available from the App Store on any iOS device.

# Publishing your Android apps to Google Play Store

The first step to publishing your Delphi Android is to create a Google Play developer account on the `developer.android.com` website.

Make sure that you have all required artwork properly configured in your **Project Options**. Select the **Application** node and in the **Target** combo choose **All configurations - Android platform**. Configure your graphical assets, pointing each type of artwork to the right file.

Molecule Hero artwork for Android in Project Options

In the **Uses Permissions** tab, check if you have selected all the required rights that your app will need to have, for example, access to `Bluetooth` or `Location`.

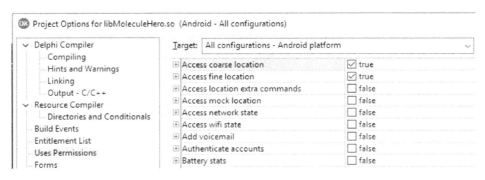

Uses Permissions tab in Project Manager

In the **Version Info** it is a good idea to increase the version number of your project. This is important if you submit a newer version of an existing app, because Google Play Store expects that a newer version of an app has a higher number than the previous one.

Version Info tab in Project Options

Finally, you need to configure a **KeyStore File** in the **Provisioning** tab. If you do not have one, you can create it by clicking on the **New Keystore...** button and follow the steps of the wizard. Make sure not to lose the `keystore` file. You will need it in the future to submit next versions of your app.

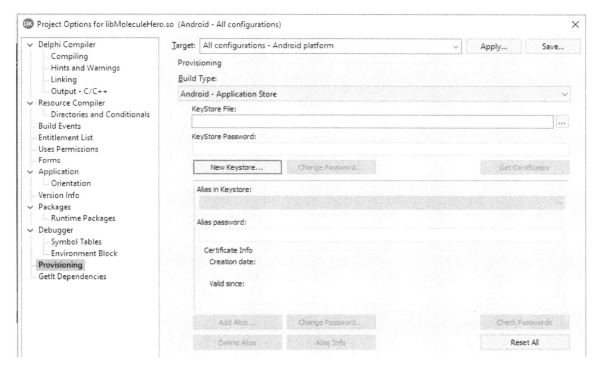

Provisioning tab in Project Options

The next step is to build a signed **Android Application Package (APK)** that can be uploaded to the store. These steps are similar to iOS. Go to **Project Manager** and select the **Release** build configuration and **Application Store** configuration in the Android target node:

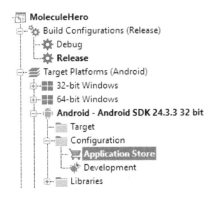

Application Store configuration for Android target in Project Manager

In the **Project Menu** click on **Build** and then on **Deploy** menu items. This should create a signed .apk file ready for submission to Google Play Store. To submit your app, log into the Google Play developer console and select **Add new application**. Select the default spoken language of your app and type in an app title to the edit box and select the option to **Upload APK**. In the APK menu option select the **PRODUCTION** tab and click on **Upload your first APK file to Production**. Then your .apk file will be uploaded to the developer console. After finishing uploading the information extracted from your .apk file will show up on the page. You will have to fill mandatory information on remaining tabs that are marked with asterisks and click **Save**. After all options are displayed with a green check mark, you can click on the **Publish this app** option. That's it. Your app is now published.

Unlike iOS App Store, you should see your Android ready for installation on any Android device in a matter of minutes or hours, and not days or weeks.

# Monetizing with adds and in-app purchases

There are different business models for mobile apps. Rather than expecting users to pay for an app, before they can use it, it is becoming more common to offer apps for free, but to provide a way to make in-app purchases. Delphi comes with a cross-platform **TInAppPurchase** component that is available on the **Services** tab in the **Tool Palette**.

TInAppPurchase component in the Tool Palette

With this component, you can sell virtual content within your app in a uniform way using the Google Play In-app Billing service on Android and the Apple iOS in-app purchase service on iOS. The source of this component can be found in the FMX.InAppPurchase unit. The details of using in-app purchases are different on both platforms and are very well documented on the Embarcadero docwiki.

Another possible business model is to embed advertisements in your apps. *FireMonkey* comes with the **TBannerAd** component that you can use to easily display ads in your app. You can find its source code in the FMX.Advertising unit. Have a glance at the icon:

TBannerAd component in the Tool Palette

Some mobile app users do not like ads popping-up, so you have to use them with care. A possible option is to have an in-app purchase to disable ads.

# Enhancing your apps

You have made it! Your app is in the App Store and you know that at least your friends are downloading and installing it on their device. But it is not the end of the life of your app. It is just the beginning. It has just made it through the first cycle from a faint idea in your mind, through development and testing to final deployment.

Some time will pass and you will start realizing that there are things in your app that could have been done better. There are some bugs to be fixed, ways to make it faster, and ideas of how to improve user experience and add new functionality.

One important saying fact that *better* is the enemy of *good*. Why change things that are working? But the change is inevitable. The only thing that never changes is the change itself. You might be a one person app development company or part of a bigger team. Regardless of the number of people you cooperate with on your projects, it is always a good idea to have a process in place to release new versions of your apps. It could be less or more formal, but certain phases are probably always there.

It is all about understanding and setting up your development workflow. There are many methodologies for how you should organize your development work. One of the earliest was the *waterfall* model where building an information system was going through different phases. It started from *requirements* where the idea of system functionality was born. In the *design* phase the desired software architecture was documented. In the next *implementation* phase the actual coding took place and it was followed by *verification* where testing was performed to validate that a system in place provided the expected functionality. In the last *maintenance* phase the system was already in production and occasional bug fixes were made. The *waterfall* approach is no longer used, because it lacked flexibility. It did not adapt to the real-world scenarios as requirements are constantly changing. A more pragmatic approach to software development started from the *Agile Manifesto* `http://agilemanifesto.org/`, where a group of software practitioners challenged the existing *status quo* and put together a list of postulates, how development of information systems should look like.

The ideas of *agile development* continues to be very popular and proved their usefulness. Software development is not a *waterfall*. It is a continuous cycle. Releasing a version of an app starts the new cycle. An app is being used. Its usage is being monitored and analyzed. Bug reports and change requests are being submitted. After some time in production a moment comes where existing feedback needs to be prioritized and the plan for the next version is created. It should include description of new and enhanced functionality, but also success criteria and ways of how to measure it. Then refactoring and development starts followed by unit testing that verifies the desired changes have been successfully implemented and then the new version of an app can be released, and the cycle starts again.

Because this process is repetitive, people are trying to automate as much of it as possible giving rise to *continuous integration* where completing a certain phase in a cycle automatically triggers next. For example, checking in a new version of source code file may trigger running an automated unit test. If a unit test, or a whole set of sets, reports no defects found, then it could automatically start compilation of an app and possibly send notifications to project manager that a new app version was successfully built.

Delphi IDE provides many features that help with establishing your own custom automated work flows, including version control engine, code editing, refactorings, integrated unit testing, and customizable build events.

# Practical version control

The key asset that you create is code, so you really, really want to keep it safe and make sure you do not waste your work and time.

You have been very intensively working on a new app throughout the whole week. By Friday your app is already in good shape and the basic functionality works. Over the weekend you have got some *clever* ideas, made some changes to the source code, and it is Monday morning in the office and nothing is working. You wish you could move back in time and put your app in a state when it was last working. This is what version control is all about. Every time you make a change to a source code file, or any other asset that belongs to your project, this change is saved and you can easily roll back changes and get back to the last working version of your app.

Delphi IDE comes with an integrated, lightweight version control system. At the bottom of the **Code Editor** there is a **History** tab. Every time there are changes in your code and you save your code, a new copy of your file is created in a hidden __**history** subfolder where your source file exists. In the **Editor Options**, in the global IDE **Options** dialog, you can control how many recent version of each file is kept. By default this value is 10, but you can increase it up to 90. Reducing this setting does not cause the existing history files to be deleted.

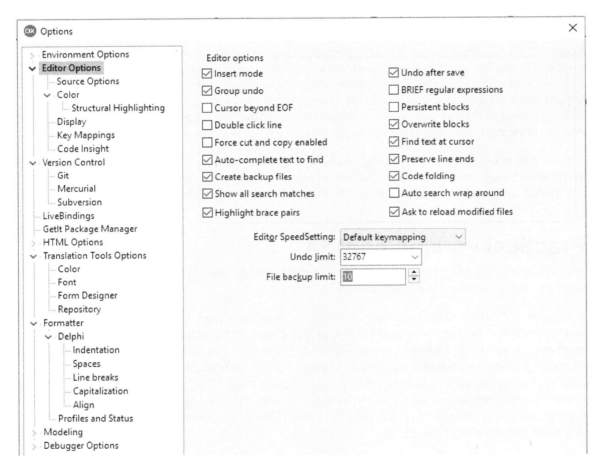

File backup limit option for controlling the number of files in the hidden __history folder

On top of built-in version control, it is also possible to configure Delphi to integrate with other popular version control software including Git, Subversion, and Mercurial. Each of these systems have different capabilities and philosophies. Probably the most widely used is Git (`https://git-scm.com/book`), because of its decentralized nature.

In order to illustrate some of the Delphi IDE *agile* functionality we are going to build a super simple *calculation engine*. It will have the potential to become a really complex scientific and financial calculator, but we are going to start from the very basics and the only capability that will be provided in the first release will be adding two numbers together. To make sure that our code works as expected we will cover it with automated unit tests.

Create a new Delphi multi-device, blank project. Save the form unit and project in the gui subfolders as respectively uFormCalc and CalcApp. Change the Name property of the form to uFormCalc. Add to the project a new unit and save it as uCalcEngine. Save all.

Let's declare a TCalcEngine class. When you type in the Code Editor the lines of code that have been changed since the last save are marked with a yellow color in the editor gutter:

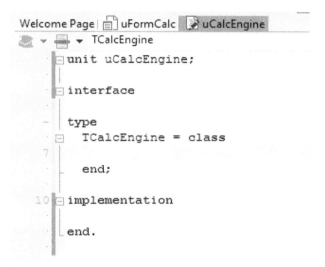

Click on **Save all**. Changed lines became green again. Declare the Add public method that will take two integer arguments and return an integer. Press *Ctrl + Shift + C* to invoke class completion and enter just one line of trivial code to implement this method. Shown in the following code block:

```
unit uCalcEngine;

interface

type
  TCalcEngine = class
  public
    function Add(a, b: integer): integer;
```

```
  end;
implementation
function TCalcEngine.Add(a, b: integer): integer;
begin
  Result := a - b;
end;
end.
```

Save all again. Click at the bottom of the Code Editor on the **History** tab. You can find here all existing past versions of a file that you are working on in the Code Editor. In the **Difference** tab we can compare added, deleted, and modified lines of code between any two revisions including the current version of the file marked as **File** and the content of the in-memory editor buffer marked with an eye icon:

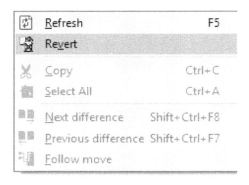

Revert context menu option in the History tab

If you right-click on any revision of a file in the **Content** tab of the **History** window and select **Revert** you can return to any previously saved version.

# Planning a release

A development cycle starts with planning. If it is the very first cycle, it also involves all conceptual and creative activities of sketching user interface and trying to figure out what the app should do. If it is one of the consecutive rounds in the life cycle of an app, it is this moment, when you need to decide what the next version of your app will look like.

The reasons why you would want to release a new version of an app could be many. Your users are reporting a bug, or you have got an idea of how to improve app functionality. Maybe the technology has changed and you can achieve certain things easier or in a way that was not possible only a few months earlier. You need to prioritize what is a *must have* and which features are just *nice to have*. When you have a clear vision about the next release, you should also try to establish success criteria and ways to measure them. Business goals also come to play here. Delphi does not have integrated requirement management functionality, but similarly to version control, most likely you would be using an external software package to manage your requirements.

# Development and refactorings

The next two phases in the life cycle of an app are very closely connected: writing code and checking if it works. Initially, it is more about writing new code, but in the next cycles the development effort goes primarily into refactoring. *Martin Fowler*, one of the pioneers of *agile movement*, defines refactoring as "the process of changing a software system in such a way that it does not alter the external behavior of the code yet improves its internal structure" (www.refactoring.com). That is the essence of enhancing your app. If there is a change in requirements you typically start from modifying the core of your app structure to be able to incorporate new functionality in a way that will be consistent with the rest of your app architecture. There will be more changes in the future to your system, so it is better to be prepared for them. The architecture of your app has to be flexible enough to adapt to future changes, but you should try not to make it too generic. Be pragmatic and defensive in changing your existing code base. Remember: *better* is the enemy of *good*.

Delphi IDE comes with a rich arsenal of refactoring tools. Probably the most commonly used is the *rename* refactoring tool. It is a very important one. Changes in your code start from a different perception of how certain parts of it should work and what they are responsible for. Naming is key to make sense of your existing code base and moving it forward to next iterations.

Drop two edits, one button and a label onto the main form of the **CalcApp** project. Add
uCalcEngine to its implementation clause. Enter **2** in the Text property of both edits.
Change the Text property of the button to + and enter into Text of the label component = ?
string. The main form of the **CalcApp** at this stage should look like this:

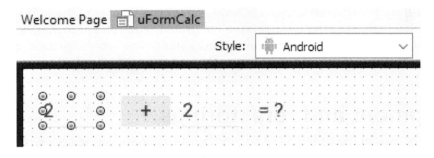

Main form of the CalcApp project in the Form Designer

Double-click on the button and enter the code to instantiate the engine and perform an Add
calculation:

```
uses uCalcEngine;

procedure TFormCalc.Button1Click(Sender: TObject);
var a, b, c: integer; ce: TCalcEngine;
begin
  ce := TCalcEngine.Create;
  try
    a := Edit1.Text.ToInteger;
    b := Edit2.Text.ToInteger;
    c := ce.Add(a, b);
    Label1.Text := '= ' + c.ToString;
  finally
    ce.Free;
  end;
end;
```

Save all. If you look into the Code Editor now, you will see that there is a problem with
naming. If we really plan to move this initial calculator engine into the future and add more
functionality to it, we need to make sure to use proper names for identifiers, or otherwise at
some point in time we are going to get lost.

There is many refactoring available in the IDE. Probably the most useful one is the *rename* refactoring. Just place the cursor in any identifier in the Code Editor, right-click and select *Rename* from the context menu. It is much more powerful than a simple *Find and Replace* option. It will change a given identifier in all files that are using it in the project including form files:

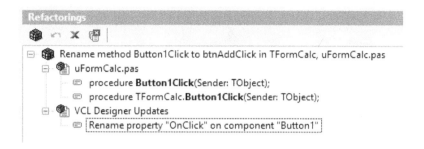

Refactorings IDE window

# Sleeping well with unit testing

Writing code is like solving a big puzzle. The more lines of code you have in your app, the more difficult it is to maintain and evolve. It takes a lot of experience to be able to properly structure your projects. When you add new features, they should not break the functionality of the whole app. Unit testing can help with making sure that every piece of code that you write works as expected. Some developers start writing their code from implementing unit tests that will prove that the code they will write later works.

Delphi IDE comes with two integrated unit test frameworks: DUnit and DUnitX. The first one is older and is not actively maintained. The second one, DUnitX, is newer and is leveraging modern language features such as custom attributes, which were not available in older Delphi editions.

Unit testing, refactoring, and version control are pillars of agile development. When you have just completely changed the internal architecture of your app, you want to make sure that it still works. Running a number of unit tests can help you have good sleep and not worry about changes that you made to your code just before the deadline.

The CalcApp project is still open in the IDE. Right-click on the project group in **Project Manager** and select **Add New Project** from the context menu. In the DUnitX category double-click on the **DUnitX Project** icon:

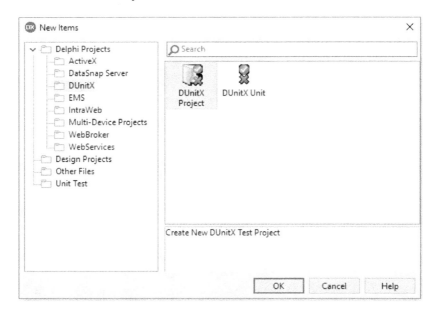

New DUnitX Project in Delphi New Items dialog

In the new unit test dialog, check all options and enter `TTestCalcEngine` as the name of the test class to be generated by the wizard:

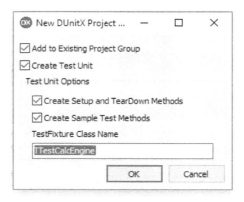

New DUnitX Project wizard options

Click **OK** and a new test project will be generated and added to the existing one. Click on the **Save All** button and save the new unit with test class as `uTestCalcEngine`, the DUnitX test project as `TestCalcEngine`, and the project group as CalcEngineGrp. Add the `uCalcEngine` unit to the new project:

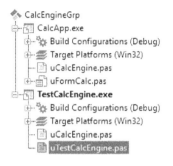

CalcApp app and unit test projects in Project Manager

The IDE wizard has generated a unit test project with a sample unit test class decorated with DUnitX custom attributes. That's an important difference as compared to the DUnit framework where test classes had to be inherited from a certain class. In DUnitX any class can be used for testing as long as it has a `TestFixture` attribute applied. DUnitX is heavily based on RTTI and with custom attributes you can mark methods to be called and what parameters need to be passed to them.

When we click on the **Run** button the unit test runner will be launched and will automatically execute all tests reporting their output. A DUnitX test fixture class can have methods marked with `Setup` and `Teardown` attributes. The `Setup` method is called before all tests are run and `Teardown` is called afterwards. These methods can be used to instantiate an object to be tested and free it.

The actual testing happens in methods marked with the `Test` attribute. The `FCalcEngine` instance is available for testing so we can directly call its methods and check that they return proper results. In the DUnitX framework there is an `Assert` class that is used to check for certain conditions. For example, when we add two and two, we are expecting that the result will be four. If this is true, the test has passed; otherwise it has failed.

When designing unit tests, it is important not only to check if a test feature works with standard arguments, but also with test corner cases, such as passing illegal parameter values. For example, if we divide by zero, there should be an exception raised.

Methods on the test class to be called by the test runner need to be marked with `Test` or `TestCase` attributes. The `TestCase` attribute can be applied multiple times and it can contain parameter values and expected results as its arguments. For example, we could implement our test class in the following way:

```
unit uTestCalcEngine;

interface

uses
  DUnitX.TestFramework,
  uCalcEngine;

type
  [TestFixture]
  TTestCalcEngine = class(TObject)
  private
    FCalcEngine: TCalcEngine;
  public
    [Setup]
    procedure Setup;

    [TearDown]
    procedure TearDown;

    [Test]
    procedure TestAddSimple;

    [Test]
    [TestCase('TestA','1,2')]
    [TestCase('TestB','3,4')]
    procedure TestAddParams(const a, b: integer);
  end;

implementation

procedure TTestCalcEngine.Setup;
begin
  FCalcEngine := TCalcEngine.Create;
end;

procedure TTestCalcEngine.TearDown;
begin
```

```
    FCalcEngine.Free;
end;
procedure TTestCalcEngine.TestAddSimple;
begin
    Assert.AreEqual(4, FCalcEngine.Add(2, 2));
end;

procedure TTestCalcEngine.TestAddParams(const a, b: integer);
begin
    Assert.AreEqual(a + b, FCalcEngine.Add(a, b));
end;

initialization
    TDUnitX.RegisterTestFixture(TTestCalcEngine);
end.
```

Using the `TestCase` attribute, we can make the unit test runner call a single method multiple times passing different attributes. If we run the unit test right now, we should see the output with the message that all three tests have been passed.

Hey! What's wrong? If we look at the `Add` method implementation, we will see that we have made a typo and instead of +, there is a – operator. Fix this, save all, and run the test again.

```
********************************************************************
*          DUnitX - (c) 2015 Vincent Parrett & Contributors        *
*                    vincent@finalbuilder.com                      *
*                                                                  *
*          License - http://www.apache.org/licenses/LICENSE-2.0    *
********************************************************************

DUnitX - [TestCalcEngine.exe] - Starting Tests.

. . . . . .

Tests Found    : 3
Tests Ignored  : 0
Tests Passed   : 3
Tests Leaked   : 0
Tests Failed   : 0
Tests Errored  : 0
Done.. press <Enter> key to quit._
```

That is much better. It looks like our calculation engine works correctly.

This is a very simple example, but this approach to testing is very powerful. Ideally, every public method of any class that we have implemented should be covered by unit tests. After every modification of code, we should run all unit tests to verify that everything works as expected. Then we can proceed and check-in new changes to our version control system.

# Continuous integration and deployment

The more we can automate our developer work, the better. Ideally, the whole release cycle should be automated. In a typical scenario, every change committed to the source code system should trigger running unit tests, and if they are successful, they should automatically build a new version of our app.

There are existing third-party commercial and open source continuous integration packages. The most popular ones are Final Builder, Jenkins, Hudson, and Cruise Control. Other systems can be configured as well. Delphi IDE provides configurable pre- and post-build events that you can use to execute arbitrary Windows shell commands or batch programs just before and after a compile. As parameter values sent to external programs you can use useful macros that resolve, for example, to the name of a current project.

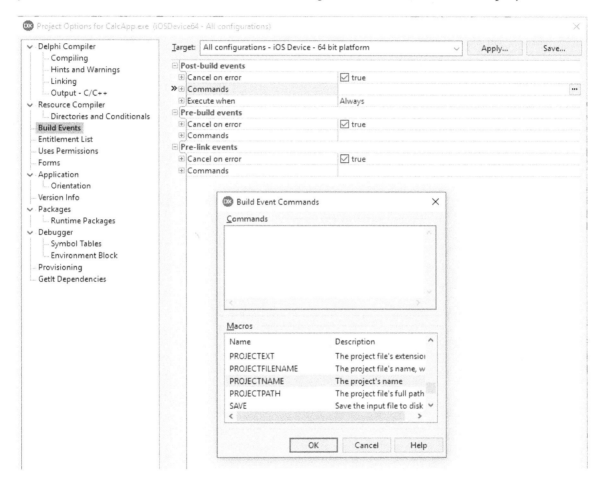

PROJECTNAME macro in Build Event Commands dialog

It is also possible to build your apps using Delphi command-line compilers that do not need the IDE to work.

# Summary

Your app is in the App Store now and you have become a developer superhero that writes code once and natively compiles it to all major mobile and desktop platforms from the very same source code files. Nobody can beat your productivity!

In this chapter, we have walked through steps necessary to prepare and publish your Delphi apps to major App Stores. When your app is there in an App Store, it is not the end of its life. We have also discussed here a typical life cycle iteration of an app from change requests, planning, development and testing, and finally to automatic deployment.

It is your move now!

# The Road Ahead

You have done it! You have become a developer superhero and now you have all the necessary skills to rapidly create stunning mobile apps from one code base in record time!

In this chapter, we are going to review some of the most important mobile development trends and think about all kinds of innovative and successful mobile apps you can now build!

This chapter will cover the following points:

- Review of what we have learned
- Trends in mobile development
- Ideas for new and innovative apps for you to build

The objective of this chapter is to show you the road ahead to be successful in the bright new world of mobile app development!

## What we have learned

Throughout this book, we have made the journey through different topics related to Delphi programming from the perspective of building mobile apps.

The main focus in the first chapter was to install and configure the Delphi **Integrated Development Environment (IDE)** for cross-platform mobile development. That's the single, biggest feature of Delphi cross-platform development: from one source code base, from one project, just by switching target platforms in the project manager, you can natively compile your code to all major mobile and desktop platforms, including Android, iOS, Windows, Mac, and Linux.

The second chapter was all about the Object Pascal programming language. From basic concepts and the structure of a Delphi program, we quickly moved to understanding more advanced constructs, such as anonymous methods, generics, custom attributes, and using **Runtime Type Information** (**RTTI**). Fluency in Object Pascal coding is very important when it comes to writing your own code, or understanding the source of the FireMonkey cross-platform library or other Delphi frameworks. The third chapter covered some of the everyday skills that are useful to have, including writing multithreaded code with the **Parallel Programming Library** and processing JSON and XML data. Armed with this knowledge, we could start with building 2D and 3D graphical user interfaces in the next two chapters. In the fourth chapter, we built a complete *Game of Memory* app and a few smaller projects. In Chapter 6, *Building User Interfaces with Style*, we looked deeper into custom styling to be able to create more sophisticated user interfaces and understand the possibilities that the FireMonkey framework offers.

The following chapters focused on specific technologies and frameworks. We learned how to write cross-platform code to work with different frameworks available on iOS and Android platforms, including responding to mobile app life cycle events, working with sensors, embedding maps, accessing cameras, address books, and more. The next three chapters were focused on working with data and building complete mobile solutions. In Chapter 9, *Embedding Databases*, the *To-Do List* app was introduced with data stored in the embedded mobile database using the Delphi FireDAC database access framework. In the next chapter, we learned about integrating with different types of web services, including SOAP XML and the newer REST API services. The *To-Do List* app was refactored and the data moved to the **Amazon Simple Storage Service** (**Amazon S3**), which we accessed with the powerful Cloud API framework. In the following chapter, we converted the *To-Do List* app into a multitier architecture where underlying data was exposed as REST APIs using WebBroker and RAD Server mobile backend architectures.

The last chapter covered practical aspects of deploying Delphi mobile apps to app stores and using agile techniques such as version control, refactoring, unit testing, and continuous integration to constantly improve your apps.

When your app is in the App Store, it is not the end of its life. You also want to have an eye on emerging technologies that you could use in existing and new app projects.

# Staying on top of everything

Ideas about how you should structure your software architectures are changing at a faster pace than ever. Clearly the technology is becoming more complex, and there are plenty of things to look at. From the perspective of the mobile developer, there are mobile platforms themselves, with new capabilities added with every new operating system version, there is the exploding world of IoT with new standards popping up, and also the quickly changing world of backend services that are no longer just about accessing a relational database through a server code, but myriads of cloud services you can integrate with.

# Apps everywhere

Mobile platforms keep evolving. With every new version of Android and iOS mobile operating systems, existing frameworks are being constantly improved and new ones are being added, such as speech recognition or mobile payments. The types of devices you can deploy your apps on grows. Delphi already provides support for building apps to Google Glass, but other targets, such as Android-based TV sets or cameras, can be used as deployment targets today.

Mobile devices and user experience will continue to evolve, and easier ways of interacting with data and services will be emerging. **Virtual reality** (**VR**) is very different now than its humble beginnings, and it will continue to grow. There are already many mobile apps that provide an **augmented reality** (**AR**) experience where the virtual world is projected into a view of the real world. Other mobile devices based on the metaphor of glasses will be built to make AR the primary way of interacting with computer systems. Apple, Google, Microsoft, Facebook, and other software giants are putting a lot of effort into making these devices the next smartphones.

# Serverless backends and NoSQL

*Serverless* architectures, *containers*, and *microservices* are some of the hot buzz words you can hear here and there. With *container* technology getting more mature, it is becoming practical to start and stop a virtual machine just to execute one function. Cloud web services vendors, such as Amazon, provide the underlying infrastructure for building new kinds of architectures where you can just deploy the source code of a remote function (`https://aws.amazon.com/lambda/`) that you want to execute, and the whole complex aspect of provisioning virtual machines, scaling, and load balancing becomes transparent to software architects. With technologies such as *API Gateway* (`https://aws.amazon.com/api-gateway/`), you can create, version, and manage your own REST APIs at any scale with lots of flexibility and little hassle.

Traditional SQL relational database management systems are no longer the only choice for storing data. NoSQL and other types of data stores, such as graph databases, are gaining more and more popularity. Some of the most interesting offerings in this space are the MongoDB open source NoSQL database (`https://www.mongodb.com/`), the Amazon DynamoDB NoSQL database (`https://aws.amazon.com/dynamodb/`), where you can configure its desired response time, and the Neo4j graph database (`https://neo4j.com/product`), which offers a whole new way of modeling data, where relations between the data are as important as the data itself.

# Internet of all kinds of things

Software companies and analytics agree that IoT is the next big thing, but they have different opinions on how the details will look. There are different IoT use cases and they will be driving the adoption of particular technologies. Communication protocols are a fundamental aspect of IoT, and there are many competing technologies, all with their strengths and weaknesses. Beyond HTTP and Bluetooth's established and widely adopted specifications, there are many more, such as MQTT, CoAP, LoRaWAN, NB-IoT, and others.

The first two, MQTT and CoAP, are emerging protocols that are based on internet stack but optimized for communication between devices. **MQTT or MQ Telemetry Transport** (`http://mqtt.org`) is a lightweight connectivity protocol based on the TCP/IP stack that uses the publish/subscribe method for the transportation of data. MQTT is a many-to-many communication protocol for passing messages between multiple clients through a central broker. Producers and consumers of messages are decoupled. CoAP is a web transfer protocol based on the REST model (`http://coap.technology/`). It is a one-to-one protocol for transferring states information between a client and a server. It is mainly used for lightweight **machine-to-machine** (**M2M**) communication because of its small header size. It is designed especially for constrained networks and that is where its name comes from: **Constrained Application Protocol (CoAP)**. CoAP is similar to HTTP, and reading sensor values is like sending an HTTP request. CoAP is built upon the UDP stack, unlike HTTP or MQTT. This makes it faster and more resource optimized. However, this also makes it less reliable than HTTP or MQTT. CoAP is a compelling option for systems where continuous streaming capability is crucial, as in the case of sensor networks for monitoring environmental conditions.

Another interesting IoT realm is **low power, wide-area networks** (**LPWAN**). They are actively being looked upon by different mobile network operators. With this technology, you can send and receive small data packets over long distances while using very little power. Some of the key technologies in this space are LoRa and NB-IoT. All of them differ in the details of radio transmission, the frequencies they use, and the types of modulation. LoRa wide area networks (`https://www.lora-alliance.org/`) are using unlicensed radio spectrums, but are based on the proprietary modulation system from Semtech Corporation. LoRaWAN can be used in a non-mobile operator network, and can be crowd-sourced, like in the case of The Things Network initiative (`https://www.thethingsnetwork.org/`). **NB-IoT** stands for **NarrowBand IoT** and is already offered by some mobile operators. Communication chips are not expensive, but you need to have a SIM card from a mobile operator. NB-IoT uses a licensed radio spectrum.

The world of IoT will continue to evolve very quickly and has the potential of becoming the next big thing.

# Your next Delphi mobile app

Your next Delphi app will obviously be very cool and successful. Think big and start small. There are many sources of inspiration and places to learn about Delphi.

Beyond the Delphi home page (http://www.embarcadero.com/products/delphi) and Delphi rich online documentation (http://docwiki.embarcadero.com/RADStudio/en/), there is also a vibrant community of developers (http://community.embarcadero.com), where you can read news, blogs, articles, and learn about online webinars and live Delphi events organized in your neighborhood, and ask questions.

Delphi community site app competitions for the coolest app are regularly organized. Check out what other Delphi developers are building and you will be surprised about all the kinds of interesting apps being built with Delphi, such as the Skype Windows client. I'm looking forward to seeing your next great app winning at the Delphi community site!

# Summary

I hope that you have enjoyed reading this book as much as I did writing it. That was a great journey. Delphi is fun. I'm sure that the elegance of the Object Pascal language and the technical excellence of Delphi Integrated Development Environments will continue to enchant a growing number of software developers now and in many years to come.

# Index